PUBLIC SPEAKING
CHOICES AND RESPONSIBILITY

PUBLIC SPEAKING
CHOICES AND RESPONSIBILITY

WILLIAM KEITH • CHRISTIAN O. LUNDBERG

WADSWORTH
CENGAGE Learning

Australia • Brazil • Japan • Korea • Mexico • Singapore • Spain • United Kingdom • United States

![WADSWORTH CENGAGE Learning]

Public Speaking: Choices and Responsibility
William Keith, Christian O. Lundberg

Editor-in-Chief: Lyn Uhl

Publisher: Monica Eckman

Development Editor: Elisa Adams

Editorial Assistant: Colin Solan

Media Editor: Jessica Badiner

Market Development Manager: Linda Yip

Content Project Manager: Dan Saabye

Art Director: Linda May

Manufacturing Planner: Doug Bertke

Rights Acquisition Specialist: Alex Ricciardi

Production Service: MPS Limited

Text Designer: Diane Beasley

Cover Designer: Riezebos Holzbaur Group

Cover Image: Diana Ong/SuperStock/©Getty Images

Compositor: MPS Limited

For product information and technology assistance, contact us at
Cengage Learning Customer & Sales Support, 1-800-354-9706

For permission to use material from this text or product,
submit all requests online at **www.cengage.com/permissions**
Further permissions questions can be emailed to
permissionrequest@cengage.com

Library of Congress Control Number: 2012952971

Student Edition:
ISBN-13: 978-0-495-56986-2
ISBN-10: 0-495-56986-0

Wadsworth
20 Channel Center Street
Boston, MA 02210
USA

Cengage Learning is a leading provider of customized learning solutions with office locations around the globe, including Singapore, the United Kingdom, Australia, Mexico, Brazil, and Japan. Locate your local office at:
international.cengage.com/region

Cengage Learning products are represented in Canada by Nelson Education, Ltd.

For your course and learning solutions, visit **www.cengage.com**

Purchase any of our products at your local college store or at our preferred online store **www.cengagebrain.com**

Instructors: Please visit **login.cengage.com** and log in to access instructor-specific resources.

Printed in the United States of America
1 2 3 4 5 6 7 16 15 14 13 12

Contents

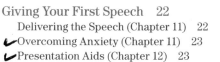

3 Understanding Audiences and Publics 47

4 Becoming a Skilled Listener 65

5 Choosing a Topic and Purpose 85

Jeff Greenberg/Alamy

9 Organization 173

10 Verbal Style 197

Digital Vision/Getty Images

11 Delivery 215

Jeff Greenberg/Alamy

Preface

Those of us who teach public speaking know that the ability to engage an audience with skill, elegance, and clarity can make a decisive impact in the lives of students. The difference between success and failure in a student's academic work, personal relationships, and vocational path can often turn on the ability to create ethical and effective speech. Although future personal success is one important reason a student should cultivate skill in public speech, it is not the only reason. In an increasingly globalizing and information-saturated world, educating more engaged, informed, and responsible public speakers may well be one of the last and best hopes for our civic and democratic life together. In an era of hyperpartisan politics and creeping disillusionment with public discourse and the political system, our best recourse may be turning to the ancient arts of rhetoric and public speaking. These arts can teach us, once again, how to really listen to, respond to, and respectfully engage with our fellow citizens. Thus, this book seeks to remake an art with ancient roots for modern times, or, to put it in more contemporary terms, to remix an ancient beat for the information era.

We wrote *PUBLIC SPEAKING: Choices and Responsibility* because we believe firmly that public speaking matters profoundly to our personal and collective futures. We hope this text embodies a vision of public speaking that is accessible, easy to engage, and relevant to our students without sacrificing the most important lessons the tradition of public speaking has to teach us. While many approaches to public speaking present a catalogue of tips and techniques for giving a speech, we have attempted to create a simple framework for helping students learn to be better public speakers.

This framework is easy to understand and teach, and better yet, it pays homage to the best insight of the traditions of public speaking, which is that addressing any audience is about *making choices* and *taking responsibility*. For us, "making choices" means seeing every public speech as a collection of decisions that starts with inventing a topic, moves through effective research, organization, and delivery, and ends with successful interaction with an audience. "Taking responsibility" means owning your choices, both by making them very intentionally and by accepting the obligation to be responsive to the audience.

In making these two concepts the core of the book, we believe we have provided a set of guiding principles that ties many of the best insights of public speaking pedagogy together around a central theme and that satisfies the demands of the current generation of students for broader civic and social engagement. The style of the book also reflects our concern not only to engage students but also to inspire them to use their voices to make a difference in their communities, future workplaces, and the broader public sphere. Many of our examples are directly relevant to student's everyday lives; others are drawn from issues that occupy the front pages of newspapers, websites, and social media sources. In both cases, our goal is to provide students with examples that are relevant and engaging and that demonstrate the importance of public speaking to the broader health of civic life.

To create a text that is intuitive, easy to teach and learn from, and engaging to students, we have placed special emphasis on significant themes. In the introductory chapter we emphasize the world-changing power of public speech, and we introduce students to our central concepts of making choices and taking responsibility for them. Our goal here is to "put the public back in public speaking" by introducing students to the idea that every speech both targets a specific strategic goal (informing or persuading an audience, for example) and simultaneously forms a part of the larger public conversation around issues important to each of us. In addition, students need to understand that this is also the best approach to speaking in professional and business contexts. Speeches here need to be well argued and researched and clearly organized, just like those in the civic context. If a "public" is a group of people with a common set of concerns, then there are publics both internal and external to any business or organization. The basic skills of good choice-making can be applied to nearly any context.

To help get students up and speaking, and more importantly, to give them a basic understanding of the choices that go into an effective public speech, in Chapter 1 we provide a brief, early overview of the process of creating and delivering a public speech. Perhaps most significantly for many first-time speakers, this chapter tackles the issue of speech anxiety head on, offering effective introductory advice for dealing with public-speaking jitters.

Because this book is so centrally concerned with the idea of responsible speaking in personal, work, and public contexts, Chapter 2 on ethics is the first substantive chapter of the book. We believe our approach to ethics will resonate with contemporary students because instead of simply producing a list of dos and don'ts, we have provided a set of principles for thinking about ethical public speaking practice as an intrinsic element of every communicative interaction. The chapter treats all the standard topics in an ethics chapter—including properly citing sources, accurately representing evidence, avoiding deception and prejudicial appeals—but it does so in the broader context of encouraging students to think about the health and quality of the relationship they are establishing with their audience.

To be ethically sound and strategically effective, good public speaking should begin and end with thinking about the audience. In Chapter 3 we discuss how thinking about the audience influences the choices speakers make and the ways they might take responsibility for the audience in composing and delivering speeches. Not only do we talk about skills at the core of good public speaking in this chapter—for example, analyzing and adapting to your audience—but we emphasize thinking about public speaking as an opportunity for engaging the audience in a conversation around issues of personal and public concern. Our goals in this chapter are to take advantage of the current sentiment among students, promoted in colleges and universities, for greater public and civic engagement and to demonstrate to students that in addressing a specific audience, they are also making their views known in the context of a broader public conversation.

For the model of public speaking as a part of a broader public conversation to work, we believe a public speaking text should present more than just the best ways to speak to an audience. Thus, Chapter 4 addresses how we should listen. One of our goals is to help students be better audience members and more responsive speakers by emphasizing the role of active, critical, and ethically sound listening. We include detailed advice on eliminating impediments to good listening, taking good notes, and giving constructive feedback. But perhaps more importantly, we believe that privileging listening in the public speaking classroom is a pivotal first step toward improving the quality of public conversation in that it emphasizes paying attention to the claims of others as a necessary part of participating in a robust and respectful public conversation.

In the subsequent three chapters, we move from a basic framework for making choices and taking responsibility in public speech toward a practically oriented treatment of how to make effective choices in selecting a topic and purpose

(Chapter 5), giving an informative speech (Chapter 6), and giving a persuasive speech (Chapter 7). Chapter 5 provides students a practical rubric for making good speech choices that best balance their interests, their goals for interaction with the audience, and the nature of the public speaking situation. We provide easily implementable solutions for picking a topic area, defining a purpose, generating a thesis statement, and focusing the speech in light of the occasion and character of the audience.

Chapter 6 focuses on informative speaking by beginning with thinking about how our contemporary context and news media in particular have changed the way we think about information. More than ever, the culture broadly, and our students specifically, have begun to think about the notion of "spin" in presenting information. Our goal in this frame is to help students think about responsible choices for presenting information in a way that is clear, well organized, and useful for the audience. This chapter returns to theme of topic selection to deal with the unique challenges of picking a good informative topic and then moves on to discuss techniques for informative speaking and the set of choices a speaker might make to ensure that information is helpful for the audience.

Chapter 7 updates from Aristotle's three modes of proof—logos, ethos, and pathos, or rational argument, the speaker's character, and emotional appeals—to give concrete guidance to students in composing and delivering an effective speech. Though our inspiration is ancient, we draw from contemporary examples to provide a basic framework for thinking about how to best convince modern audiences through appeals to reason, character, and emotion. This chapter places special emphasis on processes of reasoning, not only to help students give better speeches, but also to help them sharpen their critical thinking skills.

But public speaking is about more than simply using appeals to logic, character, or emotion. It is also about teaching students to make claims that are well supported by evidence. A culture of search engines and social media have fundamentally changed the way students relate to information, and any public speaking pedagogy worth its salt needs to take this sea change in information culture into account. Chapter 8 faces head-on the unique challenges of researching in a digital world, providing students with a detailed guide to navigating a research context substantially more challenging than it even was a decade ago. Once again emphasizing the central role of making choices and taking responsibility, our chapter on research provides a detailed, easy-to-follow, step-by-step protocol for designing a research strategy. Because contemporary students research primarily online, we start with a discussion of all the research options available to them and provide concrete instructions for effectively searching the Internet and other sources. Given changes in student research practices, we place a heavy emphasis on methodical searching, including designing and keeping track of search terms, and on focusing research efforts amid the near-avalanche of online sources from which students can choose. Because today's student often struggles with what to use and how best to use it, we devote parts of the chapter to evaluating the credibility of sources and to thinking critically about the role evidence plays in the composition of a good speech.

Chapter 9 teaches students how best to integrate their claims, arguments, and evidence in a lucid and compelling format that effectively engages an audience. Our chapter on organization presents a rubric from thinking about introductions, signposting, the body of a speech, and a good conclusion. But instead of simply offering a catalogue of possible speech formats or deferring to the nature of the topic for inventing an organizational pattern, we discuss organization as a choice that, like any other, entails specific advantages and drawbacks. Thus, students should come away with a set of resources for developing a capacity for critical thinking about organizational choices.

Chapters 10 and 11 deal with verbal style and delivery, applying the same basic framework for making choices and taking responsibility that we have woven throughout the text. Chapter 10 addresses the best of the rhetorical tradition's reflections on lively language use, borrowing from a wide range of contemporary and pop culture discourses to discuss effective choices for the use of figures and tropes, including treatments of repetition, contrast, comparison, substitution, exaggeration, and personification. We conclude this chapter by reflecting on the ways the speaker's topic and the occasion might serve as a guide to the style choices good speakers make. Chapter 11 extends this same line of thinking to choices to make in delivering a speech. To help students negotiate these choices, we discuss different types of delivery—from memory, from a manuscript, extemporaneously, with the help of a presentation aid, and so on. We conclude this chapter with sections on how best to practice and effectively handle audience interaction.

We follow physical delivery with a detailed and visually rich chapter that applies the principles of choice and responsibility to the use of presentation aids. Whether the student is using a static visual aid such as a chart, moving images, an audio clip, or presentation software, we believe applying the basic framework of choices and responsibility can provide important insights. Chapter 12 includes an integrated section on how to give a demonstration speech, which by its nature has a multimedia element. It concludes with a pragmatic, detailed discussion about integrating presentation software into a speech without leaning on it as a replacement for good public-speaking practices. Here we discuss a number of messy but critically important practicalities that go into effective presentation software use, including how to think about delivery with presentation software, how to practice with and use presentation software in the classroom, and how to develop a backup plan.

Chapter 13 concludes the text by focusing on other types of speeches and speech occasions. Although a first course will appropriately focus on basic informative and persuasive speeches, with classmates as the main audience, students will encounter many other speaking situations in the world, and these will present new communication challenges. We believe the skills to meet these challenges are extensions of the skills already learned. Students can easily learn to give effective and compelling speeches at life transitions and ceremonial occasions, and at work in group presentations.

So, we believe we have produced a public speaking curriculum that is

- Comprehensive, but systematically organized around a coherent system for making good speech choices and taking responsibility for them
- Simple to learn and to teach, always returning to the themes of making choices and taking responsibility
- Rich in practical advice and concrete detail for composing and delivering speeches
- Focused on the biggest struggles and conceptual issues public speaking students face
- An effective "remix" of ancient arts for the modern world—faithful to the best insights of the rhetorical tradition but responsive to the contemporary student in its use of examples, composition and delivery practices, and style
- A curriculum that puts the civic and relational character of public speaking in the foreground of choice making

We have included a number of instructional features we think advance these goals. We have tried to compose a visually engaging book, with images that match the diversity and vitality of contemporary public culture. Each chapter begins with a vignette that ties the actual work of students to the content of the chapter in story form and ends with review and discussion questions. We have also included two major kinds of interactive features in the text to keep students engaged. **Try It!** presents an exercise the student can do while reading the text, providing an immediate opportunity for hands-on practice with the concepts in the book. Instructors can use the Try It! boxes for in-class work, group work, think-pair-share exercises, or homework. The second feature, **F.A.Q.** (or Frequently Asked Questions), channels the spirit and style of its online inspiration. F.A.Q. boxes anticipate and answer student questions about various parts of the text, providing a brief interlude for thinking beyond the immediate curriculum and toward some of the bigger questions implied in learning public speaking.

Special resources for students and instructors designed to streamline teaching and facilitate learning complete the learning package for *PUBLIC SPEAKING: Choices and Responsibility*.

Resources for Students

PUBLIC SPEAKING features an outstanding array of supplements to assist in making this course as meaningful and effective as possible. **Note:** If you want your students to have access to the online resources for *PUBLIC SPEAKING*, please be sure to order them for your course—if you do not order them, your students will not have access to them on the first day of class. These resources can be bundled with every new copy of the text or ordered separately. Students whose instructors do not order these resources as a package with the text may purchase them or access them at **cengagebrain .com.** *Contact your local Wadsworth, Cengage Learning sales representative for more details.*

CourseMate

Cengage Learning's Speech Communication **CourseMate** for *PUBLIC SPEAKING* brings course concepts to life with interactive learning, study, and exam preparation tools that support the printed textbook. Watch student comprehension soar as your class works with the printed textbook and the textbook-specific website. **CourseMate** includes an integrated eBook, student workbook, interactive teaching and learning tools including quizzes, flashcards, Interactive Video Activities, Making Choices Simulations and Engagement Tracker—a first-of-its-kind tool that monitors student engagement in the course. Visit www.cengage.com/coursemate to learn more about CourseMate. Students can access (and purchase access if necessary) at www .cengagebrain.com.

Interactive Video Activities

Interactive Video Activities give your students a chance to watch videos of real speeches that correspond to the topics in *PUBLIC SPEAKING*. Each speech activity provides a video of the speech; a full transcript so that viewers can read along; the speech outline—many in notecard, keyword and sentence form; evaluation questions so that students are guided through their assessment; and a note-taking tool. While viewing each clip, students evaluate the speech or scenario by completing short answer and multiple choice questions or by embedding notes into the video and submitting their results directly to their instructor.

Making Choices Simulations

Making Choices Simulations help students identify the moments of choice in preparing a speech, and guide them in making ethical decisions based on their audience and speaking goals. These simulations are built around key topics and concepts in the book, from choosing a focus and theme to selecting sources and visual aids and more.

Speech Studio 2.0

This online video upload and grading program improves the learning comprehension of your public speaking students. With **Speech Studio 2.0**, students can upload video files of practice speeches or final performances, comment on their peers' speeches, and review their grades and instructor feedback. Instructors create courses and assignments, comment on and grade student speeches with a library of comments and grading rubrics, and allow peer review. Grades flow into a gradebook that allows them to easily manage their course from within **Speech Studio**. Grades can also be exported for use in learning management systems. **Speech Studio's** flexibility lends itself to use in traditional, hybrid, and online courses.

Speech Builder Express 3.0™

This exclusive program guides students through every step of the speech-building process. Nine simple steps provide a series of critical-thinking questions that guide students to effective speech delivery. Links to video clips and an online dictionary and thesaurus help students pull all aspects of their speeches together. Tutorial help is included for every aspect of the speech building process. Any portion of the outline can be e-mailed to the instructor.

- Speech Communication **CourseMate** (with eBook, Speech Builder Express™, and InfoTrac®) for *PUBLIC SPEAKING* Printed Access Code: 9781285072272
- Speech Communication **CourseMate** (with eBook, Speech Builder Express™, and InfoTrac®) for *PUBLIC SPEAKING* Instant Access Code: 9781285072289
- Speech Communication **CourseMate** (with SpeechStudio 2.0, eBook, Speech Builder Express™, and InfoTrac®) for *PUBLIC SPEAKING* Printed Access Code: 9781285072340
- Speech Communication **CourseMate** (with SpeechStudio 2.0, eBook, Speech Builder Express™, and InfoTrac®) for *PUBLIC SPEAKING* Instant Access Code: 9781285072357

WebTutor

The WebTutor™ for WebCT® and Blackboard® provides access to all of the content of this text's rich CourseMate and eBook from within a professor's course management system. CourseMate is ready to use as soon as you log on and offers a wide array of Web quizzes, activities, exercises, and Web links. Robust communication tools—such as a course calendar, asynchronous discussion, real-time chat, a whiteboard, and an integrated email system—make it easy to stay connected to the course.

- Instant Access Code for WebTutor with eBook for WebCT® 9781285072012
- Instant Access Code for WebTutor with eBook for BlackBoard® 9781285071992
- Printed Access Card for WebTutor with eBook for WebCT® 9781285072326
- Printed Access Card for WebTutor with eBook for BlackBoard® 9781285072296

InfoTrac College Edition™. This virtual library's more than 18 million reliable, full-length articles from 5,000 academic and popular periodicals allow students to retrieve results almost instantly.

CengageBrain Online Store. CengageBrain.com is a single destination for more than 15,000 new print textbooks, textbook rentals, eBooks, single eChapters, and print, digital, and audio study tools. CengageBrain.com provides the freedom to purchase Cengage Learning products à la carte—exactly what you need, when you need it. Visit **cengagebrain.com** for details.

A Guide to the Basic Course for ESL Students. Written by Esther Yook, Mary Washington College, this guide for non-native speakers includes strategies for accent management and overcoming speech apprehension, in addition to helpful Web addresses and answers to frequently asked questions.

Resources for Instructors

PUBLIC SPEAKING features a full suite of resources for instructors. These resources are available to qualified adopters, and ordering options for student supplements are flexible. Please consult your local Wadsworth Cengage Learning sales representative for more information, to evaluate examination copies of any of these instructor or student resources, or to request product demonstrations.

Instructor' Resource Manual Written by Terri Metzger of California State University San Marcos, the Instructor's Resource Manual provides a comprehensive teaching system. Included in the manual are suggested assignments and criteria for evaluation, chapter outlines, and in-class activities. All the Web Connect links and activities listed at the end of each chapter of the student edition are included in detail in the Instructor's Manual in the event that online access is unavailable or inconvenient.

The Teaching Assistant's Guide to the Basic Course. Written by Katherine G. Hendrix, University of Memphis, this resource was prepared specifically for new instructors. Based on leading communication teacher training programs, this guide discusses some of the general issues that accompany a teaching role and offers specific strategies for managing the first week of classes, leading productive discussions, managing sensitive topics in the classroom, and grading students' written and oral work.

Power Lecture. This one-stop lecture tool makes it easy for you to assemble, edit, publish, and present custom lectures for your course, using Microsoft PowerPoint®. The PowerLecture lets you bring together text-specific lecture outlines and art, along with video and animations from the Web or your own materials—culminating in a powerful, personalized, media-enhanced presentation. The CD-ROM offers an electronic version of the Instructor Resource Manual, ExamView® software, videos, and JoinIn™ on Turning Point® lecture slides. Todd Brand, Meridian Community College, prepared the JoinIn quizzes. The PowerPoint slides were prepared by Ron Shope, Grace University.

Instructor Workbooks: *Public Speaking: An Online Approach*, *Public Speaking: A Problem-Based Learning Approach*, and *Public Speaking: A Service-Learning Approach for Instructors*. Written by Deanna Sellnow, University of Kentucky, these instructor workbooks include a course syllabus and icebreakers; public speaking basics such as coping with anxiety, learning cycle, and learning styles; outlining; ethics; and informative, persuasive, and ceremonial (special occasion) speeches.

Guide to Teaching Public Speaking Online. Written by Todd Brand of Meridian Community College, this helpful online guide provides instructors who teach public speaking online with tips for establishing "classroom" norms with students, utilizing course management software and other eResources, managing logistics such as delivering and submitting speeches and making up work, discussing how peer feedback is different online, strategies for assessment, and tools such as sample syllabi and critique and evaluation form tailored to the online course.

Service Learning in Communication Studies: A Handbook. Written by Rick Isaacson and Jeff Saperstein, this is an invaluable resource for students in the basic course that integrates or will soon integrate a service learning component. This handbook provides guidelines for connection service learning work with classroom concepts and advice for working effectively with agencies and organizations. It also provides model forms and reports and a directory of online resources.

CourseCare Training and Support. Get trained, get connected, and get the support you need for the seamless integration of digital resources into your course. This unparalleled technology service and training program provides robust online resources, peer-to-peer instruction, personalized training, an a customizable program you can count on. Visit cengage.com/coursecare/ to sign up for online seminars, first day of class services, technical support, or personalized face-to-face training. Our online and onsite trainings are frequently led by one of our Lead Teachers, faculty members who are experts in using Wadsworth Cengage Learning technology and can provide best practices and teaching tips.

Flex-Text Customization Program. With this program you can create a text as unique as your course: quickly, simply, and affordably. As part of our flex-text program, you can add your personal touch to *PUBLIC SPEAKING* with a course-specific cover and up to 32 pages of your own content—at no additional cost.

Acknowledgments

I would like to thank all the students I've taught over the last 30 years; I have learned so much about teaching public speaking from them. I also owe heartfelt appreciation to the teaching assistants I've worked with at Oregon State University and the University of Wisconsin–Milwaukee. Their creativity, freshness, and passion have kept me inspired more than they know, and they have improved my teaching immensely. Chris Lundberg is the best co-author imaginable, and I owe him more than I can say: Ευχαριστό εκατονταπλάσια, φιλή μου. And finally, enormous thanks to my wife Kari—you make everything possible.

—*William Keith*

I would like to thank Bill Keith for being a fantastic co-author and colleague, and Beth Lundberg for putting up with us in the process of writing this book.

—*Chris Lundberg*

The authors would like to thank the amazing editorial team at Cengage, including Monica Eckman, as well as Elisa Adams, Barbara Armentrout, and Edward Dionne.

—*William Keith and Chris Lundberg*

Reviewers

We are grateful to all the reviewers whose suggestions and constructive criticisms have helped us shape this book.

Brenda Armentrout, *Central Piedmont Community College*
Joseph Averbeck, *Marshall University*
Thomas Benson, *Penn State University*
Marcia Berry, *Azusa Pacific University*
Sakile Camara, *California State University Northridge*
Nick Carty, *Dalton State College*
Mark Chase, *Slippery Rock University*
Jodi Cohen, *Ithaca College*
Doug Cole, *Elizabethtown Community and Technical College*
James Darsey, *Georgia State University*
Deanna Dannels, *North Carolina State University*
Katrina Eicher, *Elizabethtown Community and Technical College*
Lisa Eutsey, *Dine College*
Michael Fleming, *Mt. San Jacinto College*
Bonnie Gabel, *McHenry County College*
Susan Gilpin, *Marshall University*
Deborah Haffey, *Cedarville University*
Daria Heinemann, *Keiser University*
Kim Higgs, *University of North Dakota*
Lawrence Hosman, *University of Southern Mississippi*
Mike Hostetler, *St. John's University*
Macdonald Kale, *California University of Pennsylvania*
Jim Kuypers, *Virginia Tech*
Rona Leber, *Bossier Parish Community College*
Richard Lindner, *Georgia Perimeter College*
Matt McGarrity, *University of Washington*
Terri Metzger, *California State University San Marcos*
Diane Monahan, *Belmont University*
Dante Morelli, *Suffolk County Community College*
Phyllis Ngai, *University of Montana-Missoula*

Kekeli Nuviadenu, *Bethune-Cookman University*
David Palmer, *University of Northern Colorado*
Shelly Presnell, *Shasta College*
Rebecca Roberts, *University of Wyoming*
Anand Rao, *University of Mary Washington*
Hannah Rockwell, *Loyola University Chicago*
David Rosman, *Columbia College*
Neely Sheucraft, *Nashville State Community College*
Brent Sleasman, *Gannon University*
James Spurrier, *Vincennes University*
Tim Steffensmeier, *Kansas State University*
Mark Strother, *Ivy Tech Community College*
Joseph Tabarlet, *University of Mary Hardin-Baylor*
Barbara Tarter, *Marshall University*
Diane Todd, *Robert Morris University*
David Williams, *Texas Tech University*

PUBLIC SPEAKING
CHOICES AND RESPONSIBILITY

PART
One

Fundamentals of Good Speaking

Diana Ong/SuperStock/©Getty Images

LEARNING GOALS

- Understand the basics of the communication process
- Explain why public speaking is powerful and worth mastering
- Identify the skills necessary to compose and deliver a speech
- Describe the choices at each stage of the speech creation process

CHAPTER OUTLINE

Jim West/Alamy

Public Speaking

Danielle has a problem. Rather, her town has a problem. Supplies at the local blood bank are starting to get low, and this could be a problem for the local hospital and trauma center. As the head of a student volunteer group, she has been assigned to give speeches to different groups on campus, trying to persuade them to donate blood. As she thinks about her task, it seems pretty intimidating. So many students! They are all so busy! Who cares about blood donation while they are trying to make rent or scrounge up some extra money for social activities? Danielle imagines herself standing in front of lecture classes and social groups like fraternities and sororities, and she feels lost. Should she just get up and say, "Please donate?" No, it needs to be more than that: She needs to give a short speech. But how should she even get started?

Overview

If you want to be an effective speaker, first you'll want to understand a few basic principles about public speaking as a communication activity. This chapter will give you an overview of the communication process, highlighting the difference that public speaking can make in your life and in the lives of the people listening to you. You will learn about the process of composing and delivering a public speech, focusing on the variety of choices you have to make when you give a speech. Finally, to get you started on the process of composing and delivering a speech, we will walk you through the basic elements of speech preparation, which are the topics of the subsequent chapters. ❭

Introduction: Why Learn Public Speaking?

Caution: The contents of this book can be dangerous. Dangerous—but also powerful. Whether used for good or for ill, speech is one of the most powerful forces in human history. Sometimes it has been used to unite people around a common democratic goal—for example, to advance the cause of civil rights. Other times dictators have used speech as a powerful weapon. But however it is used, speech can change the world. More importantly, *your* speech can change *your* world in big and small ways.

The principles we'll introduce will help you give better speeches in almost any context—even when your goal is modest. They will help you learn to be a better public speaker—clearer and more persuasive, but also more engaged, responsible, and well-reasoned.

We often hear that public speaking is just about clear communication. It is in part, and people sometimes assume that anyone can do it without much effort or thought. But performance counts too—actually getting up and talking in front of other people. You may be surprised to find out by the end of this course, however, that getting up and speaking in front of other people can be the easy part. In this book, we would like to introduce you to the range of skills that go into preparing, producing, and delivering a speech, and that will make you a more effective advocate for yourself and for the people and ideas you care about.

You may not be in this class for the sake of changing the world: Many students take a public speaking course because it is required. But taking this course, working through this book, and adopting your instructor's advice on how to be a better public speaker will make you more successful not only in class but also in your everyday life and beyond the classroom.

You are about to become part of a tradition of skills that stretches back thousands of years. So stick with us: We hope to convince you of the power of words, of the world-changing capability that each of us has if we learn how to develop and use it responsibly.

Whatever brought you to this class, public speaking is important not only for your education and career, but also for your life and for the health of our democracy. We will argue that *speech is powerful* and that *speech matters*.

Speech Is Powerful

rhetoric   Term from ancient Greek for the study of how words can persuade an audience.

The study of public speaking began in ancient Greece. For the Greeks, public speaking was part of the broader field of **rhetoric**, or the study of how words could persuade an audience. In the modern world, many people associate public speaking with manipulation, and the term *rhetoric* with "empty talk." They may say, "Let's have less rhetoric and more action." Although it is true that talk is sometimes empty, good speech can also be a form of action, motivating people to make important changes in the world. To see why, the first thing to understand is that because speech is powerful, *your* speech can be powerful.

The Power of Public Speaking to Change the World

One of the first people to write about the power of public speech, the Greek philosopher Gorgias of Leontini, claimed that "speech is a powerful lord." Twenty-five hundred years later, abundant evidence supports Gorgias's insight. Speeches have been used for good and bad ends. They have introduced and converted many to the world's great religions. They have helped elect presidents and overthrow dictators. They have begun wars and ended them. Winston Churchill's and Franklin Roosevelt's speeches rallied the British and U.S. populations during World War II. In the 19th century, Elizabeth Cady Stanton spoke out to make people aware of the rights of women. In the middle of the 20th century, the speeches of Martin Luther King showed people in the United States how to think differently about civil rights and issues of race and racism.

We need the power of words *to speak a better world into existence*. Speech, used effectively, should not only motivate us to make changes on our campuses, in our communities, and as a nation. It should also help us make better decisions about the kinds of changes. We need to speak with clarity and conviction, but we also need to listen and be attentive to other people's viewpoints. Thus, one of the biggest challenges of our time is to learn how to speak in a way that generates cooperation and insight and that avoids division and narrow-mindedness.

But what can learning how to speak well do for you? After all, you will probably not be in the position of addressing the nation in a time of war or convincing Congress to change a law. The point of this course is not to change you into an Elizabeth Cady Stanton, Winston Churchill, or Martin Luther King.

 **Why start by talking about the Greeks?**

Our culture has inherited a number of ideas about communication and political institutions from ancient Greek and Roman (also called "classical") practice. The founders of the United States used them as models. Many classical principles and terms they developed are still useful and relevant; for example, in Chapter 7 we'll examine persuasive appeals in speaking through the lens of the classical distinction between *ethos, logos*, and *pathos*.

FAQ *Can speeches really change the world?*

Here are some speeches that helped to change the course of history. If you would like to learn more about any of them, access your CourseMate at CengageBrain.com and look in Web Links under Chapter 1.

"Against Imperialism," William Jennings Bryan
"Acres of Diamonds," Russell H. Conwell
"Mercy For Leopold and Loeb," Clarence Darrow
"Statement to the Court," Eugene V. Debs
"Farewell Address," Dwight D. Eisenhower
"1976 DNC Keynote Address," Barbara Jordan
"Inaugural Address," John F. Kennedy
"I Have a Dream," Martin Luther King
"Every Man a King," Huey Long
"The Ballot or the Bullet," Malcolm X
"Farewell Address to Congress," General Douglas MacArthur
"Pearl Harbor Address to the Nation," Franklin D. Roosevelt
"The Fundamental Principle of a Republic," Anna Howard Shaw
"Declaration of Conscience," Margaret Chase Smith

The Power of Speeches to Change Your World

Even though speeches can change the world, common sense tells us they can also make a big difference in your individual history. Every day, people speak in courtrooms, boardrooms, and classrooms to persuade others of their points of view or to inform others about things they need to know. A good speech can make all the difference in winning a lawsuit, pitching a business idea, or teaching people about something that might significantly change their lives. And, ultimately, that is the point of this book: Because speech is such a powerful tool, we should learn to use it as effectively and as responsibly as we can.

The skills you will learn here will also make you a more effective speaker in your career. If you want to come across as the candidate to hire when applying for a dream

Can speeches really make a difference in my life?

Here are some examples of the kinds of speeches that can change the course of your life if you deliver them effectively:

- The speech you give as an answer to the job interview question, "Tell us a little bit about yourself"

- The speech you give when you pitch an important business idea

- The speech you give when you are trying to persuade people in your community (for example, a town council or neighborhood association) to change something in your community that needs changing

- The speech you give when convincing a loved one to do something—to enter a long-term relationship, for example, or to support you in an important endeavor

- The speeches you give to convince others to vote for a candidate or a law that affects your everyday life

job, being well spoken is a crucial part of your success. If you prepare well for the interview, thinking about how to present yourself as a fitting and capable candidate, if you perform well by speaking clearly and articulately, if you make a persuasive case, and if you invite the participation of the interviewers by fostering a good dialogue, you can be a shoo-in for the position. By the same token, if you pitch a business proposal to a supervisor, client, or a lender, you will need to project an attitude of competency and meticulous preparation as well as speak articulately and build a relationship with your listeners.

The basic principles are similar for any speech, whether it is delivered on the Senate floor, in a State of the Union address, in a business meeting, or before a local community group. In each instance, you need to plan carefully what you will say and how you will say it, and you need to build a relationship with the audience.

◼ Speaking Connects You to Others: Democracy in Everyday Life

democracy A system of government where people govern themselves, either through direct votes on policy issues (*direct democracy*) or by electing officials who deliberate and make decisions on their behalf (*representative democracy*).

A good public speech, no matter what the context, ultimately strives towards the best ideals of **democracy**. If you have a dollar bill in your pocket, take it out. The Great Seal of the United States is reproduced on the back of the bill. On the left side is a pyramid inside a circle, and on the right side is a circle with an eagle in it. The eagle has a small scroll in its mouth. If you look closely, you will see the Latin phrase *E pluribus unum*, meaning "From many, one." The many people who make up the United States are all united—we are all in this together.

"From many, one" on the U.S. dollar bill expresses the essence of democracy.

Democracy only works, or at least we will only be able to make it work, if we respect the fact that we are many people with substantial differences in opinion, race, class, sexuality, gender, religion, and belief. But we also strive to make from these differences a common identity or at least a common commitment to democracy and the well-being of our fellow citizens.

Public speaking, at its best, is about respecting that common commitment—public speaking is about the **unity** of democracy. But it is also about respecting the **pluralism** of democracy—namely, that we need to speak and listen in a way that preserves the important differences that make each of us who we are.

Now you may be saying to yourself, "Wait a minute. I was hoping to get some communication skills out of this class that I could use in business, for my job." In fact, you will get that, and more. Successful and effective persuasion and informative speaking in politics, business, and even personal life can invoke the highest democratic values. Why? Because speakers who make good decisions consider the effects of their words on all **stakeholders**, or all the people who have something at stake in the decisions. Skilled speakers not only know how to adapt to their audience of stakeholders, but they understand their audience's diversity.

 Can speeches really make a difference on campus?

At most schools, the student government controls thousands of dollars for student programs. In addition to university policy, what determines how that money is spent? Typically, elected members of the student government decide. How? They get together in a room and talk. If you are in favor of spending money on a particular activity or club, you'll speak up in favor of it. Here's a case where your ability to be clear and persuasive with your peers could change the quality of campus life for a huge number of students. No matter how strongly you believe in your cause, your speech is what makes your beliefs matter.

FAQ *What do pluralism and unity mean for public speaking?*

Pluralism means that our democracy is made up of people who are different—they have different backgrounds, including differences of class, race, gender, sexuality, religious orientation, and geographical origins. But pluralism is more than just our different backgrounds. There is also difference in democracy because we have different ideas and beliefs.

Unity means that these differences are not disabling: We are all members of the same national public.

unity   Harmony among related parts.

The Conversational Framework

In this book we'll distinguish different approaches to communication, especially public communication. Speakers are never *just* informing and persuading; there is always a larger context that creates mutual responsibilities between speakers and their audiences. To sharpen the picture, let's compare advertising and democracy as contexts for communication. They represent fundamentally different approaches to public discourse and different ways of understanding this mutual responsibility.

pluralism   The coexistence of numerous ethnic, cultural, political or religious groups in one nation.

stakeholders   The people who have something to lose or gain as the result of a decision or policy.

In advertising, a company is trying to sell something, to get someone to buy something. Ads target specific groups of people called market segments—men between 30 and 40, for instance, or working women who live in urban areas, or Twitter users. Advertisers are successful when sales increase; their responsibility to their audience is fairly limited and communication is usually just in one direction.

In contrast, in the context of democracy, communication is among people or citizens "thinking together." Decisions should emerge as a result of the mutual exchange of arguments, information, and points of view. Democracy is big and messy; imagine it as an enormous system in which different ideas and arguments circulate, being expressed (and maybe changed) at many different points. Sometimes it's you and a friend talking about what the government should do about student loans; sometimes it's you reading a debate about student loan finances in the newspaper or on a website.

Sometimes it's your roommate watching an argument being mocked on a satirical news show, and sometimes it's your parents attending a community meeting to hear what people say.

If you're paying attention, you are part of the larger public dialogue, and you might even be putting in your two cents. Even if you don't see yourself as particularly political, you might be surprised if you keep track for a few days of how often you think and talk about public issues; you can't help it—they matter.

Clearly this is very different from advertising. Democratic conversation, or dialogue, aims to solve problems, not to sell products. It involves everybody, not just a target consumer audience; to be successful, arguments have to be adaptable to both men and women, older and younger, and of different races, religions, regions of the country, income and education levels, and so on. Adverting bypasses differences like these by selectively targeting a smaller audience of people that have something in common.

Suppose a student is going to give an informative speech on a surprising or controversial topic, such as the campus need for transgender bathrooms. An advertising approach would probably start by defining the target market as the types of people most likely to be sympathetic to sexualities different from their own and would ignore everyone else. It's hard to imagine, however, how the student would give a speech to a class and ignore many or most of the people in it.

In contrast, in a democratic conversation or dialogue, the speaker would begin by identifying the larger public issues that connect to the availability of transgender bathrooms: equality, civil rights, and the increasing acceptance of gay and transgender people. The speaker would be placing the issue of transgender bathrooms within larger discussions that have been going on for 10, 50, or maybe 150 years, portraying the issue as part of a larger conversation about civil rights or equality.

Or for another example, consider a speech about yoga. In a public speaking class, is it the speaker's job to "sell" yoga to her classmates? Probably not. But she could

Democracy relies on mutual exchanges of opinions and information, often through public speaking.

present the information she gained from her research on yoga in the context of public conversations about health, athletic performance, or even spirituality.

Our point here is that while you are learning many new techniques in public speaking class, such as outlining, research, and delivery, you will also learn new ways of understanding the kind of communication that makes up truly *public* speaking. It isn't quite like talking to friends about movies and music, and it isn't like a sales pitch. Public speaking is the adventure of taking your turn in one of the amazing ongoing public conversations that are happening right now.

In short, speech is powerful, and it matters in ways you may not have thought too much about, but after taking this course, you'll never hear a speech the same way again. Now let's look at an overview of the actual process.

The Communication Process

In this book, we'll often refer to communicating in the context of public speaking as *rhetoric*, but with a different meaning than you're used to. As we noted, today the term *rhetoric* is often negative and refers to discourse that is empty, insincere, and pompous. In its classical sense, however, rhetoric is about the art of speaking, and it requires at least three components:

- a speaker,
- a listener, and
- some means of getting information between them.

There might be a conversation between two people or among several people, as in a group discussion. Or, as in public speaking situations, there might be one speaker and a large audience. Or the medium might change: One person writes a letter or email to another, or a letter is published in the newspaper and read by thousands of people. Even though the "speakers" and "listeners" are not physically present, we can still use the terms *speaker* (writer) and *listener* (reader) because the communication situations are parallel: In all of them, the speaker is trying to accomplish something with the listener, using language. Of course, there are also differences: Speakers in person generate nonverbal cues to meaning, and for writers, layout, design, and color can communicate more than the words say or sometimes something different from what the words say.

For most of us "speaking" involves opening our mouths and having words come out. But if you are Deaf, speaking means using your hands to create American Sign Language (ASL) or American Signed English. And what about the many of the public speeches that are written out in advance, some existing only as texts? Many "speeches" inserted into the *Congressional Record*, for example, have never been spoken aloud. We mention ASL and written speeches to emphasize that "speaking" is a complex phenomenon and to encourage you to think about what speech is and how it is generated.

Try It! *Your Rhetorical Situations*

Make a list of the most common rhetorical situations you engage in:

- Who are the most common listeners? Why?
- Are these situations usually face-to-face or electronic? Why?
- Which ones are easiest? Most difficult? Why?

"Speaking" is a complex act that uses many forms, including sign language, shown here as Tai Lihua of the Chinese People's Political Consultative Conference (left) joins a panel discussion in Beijing with the help of a sign language interpreter.

Yan Yan/Xinhua/Photoshot/Newscom

The *Public* in Public Speaking

An audience is not the same as the people listening or reading by chance; people who happen to overhear a conversation are not the audience for the conversation. Audiences are made up of a variety of people, with different beliefs, values, and life experiences. And the speaker wants something from all of them—their attention, their patience, their comprehension, their openness, a change of mind, a change of action.

Much of the time speaking (and writing) is not only an expression of the speaker's thoughts but is also in an important sense tailored *for* the audience. Speakers need to know something about their audience so that they can adapt to them. Just as in ordinary conversation, you say different things or the same thing in different ways depending on whom you are talking to, speakers adjust their topic and presentation to their audience. **Adaptation** is one of the central concepts of rhetorical communication.[1]

Is the audience ever more than just the people in the room with the speaker? To explain why it is called *public* speaking, we need to consider the concept of a **public**, or a group of people who share a common set of concerns.

In Figure 1.1, the speaker is attempting to influence or inform an audience whose members belong to more than one public. For example, the audience at a PTA meeting will be part of the public that cares about the fate of children as well as the public that pays taxes. If the speaker is making an informative presentation about the current state of student achievement in the district, she will need to think about a particular public in deciding what information is relevant and how to frame it.

Yet the diagram in Figure 1.1 is incomplete. Why? Because it pictures the speaker as separate from or outside the public. However, when you are speaking *to* an audience in public, you are speaking *with* an audience composed of fellow members of your public. The speaker portrays herself and the audience not as opposed to each other ("I care about one thing, and you care about something else") but as part of the same public ("Here is what *we* care about"), as shown in Figure 1.2.

adaptation Adjusting a topic, arguments, and presentation to fit a particular audience.

public A group of people who share a common set of concerns.

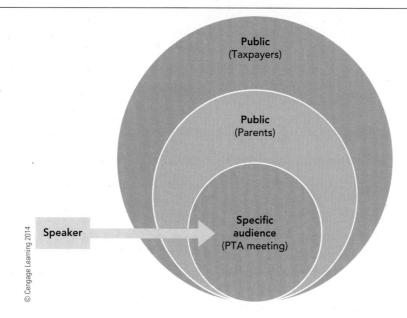

FIGURE 1.1
Audience members belong
to more than one public.

So whether we're looking at informative, persuasive, or special-occasion speaking, we'll generally talk about the *public* as a way of talking about the context for an audience. This is important because speakers need to understand who the audience is if they're going to adapt their information to them. For example, if you were giving an **informative speech** on the idea of a taxpayer bill of rights, the public would most likely be "people concerned about tax policy." If you were giving a **persuasive speech** arguing for changes to make student loan programs more widely accessible, the relevant publics would be "people concerned about access to education" and "people who believe education is essential to the economic success of the United States." Even a **special-occasion speech**, such as a eulogy at a funeral, can be addressed to a public; if the deceased volunteered at the Humane Society, his friends will talk about how his accomplishments mattered to people who care about animals.

The concept of the public allows us to distinguish public speaking from advertising and other forms of private and personal communication. (More about this in Chapter 3.) The concept of the public provides a means for you to connect to an

informative speech   A speech whose primary purpose is to educate the audience about a topic.

persuasive speech   A speech whose primary purpose is to change the audience's opinion about a topic or to encourage them to take a particular action.

special-occasion speech   A speech made on the occasion of a life transition (such as a wedding) or at a professional event (such as introducing a speaker).

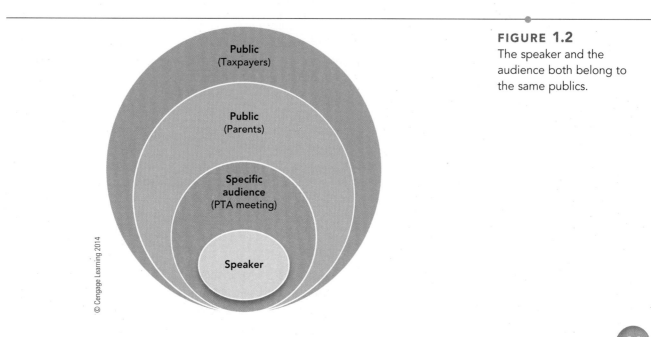

FIGURE 1.2
The speaker and the audience both belong to the same publics.

audience in an ethical and effective way by focusing on interests that concern them not just as students in a classroom but also as members of a broader citizenry. When you speak in class, you will be addressing a public only if the things you talk about implicate the interests of your audience members not just as fellow classmates but also as members of a larger national public.

Speaking Is About Making Choices

It may seem a little strange to think about speaking as making choices. Isn't speaking just saying what you're thinking? However, if you reflect for a moment, you may realize that you are often sure of what your thoughts are only as you are saying them, and you may say them differently depending on the person you're talking to.

choices In public speaking, the choices are about topic, information and arguments, organization, visual aids and other supporting materials, and type of delivery.

In creating a speech, you make **choices** about what to say. Two thousand years ago, when public figures in classical Greece and Rome wanted to give a speech, they might turn to a rhetorician (called a *logographer*, or "speechwriter") to figure out how to compose and deliver the speech. Now, most of us do this for ourselves. Ancient rhetorical practice was organized around the canons (rules or principles) of rhetoric, which broke the process of speaking into five parts: (1) Come up with content, (2) organize it, (3) choose words for it, (4) memorize it, and then (5) deliver it.

We teach public speaking a little bit differently 2,000 years later, and in this book we propose a simplified and updated model that focuses on the choices you will need to make to give a successful speech.

> First, *preparation*: How will you prepare your speech? What do you want to say? What information and arguments will you use to support your claims? How will you organize the speech and move from point to point? What words, images, or technology will be important to creating a compelling experience for the audience?
>
> Second, *performance*: How will you deliver or "perform" you speech? What tone, pace, and gestures will you use? You will need to make sure that you speak clearly, loud enough for the audience to hear, and you will need to eliminate distracting speech and body tics. Few speeches are memorized nowadays, but you'll have to decide how to master the information in your speech and create materials like notecards or slides that allow you to deliver it.

delivery The act of making a speech to an audience.

When you think of public speaking, performance, or **delivery**, is probably the part of the process you think of first. Images of shaking knees, sweaty palms, and a nervous stomach may come to mind, but effective preparation can result in more comfortable performances. Preparation means planning the best way to present your message so that the audience will respond favorably. You need to ask what the audience's interests are in this topic and in listening to you talk about it; you also need to think about their expectations and predispositions. Finally, you need to give the audience a stake in what you are saying by providing them an opportunity to participate. They may respond by asking questions, and you need to have a strategy for dealing with their questions, but you also need to give them an opportunity to participate by changing their beliefs and or actions as a result of the speech.

▣ Preparation

The moment when you stand up and give your speech may not be the most important, or even the most difficult, part of the process. Although the performance components may trigger the nerves that make your stomach shaky as you think about giving a speech, the *preparation* that goes into deciding what to say is more difficult and probably more important than the performance. Great delivery with nothing much to say isn't effective communication. We all admire and enjoy a great performer, and sometimes we assume that a musician's or actor's talent is responsible for the impressive concert or play. In fact, no matter how talented, the artist has put a huge amount of careful preparation into creating that compelling event for the audience.

Try It! *Preparation Choices Checklist*

Run through the following checklist when you are preparing a speech:

- How do I want to structure the speech?
- What arguments do I want to use?
- What kinds of research will be most helpful to do and to present to the audience?
- What sources and ideas will the audience find most credible?
- Am I taking into account possible objections or rebuttals to my arguments?
- What is the product of my preparation? A memorized speech, notes, images? And how should I use them?

The most critical part of speaking may well be the thought that goes into it. Why? First of all, good delivery depends on good preparation; The preparation that you put you put into your speech beforehand may be one of your best defenses against feeling nervous about or even overwhelmed by public speaking.

Speaking should be *communication*. You should say what you think, or better yet, you should present the best information and your most thoughtful opinions on your subject matter. In contrast to acting, which involves saying *someone else's* words, public speaking is speaking your *own* mind. In the case of actor, it's unclear exactly who is communicating to the audience. The writer? The actor? A combination of them? In public speaking, it's all you. You are both writer and actor. So although the way you give a speech may be a kind of performance, it is important to think of speaking as a process that allows you to say what you think to someone in particular.

Michael Newman/PhotoEdit

Public speaking is above all *communication*.

Deciding what to say implies making some important choices based on your opinions and on the materials and tools that are available to you: ideas, arguments, images, words, and metaphors. This means that you have to put work into preparing your speech, a process we call invention. As illustration, let's look in more detail at the kinds of choices speakers make when they prepare speeches that inform and persuade an audience.

Informing

Many times as a speaker you are trying to convey information to an audience. Sometimes you are in the role of an expert, sometimes a sort of teacher; in other cases you are more like the messenger delivering the news, like a reporter. In each case you're trying to get information across to the audience clearly and effectively.

Some people mistakenly assume that if you know what you're talking about, you'll automatically be clear, but that's not necessarily true. Think back to some of your least favorite teachers. They may have been experts, but they may not have been very good at communicating their knowledge.

Why is that? How can expertise and good communication be two different things? It happens because communication is not only about the knowledge in the speaker's head but about the audience as well. The audience can't understand things they don't understand. That seems obvious, but many speakers disregard it. To explain or clarify something to an audience, you have to assume that they don't already understand it, and then choose to explain it in terms their current knowledge.

Making Choices: Example 1   Suppose you are faced with explaining a new university regulation to a group of students on your campus. The university has decided "any drug or alcohol-related tickets or arrests involving students will have academic repercussions." Right now, you (like the hypothetical audience) are probably wondering what that means—"repercussions"? As a speaker, you have some choices.

- First, you have to decide what your role will be. Are you speaking on behalf of the university or as just a student?
- Even though you'll cover the same information in either case, if you are speaking as a student, you'll highlight benefits or consequences for students, including yourself. If you speak on behalf of the school, you may feature the reasons for the decision and what it means for the school.
- Depending on which way you go, you'll change the order of points (probably putting the ones most important to the audience last), and you'll change any charts or illustrations you use, since these highlight the things that will be most memorable for the audience about the information.

Persuading

Sometimes we want more than just to have the audience understand us; we want them to believe or do something. By *persuasion*, we mean all the ways a speaker can attempt to influence an audience, from informing them about a topic to arguing they should change their beliefs or inspiring them to action. All of these are "persuasive" in the sense that they are attempts to influence the audience. Even in an informative speech, you adapt it to the audience, trying to make sure they not only understand but also care about the information.

Making Choices: Example 2   You are probably so used to making choices about what to say that you don't realize that you are always choosing what to say and how to say it. Here's a simple interpersonal example. Suppose you'd like to get your friend Brian to go to a movie with you on a Friday night. You start with "movie" and "Brian," but from there you have a lot of choices. You have to decide whether you think he will automatically want to go to a movie, or if you'll have to convince him. If you're going to convince him, you'll consider what would motivate him. Is he looking for a relaxing time after a hard week? Is he bored with his job and looking for excitement? Does he enjoy dinner before a movie, or does he love a big bucket of popcorn with his flick? You might research what movies are playing, and you may choose one based on what kind of movie Brian likes. Or you may try to convince Brian to see the movie *you're* interested in. If Brian were someone you didn't know well, you might have to approach the request more formally; with a fairly close friend, you can be pretty informal.

Without realizing it, all of these choices may flash through your head before you decide to say to your friend, "Hey, bud, want go and check out the midnight showing of *Donny Darko*? You know you love that flick, and we can grab some food afterward." Your process for public speaking will be similar: You need to interpret the audience and purpose (whom you're talking to and what you want from them), and as the next example shows, there are *always* choices about that interpretation.

Making Choices: Example 3   Let's say you need to give a presentation to the city council asking for a change in the zoning laws for a skateboard park. Your audience is the city council members, who will vote on your proposal. So what are your choices? You probably don't need to know much about the city council members personally, because they probably don't make zoning decisions based exclusively on their being a man or a woman or white, Asian, or Hispanic. Their decisions are more likely based on their functions as city council members: interpreting the law and serving the public interest. What you want to say about your topic is to a large extent determined by what you want to convince them to do, but your approach to your audience and how you want to persuade them requires some strategic choices.

Responsible public speakers approach different audiences in different ways. A town council meeting is different from a classroom and from the halls of Congress.

Why should the city council change the zoning laws? Because it benefits you and your friends? Naturally, you think that it does, but will that move city council members? Probably not. Can you argue that it benefits them? Yes, but be careful: You're not talking about benefiting the council members personally, but rather you are arguing to their *role* as council members—they should care about the benefits to the city. How would the new park benefit the city? Presumably it will generate some tax revenue and perhaps some part-time employment.

However, because they have to think about the good of the city, they'll have to consider two problems: What if noise from the park bothers the neighbors or skaters get rowdy? You'll need to clearly address those issues, or you can't expect the council to take you very seriously. As you decide what to argue, you also need to think about language choices. You might think about how you want to address the members ("Sir" and "Ma'am" versus "You guys"), and about how you want to describe the skate park. Will it be in terms that get them visualizing it ("Imagine all these kids exercising and staying out of trouble") or in terms that support your argument ("Data on skateparks show they are good civic investments")? You might use analogies to national or state parks. You may even think about how you'll dress for the occasion—will it be in skater clothes or something more formal? You'll have to consider which would be better and why. Skater clothes might show you're in touch with the future users, but something more formal might show that you should be taken seriously.

The Speaking Process: Thinking, Creating, and Speaking

Now that you have an idea about a public speaker's choices, let's look at the actual process. What do you have to do to give a speech? It's useful to see preparation as having two parts: the analysis and the "writing" of the speech. First, you will need to *think*—analyze—what you want to say in the particular situation for your particular audience. Then, you will need to *create* a speech that is well organized, crafted for maximum effect, and has good supporting arguments. After that, you are ready to *speak*; you will need to deliver the speech in such a way that it will not only be listened to but also be heard and acted upon by the audience. Here is a brief outline of the process:

Think:

- *Choose a topic:* What things are important to you that you would like to say to your audience?
- *Audience:* Who will be listening, and what is their interest in the topic?
- *Goals:* What do you want the audience to do, either by learning, acting, or changing beliefs?

Create:

- *Arguments:* What claims, propositions, or ideas would you like the audience to believe?
- *Research:* How will you support your arguments with evidence, statistics, quotes from experts, and other materials that lend credibility to your case?
- *Organization:* How will you put your points together so that they have a clear pattern that is easy for the audience to follow?
- *Words:* How will you phrase your ideas so that they are both clear and compelling to the audience?

Speak:

- *Delivery:* What choices will you make about the performance of the speech? How will you act (for example, will you make an effort at eye contact), and what choices will you make in verbal style (tone, pitch, rate, emphasis, clarity) to make sure that your speech has maximum persuasive effect?
- *Anxiety:* What strategies and techniques will you use for managing your nerves?

Thinking Through Your Choices

To preview how the chapters of this book will walk you through these steps of the speaking process, we'll use the example at the beginning of the chapter, in which Danielle was trying to figure out how to give a speech persuading other students to donate blood. Each part of speech preparation involves a set of choices; Danielle needs to recognize both *what* her choices are and *how* to make them responsibly. First, the analytic part of preparation: Think about who your audience is and what your goals regarding them are.

Your Responsibilities (Chapter 2)

First, Danielle has to orient herself to what we'll call the *ethical* dimensions of this speaking situation. She needs to ask herself what her relationship is to her audience. Does she want to get donations, and she doesn't care how she gets them? Even if Danielle isn't willing to lie to get people to donate, she might still employ half-truths or misleading statements. This stance toward the audience shows a lack of rhetorical or communicative responsibility, because it divides Danielle from the audience ("I'm persuading *you*"). A more responsible approach would create a context where Danielle and the audience together are coming to understand the mutual benefits of blood donation ("*We* need to do something about the local blood shortage"). Before Danielle can start thinking about what to say, she needs to clarify what she intends to do with, or to, the audience in this situation.

Your Audience (Chapters 3, 4)

Now, Danielle must think about the nature of her audience. She can think about her audience in general terms, especially the obstacles that might prevent them from being blood donors already. Some students are busy with schoolwork plus jobs or family or all three. Other students may be uninterested. Either way, Danielle knows that her speech needs to be entertaining and informative and that it must give the audience a reason to show up at the blood donation station and be poked with a needle for little or no compensation.

After she takes these general issues into account, she might think more specifically about the actual group she will address—is it a random sampling of students in a course, a volunteer group, or a campus social group? Here, Danielle will need to think about why people are in the audience in the first place and then to think about how she can use the picture of the audience that she is developing to motivate them to give blood. Finally, she'll probably realize that there are a couple of specific fears about blood donation that might come into play with any audience: Some people are afraid of blood, and some people are freaked out by needles; she'll have to take those fears into account at some point in her speech. In addition, some people fear (wrongly) that they can get a disease just from giving blood.

How would a responsible speaker motivate others to donate blood? What would *you* say if you were the speaker?

littleny/Shutterstock.com

Her issue—the blood supply—is one that concerns us all, and so it is a *public* issue. What kind of public is her audience of college students relative to the issue of blood donation? Despite all the differences between students (older, younger, urban, rural, male female), can she find a common characteristic that gives them a reason to say yes to blood donation?

Here is where Danielle's rhetorical creativity comes in. She can *describe* the audience to themselves. They are busy college students, yes . . . but they are also people who might get sick or injured and need some blood at the hospital. "Potential blood-bank users" may not be how the students think about themselves, but it's a true description, and it's relevant to Danielle's purpose: It transforms the audience into a public, with a mutual interest in blood donations. Another possible public would be "people who value public service." Many college students either fall into this group or wish they did, and Danielle can give them the opportunity to perform a public service.

Danielle needs to speak in a way that helps the audience listen and *want* to listen. This includes the use of tone, pacing, and transitions to keep the audience involved. Danielle also needs to present arguments in a balanced way that takes into account the needs, expectations and predispositions of the audience. She also needs to present herself as a person who is open to and respectful toward the opinions of the audience. She needs to give them all the evidence that they need to make an informed decision, and she needs to provide them with concrete steps that they can take if they choose to donate blood. Finally, Danielle should allow the audience time to ask questions, if this is appropriate, and to answer the questions in a clear, engaging, and nonconfrontational way.

Your Goals (Chapter 5)

Danielle has to assess the situation. In this case, she already has a topic (sometimes that's not the case). What are her goals? She should clearly distinguish between her personal goals (what she wants to accomplish) and her goals with the audience (what she wants her speech to accomplish). She can't just say, "Hey, donate blood, because if I get in good with the blood bank people, I'm set for an internship, and that would be a big résumé booster." That's her personal goal; she will benefit if she can get more blood in the blood bank by recruiting more donors. Her goal *with the audience* would be to persuade them to voluntarily donate blood through the campus program. But this goal has some inherent challenges: Why donate blood on campus for a few cookies when you might be able to get money somewhere else for selling your blood *plasma*. Danielle would like to get students to want to show up at one of the campus sites. She doesn't need to control or manipulate them or make them into better people; she just needs to get them to see why it would be right to donate. Danielle wants to choose a goal that is not only appropriate to the situation but also defensible.

Creating Your First Speech

Once Danielle has made some tentative decisions about her audience, her goals, and the audience's relationship to her topic, she has to start creating her speech, which is the second part of preparation.

Information and Arguments (Chapters 6, 7)

In order for Danielle to persuade her audience, she'll need to provide information about blood donation and, for this specific situation, reasons why students should donate, and then she'll have to choose the best ones. (Her choices here will both determine and depend on her research, as discussed in the next section.) These reasons will be **arguments**, whose conclusion is "I should donate blood." Arguments give reasons and evidence, and Danielle has several choices. She can choose examples as evidence:

argument A claim backed by reasons—logic and evidence—in support of a specific conclusion.

> **Here is a person who was saved by donated blood.**

She can make public arguments:

> **Donating blood is an important public service.**
> **You or someone you love might be in an accident some day, and you want make sure the local hospital has a ready supply of your blood type.**

She can also present arguments based on emotion:

> **When one of your family members is hurt, there is nothing more comforting than knowing that there is an army of volunteers who are there to support you, even though they don't know you, because they were willing to give the gift of their blood.**

Danielle should brainstorm many arguments from which to choose the ones that her audience is most likely to understand and that connect to them the best. She may have to confront the fact that her reasons for donating blood may not be the same as the audience's reasons. She can choose to use any, all, or none of the following brainstormed reasons to make her case:

- It's fun!
- You can help others.
- You have an obligation to help.
- The blood bank needs you.
- Other people will need your help.
- Sick people need your help.
- It's easy.
- You'll feel great about yourself after you do it.
- There's no risk in giving blood.
- What if you needed blood?

What will help her choose among these? She'll need to select the arguments most effective with the particular audience/public she has chosen to address. Even if there are many good reasons to do something, they aren't equally good to everyone. If she has chosen to address her audience as college students, which of these arguments will mean the most to them *as* college students? The ones about idealism? Community? Ease of giving? We'll return to these questions in the chapter on persuasion and discuss how reasoning will help make this choice.

■ Research (Chapter 8)

Once Danielle has chosen lines of argument, she'll need to do some research to find the facts and information that will fill out her reasoning. She could, of course, just get up and freestyle her speech, but this would be a failure of her responsibility to her audience. To become thoroughly informed, Danielle needs a research strategy: She needs to figure out where the best sources are and then read enough of the literature on blood donation to make some reasoned conclusions. In order to do this, she'll need to have an organized approach to research that evaluates multiple perspectives, instead of just cutting and pasting from a discussion board or a wiki.

Danielle has an enormous variety of sources to choose from: interviews, news stories, pamphlets, journal articles, web pages, Wikipedia, books, and so on. But she needs carefully choose her sources and allow the audience to evaluate their credibility. She also needs to use the research responsibly, offering as full a picture of the facts as possible. Her speech will be more effective if all the statistics are from credible sources, such as the American Red Cross or the American Medical Association, than from something like www.saveavampiregiveblood.

Good research makes Danielle more credible, and it can give her more choices about how to present her reasoning. But most importantly, research fulfills the trust she wants the audience to place in her. If she says that donation is safe, she needs to have the research to back that up.

■ Organizing (Chapter 9)

Once Danielle has chosen her arguments and assembled research to support them, she is ready to choose how to organize her speech. This happens at two levels. First, she has to decide the best order for her two or three main arguments. Perhaps civic

Persuasive speakers know they must rely only on credible sources to back up their words. The American Red Cross website, for instance, is a reliable source for information about blood donation.

The American Red Cross; http://www.redcross.org/donate/give

duty is her strongest argument, but if people fear disease or needles, she may need to focus on that first in order to clear away misunderstandings. Otherwise, audience members may not be able to hear her powerful arguments about civic duty because they are thinking, "Wait! Isn't this dangerous?"

Second, she has to decide how to structure the body of the speech. What is the best order for her points? If the most important one goes last, which one *is* most important? How are the points related to each other? Their relationships (for example, just another reason or cause and effect) will help her choose clear transitions between the points, which will help the audience understand her argument more precisely.

She also needs to decide how to **frame** the speech in the introduction and conclusion. The introduction will, in a sense, introduce the audience members to themselves and also set the tone for the speech while previewing the arguments. The conclusion will bring the arguments together in an appeal for action.

frame The context for the information or arguments of a speech, often articulated in the introduction and conclusion.

The first few sentences basically lay out the relationship between speaker, audience and topic. Look at some possibilities and what they are likely to mean to the audience:

1. **If you give blood, I could win a prize in a competition my sorority is having.**
   Meaning to audience: The blood donation is a means for the speaker to benefit.

2. **If you give blood, the survivors of the recent disaster will do much better.**
   Meaning to audience: The donation will help others.

3. **If you give blood, you'll feel great about yourself, proud of your engagement.**
   Meaning to audience: The donation will help the audience members.

Danielle needs to choose a frame that will effectively *introduce* her arguments to the audience, so it needs to be consistent with them. Introduction 1 wouldn't work with a speech that was mainly about altruistic reasons for audience members to give blood. In a speech that focused on how blood donations help others, the conclusion would need to support the frame by providing a vivid example of someone whose life was saved or improved thanks to donated blood.

Finding the Words (Chapter 10)

An important set of choices involves the words that Danielle will use when she speaks. Not every single word, but the key terms that connect her and the topic to the audience. For example, what is the subject of the speech? It's about blood (which is intrinsically gross to a lot of people), and she is asking her audience to do something with the blood. But what? Is it

a donation?
a gift?
a contribution?

Of course, these words have similar meanings, but they have slightly different implications. *Contribution* suggests a group effort, whereas *donation* makes the blood sound equivalent to money (and the common metaphor for the place where the blood is stored a blood "bank"). *Gift* is an emotionally and culturally charged term that seems more personal than the others; people who have never made a donation or contribution in their life know all about gifts. The right word would depend on the frame of the speech and the choices Danielle has made about her arguments.

For another example, what words could Danielle use to say that blood donation is a "good" thing?

worthy	excellent
valuable	honorable
necessary	helpful
commendable	admirable
splendid	cool
marvelous	really fine
precious	awesome

This may seem like too many choices, but spending some time choosing the three or four key terms in the speech will help you get the parts of your speech to hold together. In addition, it can also help you set the tone of the speech. Notice, for example, that the choices at the end of the list are much more informal and slangy than the earlier ones. In some situations, this might be appropriate; in others it might not be—depending on the choice of audience and frame.

Language choices can go well beyond vocabulary, as we'll see in Chapter 10. They include uses of language such as metaphor and other tropes. An exciting or appropriate metaphor, such as Martin Luther King's "I've been to the mountaintop," can easily pull together a whole speech and help the audience not only understand it but remember it as well.

Suppose that Danielle has decided that the right frame and audience for this speech is that students should see themselves as members of a larger community and take some responsibility for what happens in that community. One choice that would help her to express this idea vividly to the audience would be a figure of speech that makes the plastic bag of donated blood a symbol for community itself—"This is community in a pint-sized bag." The complexities of public health problems and the volunteer blood donation system can be reduced to the image of the bag itself, allowing students to imagine their connection to the larger community when they imagine the bag. Rather than being scary or icky, the bag of blood becomes a symbol of hope and commitment.

Giving Your First Speech

Danielle, like most people, imagines that the hardest part of the process is delivering the speech. As we'll discuss later, that's probably not true—though it is true that people worry about it the most!

■ Delivering the Speech (Chapter 11)

Many of Danielle's choices about delivery involve how she will prepare and practice the speech. She'll have to decide if it will be extemporaneous (spoken from notes) or written out and either read or memorized (the more difficult options). Once she decides on a type of preparation, she'll have to practice it, either by herself or in front of a small, friendly audience, thinking especially about staying within her allotted time.

Of course, delivery matters. Danielle will want to deliver her speech clearly, not too fast or slow, and with appropriate feeling and emphasis. In Chapter 11, we'll talk about how to practice your speeches and refine all these elements.

◼ Overcoming Anxiety (Chapter 11)

Anxiety will probably be a problem for Danielle, as it is for everyone, including some of the most seasoned speakers. Though we will address this topic in greater detail in Chapter 11, for your first speech in public speaking class, you can remind yourself that your classmates are in the same boat as you, and you can focus on the all the preparation that you have done and just let the speech give itself.

◼ Presentation Aids (Chapter 12)

Danielle knows that her audience will appreciate visual images or media accompanying her speech. She may decide to bring some pictures or to use a program like PowerPoint to highlight important points, display graphics, and show images. First, she will have to consider a number of logistical issues, especially whether the setting is media friendly one. Danielle will have to decide just how image-rich she wants her presentation to be. If she uses too many images, props, or slides, the audience may either feel overwhelmed or may be distracted from what she is trying to say. If she relies too much on the images or media, she is at risk of letting the media use her instead of using the media to enhance her speech. She will have to decide what images and text enhance her message and what ones drown it out. We will discuss these issues at length in Chapter 12, with the goal of giving you some ways to manage visuals in your speech.

If all this seems like a lot to think about in preparing a speech, keep in mind that we'll give you techniques for breaking the process into easy, manageable steps. Moreover, if Danielle does all these things, she will not only have the confidence in her speech that she needs to counteract her anxiety, but she is also likely to give a powerful and effective speech. Even better, Danielle's speaking abilities will improve with every speech that she composes using this process—as will your speaking abilities. The skills that Danielle is honing in making a speech about giving blood will help her in the future, preparing her to make the kind of speeches that will change her personal history for the better, and perhaps make a difference in the lives of those around her.

Visual aids are often helpful in emphasizing your important points when used effectively.

Making Responsible Choices

Let's bring the concepts and processes of this chapter together. What you learn in a public speaking course is how to make good communication choices and how to take responsibility for them. Our aim in this book is to expand the choices you have in speaking and give you more and better ways of making those choices, enabling you to take responsibility for them.

■ Good Speeches Are the Result of Choices

What's a *good* speech? When the speaker is free from nervousness? When it gets big applause at the end? Most people imagine a good speech has something to do with getting what you want or transmitting information properly or getting the audience to think as you do. Although these outcomes may happen, they don't by themselves define good communication.

"Good communication" is a bit ambiguous, because it is pulled between choices that are *practically* good (they are effective in persuading your audience, getting what you want in the short run) and choices that are good because they are *responsible* (they are what you would want if you were in the audience). The best communicators make choices about how to write and deliver a speech that are both practically effective and ethically responsible. *Responsible* and *ethical*, for this context, are intertwined—taking responsibility for your choices is an ethical stance. Thus, your communicative ethics are revealed in the choices that you make in crafting a persuasive speech as well as the choices that you make in terms of your orientation to your audience (the kind of relationship are you creating with them as you step up to speak).

There are many possible good relationships with an audience. They depend on the specific case, and a good persuader can tell the difference between an appropriate and inappropriate approach. So, good rhetoric, or good communication, is actually pretty straightforward (though not simple in practice). It's about making choices and being willing to take responsibility for them. The responsible and ethical speaker chooses the appropriate goals for the audience and situation and the appropriate means to achieve those goals. In this sense, the story of Danielle serves as an example of what a speaker needs to do to give a good speech: making the best choices for the audience and the situation.

■ Taking Responsibility Means Respecting the Audience

Rhetoric and persuasion get a bad name when they are used irresponsibly—when the means or the goals disrespect the audience, ignore their interests, or treat them as less than fully rational participants in the process. There's a simple way to prevent these abuses: Be ready to take responsibility for your choices. Imagine, at any point in a speech, someone in the audience asking, "Why did you say that? Argue that? Use that metaphor? Organize your speech that way?" If you can give an answer, then you're taking responsibility. If you can't, then you are not living up to the requirements of public persuasion.

Many people find ways to reject responsibility for their own talk. Here are a few:

- Well, I don't know why I said that—it seemed OK to me.
- Oh, I hoped you weren't going to notice that.
- One of my sources argued that, so why not?
- It seemed like the only way to do it.

- The material just seemed to require this presentation style.
- Everybody does it this way.
- It's just conventional to say that—who cares?
- It's the truth.
- There isn't any other way to say it.

If you're not taking responsibility, then either you don't respect your audience or you don't care about being effective. Respecting the intelligence of the audience and treating their potential points of disagreement respectfully is an important part of persuasion and will make your speech more successful. As we pointed out earlier, the "public" part of public speech is connected with the best ideas of democracy, and democracy requires respect for disagreement.

Summary

Let's put it all together: *public* and *speaking*. Public speaking is powerful because it is communicating with other people in a way that respects their interests and also holds open the possibility of change. Speech changes society and can change your life as well. Public speaking addresses other people not only as individuals but also as members of a public, as fellow citizens in a democracy, as people motivated by common interests. Public speaking is deliberative, which means that the goal of a public speech is to create knowledge, to make better and more well-informed decisions about issues of common concern. Finally, public speakers make choices and take responsibilities for them; they make choices about content, organization, words, delivery, and visual aids to create a compelling speech.

Access an interactive eBook, chapter-specific interactive learning tools, including flashcards, quizzes, videos and more in your Speech Communication CourseMate for *Public Speaking*, accessed through CengageBrain.com.

QUESTIONS FOR REVIEW

1. Why will it benefit you to become a better public speaker?
2. Why does public speaking matter?
3. What's the relationship between preparation and performance?
4. What are the elements in a good public speech? What does a speaker have to think about in preparing a speech?
5. What does the idea of "public" mean in public speaking?
6. What is communication? What distinguishes public speaking from communication more generally?
7. How is public speaking related to democracy and to civic life?
8. How do speakers take responsibility for their choices?

QUESTIONS FOR DISCUSSION

1. How do you think public speaking will make a difference to your life, both as a speaker and an audience?
2. Can public speaking's connection to democracy extend to everyday speeches, especially in business and personal settings?
3. What are examples of irresponsible speech? What are the negative effects of irresponsible speech?
4. In your opinion, what makes a speech succeed or fail? What makes one speech persuasive and another fall flat?
5. Do you think the idea of a public is relevant in our current political and social situation? Is it too idealistic? Can one individual make a difference in public life?

LEARNING GOALS

- Explain what it means to communicate ethically
- Identify the main reasons why ethics matter to public speaking
- Identify various ethical pitfalls for speakers
- Apply the seven principles of ethical public speaking to your own speeches
- Define plagiarism and explain how to avoid it

CHAPTER OUTLINE

Introduction: Why Ethics Matter in Public Speaking

Ethical Pitfalls in Public Speaking

Seven Principles of Ethical Public Speaking

How to Avoid Plagiarism

How to Create an Ethical Speech

Avoid Fallacies and Prejudicial Appeals

Ethics and the Responsible Speaker

Lamont had a great idea for a speech that he wanted to give on lowering the drinking age. He thought that it would be particularly persuasive to his audience to argue that lowering the drinking age would result in safer conditions for underage drinkers on campus. There was only one problem: He had researched heavily, and he found very little evidence in support of his thesis. He did find a few quotations like "Some would argue that reducing the drinking age would make on-campus drinking safer, but . . ." The *but* was the problem. All the evidence he found argued against the thesis that he wanted to put forward. He knew that evidence supporting his case existed somewhere, but he simply couldn't find it. There was an easy fix, thought Lamont: Why not just eliminate that pesky *but* and cite the sources he had found as if they supported of his thesis? After all, would anyone really notice?

Overview

In this chapter you will learn why ethics matter in public speaking. This chapter will help you be more aware of the practices that contribute to or detract from ethically sound relationship building with your audience. It will help you make choices based on mutual responsibility and good reasons rather than on manipulation and deceptive arguments. We will address the implications of deceptive, biased, and poorly reasoned speech as well as provide positive principles to help guide your public speaking choices. We will also address the issue of plagiarism, or using other people's work without giving them proper credit. Finally, we will discuss how to create and deliver speeches that contribute to an ongoing conversation with your audience. You may want to revisit this chapter as you work through the book. ❭

Introduction: Why Ethics Matter in Public Speaking

ethics Rules or standards that govern people's conduct, or habitual moral behavior.

The Greek term *ethos*, which is the root word for *ethics*, means both "character" and "habit." **Ethics** can be defined as the principles that govern people's actions, or as habitual moral behavior. Some of the ethics of public speaking are probably obvious to you: You should not fabricate quotations or facts; you should not misrepresent the sources that you quote; you should not intentionally mislead your audience; and you should not knowingly use weak logic or faulty arguments. Most people agree that these practices are ethically shaky, whether in day-to-day conversation, in speeches delivered in or outside the classroom, or in another means of communication (such as writing, texting, or instant messaging).

In a public speaking class, unethical speech can affect your grade. But unethical communication practices can also harm your reputation, limit your effectiveness as a communicator, and damage your relationship with the people with whom you are communicating. What if you persuaded members of your audience to make a significant change in lifestyle based on shoddy evidence? What if this change harmed their health or well-being in some way?

When ethics in public speaking is based on the relationship between speaker and audience, the goal of public speaking becomes more than simply influencing or informing them. "Effectiveness" in the narrow sense of getting your own way is not a good test for ethical acceptability. Throughout history, speakers have used deception and manipulation to persuade audiences to do things that were wrong. The fact that a speech is effective in moving an audience does not mean that the speech is ethically good.

Because your words can affect your audience, you need to steer your listeners in a direction that is both effective in changing their minds *and* good for them. To do this, your speech needs to be based on

FAQ — *Why do I need to worry about ethical choices? Aren't I just delivering information from my research?*

In a sense, yes, often you are relaying things you've learned to the audience. But you don't relay *everything*—you can't—which means you're making choices. And if your audience questions your choices ("Why didn't you mention . . . ?"), you need to be able to take responsibility and explain the reasons for your choices. So, every communicator, no matter the context, by definition is forming some kind of ethical relationship with the audience.

Ashwini Bhatia/AP Images

The goal of ethical speaking is to create a trusting relationship with the audience, a skill at which the Dalai Lama, for instance, excels.

sound evidence and arguments. If your goal in public speaking is to connect with your audience on a topic of importance to you, you should do everything you can to build a good relationship with them. This relationship is the most important component of public speaking, and it is the core from which all the choices you make should flow.

Your choices entail more than just avoiding ethical pitfalls like lying, misrepresenting sources, and knowingly making weak arguments. Ethical public speaking also requires responsibly using and citing evidence in your speech, employing sound reasoning, and delivering your speech in a clear and accessible manner. Good speakers take these steps to nurture their relationship with their audiences.

Ethical Pitfalls in Public Speaking

Deceptive speech, inappropriately biased speech, and poorly reasoned speech represent potential pitfalls in building an ethically sound relationship with your audience. In this section we highlight what you should try to avoid in speaking. Let's start with lying, or the pitfall of deceptive speech.

Deceptive Speech

Consider the following thesis for a speech:

Lowering the drinking age to 18 will help young people, and college students in particular, to drink less.

Wait—is that true? Will lowering the drinking age help young people drink less? Would there be anything wrong with defending that thesis if it weren't true?

Is it morally wrong to say something untrue? Your reflex response may be "Of course it's wrong," but this is a more complex question than it may first appear. In everyday speech, we often say things that are untrue, but our intention is not always to deceive. Sometimes we just have the facts wrong. For example, if you argue in a speech that 80% of college students binge drink, you may simply be mistaken but not necessarily lying.

However, if you decide it's OK to say, "Everybody on campus drinks," because everyone exaggerates now and then, your choice will be hard to justify. That little bit of hyperbole for the sake of making an argument can have serious negative effects, because students' drinking habits are heavily influenced by their perceptions of what "everyone" is doing.[1]

What makes an intentional lie wrong is that the misrepresentation or omission is *done for the speaker's advantage*. Liars know the truth but either hide it or make the audience believe something different, and usually they do so for their own benefit. For example, if you're trying to convince an audience that a particular political candidate is terrible when she is not, you are probably doing so in the hope that people will vote for your favorite candidate. An intentional lie deceives for the purpose of accruing some benefit for the liar.

Sometimes, however, an intentionally deceptive statement does not have a destructive or self-serving purpose. For example, if a friend asks whether you like the new shirt he bought, you might say yes even if the answer is no. The motive behind socially acceptable white lies like this one is to avoid hurting someone's feelings, whereas the goal of intentional deception, such as lying about an opposition candidate, is to benefit the liar. The difference is motive.

Try It! *When Lying Might Be Ethically Defensible*

Of course, if you were protecting an innocent person from a murderous mob by hiding him in your house, you might be justified in telling the mob he is not there. Even though honesty is a good ethical goal, protecting the life of an innocent victim might justify a bit of deception to avoid a more significant ethical evil.[2] Brainstorm more instances of ethically defensible lies.

Despite the distinctions between different kinds of lies, most of us agree that lying is an ethically undesirable choice, and the ethical goals for our speeches ought to be avoiding harm, promoting good, and maintaining the quality of our relationships. Thus, though lies may be acceptable in some narrow instances, they are not justifiable in public speaking, because the goal of a good relationship in public speaking is to give the audience as accurate a version of the facts as possible so they can make a good decision on the basis of the evidence presented.

Try It! *Reasons to Be Honest—and Not to Be*

Make a list from your personal experience of all the advantages and disadvantages of honesty in communication. Then compare them to the lists of other people in the class. How similar or different are they? What do you think accounts for the differences?

Deceptive speech has three important drawbacks for your audience and your relationship to them. First, deceptive speech practices can harm your audience by inducing them to act on or believe in things that are untrue. Second, deception can damage your credibility. If your audience begins to wonder whether you are being deceptive, either because something doesn't sound quite right or because they know the truth about your claims, you will lose credibility. Third, the technical choices you make in speaking—deciding what to say, how to say it, what details to include, what to leave out—are ethical choices. If you are willing to lie for a public speaking grade, you are cultivating a habit that may be harmful to your character.

Inappropriately Biased Speech

All speeches come from a viewpoint that is unique to the speaker. The question, however, is whether you let your personal perspective, or *bias*, shape *all* the evidence or information you present in your speech. Because an ethical public speaker respects the intelligence of the audience, your goal is to make your case while letting the audience make up their own minds based on their own reasoning skills. As a result, when you are speaking you ought to make choices do not rely on bias and that allow listeners to see multiple legitimate positions on your topic.

bias Your own personal perspective.

It's important, however, to distinguish between bias and advocacy. **Advocacy** is presenting a strong case for your perspective or leading your audience toward a change in belief or an action. Being an advocate means you are willing to give alternate perspectives a fair hearing. You may be advocating lowering the drinking age, but as an advocate you're aware of, and address, the reasons why people might disagree. Showing bias, on the other hand, means that you intentionally misrepresent, leave out, or unfairly downplay alternative perspectives. Biased presentations ignore the fact that reasonable people can and do disagree.

advocacy Making a case for a perspective, a change in belief, or a particular action.

Think about it this way: As a speaker who is providing information, you will be at your best when you treat your topic the way you expect your teachers to treat topics: You give the fullest picture possible, without leaving out facts or ignoring areas of dispute. For example, if you were giving an informative speech about the effects of lowering the drinking age, you would present the evidence on both sides. By the same token, if you were giving a persuasive speech, you would certainly advocate your position, but not by leaving out or discrediting alternative viewpoints. For example, in a persuasive speech advocating lowering the drinking age you might legitimately say the following:

> **Some scientific evidence justifies the claim that legal drinkers are, on average, more responsible drinkers.**

In contrast, this would be an inappropriately biased statement on the topic:

> **Just think about the negative effects of Prohibition. Obviously, setting the drinking age at 21 makes things worse in the same way.**

The difference between advocacy and bias is a matter of the choices you make. Notice that in citing "some scientific evidence" in the first example above, the advocate does not back off her claim that lowering the drinking age is good. Instead, she qualifies it with the word *some* to acknowledge disagreement.

An advocate presents a strong case for his or her position and gives other perspectives a fair hearing.

In the second example, the speaker chooses to ignore criticism altogether, which can be a surprisingly ineffective persuasive strategy. Listeners who disagree with the speaker will be put off by the suggestion that they are being unreasonable. In contrast, the first statement is on solid ethical ground because it respects the intelligence of the audience, acknowledges an alternative viewpoint, and suggests there are sources they could consult to come to a reasoned decision on their own.

Poorly Reasoned Speech

Deception and bias are two common ethical pitfalls in public speaking, and the third is poorly reasoned speech. We will show you how to create a well-reasoned speech more extensively in the chapters on research and persuasion. For now, we will discuss the ethical implications of knowingly making poor arguments.

What is an argument? It is not a shouting match or a heated back-and-forth between two or more parties. An **argument** is a **claim,** or something you would like to prove or get another person to agree with, that is supported by some **grounds,** that is, evidence, expert opinion, data, or logical chain. **Reasoning** is the process of making good arguments that are well supported by good grounds.

There are a number of ways the process of reasoning can go wrong. Here are some examples:

argument An assertion (a claim) supported by evidence, expert opinion, data, or a logical chain (grounds).

claim A statement to be proven or agreed to.

grounds Evidence, expert opinion, data, or a logical chain in support of an argument.

reasoning Making good arguments that are supported by good grounds.

- *Claims without any support.* If you say, "Eating a strict diet of rutabagas is the path to a healthy life," but you don't provide any data, expert opinion, or studies to back up the claim, your argument that is incomplete and therefore poorly reasoned.
- *Claims with weak support.* If you say, "You should invest heavily in pork bellies, because I read a really great advertisement from the Pork Council that said investments in pigs will really pay off," you have provided some grounds for your claim, but because your support is a small and arguably biased sample, it does not justify your claim.
- *Claims with inappropriate support.* If you say, "You should go to Disneyland for spring break, because the FDA recently found that vaccines are safe," you have provided support that does not justify your claim. Though most examples are not this obvious, speakers commonly cite evidence that has little to do with the conclusions they want the audience to make.

One of your most important choices in preparing a public speech is how you will back up what you are saying with data, studies, logic, and expert opinion. If you intentionally make claims without support or with weak or inappropriate support, you can all too easily mislead your audience. If your audience recognizes your poor reasoning, that will damage your relationship with them and your ability to inform or persuade them. If they do not realize that you are making claims based on shoddy support, they may end up acting against their best interests.

Seven Principles of Ethical Public Speaking

Now that you know what to avoid, what steps can you *take* to ensure your public speaking choices are ethical? Here are seven principles that will help you be an ethical and credible speaker:

1. Be honest.
2. Be open.
3. Be generous.

4. Be balanced.
5. Represent evidence responsibly.
6. Take appropriate risks.
7. Choose engagement.

Let's see how each of these principles works in practice.

Be Honest

Honesty really is the best policy. However, it's easy to forget that sometimes. Given what you know about your audience and what you want to achieve in your speech, you may be tempted to say things that aren't lies but that you know will mislead. For example, it would be misleading to claim that real estate is a foolproof investment because "in 2006 investors were routinely seeing 20% growth!" The real estate market worsened significantly in 2008, so your implication that it has remained the same since 2006 is just not true.

The more complete the information you give your audience, the more honest you are about the topic. Sometimes being honest means letting the audience see the limitations of your argument or your supporting data. You might think about being honest in these terms: It is always better to back your facts and claims with reasoning that *you* would find clear, well supported, and logically sound.

Feverpitch, 2010/Used under license from Shutterstock.com

It would be dishonest to pretend in a speech about investments that the real estate market has not suffered in the last few years.

Try It! *The Consequences of Dishonesty*

Think back on a couple of lies you have told, whether they were small or big. Think about why you told them. For each one, do you think that the other person, if he or she knew the truth, would still consider you an honest person? Why or why not?

Be Open

Do you have a specific motivation for making an argument? Perhaps you have direct personal experience with the issue, or perhaps you want to talk about the benefits of a product that you sell in your spare time. Open communicators ensure that their audience understands their motivations for talking about an issue are clear; less ethical communicators are sometimes selective about what they reveal about their motives and predispositions toward the topic.

If you have a personal motive, such as a specific experience with or a vested interest in your topic, you should say so. Not only is your openness likely to increase your persuasive appeal, but it also tells your audience why you are interested in the topic.

Openness applies not only to your topics but also to the kinds of reasoning that you use. For example, your political position influences the kinds of arguments you make. Explaining where you stand gives the audience a chance to think critically about your speech and points of agreement or disagreement. In addition, being open means being open to having your opinion changed—we discuss this idea up in Principle 6: "Take appropriate risks."

Be Generous

Ethical public speaking requires that you place the audience's interests above your own. You should use your speaking time for the good of the whole as opposed to pushing an agenda that benefits only you. A public is a community, and your speech should put the community first.

You won't always have just one goal in speaking. Your primary concern should be to help the audience by informing them about your topic, but realistically, you may be pursuing other goals at the same time, like getting a good grade or impressing that special someone in the second row. Those are legitimate goals. But you should convey to the audience the sense that you are speaking primarily for *their* benefit. Try to make sure that your audience will recognize that you want to expose them to some sound reasoning or to become aware of a beneficial change in their thinking or actions.

As an audience member, you don't like to think you are being manipulated for the speaker's gain. Choosing to speak for the benefit of your listeners is the ethical option because you have your *and* their best interests at heart. Your common interests help you form a genuine connection with your audience.

Be Balanced

balance Presenting alternative perspectives fairly.

Balance, or presenting both sides fairly, is the other side of the bias coin. Some speakers always try to balance their presentations, acknowledging views they don't agree with, but others focus exclusively on their own side, hoping the audience will forget the other side. The extent to which you include objections to, evidence against, and counterarguments to your position determines the level of balance in your speech.

More importantly, you should treat these arguments with the respect they deserve. In fact, you probably appreciate it when a speaker interprets your position fairly before critiquing it. Philosophers call this the Principle of Charity ("Always interpret others in a way that maximizes the truth and rationality of what they say"), and it's most closely associated with the work of Donald Davidson.[3]

Here is an easy test of your speech's balance: Ask yourself whether a person who holds an opinion opposite yours will think you are being fair in your presentation of their argument. Are you are giving the best possible version of the opposing argument? Have you captured the nugget of truth in it? People on the other side of a dispute are rarely stupid or crazy, even if you vehemently disagree with them.

When we address hotly contested issues, we should treat opposing viewpoints with the same respect we would like our arguments to receive. Choosing to give a balanced presentation of the facts in your speech is ethical because it allows the audience to come

As a listener, you don't like to feel manipulated. What strategy does that suggest to you as an ethical speaker?

to an informed conclusion. In addition, your speech may be persuasive because you have chosen to address the counterarguments against your position fairly and disarm them.

Represent Evidence Responsibly

When you cite a piece of evidence (such as survey results, statistical data, or a quotation), the audience should know the name of your source, what your source said, and where they can find the source if they are interested in fact-checking or exploring the topic further. Why? First, it is unfair to not give credit to someone else's work—this is plagiarism, the academic equivalent of stealing (look up your school's policy against plagiarism on the school website). Second, if you pass off someone else's work as your own, you deny your audience the ability to truly assess the credibility of the claim you are making.

Responsible use of sources requires the following:

- A citation that is complete enough to allow audience members to find it easily if they wanted to check on it themselves.
- A fair presentation of what a quotation says or what data means if audience members don't or can't look your source up. It undermines your audience's ability to think about your claims when you modify quotations or data to suit your needs. Let the opinions and work of others speak for themselves.

The irresponsible use of sources has become easier to spot, thanks to Internet search engines. Your instructor or classmates can do a quick search and easily catch you modifying or creatively "borrowing" ideas from others. The consequences for your grade, your credibility as a speaker, and even your academic standing could be severe. More importantly, it is a good ethical habit to properly present and attribute the work of others that informs your speech—you would expect the same from someone using your speech or writing.

Take Appropriate Risks

Risks in public speaking include building relationships, taking stands on issues, and giving your audience information that helps them think differently about a topic.[4] You are not only putting yourself on the line by giving a speech, but you are also putting your ideas up for public scrutiny. Though taking such risks can seem uncomfortable, the alternative is to give speeches about topics that everyone already knows about or that they already agree with.

The choices you make in regard to risks entail two ethical challenges. The first challenge is taking a large enough risk. You might not step out of your comfort zone to speak to audience members who disagree with you; you might just "preach to the converted." In doing so, you invite the following question: Why didn't you take the opportunity to do something meaningful, to make a change in your audience's opinions, actions, or understandings of the world for the good?

The second challenge is taking risks that are too large, straying into territory that you do not have good support for or that your audience will be unable to hear. For example, a speech insisting that everyone should join a doomsday cult because aliens are about to take over the world would be taking too large a risk in terms of what could be proved and in terms of what most audiences would find plausible and be able to evaluate and act on.

[handwritten: trouble with that]

Thus, one of the principles for composing an ethically good and persuasive public speech is to take on an appropriate degree of risk for the situation and for who you are. Test your choices using the self-risk test: Are you willing to put your beliefs and commitments at risk in an ongoing public dialogue? Do you approach the potential interaction with the audience as if it might change your mind at some point? In other words, do you go into the speech thinking, "Well, I hope this works, but I'm open to modifying my views based what I hear"?

Choose Engagement

[handwritten: break out of shell]

Done well, a good public speech is an invitation for vigorous public conversation—for an exchange of ideas and opinions that benefits the speaker and the audience.[5] When we talk about civic engagement in this book, we don't mean just speaking in a particular space (a city council meeting, public hearing, or community organization's gathering) but making speaking choices that open you to a potential dialogue with your audience.

A lecture is one-sided, but a conversation requires back-and-forth. Speakers can actively discourage audience participation—they can go well over time limits, they can speak in an inaccessible or an intimidating manner, or they can ignore obvious cues that the audience has lost interest, can't follow what is going on, or would like to ask questions. To make your speech the opening to a conversation, you should choose to invite your audience to participate in your speech. This does not mean letting them have their say in the middle of your presentation. It means you are speaking in a way that allows them to understand, digest, and engage with your ideas.

What might get in the way of your audience's engagement in your speech in this way? You might speak too quickly; you might use obscure or jargon-laden language; you might bombard them with too many facts; you might speak in a boring monotone or otherwise fail to hold their attention. Speaking in a way that stifles audience participation and response is unethical not only because it harms your relationship with the audience, but also because it prevents ideas from undergoing public scrutiny.

Engaging with the audience is a skill you can learn. You don't have to have Oprah Winfrey's charisma to make engagement work for you in a public speaking situation.

For the audience to engage your speech, you need to present your ideas simply, with structure, and at a pace that is digestible for the majority of the people listening to you. These are skills you'll develop as you practice your speech, and we'll discuss some specific ways to improve them in the chapters that follow.

As you might guess, engagement also means that you are open to audience feedback in the form of questions or commentary on your speech. You should engage audience questions (if the program or speaking format allows them) as thoughtfully and deliberately as possible, and you should see feedback as an opportunity to sharpen your speaking skills. (Check out Chapter 13 for more on dealing with audience questions.)

Inviting your audience to express their viewpoints is ethical because they contribute to an ongoing conversation about important issues. Whether your audience provides feedback in class or in conversations after class, the best goals of public speaking are served when your speech is an invitation to a larger conversation about an issue.

How to Avoid Plagiarism

If you compose and deliver your speech following these seven principles, you will be well on the way to giving an ethically sound speech. However, one breach of these principles is so important that it must be discussed in depth—plagiarism. **Plagiarism** is the act of using the language, ideas, or arguments of another person without giving the person proper credit. Several of the seven principles we just discussed offer strong ethical reasons for avoiding plagiarism:

> **plagiarism** The use of the language, ideas, or arguments of another person without giving proper credit.

- Plagiarism is not *honest* (Principle 1). If you do not give proper credit to your sources, you are implicitly claiming that the language, ideas, and arguments in your speech are entirely yours.
- Plagiarism does not respect the spirit of *openness* (Principle 2) because it conceals your sources, which prevents your audience from evaluating their credibility.

- Plagiarism is not *generous* (Principle 3) because it does not give other people credit for the work that they have done in writing, thinking, and making their ideas public.
- Finally, plagiarism does not *represent your evidence responsibly* (Principle 5), because your audience needs to know who created a quote, an argument, or an idea in order to understand its context and to track down and fact-check what you say.

We live in a culture awash with remixes and mash-ups of songs and movies, in which the laptop's cut-and-paste function has made it easier than ever to use other people's creations, ideas, and creative work—with or without attribution. It is unavoidable that you will be influenced by the ideas and styles of arguments from the sources you read while researching your speech, but "borrowing" without crediting the source is clearly unethical. To illustrate, let's consider some examples, from the most blatant acts of plagiarism to a few practices that are on the borderline of ethical behavior.

- *Blatant and egregious plagiarism:* If you find a speech online and you read it word for word, passing it off as your own, you are clearly plagiarizing. What your instructor expects from you, and what audiences expect from you outside the classroom context, is not simply to stand in the front of the room and say something. You must do the work to research the speech, compose and organize your arguments, and really think through your topic. Delivering someone else's speech as your own is a clear-cut case of intellectual theft, and you should not do it.
- *Uncredited "borrowing" of quotes, facts, and figures:* Sprinkling into your speech large portions of text copied from other places without giving credit is plagiarizing, even if you composed the material that surrounds the copied parts. If you use a quotation in a speech, you need to say where it came from, and you need to include that information in your speech's bibliography (see Chapter 8).
- *Paraphrasing or minor modifications:* **Paraphrasing** is rewriting or modifying text so its original idea and flow of argument are essentially unchanged. Speakers do this because it is easier to paraphrase an idea than it is to create original ideas and arguments. So, if one of your sources says,

paraphrasing Making minor modification of the wording of someone's idea or argument; requires citing the source.

> **Global warming will create significant environmental effects, including inducing a rise in sea levels that will threaten coastal areas,**

and you simply replace a few words, saying,

> **Global climate change will produce a number of significant environmental effects, including a rise in ocean levels that will threaten our coasts,**

you are plagiarizing. The rewritten version of this sentence contains only a few minor changes in phrasing; the original idea is unaltered. If you want to use a paraphrase like this in your speech, you must cite the original source.
- *Appropriating ideas:* All public speeches will borrow ideas from other people's work to some extent, and this is actually one of the great benefits of public speaking—it takes work that authors and researchers have done into the broader public sphere in front of a new audience. There is a risk here, however. If you introduce into your speech an idea that you would not have come to on your own, you must give credit to the source where you found the idea.

When it comes to plagiarism, you have a choice: giving credit or inappropriately taking someone else's words, ideas, or arguments. When in doubt, give credit! Chapter 8 describes how to take good notes as you research your topic, so you will not forget or misplace critical source information.

How do you avoid plagiarism in your speech? There are two easy steps you can take to stay on the safe side.

1. *Give credit for every quotation, idea, statistic, and argument you use in your speech.* This step is as simple as preceding the quotation or fact by saying where you got it from: "The Worldwatch Institute claims that global warming will induce a rise in sea level" or "The Heartland Institute produced a study that claims global warming is not a result of human emissions." Or you could start your speech with a quote, and then immediately follow it with "This quote, which was drawn from the Intergovernmental Panel on Climate Change, underscores the importance of addressing climate change," for example. "preceded the citation"? otherwise this is a bit awkward,."
2. *Provide complete citation information in your bibliography.* You need to include the author's name, title of the work, date of the publication, page numbers, and other information that will enable audience members track down the source; Chapter 8 will cover the details of citing a source and compiling a bibliography.

The bottom line is that you will use a variety of different materials, which all will influence your speech in some way. If you give proper credit to these sources,

- you will advance your case with rigor and strength,
- you will act generously, and
- you will give the audience the chance to engage with your materials.

If you do not give proper credit, you are engaging in an intellectual version of stealing, and your speech, your ethos, and your character will suffer accordingly.

How to Create an Ethical Speech

What other kinds of ethical concerns should you be thinking about in preparing your speech? From the moment you decide to speak about a topic that interests you and is important to you, you have a number of choices to make regarding how you will present and organize your material for your audience. These include choices about respecting your audience and your topic, presenting more than one side, dealing with disagreement, and avoiding prejudicial language.

Respect Your Audience

The seven principles of ethical public speaking ultimately imply that public speaking should be about *relationship* and *conversation*. Because a public speaking situation is about building a relationship with the audience, it's fundamentally a *cooperative* setting. The speaker and the audience are working together to come to points of agreement and to mark off points of disagreement. When the audience and the speaker disagree, their disagreement should be understood in the broader context of the cooperative relationship. Although it is easy to get into a heated exchange with a stranger whom we will never see again, we are more careful about how we disagree with our friends, or with anybody with whom we have an ongoing friendly relationship.[6]

The choices that you make in public speaking dictate the ethical character of your relationship with the audience. Is that relationship premised on honesty or deception? Are you open about how you came to your conclusions and to having your opinion changed, or are your processes of reasoning closed off to the audience? Are you speaking in a generous and balanced manner, or are you unfair toward people who might disagree with you? Are you representing the work of others fairly and in a way that helps the audience to evaluate your case, or are you misappropriating or hiding your sources? Are you open to risking yourself and your ideas for the sake of your audience, or are you unwilling to put your ideas on the line? Are you choosing engagement, or are you attempting to manipulate or otherwise exclude your audience's participation? Obviously, if you want to build a relationship that is both effective and ethically sound, you want to make choices that emphasize the seven principles of honesty, openness, generosity, balance, fair representation of evidence, appropriate risk taking, and engagement.

At the core of all these principles is reciprocity, or the Golden Rule. As a speaker, you should think, speak, and argue like you would like to be spoken to. Put another way, you should employ the same perspective toward the speech that you are asking your audience to take. Obviously, you want your audience to pay attention, listen thoughtfully, and be open to change on the basis of your speech. Consequently, you should choose speaking practices that allow your audience to pay attention, that create the opportunity for them to listen thoughtfully, and that give them the opportunity to make an informed change in opinion based on clearly cited, well-documented, and solid evidence.

To apply the Golden Rule, ask yourself these questions at each point in the composition and delivery of your speech:

Have I made any choices I'd want to conceal? Why?

Do my choices respect the audience's freedom to choose based on solid arguments?

Would knowing my purposes and techniques change anything for them?

Finally, you may also have a responsibility to an extended audience, a *community* of relevant people. If you are talking about AIDS prevention and your audience doesn't know very much, it might be easy to mislead them, intentionally or not. But you can check your ethical intuitions by making yourself responsible to a community of people who *do* understand AIDS prevention. If you'd be willing to take responsibility for your speaking choices with an expert in the audience, or if you'd be comfortable having your remarks on the front page of tomorrow's paper, then you're respecting your extended audience. If you wouldn't be comfortable, ask yourself why. What about your speech *wouldn't* you like to take responsibility for?

Respect Your Topic

The next important choice is how you will respond to the research that you have done on your topic. We call this "respecting your topic" because whatever your preconceived notions, research and expert opinion should guide how you think about your topic. Respecting your topic means that you should compose a speech based on your research rather than cherry-picking research to support your preexisting views.

Realistically, when most people prepare a public speech, they often already know what they would like to say. What this means in practical terms is that people often research their topic to find evidence that supports their preexisting opinions. Letting your agenda drive your research as opposed to letting your research drive what you will eventually say may result ethically suspect choices. It violates the rule of reciprocity regarding opinion change and the principle of risk. You cannot expect your audience to be open to your opinion if you are unwilling to be changed by your research or to follow where it is leading you. Of course, you may find after extensive research that your opinion still seems right. If so, good for you, but remember that it is important to go through the process of not only checking but also shaping your opinion as your research dictates.

A number of concrete practices can help you be responsible to the existing body of research on your topic.

1. *Pull research from a broad set of sources.* If, for example, you are politically liberal, you will naturally be tempted to go to primarily liberal sources, and if you are a conservative to go to primarily conservative sources. Picking your sources on the basis of their ability to confirm your biases closes you off from the variety of differing perspectives on your topic, and is ultimately irresponsible to the broader lines of thought that make up the literature on your topic. So, for example, if you want to make the case that the war in Iraq was bad, or was good, for national security, you need to do research in both conservative and liberal publications. Similarly, if you are giving an informative speech about health food, you should balance your research with sources on conventional as well as alternative medicine.

2. *After researching a number of perspectives, make some choices about which arguments are the most credible.* This requires hard work and thinking. Which sides of the argument are most appealing to you? Why? Which claims are most well supported? Who offers the best evidence and arguments? On the basis of these choices, you should start to form an opinion about what you want to say about your topic, primarily based on what are the most defensible conclusions.

3. *Once you have started making preliminary conclusions, ask yourself who would disagree and on what grounds.* This question will help you check your natural tendency to let sources that appeal to you do all the work for your speech without considering alternative arguments.

4. *Be willing to revise your conclusions based on new evidence.* If you have formed a provisional opinion about your topic based on your reading but you stumble across some really compelling new evidence, you have to be willing to change your mind.

5. *Include the main disagreements between differing perspectives that led you to decide on the case you want to make,* or the angle on your informative topic that you want to take. For example, if you are giving a speech about health care policy and you would like to argue that reform is worth the costs, you should cite the opposing arguments and explain why you came to your position despite the good objections of some critics.

In the end, respecting your topic is about letting evidence and arguments influence what you will say as opposed to simply confirming what you already thought. This practice is ethical because it both forces you to be honest about your views in your speech and ensures that your audience can make a well-informed decision about your topic.

Suppose you want to give an informative speech about the health benefits of running, which promotes heart health, bone density, and weight control. What is the other side of the picture that balances these benefits, and where would you find out about it?

■ Present Other Views and Treat Them Fairly

It is important to inform your audience about divergent viewpoints. Here we would like to suggest a few techniques for treating disagreement fairly.

People with opposing viewpoints don't disagree on absolutely everything. Usually the big disagreements in public life are about priorities or a few critical assumptions. Think about our public debates on the role of the government in promoting social goods (such as health, education, welfare, or any number of social policy issues). Though the tenor of public debate may not respect this fact, most well-intentioned advocates on both sides of any crucial issue agree about more than they disagree about.

Some people, for example, think that the government should stay out of the health care, while others think that the government ought to take a more active role in ensuring health care coverage for all U.S. citizens. The advocates on either side of this issue agree on a surprising number of things. Both sides would like to expand access to health care and to lower the cost of coverage. Both sides would like to promote efficient and effective health care delivery. Where the two sides disagree is usually whether the government's intervention hinders or helps to achieve these goals. In order to treat such disagreements fairly, you can employ the following techniques:

- *Foreground shared commitments.* What goals and values unite the majority of opinions, even ones that differ, around your topic?
- *Be clear about the central points of dispute.* Your job as a speaker is not only to say what you think but also to specify your position on grounds those who disagree with you would recognize. If you do this carefully, you will not only help your audience make an informed decision, but you will also put yourself in a good position to discuss the merits of opposing viewpoints.
- *Make the best possible case for alternative viewpoints.* Audiences know when you are intentionally presenting alternative opinions in a bad light. If you want your audience to engage with your topic and, more importantly, to grant you credibility in talking about it, you should present opposing viewpoints in a charitable light.
- *Make your grounds for disagreement explicit.* Once you have framed alternative viewpoints, be explicit about why you do not agree with them, and present a well-reasoned case for your position in the light of potential objections.

When should you identify opposing arguments? Probably throughout your speech, whenever they become relevant. For example, if your speech about raising the gas tax has three major points (raising the tax will create incentives for conservation, lead to the development of more efficient technologies, and produce significant new revenue), you might use an opposing argument as the introduction to a major point in the speech:

Raising the gas tax will create greater incentives for efficiency. Because an increased tax makes operating a car more expensive, drivers will have an economic incentive to cut out unnecessary travel. Some have argued that raising the tax will not have this effect, however. For example, a study by Gas Inc. argued that demand for driving is inelastic—that is, raising the cost of driving does not reduce gas use, because people will simply pay more to go where they want to go.

At this point, evidence to the contrary would usually be introduced, often preceded by the conjunction *but*:

But recent studies of states that raised their gas tax show that the cost of driving is a significant factor in the choices drivers make about where to go.

To complete the argument in an ethical and balanced way, at this point you would say why you believe one study and not the other:

This historical data from state gas taxes shows that the conclusions that Gas Inc. came to are not quite right. At a certain point, increases in the cost of gas do affect driving behavior, inducing more people to carpool, use mass transit, or avoid unnecessary trips.

Being balanced does not mean that you cannot advocate for one side. Rather, being balanced means presenting multiple perspectives on an issue and then providing your audience with the grounds that brought you to your conclusions.

Avoid Fallacies and Prejudicial Appeals

In public life, speakers make choices about not only *what* they are arguing or asking for but also *how* they argue or ask for it. You don't have to be on a college campus for long before you are solicited by people gathering signatures for petitions. They often begin by asking, "Do you have a minute for [the issue]?"—for example, "Do you have a minute for the environment?" This is, by definition, a loaded appeal. It is set up to make you feel like a loser if you say no.

An **appeal** is an attempt to influence the audience. Some appeals rely on the strength of the evidence or logic that undergirds them, and other appeals rely on prejudicial language. Language is prejudicial when it attempts to distract the listeners from thinking critically and making a decision based on the merits of the evidence.

appeal An attempt to influence an audience.

In this section, we'll describe name calling, glittering generalities, inappropriate testimonials, the plain folks appeal, card stacking, and bandwagoning—a few of the logical fallacies and unethical appeals that rely on drawing your attention away from the merits of a claim.

Name Calling

Name calling is sticking a label on people or ideas that prejudges them as good or as bad.

We can't afford civil liberties for *terrorists*.

When you call somebody a "terrorist," you have already made a number of judgments about what they did and why. However, you've provided no evidence or arguments, just assertions hidden under a negative label.

We must reject marijuana—it's a *drug*.

The implication "therefore it's bad" isn't supported by any arguments, so this name calling is just a way of short-circuiting real dialogue. After all, ibuprofen is a drug, and it's widely regarded as beneficial.

Glittering Generalities

Glittering generalities connect a person, idea, or thing to an abstract concept, whether positive or negative. The speaker expects the goodness or badness of the abstract concept to transfer to the topic, just by being mentioned in the same sentence.

It's the *patriotic* choice.

Everybody on every side of every issue thinks their position is the patriotic one, and they may be right. In a democracy, equally patriotic people can disagree, so it's unfair to attempt to bypass discussion through an appeal to patriotism.

How should you react when speakers use shorthand expressions like "job killing" or "death tax"?

Inappropriate Testimonials

Inappropriate testimonials rely on good will toward a celebrity rather than expertise.

Hey, it's the *president* recommending this.

No matter who is president, just being president is not adequate support for an argument. Of course, not all testimonials are unethical, because we should be influenced by people we trust in the areas where they have expertise or experience. But "Trust me" (or "Trust him") isn't a substitute for real reasons and dialogue.

Plain-Folks Appeals

Pretending to identify with the audience's (assumed) tendency to avoid complexity or unfamiliar ideas is a plain-folks appeal.

I don't know much about economics, but I know I can't run a deficit in my bank account.

Perhaps the economy would be easier to manage if the federal budget were like our personal bank accounts, but it isn't. There are good deficits and bad ones in a national economy, and you have to make the case for your view, not just throw up your hands.

Card Stacking

Card stacking (as in stacking the deck in a card game) uses evidence selectively to prove a point, especially by allowing one or two extreme examples to stand in for a whole range of evidence.

Cheating is rampant on this campus! Did you hear about those crazy cheaters in Biology 101?

A card-stacking argument that student cheating is a widespread problem might focus on a few shocking episodes and never bring up the majority of students who are honest in their course work.

◼ Bandwagoning

Arguing that "everyone" believes or is doing something is an attempt to get the audience on the bandwagon.

Everybody knows that big banks can't be trusted.

This kind of claim isn't a logical argument. It's more like bullying, implying there's something wrong with *you* if you don't believe what "everyone" believes.

In conclusion, composing an ethically sound public speech requires making choices that treat your audience as you would like to be treated. You would like to hear good information and arguments presented in a clear, compelling, and honest manner. You would like to be able to have a basic grasp of the various perspectives on the issue, and you would probably like some guidance on how to sort through the different claims regarding a change in opinion or action.

Summary

Public speaking can go ethically wrong in a number of ways: lying, misrepresentation of facts, poor reasoning, plagiarism, poor citation of sources, and intentional use of manipulative or deceptive appeals. All of these ethical lapses can damage the relationship between you and your audience. You should feel great after having delivered a well-researched, well-thought-out speech, and you should feel even better if you do it in a way that you can be proud of from an ethical perspective.

Cultivating ethical public speaking as a skill can make an important difference in your life and perhaps even in the world. Maybe someday you will convince business colleagues to undertake a profitable change, or you will help your community overcome a pressing challenge. The key to making a difference, whether large or small, is to see each public speaking opportunity as a chance to build a relationship with an audience and to point the audience toward some greater good. Each chance you have to speak lets you take part in a larger ongoing conversation and to make positive changes.

Access an interactive eBook, chapter-specific interactive learning tools, including flashcards, quizzes, videos and more in your Speech Communication CourseMate for *Public Speaking*, accessed through CengageBrain.com.

QUESTIONS FOR REVIEW

1. How do relationships and conversations relate to communication ethics?
2. What are the seven principles for ethical communication?
3. How is bias an ethical problem for speakers?
4. Choose three of the prejudicial appeals described in the chapter and give an example of each.

QUESTIONS FOR DISCUSSION

1. Is it always wrong to lie? Explain why or why not and give examples to support your answer.
2. Choose three of this chapter's principles for ethical speaking and give an example of how a speaker might fail to uphold each of them. How could each of these ethical lapses be corrected?
3. How do you usually evaluate whether communication is ethical? List your personal criteria and be prepared to defend them.
4. Do you disagree with any of the principles in this chapter? Why or why not? Use examples to prove your point.
5. We have identified a number of ethical faults in this chapter. In your opinion, which are the worst? Which are nearly acceptable, and when? Give examples to back up your claims.

- Analyze the character of audiences

- Explain how the identity of the audience influences your choices, and explain how your choices influence the identity of the audience

- Define and distinguish between the literal audience and the rhetorical audience

- Define and distinguish between marketing and engagement as approaches to the audience

- Understand how your interaction with an audience fits in the broader context of the public and democratic conversation

Radius Images/Alamy

CHAPTER 3

Understanding Audiences and Publics

Looking out over the class, Aliyah wondered how she was going to do it. How would she connect with all these different people! She didn't know any of them and didn't think she could figure out how to talk to people she didn't know. Where should she even start in thinking about her speech? Though she was passionate about a number of topics, how could she know if the audience would feel the same way about them? She just didn't know how to start writing a speech for a group of people so diverse and mostly unknown to her.

Overview

Understanding and connecting with your audience is crucial if you want to give a successful speech. In this chapter, we begin by providing you with a way of thinking about audiences and gradually move outward to the ways your interaction with a specific audience is part of a broader public conversation. To start, we offer a set of tools for analyzing your audience. Second, we provide you with resources for adapting your speech to your audience, with the goal of helping you to make effective choices about the best ways to engage them as you persuade or inform them. Next, we discuss the idea that audiences are also part of a larger public dialogue. We conclude this chapter with an argument for understanding your audience as part of a broader public conversation, and we talk about your responsibilities to them. ❯

Introduction: Those People Sitting in Front of You

Effective public speaking requires that you connect with your audience. If you deliver a carefully researched, well-argued, stylistically powerful speech, but you fail to engage your audience, your speech will not be effective. Connecting with your audience requires you to develop skills in analyzing your audience and, on the basis of analysis, adapting your speech to it and engaging its members.

- Analyzing your audience means thinking about the makeup and motivations of your audience, so that you have a sense of the best way to make your case to them.
- As we discussed in Chapter 1, adapting to your audience means writing, framing, and delivering your speech in a manner that will maximize the chances that they will not only hear you but may also change their opinions, beliefs, or actions in response to your speech.

Analyzing and adapting to your audience are fundamental skills for responsive communication. Communication is always directed to another person in some way. Letting the other person know what is on your mind is the goal of *expressive communication*. In contrast, the goal of *responsive communication* is to engage the other person and elicit a response, so it must take into account his or her opinions, motivations, beliefs, and character. Inexperienced speakers often focus on themselves: "What do I think?" "What do I feel like saying?" Although of course the speech starts with the speaker—you have to have something you want to say—to be effective, you need to include the audience in the choices you make in both planning and speaking.

In public speaking, you want not only to make your opinion known but also to influence how your audience thinks about your topic—whether your goal is to inform your audience, to persuade them to take action, or to honor someone on a special occasion. In each of these cases, achieving your goal requires making choices to carefully tailor your speech to the audience.

Though you have specific goals in mind for each audience to which you deliver a speech, a public speech is also a turn in a larger conversation. As a communicator, you should think about your audience as a partner in an ongoing public conversation. Your goals in speaking and your choices in composing and delivering your speech should move a public conversation forward. Thus, for any public speaking situation, you will need to develop an understanding of the audience in order to foster a relationship with it and to strengthen the quality of public conversation in your community and beyond.

We begin by giving you tools for analyzing and engaging specific audiences: asking who, what, where, when, and why questions about each audience and viewing them as a rhetorical, as well as a literal, audience.

Audience Analysis

Audience analysis is thinking about the beliefs, values, experiences, and motivations that characterize your audience. Of course, an audience is usually made up of people with different, beliefs, values, experiences, and motivations. Still, you can try to answer some questions about the general tendencies of your audience. You might think about these questions as the who, what, where, when, and whys of audience interaction:

- *Who* is in the audience?
- *What* opinions does your audience already have about the topic you are presenting?
- *Where* are you addressing the audience? What things about the context or occasion might influence your audience members' interest and dispositions?
- *When* are you addressing the audience? This is not just a matter of the time of day, but also why your topic is timely for the audience.
- *Why* would your audience be interested in your topic? Why should these people make a particular judgment, change their minds, or take a specific action? In other words, how does your goal intersect with their interests, concerns, and aspirations?

This analysis will help you figure out how to make effective choices in your speech.

Skillful public speaking requires identifying the common factors that unite an audience's opinions and the possible points of persuasion. A good speaker can also convince the audience to find new areas of commonality. But this task requires more than simply identifying who is in the audience and what they think.

The important distinction here is between the **literal audience**, or what the audience is as you get up to address them, and the **rhetorical audience**, or what the audience can become when you convince them to think about themselves—and your topic—differently. The literal audience is the group of people sitting in front of you, who have opinions and ideas that are all their own; they are the audience of marketing and advertising. The rhetorical, or possible, audience is who your speech can transform them into by convincing them to think differently about their worlds. The rhetorical audience is the audience you choose to address. Let's look at each audience in detail.

> **audience analysis** Surveying your audience's beliefs, values, experiences, and motivations.

> **literal audience** The group of people sitting in front of you, as you begin to speak; they can be described in demographic categories.

> **rhetorical audience** What the literal audience can become when you convince them to think or act differently.

The Literal Audience: Demographics

Analyzing the literal audience requires that you make a series of educated guesses about the commonalities between the people in the room. These guesses are based on knowledge (or assumptions) about the demographics of the audience. **Demographics** are the standard categories we use to understand who people are. They are classifications that can give a rough picture of important characteristics of the audience, such as the following:

> **demographics** Population characteristics, such as age, gender, or income.

Age	Political commitments
Gender	Sexual orientation
Race	Educational level
Socio-economic status (class)	Occupation
Religious beliefs	Income

For example, you know that all the people in your public speaking class are likely to be enrolled at the school. Because they are students, you can make some

Demographics help us understand some superficial characteristics of a group of people, such as age, gender, and race. For a public speaker, however, a deeper understanding of the audience is necessary—and possible.

Jim West/Alamy

Try It! *Experimenting With Demographics*

Pick a topic that is interesting to you and that would interest the audience in your public speaking class. What will you do to adapt this topic to an audience of college students? Now imagine giving the same speech to a middle-aged business or professional audience from diverse backgrounds. How would you modify your approach to address that audience? Finally, imagine that you are giving a speech on the same topic at a senior citizens center. What difference would this change in audience make for your speech?

educated guesses about how they think about the world and what issues concern them (20-something college students think about the world differently than older or younger people do). You can also make educated guesses based on their age about other things that might influence your speech, such as media consumption habits, political leanings, and a number lifestyle issues. For example, most people under 40 have never used a typewriter or rotary phone.

You might also make guesses about your audience based on their educational level or professional experience, which will dictate the kinds and complexity of topics that you can treat. You might even make some guesses about your audience based on its racial or gender composition—though you need to be careful to avoid stereotyping. Different life experiences because of race and gender influence how people think about the world, but it is dangerous to presume that people can be defined by their race or gender. It's also important to remember that you can't tell someone's race, age, or maybe even gender just by looking across the room at them. Someone with light skin may self-identify as African American, and our age guesses can often be wrong.

Although demographics can be useful, you shouldn't assume you automatically know what someone thinks or values because that person is female or male, Chinese or Jewish, 15 or 50, or a college professor or a plumber. Instead, you should take the diversity of your audience as a clue to the diversity your speech must address.

Problems With the Demographic Approach

Relying on demographic data alone won't allow you to make good choices about how to engage with your audience. Why? Your information may be incomplete or inaccurate. Even if you get the demographics right, you can't assume you know people's positions or values based on their demographic characteristics. Generalizations are really just stereotypes, and they are often an undependable way to assess to people's actual beliefs or commitments.

Another problem is that if the audience doesn't fit the demographic implied by the topic, they have no reason to listen. If the speech argues, "Women should get yearly pelvic exams," then men in the audience have no reason to listen—unless you expand the audience to all people who care about the health of women. For another example, suppose the speaker starts a speech about a new diabetes testing device with the question, "Do you have diabetes?" That makes sense for the topic, but if the answer is no, then those audience members will tune out. They have no reason to care about the device—unless you expand your definition of the audience to include everybody who cares about someone who has, or could have, diabetes.

A focus on demographics can also lead away from finding a common ground for the audience. Demographics focus you on differences and toward treating the audience as a fragmented set of groups, rather than as a single group you are trying to persuade or inform. The fragmentation makes it hard to make choices: Do you choose arguments for the men or the women? For the rich or the poor? White or Asian?

Your challenge, then, is to make choices in your speech that cut through the inherent diversity of your audience to find commonalities and address your speech to them. Use demographic information about the audience as a starting point, but then move beyond these differences to find points of commonality. For example, if you are giving a speech about the negative effects of Title IX (the federal law that requires funding equity for men's and women's sports teams), and your audience has both men and women in it, you will of course find a way to address male and female students' concerns simultaneously. But suppose you have an all-guy audience. Does that mean you can assume that no one is in favor of Title IX? Of course not. Not only may some audience members have a sister or girlfriend who benefits from Title IX, but some men may favor it in principle, even if it decreases funding for their favorite sport.

The Rhetorical Audience

Speakers can make better speech choices by focusing on the audience they want to create rather than on just the demographic characteristics of the bodies sitting in the room. It's not the audience you are given that should guide your choices—it's what you *make* of the audience. What makes your speech effective is your skill in designing the persuasion that provides you with an audience suitable for persuasion, or a rhetorical audience.[1] The answer to questions like "Which arguments should I use? Which evidence should I offer?" is always "What makes my point best to my rhetorical audience?"

How do you create a rhetorical audience? By *addressing* them in a particular way, you can create a particular relationship, a particular "us."[2] You are already familiar with the idea of "addressing" an audience, because you do it interpersonally. When you greet someone, you use some form of address. To a friend, it might by "Hiya, Rudy." To the clerk at the convenience store, it's likely to be "Hi," with no name. To a teacher, it might be "Hello, Dr. Jones." But if you went up to Dr. Jones one day and said "Hi, Bob," it would cause some confusion. When you address someone as a friend or as a teacher or as a sales clerk, you are defining your relationship.

The same process operates in many communication contexts. Suppose you ask a fellow student out for coffee. Are you asking the person "as a student, let's talk about the homework" or "as a potential friend, let's get to know each other," or "as an expert, please will you tutor me." "Student," "friend," and "tutor" are different roles one person can inhabit, and so they are different rhetorical audiences.

You should make clear, in your approach, which audience (which role) you are addressing. You might even address—and so bring into existence—a role the other person didn't even think of: "Hey, are you worried about the tuition situation here? I am. I think we need to talk about what can be done." Now the audience is not "fellow classmate" but "fellow tuition-payer at our school." The other student may not have ever thought about himself or herself that way before, but your mode of address invites him or her to take the role of tuition-payer in listening to you.

The point about rhetorical audiences is that you are not simply bound to what a demographic analysis can tell you about an audience. You can also invite the audience to relate to your topic through a different lens—through a lens that you create. The ways that you may invite an audience to engage a topic are bounded only by your rhetorical imagination and creativity.[3]

Try It! *The Rhetorical Audience*

What's the difference between literal and rhetorical audiences in the same situation?

Directions: Describe both a literal and a rhetorical audience for each of the following speech goals. For example, if the speech goal is to persuade people to recycle, a literal audience would be "the 18- to 30-year-old students in front of you who are mostly from the city you live in and work part-time jobs," and a rhetorical audience would be "people who care about saving the earth."

- Persuade someone to avoid texting and walking at the same time.
- Persuade someone to take a public speaking class.
- Give a wedding toast.
- Inform an audience about a proposed piece of legislation.

How do the answers differ? What does this tell us about audience?

The "As" Test

How do you figure out what audience to create? You can start, if you like, with demographics, and ask yourself about likely roles that cut across categories and include the whole group. From among those roles, ask yourself which ones would make your audience most open to changing their perspective on your topic. Or you can start with your topic (which you intuitively thought was appropriate to this group), and try to imagine the different possible audience roles for which you could design arguments.

A useful tool for choosing a rhetorical audience is the **"as" test**. For example, instead of addressing your audience in their roles as 20-somethings and college students, you could address your audience *as*

> **"as" test** A tool for choosing a rhetorical audience as people in a specific role in order to change their perspective on your topic.

Americans	curious people
citizens	voters
consumers	taxpayers
music lovers	drivers
achievers	people who care about their health
compassionate people	

Many more roles are possible. In principle, a rhetorical conception of your audience allows you to pick a role or perspective that not only helps them relate to your topic but also invites them to forge commonalities despite demographic differences.

The rhetorical role of the audience can influence a number of choices that you make in your speech. You might address the audience directly in their rhetorical role. For example, in a speech about online piracy, you might say, "As consumers of media, all of us are concerned with the quality of music that contemporary artists are producing." Inviting an audience to take up a specific role can also influence your choices about words and verbal style. For example, if you want to invoke the idea of people who have to make difficult choices about what they can and can't afford during a financial downturn but you want to avoid inviting the audience to think of themselves as cash-strapped consumers, you might say, "Budgets are tight, resources are not infinite, and we have to make some difficult choices about health care."

A limitation to the idea of the rhetorical audience is that you cannot magically make the audience into anything that you want it to be. You will need to use judgment about what roles you think your audience might be willing to assume. If you want to give a speech on the benefits of recycling, you can't assume the rhetorical audience is "people who care about recycling." That sounds good—it's

Hillary Clinton appealed in 1995 for women's rights to be regarded as human rights, invoking the audience in Beijing as members of the human community.

convenient!—but it misses a crucial point. You are speaking about recycling because you think some people don't know a lot about recycling or don't care about it very much. If you assume they already know a lot, why are you speaking? Instead, you might choose as your rhetorical audience "people who care about the environment" (because recycling helps reduce pollution and garbage) or "people who care about prices" (because recycling can make certain products cheaper). In general, a rhetorical audience of "people who wanted to hear this speech and agree with it" doesn't help you make choices that will help you reach people in your audience who don't fall into that category.

From "Me" to "Us"

As you think about the audience you will choose to address, you are directing your attention, to an extent, away from yourself. Most of the choices you make in planning your speech take your audience into account. But your orientation towards your audience is also a component of your speech. Sometimes speakers can appear to be lecturing or talking down to their audiences, because they create a distance between themselves and the audience. Listen to the difference in these two pairs of theses:

> **You** should all do more recycling.
> **We all** need to do more recycling.
>
> **You** need to know more about energy conservation.
> **We all** could be better informed about energy conservation.

In the first sentence of each pair, the speaker seems to be saying she is different from the audience: smarter, more knowledgeable, and more moral. They may find that off-putting, as if they were children being lectured. In the second sentence of each pair, the speaker includes herself in the speech. This makes a lot of sense. If you are calling a community into being, asking the audience to see themselves as all affected by a problem, you will be more effective if you are speaking as a member of that community.

Similarly, whenever you listen to a speech and evaluate it, you should ask yourself, "Who does the speaker think I am? What does he or she want from me? Is that appropriate?" You should expect the speaker to address you in terms you can relate to. For example, if the topic of the speech is obesity, and you feel you are pretty fit, you may think, "What has obesity got to do with me?" You should expect the speaker to address people like you in the speech: "Obesity is everyone's problem, because . . ."

Adapting Your Speech to Your Audience

Adapting to the audience doesn't mean just telling people what they already know or want to believe. It means creating a bridge between a particular version of the audience's identity and beliefs and what you want them to believe. You have several resources for building this bridge.

Identify Common Interests

What are the interests or goals your audience members, as _____ (fill in the audience you've chosen to address), could reasonably be expected to have? Tying your arguments to a goal that people would have in the role you're addressing enables you to adapt to your audience while advocating a policy or proposition they might have initially rejected or found implausible, or even presenting information they don't really care about. For example, if you are giving an informative speech on the registration process at your school, you can be sure that everyone who registers has similar interests, such as getting the classes they want and getting through the process quickly.

Make the Most of Shared Experience

In many cases, the audience you create will have a set of common experiences. You can use these for your argument: "Everybody knows how annoying it can be to stand in line and deal with the registrar." You can organize your speech in terms of these experiences: "Everybody knows the registration process: first you get the class schedule, then you attempt to register, and then you try to find another set of classes. At each stage, you're paying for things you don't need." You can also emphasize topic through verbal style: "Registering for classes is like playing the lottery."

Work from Common Premises

Your audience may share common assumptions. Bringing these to the surface can provide points to support your argument: "Getting the right courses is important, or we wouldn't put so much work into the registration process."

Be Directive

Your creation of the audience can be normative. You can tell your audience who they should be.

> As students, we *should care* about the negative influence of big sports at our school because . . .
> As U.S. citizens, we *need to be interested* in other countries' opinion of us because . . .

Two Views of the Audience: Marketing vs. Engagement

The conceptions of the literal and the rhetorical audiences imply different approaches to interacting with an audience. To see how, let's look at the differences between a familiar type of communication, marketing, and engagement, one of the principles of ethical speakers we discussed in Chapter 2. We live in a sea of advertising and marketing. Marketing is about convincing an audience to change their behavior, based on their existing beliefs and motivations, and engagement is about changing the beliefs and motivations of the audience (see Table 3.1).

Marketing

When you are selling something, your relationship to your audience has four characteristics:

TABLE 3.1	Two Approaches to Audiences
Marketing	**Engagement**
One-way process	Two-way process
Demographic segments	Commonalities
Stereotypes	Self-risk
Means to an end	Deserving of honesty

- *One-way process.* When you're selling a product or a service, your goal is not a dialogue with your potential customers. You don't expect new ideas or mutual interests to crop up; you are doing something *to* them, not *with* them.
- *Demographic segments.* Marketers divide their audiences into demographic segments: old, young; rich, poor; college education, only high school; urban, rural; and so on. Marketers are interested in difference, in finding the specific groups of people most likely to buy their product or service.
- *Stereotypes.* Through research, marketers know who is most likely to like their soda sweet, their pants loose, and their cars slow. Stereotypes like these, if based on good research, can be very reliable, but they still just generalizations: Some young people like Cole Porter, and some older people like Jay-Z. Stereotypes need to have only enough truth to generate some sales.
- *Means to your ends.* In marketing, the audience members are means, not ends in themselves, deserving of respect. Marketing is premised on using people rather than engaging them. Although a salesperson may try to convince people that she's helping them out, which might sometimes be true, in the end she just wants to sell her product because it's her job.

Advertising creates a detached, impersonal relationship with an audience.

Songquan Deng/Shutterstock.com

Engagement

Communication in any democratic framework requires a genuine engagement, recognizable by everybody involved. A democratic framework is of course an integral part of the institutions that form our government. But it can also be the framework for lots of organizational and small-group settings. Whenever a group of any size decides they are going to listen to everybody and give everyone's insights and arguments equal weight, they have adopted a democratic framework. To what does genuine engagement commit you?

- *Two-way process*. Real engagement includes both talking and listening. As a speaker you have a responsibility to treat the audience in the way you'd like to be treated, which boils down to the Golden Rule, discussed in Chapter 2. Although public speaking is part of a public dialogue, it isn't actually conversation, and your audience may not always be able to respond. But you still have responsibility to address them *as if* they were going to respond and have their turn.

- *Commonalities*. Public speaking that's engaged doesn't segment the audience and deal with every demographic difference piecemeal. Instead, the democratic imperative is to talk to the whole audience, because everybody is part of this conversation. The skilled public speaker finds a way to speak across differences of identity, beliefs, and values.

- *Self-risk*. If you see your speech as part of a larger dialogue, you approach it as if someone in the audience might change *your* mind. You can test your speech choices using the "self-risk" test described in Chapter 2: Are you putting your own beliefs and commitments at risk?[4]

President Clinton's "dialogue on race" in 1997 with a group of well-known conservatives showed that speaking on difficult topics requires being open to having your own beliefs challenged.

© Presselect/Alamy

- *Deserving of honesty.* In the public dialogue, if you are speaking to an audience who knows little about your topic, it might be easy to mislead them. As we pointed out in Chapter 2, you can assess the integrity of what you are asking your audience to believe or do by imagining that they are an audience of experts.

> ### Try It! *Marketing vs. Engagement*
> Pick an issue that is important to you. If you were marketing the issue, how would you approach your audience? How would your approach change if you opted for an engagement approach?

The Audience and the Public

The hallmark of successfully engaging your audience is their recognition of their common interest in your topic. In other words, to be an effective public speaker, you should see your speech and your audience as part of a larger public conversation. So, this section will help you understand the broader public context of your audience.

As defined in Chapter 1, publics arise out of the common experience of a shared problem. For example, the people whose drinking water is polluted by an industrial polluter form a public, as do the people angered by the lack of choice among news outlets due to reduced competition in the news business. Whether your topic is large or small, local or global, your job as a speaker is to create and address a concerned public.

You participate in public conversations in two ways in public speaking class: as a speaker addressing public problems and as an audience member participating in issues of public concern. Both these ways of participating in public matters are broader than your specific community. A community is the people who share a common location (they live in the same town) or institution (they work at the same company or go to the same school or church).

In contrast, a public, as the U.S. philosopher John Dewey explained, is a set of individuals who have a common set of interests because they perceive a common problem.[5] These individuals probably don't know each other personally, and they may never meet, but *if* they met, they would be able to relate to each other on the basis of the cost

FAQ *What makes an issue a public issue?*

Private Issue	Public Issue
Tuition bills are putting a drain on my social budget.	It would be better for the university to reduce tuition for all the residents of the state.
I hate cigarette smoke.	The university should ban public smoking for the sake of the health of the students, faculty, and staff.
I need to go on a diet.	The state and local government should work to provide resources for healthier eating in schools and universities.

© Cengage Learning 2014

> ### Try It! *Joining the Public Dialogue*
> One of the goals of public speaking is to give each of us a voice in local and national public dialogues.
> - List three factors that limit the access of average citizens to local and national dialogue.
> - Which barriers affect you most directly?

Diverse groups of citizens can be united by their common concerns.

of gasoline, pollution of local lakes and streams, the lack of good candidates for state office, or some other topic. For example, people all over the United States are concerned about the future of our safe drinking water supply. Though they each have their own private needs and perspectives, live in different parts of the country, and have different individual circumstances, they are all united by a shared concern.

Ideas that you present in a speech may influence a member of your audience to blog about them, speak about them to another community, to write an editorial, or to engage in broader dialogue beyond the classroom in some other way. The point is that your participation in the great conversation around public ideas extends beyond your specific community, because your ideas, if persuasive, may carry beyond your speaking situation.

Try It! *What Is a "Public" Problem?*

Make brief lists for each of the following:

- What problems most affect your daily life?
- What problems do you think present the biggest challenge for your future?
- What problems most affect the daily lives of your friends and family?
- What problems present the biggest challenges for your friends' and family's future?
- What problems most affect the daily lives or futures of all people in the United States?

In what ways were your answers to each of these questions similar? In what ways were they different? What does this tell you about the big "public" problems? Which should we be most concerned about? What can we do about them?

Advancing the Public Conversation

Speaking to a public is speaking to a group of people whom you treat as reasonable, interested, and engaged partners in a dialogue. In speaking to a public, you are speaking to your audience about an issue that is of common concern, using a common vocabulary. This means speaking in a way that all the players in the dialogue can have meaningful input regardless of their age, gender, sexual orientation, religion, race, or class.

In a successful public speech, the speaker and audience are on the same side. You are both the "us" discussed earlier in this chapter. The "public" in public speaking means that you establish commonalities with people you may not know personally. When you look at an audience of strangers, you don't have to panic because you don't what their personal beliefs and values are. That doesn't matter to a *public* speaker. Instead, a public speaker will ask these questions:

- What public, exactly, should listen?
- Why should they listen?
- What common goals might we share in speaking and listening to each other?

Your Responsibilities to Your Audience

Because your speaking choices define the character of your audience and the way they engage with your topic, you have a responsibility for the connections you are inviting the audience to make. Does your speech invite the audience to understand issues in a deeper, more nuanced way? Does it lead them to value and fairly evaluate the positions of all the relevant participants in the public debate?

One way to think about why your speaking choices matter to audiences is to presume that *the world we speak comes into existence*. What does that mean? It means that the world can be seen as a collection of smaller individual worlds created by people communicating. The words people speak in one place can change the way people think and act in other places. It means that the habits we use in speaking help create our social context ats well as affecting the way other people respond to us.

Try It! *Words Create Worlds*

The words we use to describe things make an important difference in how we think about them. Discuss with a small group what difference the following descriptions make in how we think about each of these topics:

- Downsizing vs. firing
- The war on terror vs. the global struggle against violent extremism
- Slacking vs. relaxing
- High fructose corn syrup vs. corn sugar

In the largest sense, *speakers are responsible for the world their choices create.* If you speak in a way that demonstrates a lack of concern for your audience, that deceives them, or that aims only for your benefit, they are likely to respond in kind. For instance, in addressing the students and administrators at a university board meeting, you should try to make the best, clearest, and most compelling argument possible. But you also hope that your audience will listen to what you have to say and consider its merits. Indeed, your argument will have the best chance if you also listen carefully and consider other peoples' viewpoints, opinions, and objections. If your audience perceives you as deceptive, manipulative, or self-serving, they will likely respond with resistance, deception, or manipulation. In public speaking, the habits of speaking we develop also imply habits of listening, responding, and being part of a community.

So, taking your audience into account is about more than just guessing their pre-dispositions toward a specific topic and saying something interesting. Public speakers are making a difference, no matter how small or large, when they speak in public, to a public. Doctors make a difference to our health and so are bound by the Hippocratic Oath, an ancient ethical code of physicians that includes this promise: "I will prescribe regimens for the good of my patients according to my ability and my judgment, and never do harm to anyone." Likewise, public speakers should "prescribe regimens" for the good of their audiences according to their ability and judgment, trying to avoid harm to anyone.

Some speeches can help the audience by giving them information they might not already have; some can change people's opinions and possibly their actions; and some have changed the course of history. Because speech is such a powerful tool, you have a responsibility for how you speak. Framing a speech about lowering the drinking age in terms of students who die in car crashes creates a different world than a speech framed around the idea that a beer or two isn't going to hurt anyone. Either frame might be effective, but which one is the responsible choice?

There are two basic tests for whether your choices are responsible in relation to your specific audience and the broader public.

In a speech at Columbia University in 2012, United Nations Secretary-General Ban Ki Moon galvanized his audience with appeals to universal human values.

- *First, does your speech create a benefit for everyone*, including you, or is your speech responsible only to your own needs and values? A speech with political implications should benefit you and your fellow citizens.
- *Second, is your speech responsible to your audience and its context?* Answering this question means understanding what arguments will motivate your audience and allow them to achieve the change you intend. Your speech should give the audience the tools they need to take action on your topic. A speech that argues for getting rid of gravity or figuring out how to go back in time is a detour into fantasy unless the speaker can provide action steps the audience can take to accomplish these goals.

In the end, these two responsibilities of public speech mean that you'll need to adapt what you say to different contexts and different audiences, as we discussed earlier in the chapter. The ways you speak at home with your family, at lunch with a friend, and in front of an audience that you don't know should differ depending on what you are trying to achieve, how you can help the audience achieve this change, and why your audience is listening.

To decide what choices are responsible for a specific speech, ask yourself these questions about your audience:

- What is the best way I can cultivate a relationship with this audience in this context?
- What expectations does this audience have of me?
- What can I expect them to do with the points I am making in the speech?
- What common goals and ideals can I reference in making my case?
- And, finally, what changes in opinion, belief, or action am I calling for?

The habits you use in addressing an audience will make a difference not only in how they respond to you but also in whether your speech can help shape the public conversation for the better. If you cultivate an ethic of responsible, engaged, well-reasoned speech in your public speaking classroom, you will be developing habits that reach beyond your time in school and encourage others in your class to do the same.

Summary

Access an interactive eBook, chapter-specific interactive learning tools, including flashcards, quizzes, videos and more in your Speech Communication CourseMate for *Public Speaking*, accessed through CengageBrain.com.

In a public speaking setting, the audience is the people to whom you are communicating and for whom you make the choices that compose your speech. These choices set the tone for your relationship with your audience. This relationship affects how you and your audience will act in the future: Because public speaking is so closely tied to democracy, public speaking provides you with an opportunity to practice decision making with others. An effective speech can not only teach people about the specific contents that you would like to impart; it can also bring the audience and speaker together in thinking about difficult public problems.

As a speaker, you'll consider not only *who* is in your audience and *what* they will want to hear, but you will need to decide *how* you want to address them. In other words, you need to know who your literal audience is and who you want your rhetorical audience to become. The "as" test will help you figure out the possible ways you might appeal to your audience, for example, as fellow students, as concerned citizens, or as members of the human race. The choices that you make in defining how you want to address your audience determine what you will say to your audience and what ideas you will select and highlight in your speech. To make the most out of a public speech, you need to make careful choices, and you need to take responsibility for the effects of these choices.

Questions for Review

1. What is an audience, and how is it related to a public?
2. How does engagement influence how you understand an audience?
3. What are the different ways that you can analyze an audience? What are the strengths and weaknesses of the demographic approach to audience analysis?

Questions for Discussion

1. It's important to think carefully about how to address your audience. What problems do you think that we need better speaking to solve? How would you address an audience regarding any of the problems you think need better critical deliberation?
2. Try to think of the last time you were an audience member and you felt you were manipulated by a speaker (or even an advertisement or infomercial). What did the speaker do or say that made you feel manipulated? How did it make you feel?
3. How will choices about how to address an audience influence your decisions in putting a speech together—choices about the order of points, possible arguments, and types of evidence?

LEARNING GOALS

- Distinguish between hearing and listening
- Contrast passive, active, and critical listening and their uses
- Define and explain some of the ethical issues that confront listeners
- Identify obstacles to listening and how to avoid them
- Evaluate which note-taking techniques work best for you
- Develop strategies for giving effective, constructive feedback

CHAPTER OUTLINE

Commercial Eye/The Image Bank/Getty Images

Becoming a Skilled Listener

Tanya is bored. This class has so many speeches, and she has trouble paying attention to them all. While other students are speaking, she thinks about her homework for other courses, her work schedule, and her plans for Friday night. She knows she should be paying more attention—the teacher keeps asking questions after each speech—but she just can't seem to focus. Tanya has noticed this also happens when she's listening to teachers in her other classes. She wishes she knew how to listen better.

Overview

If public speaking is a conversation between a speaker and an audience, then "public listening" is every bit as important as "public speaking." In this chapter you will find out how you can be a more active, engaged, and critical listener. We start by distinguishing between simply *hearing* a speech and *listening* to a speech—which entails not only hearing but actively engaging and attempting to understand the content of the speech. To further define good listening practices, we discuss the differences between passive, active, and critical listening. Because listening is one half of the circuit of a public conversation, we also address the ethics of listening, which entails a set of practices and prescriptions about how you should think about listening. Finally, we will discuss the some of the most important impediments to good listening and a number of practices that can enhance your listening experience, including taking notes and giving feedback. ❯

Introduction: Public Hearing and Listening

You cannot control how interesting the speeches are that you have to listen to in the public speaking classroom or beyond, but you can control how you choose to engage with them. So what can you do to be a better and more engaged listener?

The answer begins with the difference between listening and hearing. Sometimes as an audience member you may hear a speech, but you are not truly listening to it. You may register individual words and sentences, but you are not thinking about what you are hearing, and you retain very little of the speech the moment that it is finished. And then there are times when you hear a speech and truly listen to it—that is, you engage the ideas in the speech; you actively think about the concepts; and you have paid enough attention to have good recall.

We can *hear* a speech in another language, but we can't *listen* to it because we don't know the language. Hearing is just the act of receiving the sounds; listening is actively processing what you are hearing. If you can't *hear* a speaker, you can move closer or ask him or her to speak up. If you are having trouble *listening*, the techniques in this chapter will help you.

As an audience member, you need to know how to listen actively and critically, engaging with the speaker's message. As a speaker, you also need to know about listening, because you are trying to get people to listen to you or help them listen to you in the most productive way. The more you know about what makes messages easy or difficult to listen to, the better you will be prepared to engage with your audiences.

Types of Listening

There is no one best way of listening. What's "good" in listening depends on what you're trying to accomplish, what you want to learn from the speaker, and what you think the speaker wants from you. We'll talk more about these factors and their part in good listening, but first, what are your choices of listening styles?

■ Passive Listening

passive listening Listening that does not actively engage the ideas and arguments of the speaker.

Passive listening is listening that does not actively engage the ideas and arguments of the speaker. It makes you a bit like a sponge: You're merely soaking up what's coming from the speaker and not thinking much about it. You're not analyzing it, questioning it, applying it to yourself, or making an effort to remember it.

Passive listening is what most of us do when we're watching television or a movie. We just let the experience happen, with the words and ideas washing over us and leaving whatever traces they may while our brain goes into neutral. Entertainment media don't ask for your engagement, but a speaker does. Public speaking is a dialogue between speaker and audience. Passive listening is like zoning out in a conversation.

Passive listening is not only a bit rude to the speaker, but it probably won't produce a great experience for you either. If you expect a speaker to grab your attention and hold your interest no matter how little effort *you* make, you'll probably be disappointed and bored. You probably won't be able to produce meaningful questions and take up your end of the larger conversation.

> ## Try It! *Your Passive Listening Profile*
> Make a list of the top three situations in which you are a passive listener. What are the consequences of passive listening in these situations? How do you feel about these outcomes?

Active Listening

Active listeners aren't waiting for the speaker to make sense—they actively seek to make sense out of what they hear. **Active listening** seeks the meaning and the relevance of what's being said. Suppose a speech is about concealed carry laws, which regulate carrying a gun in your pocket in public places. An active listener will be thinking, "Why does this person care about guns? Gun laws? Why do I care?"

Meaning includes not only the topic but also the speaker's angle or position. *Relevance* is the connection between your interests and the speaker's interests, and you'll be listening to see how much those converge.

active listening Listening attentively for the meaning and relevance of the speech.

> ## Try It! *Your Personal Active Listening Challenges*
> Make a list of the three situations in which you have the most trouble being an active listener. For each one, say *why* active listening is hard for you. What could you to do to improve your listening in these situations?

We listen to a speech in real time: We can't stop it, slow it down, or rewind. That means the speaker and audience need to work together for the speech to make sense. Speakers have the responsibility to provide enough organizational structure that the audience has a chance of following their ideas and line of reasoning. The audience's responsibility is to pay enough attention to put the pieces together, to make something meaningful out of what the speaker is saying.

Making sense out of a speech takes some work. Most of us benefit from either taking notes (which forces you to create a structure for what's being said) or making mental summaries of what you hear ("OK, the first point was about the history of gun laws, and so now the second point is about current law"). Active listeners typically find speeches more interesting than passive listeners do, because a speech that makes sense—that *you* help make sense of—is always more engaging than a speech that just washes over you. Table 4.1 summarizes the differences between active and passive listening.

TABLE 4.1 Active vs. Passive Listening	
Passive Listeners	**Active Listeners**
Just take things in, not really paying attention to specifics	Engage what the speaker is saying, thinking about the meaning and relevance of the claims
Don't reflect on the content of the speech	Pay attention to where the speaker is going and put the pieces together by taking notes or making mental summaries
Do not think of questions	Think of lots of questions

◼ Critical Listening

critical listening Listening to evaluate what is well done and poorly done in a speech.

Critical listening goes a step beyond active listening. **Critical listening** is listening with the goal of evaluating what is said in addition to listening actively for meaning and relevance. An evaluation is different from a preference. If you like your hamburgers with ketchup but not mustard, or movies with action over ones with romance, that is a *preference*. However, if you are *critically evaluating* a burger or a movie, you are applying the standards that are appropriate in the context regardless of your personal preferences. "This kind of movie is not to my taste, but it is very well done on its own terms" is critical evaluation.

The same strategy applies to a speech. Critical listeners listen for what's good and bad about the speech and do not let their evaluation be affected by their personal opinion of the speaker or the subject. Critical listeners ask themselves whether the speech is effective or ineffective, whether its arguments are strong or weak, whether its supporting evidence is relevant or irrelevant, and whether its conclusions are logical or illogical. A critical listener always asks why the information in a speech is true and how we could confirm it is true.

In sum, these are the qualities of critical listeners:

1. They *think* about whether the speaker has produced appropriate evidence to justify the claims in the speech.
2. They *ask* themselves about what the speaker is *not* saying and what topics or information the speaker is avoiding.
3. They *appreciate* a well-organized, logical argument.
4. They *sort* through relevant and irrelevant parts of a speech and focus closely on the relevant parts.
5. They *assess* the strong points of a speech, and say so, but they also offer constructive criticism about the weak points.

Passive, active, and critical listeners differ in the kind of feedback they give:

- Passive listeners usually say only something about themselves, such as "I felt like it was interesting" or "It held my attention."
- Active listeners are able to say something descriptive about the speech, such as "Here's what I heard you say in your speech" or "These seemed to be your main arguments."
- Critical listeners are able to say something evaluative about the speech, such as "Here's the point that worked best," "This is where your arguments were least persuasive," or "A metaphor could have made your point clearer."

British author and former Catholic nun Karen Armstrong asks audiences to think critically and listen respectfully about religious differences in speeches on her Charter for Compassion project.

The Ethics of Listening

The choice to be a good listener has an important ethical component. As an audience member, you have an ethical and a civic obligation to listen carefully and critically. First, you have an obligation based on creating a reciprocal relationship—that is, as we discussed in Chapter 2, a relationship that goes both ways. Ethically, you have responsibility to match the speaker's effort with equal effort in listening; your willingness to listen shows respect for the speaker.

You also have an obligation to listen as you would expect to be listened to. If public conversation is a grand dialogue where everyone gets a turn, it is important to make each speaker's turn count by paying attention to a speech as you would like to be paid attention to. Just as everyone should get a chance to speak, so too should everybody be a good listener.[1]

In previous chapters we discussed the dialogic aspects of public speaking; rather than being a one-time event, a speech is a special type of ongoing conversation in which only one person speaks at a time. Your speech responds to things others have said (you may even refer to them in your speech), and you expect others to respond to you by asking questions and giving you solid feedback. As a turn in an ongoing conversation or dialogue, a speech will be effective only if the audience is listening critically enough to be able to respond.

The ethical components of listening not only include being an active and engaged listener, but they also include a set of concrete considerations. The following behaviors both allow you to listen and improve the environment for the whole audience to pay attention:

Fred "Mr." Rogers, speaking here during commencement exercises at University of Connecticut, Storrs, was more than a host of a long-running children's television show. His many speaking engagements embodied, for his audiences, an ethic of gentleness and dialogue.

CJ Gunther/ZUMA Press/Newscom

- *Be ready to listen.* You need to be fully mentally present to the moment of speaking, so you should avoid thinking about other things or performing other tasks (such as reading, doing homework, or texting) while the speaker is preparing to speak.
- *Visibly pay attention.* Your actions create a positive cue for the speaker when you are paying attention, and they create a negative cue when you are visibly distracted. Paying visible attention (eyes on the speaker, pleasant facial expression, taking notes, not fidgeting too much or playing with technology) can affect a speaker's ability to give the best speech he or she can. In addition, if you look bored or disengaged, other members of the audience might also decide to tune out. However, if you look interested, that signals to your fellow audience members that the speech is worth listening to.
- *Eliminate potential distractions for yourself and others.* This means doing some obvious things, like not talking during the speech, turning your cell phone off, not using your computer for non-speech-related activities (such as watching videos, poking your friends on social media sites, instant messaging). It also includes more subtle distractions such as preparing for your own speech or loudly shuffling notes.
- *Respect the forum.* Because public speaking can turn a classroom into a participatory, democratic forum for the exchange of ideas, your behavior should show respect the nature of the forum. You should show up on time or wait to enter the room if you are late and someone is already speaking. If you have to leave early, you should excuse yourself between speeches. Making faces or noises to indicate your disagreement while the speaker is talking

Public forums, such as this board of education meeting, can be challenging communication situations. They require participants to think hard about how to balance their need to speak with their responsibilities to other speakers.

reduces the atmosphere of mutual respect that's needed for a forum to function as a dialogue.

- *Practice good turn-taking.* Do whatever you can to respect the time in the public speaking classroom. If you are next up to speak, move to the front of the room as efficiently as possible. If there is feedback time, raise your hand and wait to be recognized. Then make your point and move on, allowing the speaker to respond and leaving time for others to give comments. Just as speakers should stay within their allotted time, audience members should make their questions or feedback concise.

Ethical listening strategies are crucial not only to the public speaking classroom but also to an ethically robust civic and community life. One common gripe about American life is that people don't really listen to each other anymore. On many major public issues, we find passionate advocates for all sides of a cause who can make their case effectively but who do not do a particularly good job of paying attention to the arguments of people on the other side. We may hear others, but we often do so only for the sake of lining up our counterarguments before we have truly listened to the logic of another person's claims. Ethical listening means listening with an open mind, attempting to give the most charitable reading possible of what others are saying, and giving them the benefit of the doubt before arguing with them.

Enhancing your skill in listening has two important benefits for you as a member of the public. First, it will allow you to listen carefully to the arguments of people that you do not agree with, which may either change your mind or at least make you a better advocate for your causes. Second, it will make you better at listening for the quality of arguments, the soundness of evidence, and the strengths and shortcomings of various positions on difficult public issues. Thus, the listening skills that you hone in the public speaking classroom will make you a more competent citizen and member of the general public.

Obstacles to Good Listening

Listening is hard work: Not only do you need to listen actively, critically, and with an open mind and to be courteous, but you also have to deal with external and internal obstacles.

◼ Distractions

You're ready. Paper out, pen in hand. Mind clear and focused on the speech that's about to start, on which you know you'll have to give comments. And then a huge truck rolls by outside the classroom. Next, you hear a little clicking sound and see the person next to you has a phone out, under the desk, and is texting. Wait, do you smell something? What is that? It must be the worst cologne ever. And then . . . you realize you've missed the introduction to the speech.

distractions Obstacles to paying full attention to a speech.

Distractions make it hard to listen because we're paying attention them instead of the speaker's words. Some distractions are built into the setting. You may be too far back to see or hear the speaker clearly. Perhaps the room is too hot or too cold.

Outside distractions of all kinds are often referred to as "noise," and sometimes they are literal noise—nothing is as annoying as a jackhammer in the background. Or someone near you is snapping gum. Or the visuals may have too much information or too small text, and in the effort to see them, you may forget to listen.

In these situations, it takes an effort of will to pull yourself back into the moment and begin to actively listen. What will help you focus? Certainly note-taking is one way. (We'll discuss note-taking strategies shortly.) Sometimes it also helps to acknowledge silently to yourself, "That jackhammer is really annoying," and then redirect your attention to the speaker.

> ## Try It! *Distraction Awareness*
> Make a list of what's distracting you right now, as you are reading, whether it's in the environment or in your head—or in your headphones. How long is that list? What could you do to shorten it?

Another kind of distraction is stereotypes, which are a kind of noise in our head that makes hard to really listen to someone. As we pointed out in Chapter 3, stereotypes are generalizations based on a single dimension of the person, such as age, gender, race, religion, or job.

> **He's talking about legalizing marijuana—he's just a pothead.**
> **She's speaking about sexual harassment. Because she's a woman, she
>   must have been a victim of it.**
> **He's too old to "get" video games.**

Such stereotypes imply that people "like that" are all alike. If you assume, for example, that all Asian students are math nerds, then you may have difficulty actively and critically listening to an Asian student's speech about the current art scene at your school.

Of course, most of us have been taught the limits and unfairness of stereotypes, but we tend to stereotype people anyway. So, as listeners, we have to be alert to whether we are stereotyping. This means being aware of the assumptions that you are making as you listen. In a sense, this means you have to listen critically to your own listening, questioning whether you are being fair to the speaker and the material.

A third kind of distraction is more subtle but perhaps easier to control. Your focus may drift a bit from listening to the content of a speech, and you may find yourself focusing on some aspect of the speaker. This is natural. The speaker might be attractive or not, charismatic or not, dressed conventionally or oddly, and we can't help but notice. We all focus at times on qualities of speakers that we do or don't like.

Although outstanding delivery or a pleasing appearance is certainly an asset, for the active or critical listener, they play only a supporting role and shouldn't become a distraction. Sometimes when the delivery is notably dramatic and engaging, audience members will be so caught up in it that they have trouble listening to what is actually being said. This is why some people are suspicious of elaborate, theatrical delivery: They fear it will lead them away from critical listening.

Sometimes audience members will be distracted by what they see as mistakes or errors in delivery: poor posture, mispronunciations, a slight speech impediment, or small stumbles over words. As active and critical listeners, we have the responsibility to do our best to listen past these things for the content of the speech. If we're actively engaged as listeners, then we realize the point of the person's speaking is not presenting a perfect appearance or delivery but sharing ideas and arguments. The kinds of flaws that matter include those we discussed in Chapter 2, such as bias in the presentation of evidence and unethical appeals.

■ Your Mental Zone

A final set of obstacles comes from inside you and is not related to the speaker. The first happens when you are not "in the moment." You might be thinking about problems at home or at work, worrying about an exam or a paper that's due, or anticipating an upcoming party. And then there is the habit of always wondering if you have any new text messages or an update on a social media site. But if you're thinking about these things, you're not really in a position to listen actively and critically. To redirect your thoughts, try admitting to yourself that you have something on your mind and acknowledge that you need to make time to think about it later. Then, turn your attention right back to the speaker so you miss as little as possible.

A second internal obstacle to good listening is preconceptions about the topic—for instance, "yoga is boring" or "gun laws are stupid." To listen critically you have to set aside your existing ideas about the speaker or the topic. After all, a person who's been boring or illogical in the past might be really interesting and logical today. Whether you like someone won't help you critically evaluate what he or she is saying in a speech.

You have to try to be open to what's being said in this particular speech. Being open means being willing to try ideas on, like a piece of clothing, to see if they might "fit" with your beliefs and values. You can ask yourself, "OK, what would I be giving up if I were to accept what the speaker is saying as valid?" Maybe you've always identified yourself has someone who dislikes conservatives. But this speech advocates a "conservative" idea. Can you listen in a way that allows you to evaluate its merits independently of whether it's conservative or not? Being open requires an active effort to put aside, or bracket, your preconceptions for the time you are listening. In the end, of course, as a critical listener, you'll make a critical evaluation what was said, and you may end up rejecting it or deciding to think about it more, and in either case you gave it a fair chance.

A third challenge to your focus is internal objections, or the "yeah, but" problem. Sometimes, when we really disagree with a topic or argument, we mentally object to every point the speaker makes, thinking "Yeah, but . . . " and generating a counterargument. In a sense, this is good, because it indicates our critical engagement with the speaker. But if we spend too much time doing mental refutations, we may miss some of what the speaker is saying. The mental noise we generate is simply too loud to allow us to focus on the speaker, and we risk misunderstanding the arguments and refuting the wrong things. The solution in this case is to refocus

Apple's CEO Steve Jobs broke through preconceptions that he was just a clever entrepreneur in his commencement speech at Stanford University in 2005, when he told three striking personal stories about formative events in his life. Check it out online.

Norbert von der Groeben/The Image Works

on the speaker and on note-taking. You can also use an asterisk or other special symbol in your notes to mark points where you think the speaker went wrong. The symbol will help you locate the points you want to ask questions about after the speech.

Taking Good Notes

Note-taking is a key tool of active and critical listening. The best listeners are often good note-takers, whether their notes are on paper (or screen) or in their heads. Why? Taking notes is a way of translating the words being said into ideas. To translate, you need to pay careful attention not just to words but also to their meaning and context. For example, the word *fair* can mean dividing things equally (everyone gets the same amount) or proportionately (each person gets a different amount according to a rule or principle like seniority or need). If a speaker says the word *fair*, as a note-taker you have to decide, based on what you're hearing, which meaning is appropriate because that will determine what you write in your notes.

Taking good notes is an absolutely crucial skill for students, and for everybody else. When words go in your ears and out your hands, you understand and remember them better. Yet note-taking can be a little mysterious—What are you going to write down? Everything? Just an outline? Key words? How will you decide what to write or skip?

Most note-takers use one or a combination of the following techniques to record the speaker's main points and show their relationship and the structure of the speech:

FAQ *If have a good memory, do I need to take notes?*

Yes. Although notes help you remember, they do more than that. They are your on-the-spot interpretation of what the speaker means, so they help you to be a critical listener.

FIGURE 4.1
Outline Style Notes

Thesis: Marijuana should be legal

I. Prohibition does not makes sense: marijuana is safer than many legal substances

II. The costs of keeping marijuana illegal are draining the criminal justice system.

III. Money saved from legalizing marijuana could go to enforcement efforts for more dangerous drugs

● *Make an outline* (Figure 4.1). As you'll see in Chapter 8, speakers should provide verbal signals—such as *first*, *next*, and *finally*—and transitions—such as *in addition* and *in contrast*—indicating the structure of their speeches. Speakers also usually identify their thesis, or main point, and use previews and reviews of their arguments. These will help you make an outline with your notes.

● *Indicate the relationship between ideas with arrows and lines.* For instance, when the speaker says, "Here's my second reason for advocating gun control," you'll know that this is the second main argument the speaker is

Dr. Hans Rosling, a Swedish doctor and public health advocate, uses slides to make his information clear. Concise, high-contrast visuals such as the ones accompanying his speech at a recent TED conference make it easy for listeners to take notes.

FIGURE 4.2
Cornell Style Notes

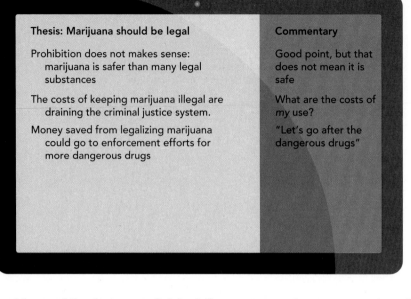

Thesis: Marijuana should be legal

Prohibition does not makes sense: marijuana is safer than many legal substances

The costs of keeping marijuana illegal are draining the criminal justice system.

Money saved from legalizing marijuana could go to enforcement efforts for more dangerous drugs

Commentary

Good point, but that does not mean it is safe

What are the costs of my use?

"Let's go after the dangerous drugs"

making, and the first one is finished. So you can mark your notes accordingly, perhaps by drawing a line across and starting a new section. Phrases like "in other words" and "for example" signal descriptive material that illustrates a point the speaker has just made. You can use these an arrow to indicate the relationship.

- *Comment on the concepts and arguments in the speech with the two-column Cornell System* (Figure 4.2). On the left side of the page, record the flow, or structure, of the speech, and on the right you can put key words, questions, and comments.

- Use a concept map or idea cloud to diagram connections among concepts or arguments (Figure 4.3). Because speeches are linear, this may not be the best way to capture a speech, but it works well for some people. To make a concept map, start by writing down the speaker's main ideas or concepts (from the thesis and the preview in the speech's introduction). Put those roughly in the center of a piece of paper, with circles around them. Then, in the course of the speech, you can create additional nodes for their subpoints. You can draw lines between the different circles to indicate relationships between the speaker's points.

FIGURE 4.3
Concept Map

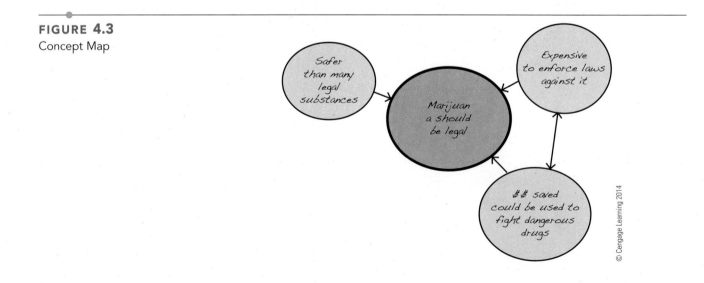

Safer than many legal substances

Expensive to enforce laws against it

Marijuana should be legal

$$ saved could be used to fight dangerous drugs

© Cengage Learning 2014

Every note-taker develops a personal system, which takes into account certain practical concerns:

- If you write too much, you'll fall behind the speaker; if you write too little, it won't be useful to you later.
- Most people find that abbreviating common words works well, in the way you would do when texting, such as *bc* for *because* and *btwn* for *between*. Some people use Greek letters for subject names, such as φ (phi) for philosophy or ψ (psi) for psychology.
- If an unfamiliar and difficult word comes up, write an abbreviation and the definition next to it the first time you write it down, such as "chthonic = © = underground." Then every time you see © in that set of notes, you know it refers to that word. But if you can't figure out your abbreviations later, then you'll have cryptic notes that you can't use.
- Should you take notes on paper or on your laptop? This really depends on how good your handwriting is, how good your typing is, and what technique you use to take notes. Outline-style notes are suited to the laptop, but if you find concept maps natural, you'll need to stick to paper.

Giving Constructive and Useful Feedback

In public speaking class, you'll be giving feedback to other speakers as a listener and audience member, and you'll be getting feedback from your audience as a speaker. This is known as **critical feedback**, or your argued opinion about what worked and didn't in a speech. Everyone needs this kind of feedback to improve as a speaker; if no one tells you what's working and what isn't, you can't grow in sophistication and effectiveness. But even **constructive criticism**—criticism that is well thought-out and useful—is still hard to hear.

critical feedback A substantiated opinion about what worked and what didn't in a speech.

How you would complete the following sentences?

When I am criticized, I feel . . .
When I am criticized, I often think . . .
When I am criticized, I tend to react by . . .

constructive criticism Specific feedback about strengths and weaknesses, with specific suggestions for improvement.

Are your reactions less than positive? You are not alone. Even criticism we know is legitimate can provoke negative feelings. Keeping in mind that other people feel about criticism the same way you do can help you deliver constructive criticism to *others* in a way that it will be heard, and it can help you hear criticism of *yourself* and take away something useful from it.

Unrealistic assumptions can sometimes act as a filter and transform criticism—valid or not—into negative feelings that prevent us from responding positively and learning how to improve. These assumptions include the following:

- Everyone should like me.
- People who criticize me don't like me.
- I don't make mistakes.
- Criticizing my work demeans me as person.

FAQ *I dislike critical people. Why do I have to be one?*

The word *critical* often means being negative to someone personally. We are using it in a more positive sense, referring to feedback that contains enough analysis that recipients can understand what they did well and where they could improve. The speaker's best friend is someone who takes the time to separate strengths from weaknesses—and talk about both.

Many us of don't like to see hands in the audience go up, but the constructive potential of feedback is important to gaining skill as a speaker.

If your instructor says, "Please rewrite this paper and edit more carefully," but you hear "You're a horrible writer," you probably won't be motivated to write an improved paper even if the teacher's criticism is reasonable.

Be aware of your reactions to criticism of your speeches. Try to keep your feelings and spontaneous reactions under control until you've reflected impartially on the feedback and consciously *decided* which elements are appropriate and useful. This isn't easy, but it's a skill that does get better with practice.

Because you're in a position to critically evaluate speeches, as a good listener you can help other speakers improve—just as they can help you. In order to play this role, you need to be able to give feedback, positive and negative, that speakers can really use.

Four tips for giving feedback the speaker can use are

1. criticize speeches, not people;
2. be specific;

People at Occupy Wall Street rallies used hand signals to give feedback to speakers.

3. focus on what can be changed; and

4. be communication sensitive.

We'll discuss each of these tips in turn.

Criticize Speeches, Not People

Just as a good teacher does, you should be criticizing or praising only *this* particular speech or *this* performance, not the person giving it. Many students want to say after a speech, "She was good." There's no question that it's great to get personal encouragement from audience members, and you shouldn't hesitate to give it ("I really enjoyed your speech, Kim"). But that isn't critical feedback.

To be useful to the speaker, you need to say *why* the speech was good:

> **Your introduction was really effective because it made the information concrete.**

The same goes for weak or ineffective speeches:

> **I found the transition to point 2 really unclear and confusing.**

Make sure you don't say things about the speech as if they were about the person. Saying "That speech was lame" doesn't help the speaker at all, and it might feel insulting and distract the speaker from other feedback that would improve future speeches.

Be Specific

"That was boring" isn't specific enough to allow for improvement. It's better to think about *why* it was boring and give those reasons without using the insulting label "boring." Try to identify the specific part of the speech you want to give feedback about:

> **I thought your evidence in point 2 was especially strong because the sources were clear and familiar. But point 3 really wasn't convincing because I couldn't follow the connections between the evidence and your claims.**

The degree to which you can be specific usually reflects the amount of thought you've put into the feedback, and speakers will take the most thoughtful and detailed criticism the most seriously. Even praise isn't useful if it's too general.

Focus on What Can Be Changed

Make sure what you are criticizing is something the person can actually change. It's pointless, for example, to critique someone for speaking English with an accent. Similarly, if the topic was assigned, the speaker didn't choose it—so no use criticizing it.

But the speaker did choose how to develop and organize the speech. If you want your criticism to be useful, try to provide specific ideas about how the speech could have been developed or written differently. It's helpful to encourage speakers to revisit their choices.

If you're listening and taking notes carefully, you can often identify one or two central choices that, if changed, would improve the speech. For example, the speaker might've been assigned the topic "crime on campus." The biggest choice in a speech with this assigned topic is probably going to be between talking about crime in abstract, statistical terms and talking about crime in personal, specific terms. This is a core choice about how to frame the speech and how it is going to relate to the audience. So as an audience member, it's less helpful to say, "Wow, crime is really boring," than to say,

It seemed like your choice to approach the topic abstractly made it hard for the audience to connect to it and get interested in it.

Be Communication Sensitive

Sometimes the way a critique is phrased can make a difference to whether the speaker takes it seriously. Wording and tone can suggest you're stating a fact rather than your opinion. For example, "This speech was underresearched" can come across as harsh. You can correct for this by remembering that your critical reaction to the speech is *your* reaction; it is not a fact, and it is therefore debatable.

Incorporating **I statements**, such as "I feel" or "It seemed to me," can soften your critique for the speaker, and they also show you acknowledge that other listeners, including the speaker, may legitimately disagree with you. So you can make the point that the speech was underresearched with I statements like these:

I wondered whether adding more research would have strengthened your argument overall, especially in point 2.

It seemed as if the second point was much shorter than the others, and I wondered how much stronger the speech would be if it were better developed.

Finally, remember that it's usually more effective to balance positive and negative feedback, so your critique doesn't seems like an endless list of "Wrong . . . wrong . . . wrong." Constructive criticism should not only describe how improvements can be made but also point out what worked well.

I felt the introduction did an excellent job of catching our attention by focusing on a famous case of government waste.

> **I statements** Judgments (criticism and praise) phrased in terms of "I" rather than "you."

Summary

Access an interactive eBook, chapter-specific interactive learning tools, including flashcards, quizzes, videos and more in your Speech Communication CourseMate for *Public Speaking*, accessed through CengageBrain.com.

Learning to listen is just as important to developing your skill as a public speaker as learning to put good arguments and eloquent phrases together. Developing your skill in listening is important because it helps you be a better audience member. By conquering distractions and learning to listen actively and critically, you can learn a lot about good speaking from paying attention to and dissecting the choices of other speakers. Effective note taking makes listening more effective. If you listen closely, you will have a better grasp of the choices that speakers make, and you can give a better assessment of the strengths and weaknesses of their choices than if you were not paying attention. In addition, your constructive feedback and criticism can help others improve. Every speech, whether you are somewhat bored or totally engaged, is a new opportunity to learn something about the right and wrong ways to give a public speech.

QUESTIONS FOR REVIEW

1. What is the difference between hearing and listening?
2. What are passive, active, and critical listening? What kinds of things does a listener do when listening passively, when listening actively, and when listening critically?

3. What distractions or challenges get in the way of good listening practices?
4. What are some ways of taking effective notes?
5. What techniques make feedback effective? What makes feedback ineffective?

QUESTIONS FOR DISCUSSION

1. Why is good listening an important skill for being a better public speaker? How might skill in listening translate to your effectiveness as a citizen or as a member of your community?
2. What kinds of feedback are most important to you? What makes you likely to take feedback seriously? What makes you ignore feedback?
3. Is it ever good to be a passive listener? Why or why not? Use examples to prove your point.
4. Find the video of a speech online. It might be a commencement address by Fred Rogers ("Mr. Rogers"), a presidential speech, or one of the examples on the site that goes with this book. Listen to it once, straight through; then listen to it again while taking notes. How different was your experience? Did you "hear" the same speech the second time, or a different one?

Creating a Great Speech

Diana Ong/SuperStock/©Getty Images

83

LEARNING GOALS

- Define topic, purpose, and thesis statement
- Analyze topic selection from the perspective of the audience, the speaker, and the occasion
- Explain how to focus a general topic area into a specific speech topic
- Frame general and specific purposes for your speeches
- Draft thesis statements

CHAPTER OUTLINE

Image Source/Alamy

Choosing a Topic and Purpose

Alicia just got a speaking assignment from her teacher, and she's not happy. The assignment says Alicia needs to give a speech, and she has to choose the topic. What does the teacher want? What will get a good grade? What will get the class excited? Alicia wonders where to even begin.

Overview

One of the most important choices that you will make in composing and delivering any speech is the topic you would like to talk about. But choosing a subject is not all there is to it. An effective public speech requires that you decide what you would like to achieve by presenting your topic in front of a specific audience, or the purpose for your speech. These two elements, your topic and your purpose, are the starting point for your relationship with the audience and for the choices you'll need to make to best achieve your goals in the speech. In this chapter we'll cover strategies for finding a topic and coordinating it with the purpose of the speech, whether it is to inform, to persuade, or to mark a special occasion. If you understand your speech as a part of an ongoing public conversation, picking a topic and a purpose can be both simple and rewarding as long as you consider your interests, the interests of the audience, and the demands of the specific speaking situation. Finally, we will discuss how to craft a thesis statement that captures the essence of your speech. ❯

Introduction: Picking a Topic and Defining Your Purpose

topic The subject of a speech focused to fit the audience, the purpose, and the situation.

A public speech is built out of specific choices. Some choices are small—the merits of one word versus another. Other choices are bigger, including how will you organize your speech and deciding the best way to make your overarching argument. But the first choice you make is the choice of what to talk about, your **topic**. All your other choices in composing and delivering a speech flow from this primary choice.

The strategy for picking a topic that we lay out in this chapter consists of two basic choices. The first choice is a topic that works for you, your audience, and the specific occasion. The second is how to narrow that topic to a specific purpose and create a thesis statement that reflects that topic and purpose.

A Strategy for Picking a Topic

Picking a topic may be easy if you are intensely interested in one or more issues. In that case, your challenge may be to decide which topic to pick. Other times, you may not know exactly what you would like to talk about.

In both cases, the advice is the same: You need a strategy for topic selection. An effective topic choice requires a bit more work that just deciding on a whim that you would like to talk about a topic that is currently of interest to you, or surrendering to the idea that you feel is the least boring.

Picking a topic requires that you coordinate three important considerations, which draw on some of the concepts about audience that we introduced in Chapter 3, in particularly the ideas of audience, public, and adaptation: A good speaker understands the audience in relation to a public, which defines a set of interests, and then adapts the speech to those interests. The three considerations for selecting a topic are your interests, the interests and needs of the audience, and the nature of the occasion or speaking situation.

- *Your interests:* First, decide what is important to you. What topics do you spend your time thinking about? What are you passionate about, or at least interested in talking about and researching?
- *Your audience's needs and interests:* What do you imagine would interest your audience about a given topic? What does your audience need to hear about the topic, and what information or persuasive claims would be useful to them?
- *The specific occasion or speaking situation:* What is the occasion for the speech? Why is the audience gathered to listen to you, and what kinds of content and ways of talking do you think they expect from you?

KRISTOFFER TRIPPLAAR/UPI/Landov

Comedian Jimmy Kimmel, speaking at the White House Correspondents' Dinner in 2012, needed to stay within the constraints of that particular occasion.

These three considerations can provide you a rubric for choosing a topic, and they will remain helpful as you move to defining the purpose of your speech.

The best topics are found where your interests, the interests and needs of the audience, and the demands of the occasion overlap (see Figure 5.1). If you ignore any of these three considerations, the quality of your speech may suffer. For example, if you are talking about something that your audience is interested in and is appropriate for the occasion but you are uninterested in the topic, you are unlikely to speak with energy and conviction, and you are unlikely to be motivated to do the work of researching and composing an effective speech. If you are talking about something that interests you (suppose you love to talk about term vs. permanent life insurance) and is appropriate for the occasion (an informative speech) but is uninteresting to your audience, you are unlikely to keep your audience for very long. Finally, if you are talking about something that is of interest to you and your audience ("Is dubstep annoying or awesome?") but that is not appropriate to the occasion, you are unlikely to give a successful speech.

FIGURE 5.1
The Three Considerations in Topic Choice

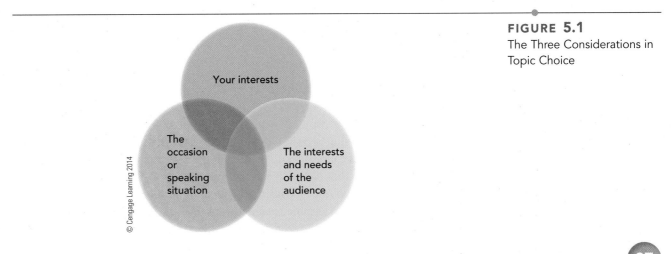

© Cengage Learning 2014

Your interests

The occasion or speaking situation

The interests and needs of the audience

What Interests You?

So, the first consideration is what topics interest you? If a list does not immediately jump to mind, you might think about markers of your interest. What kinds of TV programs and movies tend to draw your attention? Can you recognize any consistent themes? When you read or browse the Web, what are the usual subjects? Do you have hobbies or activities at work or outside the classroom that you would like to share with an audience? Even seemingly small interests can make an interesting speech topic.

Say, for example, you are one of the millions who love cooking and cooking shows. You do not have to give an informative speech on how to cook a perfect egg to make use of this interest. You could also take up issues of good nutrition or trends in food and eating. For example, you could talk about the implications of agricultural subsidies, or you could make the case for eating locally. If you are careful and creative in thinking about your interests, you are likely to discover a range of potential topics that interest you. A little later in the chapter, we'll offer a number of ways to find a speech topic among your interests.

What Will Interest Your Audience?

You should also think about the interests and needs of your audience. Instead of asking yourself, "What am *I* going to do with this speech?" it's better to ask, "What are *we* going to do with this speech?" In earlier chapters, we've discussed public speaking as conversation, and here's just one way where that orientation begins to pays off. When you've identified some topic areas of interest to you, ask yourself these questions about your audience:

- What would the audience be interested in, or could be convinced to be interested in, on the basis of the topic's impact on the audience as a group?
- What does your audience need to hear? What aspect of the general topic area should the audience be informed or persuaded about?

In other words, the more fully you are able to put yourself in your audience's shoes, the more effective your choice of topic and purpose will be.

In Chapter 3, we discussed audiences and speakers as participants in a larger public conversation. If you think about your audience as people who care about health, a whole set of topics comes to mind. If you think about your audience as people who care about jobs and careers, another set of topics comes to mind, and so on. The point is that you don't have to start with just yourself or some random topic; you can begin thinking about topic choice by thinking about the audience. In a few pages, we'll discuss in detail how to focus your topic to fit your audience's interests.

What Is the Occasion?

Second, as you choose your topic, consider the occasion. Whether you are giving a sales presentation, endorsing a political candidate, asking for an exemption from a university rule, or speaking to your public speaking class, the speaking situation may impose some constraints that can affect your topic selection. You need to talk about an issue that you can effectively fit within your time limit, and you need to talk about subject matter that is both accessible to and acceptable for an audience of your peers. Later in the chapter, we will discuss types of speaking situations.

Winner of a MacArthur "genius grant" and founder of GrowingPower.org, Will Allen of Milwaukee, Wisconsin, speaks often on the specific topic of growing affordable fresh produce in urban areas.

What Is Your Purpose?

Your purpose is another critical choice point. Your task is to figure out what topics can simultaneously suit you and your audience. Of course, at the most general level, your purpose is to give a good speech. Good speeches make a connection with the audience, advance the quality of collective conversation, and inform, persuade, or engage.

But these general goals are not specific enough to guide the choices that you need to make in composing a speech. So, to decide the **specific purpose** of your speech, look at where your interests and your audience's interests intersect. This intersection is in part your personal preference and in part the audience's need, which we discussed earlier. Your specific purpose is to fulfill a specific need for your audience as it relates to your topic.

specific purpose The need your topic can fill for your audience.

For example, imagine that you want to take up the general topic of food, and you are convinced that locally produced food is better for you, your audience, and the environment. Your general topic (food) drives toward a specific purpose. In this case, you would like to inform your audience about the benefits of eating locally or to persuade them to change their eating habits to emphasize local foods. Of course, your specific purpose could go the other way too: You could try to convince your audience that local foods are costly, more energy- and labor-intensive, and not that much better than foods that come from a distance. Either way, your specific purpose flows from your interests and your assessment of what your audience should do or think about your topic.

What Is Your Thesis?

Finally, you need to translate your topic and purpose into a thesis statement. A **thesis statement** is a one-sentence summary of the argument that you would like

thesis statement A one-sentence summary of your topic and your goal.

FIGURE 5.2
The Process of Choosing a
Topic

General Topic: What is the overlap between your interests, the audience's interests and needs, and the occasion?

Purpose: What would you like to convey to the audience about the general topic?

Thesis: How would you reduce the topic and specific purpose to a one- or two-sentence summary?

© Cengage Learning 2014

to make or the information you would like to present. This statement identifies your topic, embodies your goal, and sets the stage for all the elements in the speech that follow it. In fact, a good thesis statement will help you compose an effective speech. As you are drafting it, you can ask, "Does this fact, piece of information, point, or argument support the thesis statement and help me to advance my case?"

We will discuss thesis statements in more length toward the end of the chapter, but for now, think about thesis statements like very short movie trailers. They give a succinct idea of what the movie is about. So for our local food example, whose specific purpose is to convince the audience to eat locally, the thesis statement might be something like this:

> **We should all emphasize local foods in our diets, because locally grown food tastes great and is better for the environment.**

Notice that this statement identifies the general topic area (food) and the purpose (to get more people to eat more local food) and condenses this purpose into an argument by emphasizing the benefits of local eating for the audience. Your goal in this process of choosing, focusing, and defining your topic is the best fit possible for your audience and the situation (see Figure 5.2).

So far we've discussed how to pick a topic, define a purpose, and move toward a thesis. Next, we'll look in detail at ways to find and focus your topic.

How to Find a Topic Among Your Interests

As we've said, one place to start looking for a topic is your own knowledge and interests. Even if you want to begin with a particular public—people who are concerned about health or the environment or success or some other topic—you have to identify what publics *you* belong to or are important to you. You can start by asking yourself what you already know and what you want to know.

What Do You Already Know or Care About?

On what subjects are you expert? Does the answer tell you something about the publics of which you are a part? Everybody has many kinds of expertise, whether they realize it or not. You've done many things in your life so far, and they have given you knowledge that others may not have. Maybe you play one or more sports or a musical instrument, or maybe you are an expert gamer. Perhaps you've had jobs or internships that gave you interesting insights or knowledge. Your major classes obviously define a kind of expertise, as does any course where you mastered the material because it moved you.

Angelina Jolie began speaking out about the status of refugees after her experiences filming around the world motivated her to find out more about their problems.

Reflecting on any of these experiences might help you choose a topic area that's meaningful and relevant to you and that you can make interesting for your audience.

As mentioned earlier, be sure to consider your audience as well as yourself when you are reflecting on possible topics. For instance, with respect to our example of a speech about the drinking age in Chapter 2, people who are old enough to drink have an interest in this topic that is very different from those who are still under age. Similarly, some college students feel that alcohol is an important part of their life, and it is something they care about; however, others have little interest in alcohol or other people's alcohol consumption.

What Do You Want to Know More About?

Another great way to explore possible topics is to think about what you wished you knew more about. A particular topic, say, cloud computing or cancer vaccines, may have caught your imagination. Or you may have noticed a problem, such as a local source of pollution or a campus group that you don't think has sufficient funding.

Often, we see items in the news or while surfing around online that pique our interest. Not everything you find this way will work for a speech, but once you're in a public speaking class, it's worth keeping a little list you can go back to for ideas. Perhaps, for example, you'd like to know more about tuition, how it's set, why it goes up, or where your tuition dollars go.

FAQ — *What if I don't want to know more about anything?*

Everybody has some curiosity—you couldn't get through school if you didn't. But often people self-censor: when they think about the things that interest them; they immediately decide, "Oh, no, that wouldn't work." So when you're brainstorming, be gentle with yourself. Write down everything that comes to mind, and evaluate it only later.

Brainstorming

Suppose you've thought about what you already know and what you'd like to know, and you're still drawing a blank. Don't give up. Brainstorm instead.

First, write down a list of everything you're interested in. Try to imagine all the things you would like learn about if you had unlimited time and money. It could be anything from the moon and the stars, to how buildings are constructed, to the science of concrete, to how officials decide to site and time traffic lights, to what makes people smarter or stronger, or why college is important, or how Jon Stewart became so popular. Whatever it is, write it all down. Save this list.

Now, write down the major experiences of your life: home, family, school, travel, work, hobbies, places you've been (whether the hospital or Washington, DC), and things you've done (competed in sports, won an award, worked at a camp).

Next, go through both these lists and look for *keywords* or key phrases. These are words the come up more than once or that seem especially vivid to you.

Finally, go to a search engine (such as Google, Yahoo!, or Bing), and put in some of your keywords or phrases. Comb through the hits and see what comes up—is there something here that looks like a speech topic? You'll want to be patient doing this, because for any given search term, you'll get a huge number of hits.

You can also see how your term relates to other people by combining it with the words *news* or *current* events. Type in the words *news blood donation* and see what you get; the hits near the top are likely to be reports about research on blood, policies about donation, problems with shortages, and so on.

Cut and paste to a file the links that catch your eye. Do this for five or six of the terms on your brainstorm list, and you'll certainly have some excellent speech topics, ones that come right from your life and experiences.

Another option is to talk to a librarian at your school. If you talk to someone who deals with topics of all kinds on a daily basis, you might get some very good additions to your brainstorming.

Try It! *Finding Topics Connected to* Your *Publics*

Brainstorm some topics that matter to you. If this seems a little broad, you might begin by thinking about specific areas, using the "as" technique from Chapter 3. So, what matters to you in a particular role:

- As a student of the university—is there a service the campus needs or a policy you'd like to see changed?
- As a future member of a professional community—what should your classmates know about your career, occupation, or business interests?
- As a consumer—what should or shouldn't people be buying? Do you know something about a product or a brand that would help your listeners make better choices?
- As a citizen of your city or state—what local policies or practices bother you? What are the actions that make you say, "If I were running things, this would be done differently"?
- As an American—what federal policies or practices are working well and should be expanded? What issues should we be paying attention to that we are not?
- As a human being—there has to be something that you are passionate about that you would like to share with your audience. What is it?

Your answers to these questions indicate publics to which you belong, and to which your audience will belong as well.

Choosing One of Your Topic Ideas

Once you've generated some topic ideas, you have to think about how to choose one. Researching and presenting will be easier, and you will be more effective, if you care

TABLE 5.1	Topic Choice Dos and Don'ts
Do	**Don't**
Brainstorm by writing a list of all the things you already have opinion on.	Pick a topic you don't care about because it seems easy or feels safe, or you have already done all the research.
Pick a topic that interests you, preferably one that you care about.	Pick a topic on which you are so passionate you don't have any perspective.
Pick a topic that contains some element of controversy or that has an angle your audience may not expect.	Pick a topic that everyone already knows about.
Pick a topic about which you can explain to the audience why they should care.	Pick a topic so obscure or difficult that you won't be able to connect it to the audience in the time allotted.

about the topic. However, if you are *incredibly* passionate about the subject, beware: It might not be the best choice because you may not be objective enough to take the audience's perspective, and you may give a speech aimed only at yourself.

You probably shouldn't play it too safe by picking something that's so well known or universally understood that it's boring. Instead, go for something that seems novel or represents a new angle on something familiar.

If you have only 5 to 10 minutes to speak, then a topic that's too broad or too obscure won't work. If it would take 15 minutes to give the audience the background information to understand your point, you won't achieve your goals in a 10-minute speech.

Table 5.1 summarizes our advice on choosing a topic.

How to Focus Your Topic for Your Audience

Often the topic area you've chosen will be too broad. It would be easy to talk about a topic area like obesity or decriminalizing marijuana for an hour without scratching the surface, but you probably have only 5 to 10 minutes for your speech. You can't squeeze it all in, so you'll have to narrow your topic. Yet you also don't want to narrow your topic so much that you have nothing to talk about. Finding the happy middle is the key here. Your goal is to give a complete and self-contained speech in 5 minutes or 10 minutes, not a small part of a larger speech.

How do you narrow your topic? You have to find a subtopic, a piece of the larger topic. You've already established your interest in and connection to the topic area, so you should focus it according to the audience's likely interests. You can play around with possibilities, considering different rhetorical audiences and different subtopics, trying to find the best fit.

For examples, let's turn to topics of obesity and decriminalizing marijuana and consider the potential rhetorical audiences that would allow us to focus them.

Geography or Location

Sometimes, you can narrow a topic by looking at it in terms of "our city," "our state," or "our campus." Each location defines a particular rhetorical audience and public. For example, the epidemic of obesity strikes differently in different parts of the country, and the statistics differ significantly for urban and rural folks.

The criminality of marijuana also depends on the local laws and their enforcement. Some states and cities are more tolerant than others, so you might focus on the local obstacles to and consequences of decriminalizing marijuana.

Audience members will naturally perceive a greater relevance for something that is happening, or could happen, nearby. If you are giving a persuasive speech, local actions are more likely to be meaningful to your listeners than those on a national scale.

Past, Present, or Future

Some time frames may be meaningful than others to a particular audience, so they too can narrow the focus of your speech. Probably a student audience doesn't care much about the history of obesity, but they may care about the future. If current data project that 1 in 3 people will be obese by age 32, then in a class of 25, about 8 people are likely to become obese—and they might be anyone!

The history of drug laws, however, and how the use and possession of marijuana became a federal crime in the 1930s is important in setting a context for current debates. The history is also fascinating on its own, because it's a common assumption that drugs have always been illegal, when, in fact, attitudes about particular drugs changed radically in the past, and so they could change again in the future.

Typical Audience Interests

You can also think about what interests are characteristic of your particular rhetorical audience. With regard to the topic of obesity, college-age students might worry about the "freshman 15" (a documented 15-pound weight gain many college students experience) or about increasing numbers of their peers who are either obese or suffering conditions to which obesity contributes, such as diabetes. From another perspective, everybody at some point becomes a consumer of health care, and the prevalence of obesity lowers the general health of the population and tends to make everyone's care more expensive. Some students will be covered by their parents' health insurance, but one day everyone will be funding his or her own insurance or health care, so obesity matters even for people of average weight.

Some students may be interested in being able to use marijuana freely, but that won't be your whole audience, so framing your speech as if your whole audience were recreational drug users wouldn't be appropriate. On the other hand, if, by reducing costly drug prosecutions, decriminalization would free up government money that could help improve public schools and universities, it would serve the interest of every student.

Table 5.2 gives examples of extremely broad and narrow versions of topics (the left and right columns) and ones that would be just right for a classroom speech.

> **FAQ** *What can I do to learn more about my audience in public speaking class?*
>
> If your classmates seem like strangers to you, it's much harder to know what topics will interest them. Taking advantage of class activities, like group work or study groups, will allow you to get to know people in your class.

TABLE 5.2	Finding Your Topic Focus	
Too Broad	**Just Right**	**Too Narrow**
Persuasive speech: We need better health care.	The federal government should adopt a single-payer insurance system.	Someone should give *me* better health insurance.
Informative speech: Recreational drugs are bad.	Methamphetamine use is dangerous.	That guy in the back row is always high.
Persuasive speech: People should care about stuff more.	College students should take a more active role in local elections.	You should come to the environmental interest group meeting tonight.

Speaking Purposes and Speaking Situations

In ordinary conversations, you rarely even have to think about your goals for a particular situation. If you are at a party, your goal might be learning more about the person you're talking with and letting him or her learn about you. If you're interviewing for a job, you're sharing information in a way that highlights your skills and experience and demonstrates why you're right for the job. If you're shopping for a new TV, you'll probably go in with some questions and preferences, and you want the salesperson to tell you what you need to know to make a buying decision.

A public speaking situation requires consciously thinking about the situation and your purpose. Sometimes the situation determines the purpose. At a funeral, for instance, you need to praise the person who has passed away. In other cases, you have more freedom to set your goal. If you're talking to a community group about the problems of tagging and graffiti, you might choose between being mainly informative or mostly persuasive.

General Purposes of Speeches

The **general purpose** of your speech is the kind of communication act you would like to accomplish with the audience. The way we think about speaking purposes today is based on a set of categories from the Roman rhetorician Cicero. Cicero identified three general purposes for speeches: *docere*, Latin for "to teach or inform"; *movere*, "to move or persuade"; and *conciliare*, "to engage with the audience" (sometimes the term *delectare*, "to delight, please, or entertain," was used).

general purpose Type of communication act: information, persuasion, or engagement.

With some changes, these categories still work well for us today. When you speak, your purpose can be to provide some new information to the audience, to move them to some change in their thinking or behavior, or to comfort or inspire them. Here, in more familiar terms, are the three general purposes of speaking, which were introduced in Chapter 1:

- *Informing* is your purpose when you are giving the audience information that you think might be useful for them in making decisions or understanding events in their lives. As we'll discuss in the next chapter, speaking to inform doesn't mean you are just a passive conduit of information; as a speaker, you are choosing and shaping information in ways that will make it most effective for your audience.
- *Persuading* is your purpose when you are trying to change minds or actions of the audience. Persuasion requires you to appeal to the audience's trust, emotions, and reasoning.
- *Engagement* is your purpose when the main point is the audience's engagement with the speech itself. The speech may be funny, sad, or inspiring, but even though it may incidentally convey information to the audience or help change their minds, its primary purpose is to draw the audience into the experience.

Your *specific purpose*, which we discussed earlier, is the general purpose related to your topic and your audience. If the topic were "parking problems on campus," then the specific purpose could be "*informing* the audience about parking problems on campus," "*persuading* the audience why parking is a problem on campus and how to solve that problem," or "*having some fun* with the frustrations of the parking situation on campus." Your purpose is also related the occasion for your speech, or your *speaking situation*.

Types of Speaking Situations

Outside the public speaking classroom, the occasions that call for you to speak will often dictate what you are speaking about. You may be asked to give a pitch at a business meeting, to give a speech honoring someone, or to motivate your organization to adopt a specific policy or proposal. But in the classroom setting, you'll often have the chance to choose your topic. This is an important choice, one that demonstrates your understanding of your audience and your purpose.

The Classroom Situation   In the classroom, first, make sure you are clear on the assignment. Your syllabus will identify, for each graded speech you give, your goal or general purpose: Informing, persuading, and entertaining or commemorating are typical goals of classroom speeches.

But presenting a good speech isn't just meeting the minimum requirements for the assignment. Speaking is communicating, and classroom communication is real, in many ways. Your speech will have real effects on your classmates. It may bore them, annoy them, inspire them, enlighten them, or confuse them. Which of these you want to do depends on your purpose. If you are just going through the motions, with no real goal, then your speech probably won't be that good, and you won't be training yourself well for situations in which you do want to have a real impact.

Invited Speaking Situations   An advantage of an invited speech is that you often have information about the situation and its constraints before you go in, which helpfully reduces some of your choices. A group often has a purpose and will make clear why it's invited you to talk. For example, if the international student association at your school asks you to talk about your experiences studying abroad, you have a pretty good idea of both the topic (studying in another country) and the purpose (sharing information and insights). If someone asks to you to speak to a class or a group about a blood drive, you know you'll be talking about blood, the need for donations, and you'll be trying to persuade people to donate.

Staff Sergeant Salvatore Giunta, the first living soldier after the Vietnam War to be awarded the U.S. Medal of Honor, was invited to award a scholarship in his name at his own high school.

Everett Collection/Newscom

Being invited to speak can often reduce the uncertainty about the purpose and expectations for the situation. But even though you've been invited, you will still have to work to win over audience members, who may not know exactly who you are or why you're there.

Public Situations   In a public situation, it's likely that you'll be one of several speakers, and that a meeting has been convened for a specific purpose. In some cases, that purpose is to make a decision. At a school board meeting, for instance, members of the public will be allowed to each speak for a few minutes about a particular policy before the board votes. At a zoning hearing, citizens may get to speak about whether or not a particular business should be located in their neighborhood.

Before you speak in situations like these, you'll want to think carefully about how your contribution can make a difference to the final decision. Many times people have only a short time at the microphone, and they produce a rapid-fire list of complaints and concerns. It can often be more effective to state one solid argument that the governing body can use in making its decision.

> **FAQ** *What resources are available to me in brainstorming a topic of public relevance?*
>
> There are a number of places you can go to figure out what topics are "trending" and might be interesting. You can start by reading newspapers and news sites. You might also check out what topics are currently popular in web searches (for example at Google.com/trends) or on social media sites (like Twitter). You probably don't want to talk about specific stories you find there, but you might use these resources to discover examples for your speech or general trends that will interest your audience.

Sometimes public settings are forums or town halls. In this situation, participants are encouraged to make short speeches in which they share their feelings or experiences. This setting is often more about getting all the available points of view and isn't well adapted to argument and dialogue. In such situations, your goal is to be vivid, memorable, and relevant. You want to say something people will remember because it's relevant to the question at hand and because it reflects something personal about you.

> **Try It!** *Public Comment Opportunities Near You*
>
> Try listing three occasions in your area that allow for public comment and encourage people to step up to the microphone. These occasions might be at your school, a city agency's meeting, or a meeting of an organization. Which of these could you see yourself speaking in? Why?

Business Settings   Often business speeches are either a presentation or a pitch. The *presentation* is a kind of informative speech that shares information, either to make sure everyone is fully informed or to help managers with decision making. Presentation goals include clarity and relevance above all. You want to be sure you are telling your coworkers exactly what they need to know, and they need to understand it clearly. In general, less is more in an informative presentation; presenting only the most relevant information will help you avoid wasting everyone's time.

The *pitch* is something like a sales presentation, although what you are "selling" can be an idea, such as an advertising theme, or a service, such as your consulting or accounting expertise, or a product, such as your office collaboration software suite. The basic structure of a pitch is problem/solution (organizational patterns for speeches are discussed in Chapter 9). The presenter describes a problem and then provides the idea, product, or service that solves the problem (you may have noticed that advertisements often take this form as well). To pitch your case effectively, you have to convince people not only that you understand their problem but also that your solution is the right one. An effective pitch requires a lot of background research to ensure that you fully understand your client's or coworkers' needs and interests.

Time Constraints

Time constraints are a given in almost all speaking situations. There is a simple rule here: The more time you have, the broader your topic, the more challenging your purpose, and the more ambitious your thesis statement can be. Alternately, the shorter your time, the more disciplined you will have to be in choosing your topic and purpose. Of course, expanding the amount of time that you have does not necessarily mean that you will choose a larger topic, nor does it mean that you have to choose a more ambitious purpose or thesis statement. Nor does a short time mean you cannot achieve important goals.

This rule is important for speeches intended for the public speaking classroom. Sometimes, students can get hung up by not having enough to say to fill the allotted time. To guard against this problem, it is important to pick topics that are sufficiently fertile and purposes that are challenging enough to require the full speech time.

The more common problem with time constraints is topics and purposes that require more content than time allows. The following considerations can help you balance your topic selection with the allotted time:

- Does setting up the topic or the major issues surrounding it require a large amount of explanation? For example, convincing people to eat more local food is a simpler topic than a detailed description of American agricultural policy.
- Is your intended topic so far out of the range of your audience's expertise or experience that you will have to spend significant amounts of time defining terms or explaining arguments?
- Does the topic translate easily into a compact thesis statement? If you are having a difficult time framing a thesis statement in one or two sentences, it may be a sign that the topic you have chosen requires too many different arguments and kinds of evidence to make your case elegantly.
- Are you overloading your topic and purpose with unnecessary arguments? The easiest test of this is to sketch out the points that you would like to cover, and then to ask if each of them directly support your thesis statement.

Choosing a topic will thus require you to balance several different factors: time limits, the size of the topic, and your goals.

The Thesis Statement: Putting Your Purpose Into Words

Once you have chosen a topic and a purpose that's appropriate for your time limit, the next step is to combine the topic and purpose in a form that your audience will easily grasp: the *thesis statement*, a one- or two-sentence summary of the topic and purpose together. The thesis statement ties together your narrowed topic and your purpose.

The thesis statement should come right after the first part of the introduction (which you'll see in Chapter 9 is called the "narration") to let your audience know exactly what your speech is about.

TABLE 5.3	Informative Thesis Statements	
	Marijuana Speech (Informative)	**Obesity Speech (Informative)**
Topic:	Marijuana	The extent of obesity
Purpose:	To inform the audience about the history of marijuana	To show that obesity is widespread and to detail some causes
Thesis Statement:	In the next few minutes, we'll examine the history of marijuana as an illegal drug, from 100 years ago to the present.	In this speech, I would like to help you understand the extent of the obesity epidemic and some of its causes.

If you have trouble formulating a thesis statement, go back and reconsider some of your choices:

- Did you do enough research?
- Have you included the audience?
- Does the thesis statement fit your general purpose?

Table 5.3 and Table 5.4 show thesis statements for informative and persuasive speeches about the two topic examples we've been using, obesity and the decriminalization of marijuana.

If you were giving an informative speech about obesity, you might present your thesis statement to your audience like this:

In this speech I would like to help you understand the extent of the obesity epidemic, and some of its causes.

Or this:

Today, I'm going to analyze the phrase "obesity epidemic," explaining what obesity is and why it's an epidemic.

You don't have to say, "I'm going to inform you about obesity," to make your purpose clear to the audience, though sometimes that is a useful way to construct your purpose and thesis statement.

If you were giving an informative speech about marijuana, you might present your thesis statement this way:

In the next few minutes, we'll examine the history of marijuana as an illegal drug, from 100 years ago to the present.

This formulation also tells the audience that the organizational structure will be chronological (organized by time periods).

TABLE 5.4	Persuasive Thesis Statements	
	Marijuana Speech (Persuasive)	**Obesity Speech (Persuasive)**
Topic:	Marijuana enforcement	The extent and harms of obesity
Purpose:	To persuade the audience that marijuana is not harmless	To convince people obesity is a significant problem
Thesis Statement:	Today I'll present a significant amount of evidence why you shouldn't believe marijuana is a harmless drug.	I'd like to argue that obesity is directly or indirectly a problem for all Americans, including everyone in this room.

Former governor of New Mexico and Libertarian presidential candidate Gary Johnson speaks about the need to legalize and regulate marijuana, which is not always a popular position.

AP Photo/Damian Dovarganes

Another thesis statement for a speech about marijuana is this:

Today, I want to describe the positive and negative health effects of marijuana, for teens, adults, and college students in particular.

This statement of purpose and thesis has the advantage of including a preview of the three points of the speech (teens, adults, and college students).

A persuasive thesis statement on obesity might look like this:

I'd like to argue that obesity is directly or indirectly a problem for all Americans, including everyone in this room.

"I'm going to persuade you that obesity is a problem" is unlikely to be an effective thesis statement. Because it announces an outcome rather than an intention, the audience can take it as a challenge and mentally respond, "No, you're not!" and stop listening. It's better to state what you want to do, as in the following example, rather than your expected outcome.

Today I'll present a significant amount of evidence that proves you shouldn't believe marijuana is a harmless drug.

Try It! *Practicing Thesis Statements*

Pick two topics from your brainstorming list and turn each into a thesis statement (either persuasive or informative) that reflects your position on the topic. Check that the thesis is neither too broad nor too narrow, that it aims at an issue of common concern, and that there is a way of thinking or acting that would help or interest your audience. Would *you* like to hear a speech organized around this thesis? Do you expect that most of your audience members would?

Summary

Picking a topic can be a challenge, but only because it sometimes seems like you have to pull it out of thin air. The process of picking and refining a topic is easier if you follow a few simple steps, and if you ask a couple of questions of yourself at each step in the process.

Access an interactive eBook, chapter-specific interactive learning tools, including flashcards, quizzes, videos and more in your Speech Communication CourseMate for *Public Speaking*, accessed through CengageBrain.com.

- First, *think* about what topics matter to you or that you would like to know more about, and compare your list of interests with a list of topics that might matter to the audience. *Brainstorming* can often help you generate these lists.
- Second, *define* the situation: Where and to whom are you speaking? What is this audience interested in, or what should be important to them that they might not know already? Focusing your topic so that it is appropriate to the time that you have been given to prepare and speak.
- Next, *choose* the general and specific purposes for your speech. Given the situation and your goals, what are you trying to accomplish with your audience?
- Once you have a topic and general and specific purposes appropriate to your situation, *create* a thesis statement. Make sure the thesis is focused enough for you to do a credible job of supporting it but broad enough to be of sustained interest for you and your audience.

Picking a topic can seem daunting at first, but if you start with what interests you and think about what might interest your audience, you will likely find some good areas of overlap. If you work through each of these steps with some thought and intention, you will be well on the way to picking a topic that works for you and for your audience.

QUESTIONS FOR REVIEW

1. What factors should you consider in choosing a topic? How do speaking situations, as described in the text, make a difference to your choice?
2. What are the best ways to narrow a topic? Give examples of overly broad and overly narrow topics.
3. What are the steps in the process of brainstorming?
4. What are the general purposes for speaking?
5. What are the speaking situations, and how do they differ from each other?
6. What is a thesis statement? What makes a thesis statement effective?

QUESTIONS FOR DISCUSSION

1. What kinds of topics do you think are too difficult to talk about in public? Why?
2. What topics interest you? Is there a common thread among the topics you would like to hear about? Do you think your potential audience shares any of these interests?
3. Can you make a topic interesting if the audience is not already concerned about it? How?
4. Pick a topic you've heard about in the news that really bores you. What would it take for *you* to become interested? Do a little online research and see whether you can come up with three interesting angles on this topic.

Informative Speaking

Jorge and Sarah are talking about a presentation Jorge has to give in his biology class. Jorge thinks it's just too early in the term for the complicated ideas he needs to get across unless the other students already understand them: "How will they get the Krebs cycle? They'll just fall asleep." Sarah thinks that since Jorge understands the material so well, it will be easy for him to prepare. But Jorge knows he'll need to make some strategic choices to keep students interested as well to ensure they understand what he's talking about.

Overview

This chapter will introduce you to informative speaking. Unlike a persuasive speech (Chapter 7), where your goal is to move an audience to action, your aim in an **informative speech** is to provide your audience with a basic factual understanding of your topic. First, we will discuss the goal of an informative speech, which is to communicate new information—that is, facts and data—to your audience about your topic. You might use this information to encourage your audience to develop a new perspective on the topic or to elicit positive

informative speech A speech that provides an audience with facts and data about a topic so that they will understand it.

or negative feelings about it. Next, we will address the responsibilities of informative speech, highlighting the ways that your choices can make a difference in how your audience understands and relates to your topics. Then we provide you with some pointers for picking a good informative topic. Finally, we will discuss the kinds of techniques that you can employ to give a good informative speech, highlighting the kinds of choices that you will have to make to give an effective informative speech. ❯

Introduction: Telling It Like It Is

Not all instances of speech aim at a change in the behavior or opinion of the audience. A speaker might simply want to give an audience some helpful information that contributes to their understanding of an object, process, or event. For example, a student might listen to a speech at orientation about how to fill out a student aid form, or she might give a speech to educate other students about a student organization. In other words, sometimes speakers speak to convey information about a topic, not to persuade the audience to do something with the information.

Nevertheless, the information that you convey to your audience could influence decisions they make in the future. Each of us is confronted with a number of choices in day-to-day life: What should I have for lunch? Should I see the doctor about this cough? Should I follow a budget? Whom should I vote for? If we are making these decisions reflectively, that is, if we are actively thinking and informing ourselves about them and perhaps even discussing them with others, we are deciding on the basis of the best information available to us.

Thus, we largely navigate our worlds on the basis of the stock of information we have accumulated. So, for example, when you decide what to eat for lunch, you have a number of information-based decisions to make. Are you eating for health, convenience, or value, or are you looking for the tastiest meal you can find? Once you decide what drives your choice for lunch, then you refer to other information that helps you achieve the goal—for example, if you are eating for value, you have to know who has the cheapest lunch deal around. The same holds true for bigger decisions such as whom you should vote for: You have to find out which candidates best represent your interests and concerns.

Informative speaking is important because it adds to the audience's available information, and even if your topic seems minor, it may be useful to some of your audience members. Maybe your speech on how to eat a balanced diet will influence a person's eating choices, helping them to create good eating habits. Perhaps a speech on how to prepare a budget will influence your audience to take better care of their money. Or a speech on how to buy a good car will help your audience to save money and buy a safer vehicle.

Whatever the topic, the information you convey to your audience can affect the choices they will make in the future. For this reason, think carefully about the choices you make in presenting information to your audience. A clear, concise, well-researched, and well-delivered speech can be a valuable asset to your listeners. A speech that is difficult to follow or that contains inaccurate information might lead your audience to make some poor or ill-informed choices.

Better choices in informative speaking improve the collective decision-making capacity of your audience. As a result, informative speech can play an important if indirect role in healthy personal and even civic deliberation. So, the goal of good informative speaking is to figure out how to best present good information to your audience.

To help you focus on the kinds of choices you'll make in contributing to better decision-making through informative speaking, we begin by looking at the three goals of an informative speech.

Goals of Informative Speaking

In contrast to persuasive speech, which calls for the audience to take action (to be discussed in Chapter 7), your goal in an informative speech is to convey information (facts and data) about your topic to the audience. Though an informative speech may change the way the audience thinks about or takes action on a topic, your primary aim is to deliver information impartially. You have three approaches to choose from:

- helping your audience encounter and process new information,
- providing them with a new perspective on the topic, or
- eliciting positive or negative feelings about it.

FAQ *Why call it "informative"?*

The word *informative* comes from the Latin word *informare*, which means "to shape, form, train, instruct, or educate." To inform someone is thus to "shape, form, train, instruct, or educate" someone about the topic.

The first goal, presenting new information, depends on the choices that you make about clarity and starting with common ground. The second and third goals (new perspectives and feelings about the topic) depend on choices you make to help the audience connect the breadth of information you present with a set of concepts, organizing principles, or feelings. Though any informative speech may have more than one of the goals that follow, all informative speeches will have at least one of them.

◼ Present New Information

One of the primary goals of an informative speech is to *help your audience encounter and understand new information.* You'll want to present your informative speech in a manner that best helps the audience digest the information, because the more readily your audience can assimilate the information, the more useful this information can be for them.

The members of your audience will probably have many different orientations to your topic. Some may think they have already heard just about everything there is to know about your topic. Others may have no interest in or no frame of reference for your topic. A good informative speech addresses both these segments of the audience (and the people in between) by starting from a common base of knowledge about the topic and then adding specific new facts and data about it. So, for example, you might begin a speech about political advertising by saying,

We have all seen political commercials around election time. Candidates are always trying their hardest to get their messages out to voters strategies. But did you know that candidates are increasingly turning to highly targeted Internet advertising strategies that help them tailor their messages towards ever more specific segments of the population?

Beginning with a recognizable starting point and then increasing your audience's understanding of the issue is appropriate for both the well-informed and the less-informed members of your audience.

Now, take a look at how the following passage from another informative speech delivers new information:

One of the choices people most commonly make when they become interested in controlling their weight is to substitute sugar-free foods for sugary foods. We all know that if you want to lose weight you should limit your calorie intake, and artificial sweeteners allow us to do that without giving up our afternoon soda, our favorite candy, or a little treat after dinner. But did you know there is strong evidence that artificial sweeteners actually make it harder to lose weight? Researchers at the University of Texas Health Sciences Center at San Antonio found that artificial sweeteners cause us to underestimate the calorie content of the other foods we are eating.[1] So, even though a diet soft drink will help you avoid the calories you might have consumed if you drank its sugary counterpart, the net effect of consuming such drinks might be to increase your overall calorie count.

This passage begins with a bit of conventional wisdom ("One of the choices people most commonly make . . .") and then poses a question ("But did you know . . ."). Recent research about the topic follows that setup.

So what makes this passage effective? People like the novelty of new information, and they usually appreciate the surprise value of information that upsets conventional wisdom. This strategy helps you gain and hold the audience's attention. Whether they are accepting or a bit skeptical, they will probably listen to your supporting evidence and information more closely when they believe you are telling them something new and potentially interesting.

Journalist Michael Pollan has written and spoken widely on nutrition science and theories of healthy eating. He has mastered the skill of presenting new information in ways that allow audiences to listen and understand.

Boston Globe/Getty Images

If the information is not new or interesting for audience members, they may tune you out. If they have reason to doubt the new information is credible, they may not be willing to follow you to your conclusion.

Finally, sometimes the value of a good informative speech lies in the way it helps audience members organize information they *already* know. For example, most students have heard plenty of advice about job searches and most have some experience of their own, but a speech called "Twelve Tips for Handling a Job Search Online" can help them assemble familiar information into a concise and usable strategy.

Provide New Perspectives

A second goal of informative speaking is to *encourage listeners to adopt a new perspective* on the information you are presenting, understanding it in a new way. The way you choose to frame your content gives your audience a new context or reference point for understanding their relationship to it.

Context creates a perspective that makes the information clear. For example, humor can be a good way of looking at the relationship between advertising and politics: "You're already familiar with political advertising—we all see a lot of it on TV and billboards—but I'd like to explain just how funny it can be." Contextualizing information provides a standpoint for viewing your topic, helps you organize your content around a memorable central theme, and helps your audience link the various elements of your speech to it.

So a strategy that helps an audience think in a new way about familiar facts can be very effective. Consider this introduction for an informative speech:

> **According to the Centers for Disease Control and Prevention, 67 percent of U.S. adults over the age of twenty are overweight.[2] With so many people struggling with their weight, perhaps it is not surprising that market research conducted by General Nutrition Centers showed that 38% of the people who make New Year's resolutions resolved to lose weight in the coming year.[3] We often think of weight loss as a personal problem with important implications for our well-being, and the solution is for each of us to be healthier—exercise more and eat better.**
>
> **Without question, carrying extra weight can have significant implications for an individual's length and quality of life. But the collective size of our waistlines also has fairly significant implications for the public at large. For example, obesity exerts dramatic effects on the cost of health care. To show why this is the case, we might start with some estimates about the relationship between obesity and health care spending. According to Surgeon General Regina Benjamin, obesity and the health problems associated with it reduce annual productivity by 200 to 440 dollars per person, resulting in a massive loss in economic productivity.[4]**

This is not a persuasive speech because it does not claim that the audience *should* view obesity as a public health problem, only that it's an interesting topic because they *could*. Yet as the excerpt shows, it does introduce the audience to a new way of thinking about the problem. Its goal is to inform the audience and shape their viewpoint by connecting information they already know—the United States has an obesity problem—to another set of facts with which they are probably also familiar—the United States has a problem with the high cost of health care.

Choosing the new-perspective strategy has a number of benefits. First, it organizes the facts in the speech around a set of central themes, so it makes it easy for the audience to engage, digest, and remember the individual elements of your speech.

Benjamin Stansall/Alamy

Bill Gates, founder of Microsoft, excels at communicating clear, incisive information, whether he is talking about a new operating system or disease prevention around the world.

Second, though the strategy is not explicitly persuasive, it allows you to shape how your audience will understand the facts. Thus, this strategy adds to the stock of useful public knowledge without explicitly calling for a specific change. Third, the strategy is interesting for audience members because it can reveal new ways of thinking about familiar facts and ideas and show new connections between them.

■ Generate Positive or Negative Feelings

Another goal of informative speaking is to tie the elements of your speech to the attitudes or feelings you want the audience to hold about the topic. Although an informative speech by definition does not seek to persuade the audience toward any specific course of action, it needs a set of guiding principles that tie it together. If you provide this by organizing your informative speech around a central theme, you can also arrange its elements around a central set of positive or negative attitudes or feelings.

Consider the difference between saying a coworker is "assertive" and saying he is "bossy." These terms are not very different in meaning, but they convey very different feelings about the person described. Assertiveness is often a helpful trait at work, but no one likes someone to be bossy. Wording and other stylistic choices (discussed in Chapter 10) can influence the way an audience understands an informative speech without changing the basic content of the information presented. For instance, you could choose to describe your coworker as "achievement-oriented," without commenting on his assertiveness or bossiness at all. Decisions like this help create negative or positive feelings in your listeners about the topic of your speech.

For more examples of positively and negatively charged terms, take a look at Table 6.1, and remember that your wording choices are part of your larger strategy to convey information in an engaging, memorable, and helpful way to your audience.

Just keep in mind that if the speech is to remain an informative speech, you cannot call for a specific change in thinking or action. However, there is a world of difference between claims that political advertising "extends" or that it "erodes" public discourse. Both are informational claims, and you could present facts that support either one. Although both sides may be valid, the informative goal you select to

TABLE 6.1	Some Positive and Negative Synonyms
Positive	**Negative**
Tidy	Obsessive
Self-confident	Arrogant
Dynamic	Chaotic
Innovative	Unproven
Cost-effective	Stingy
Voluptuous	Fat
Creative	Weird
Thrifty	Cheap
Prudent	Selfish

configure your speech—whether concept, perspective, or attitude—determines how you will present the facts.

How to Choose an Informative Goal

Though any informative speech may have more than one goal, let's consider some examples of how choosing the different informative goals changes the nature of your speech as well as how you might compose a speech for each goal.

Let's look at the choices you might make in selecting information about obesity in our hypothetical speech. Imagine you are trying to convey the idea that obesity is a significant public health problem, and your goal is to inform the audience of this problem, but you're worried that people have heard this so often it doesn't seem to register with them. Let's say the basic piece of information you want to convey is "67% of U.S. adults are overweight." You could introduce this fact in a number of ways, and each option will make your audience think about it in a different way. As we saw in Chapter 3, in order to make the right choice, you first need to know your audience.

If you guess your audience members won't think obesity is an important public health problem because they are mostly young and healthy and they are generally uninterested in public health issues, you could try to create concern by choosing language that creates a little shock:

> **The United States is drowning in a sea of fat: More than two of every three citizens are overweight. Even though you might be perfectly healthy, the massive burden that obesity puts on our medical system can significantly damage your ability to get reasonably priced health care.**

"Drowning in a sea of fat" is evocative and emotive language: it implies negative feelings about the obesity epidemic.

However, if you aren't interested in shock value, or you think your audience might feel you are overselling the relevance of your information, you could choose a straightforward presentation of the facts:

> **According to the Centers for Disease Control and Prevention, 67% of U.S. adults carry excess body weight.**

But what if a neutral presentation of facts will not engage your audience and a dramatic "sea of fat" approach will turn them off? Then you might solicit the audience's goodwill with a more empathetic approach. You could personalize the presentation and address your listeners' potential resistance before offering the statistic:

Almost all of us have worried about our waistlines at some point in our lives. I know I have. Before we start to feel guilty about our weight, however, we can take comfort from the fact that none of us is alone: Almost 70% of U.S. adults struggle with maintaining a healthy body weight.

The statement that the speaker and almost everyone else has or has had a weight problem might help eliminate the audience's resistance to hearing that obesity is an epidemic because it avoids judgment and it describes excess body weight in neutral terms (as opposed to negatively charged terms like "fat") and as a problem for many people. This version avoids a potentially negative emotional appeal, and it might be a bit easier for some audiences to accept.

Try It! *Redoing Obesity*

What other approaches to an informative speech about obesity speech could you imagine?

- Describe at least two different approaches that an informative speech could take about the topic.
- How would you attempt to create positive or negative feelings about the topic in each of those two speeches?
- What role could positive feeling play in making a topic like obesity relevant?

The Responsibilities of the Informative Speaker

Informative speaking is often thought of as a neutral type of speech that just conveys information. But as the preceding section demonstrates, you make choices in an informative speech, and those choices present information from different perspectives, so informative speeches are not necessarily neutral. Because we make choices about what to say in an informative speech, we need to take responsibility for those choices.

Newspapers, television, and Internet news sites present themselves as places that give the facts and allow you, the viewer, to decide what to think. But no reporting is ever truly unbiased, because to report something is to create a picture of an event—whether in 30 seconds of news video or a few hundred words on a page or screen—and that picture is incomplete. Presenting a fact also means choosing what to say, how to say it, and what to leave out. These choices result in a specific view of the facts. For instance, one report might simply say that a suspect in last night's robbery and shooting has been apprehended, while another identifies the suspect by gender, race, and age. The audience will have different feelings about the suspect based on which report they read or hear.

When you deliver an informative speech, you have choices about which information to include, how to organize your speech, and how to deliver it. These choices imply responsibilities—you may be the primary source of information for an audience member on your topic. Thus, like a responsible journalist, you should present your speech in a way that gives your audience the best chance to learn from the information. At the end of your talk, listeners should know something worthwhile about your topic that they didn't know before.

So what are the responsibilities of an informative speaker? In short, they are the following:

- To do the necessary research to find relevant and credible information
- To present to the audience the essential facts about your topic in a way that is factually correct and true to the research that you have done
- To present the facts in a clear and accessible manner
- To provide the audience with an organized presentation of these facts they can digest, engage, and remember
- To provide information that is useful and relevant to your audience, with the goal of improving their decision making

To fulfill these responsibilities, keep the following principles in mind as you compose your speech:

1. *The facts don't speak for themselves.* "Here's all the stuff I found in my research," or a jumble of disconnected facts, is an ineffective approach even when your research is good, because it assumes the audience will work to make something meaningful out of all the pieces of information. You need to pull the facts together into a coherent picture to provide meaning for your audience.

2. *Relevance matters.* Nothing is more boring than listening to pointless or irrelevant information. To be an engaging and compelling speaker, demonstrate the relevance of your content right up front. Remember that relevance also matters when you're deciding which examples to use, because examples that click with one audience might be mystifying to another.

3. *Clarity is the result of choices.* Clarity can seem effortless when it happens, but a lot of work goes into looking effortless. Speakers are clear and easy to follow because they make good choices that are tailored to their audience. A number of techniques can increase your clarity:

- Use simple, short, direct sentences. This is especially useful when presenting a statistic. Instead of saying the tangled "A majority of experts agree that of the net percentage of return on investment for a dollar in renewable energy technologies is 6%," say, "Experts say that investments in renewable energy generate a 6% return."

Developing expertise through research is an important responsibility for an informative speaker.

- Break long lists of facts into individual sentences to give the audience time to follow your claims. For example, instead of saying, "There are five reasons why the parking problem on campus has gotten worse, including an increase in demand, an expansion in permits, and a reduction in spaces," say, "Parking on campus has become more difficult to come by. First, because of increased student and employee populations, more people are looking for spots. Second, the parking office has issued more permits than it has in the past, so there are more people looking for parking on any given day. Finally, new construction has eliminated a number of open parking spaces." The enumeration and the additional content make the individual claims clearer and stronger and also afford the audience the chance to process each of them.

The bottom line is that responsible informative speaking requires you to present facts in a clear and organized manner around a central theme or set of themes. It requires concise, direct, and carefully crafted claims, and it requires you to present the facts in your speech in a way that is true to the research that you have done.

Topics for Informative Speeches

If you are asked to give an informative speech, you may be able to choose your own topic, and choosing wisely may help you give a better speech. Many topics are easy to explain, and clarifying some topics can make for an interesting informative speech, but other topics may be too ambitious for your audience and your time limit. For example, it might be more manageable to give a general overview of global warming than to focus your speech on the mathematics that underlie climate modeling, especially if you have only a short time to speak with a nontechnical audience. This is not to say that you should dodge difficult topics, but rather that you should pick those that are reasonably translatable to, and useful for, your audience in the time you have.

Informative speeches can be about objects, events, people, processes, or ideas. Here are some suggestions for presenting those topics in interesting ways.

◼ Objects and Events

Sometimes a speech informs the audience about an object or an event—for example, navigational apps for a tablet computer or the mechanical causes of a recent plane crash. An audience might find an object or event interesting or important for these reasons:

- How often they encounter it (every day is more interesting than only sometimes; people go to class every week, but they get married or have surgery rarely)
- The role it plays in their lives (toothbrushes are more important than jellyfish to most people, and yearly checkups with the doctor are important to our health)
- Whether they can profit from knowing more about it (a little knowledge about a car's workings can reduce gasoline bills)

As opposed to a demonstration speech (discussed in Chapter 12), an informative speech about an object or an event doesn't require the subject of your speech physically in front of you, so it is important to make the topic concrete and visual for the audience.

People

What makes a person an interesting topic for a speech? It could be the person's *accomplishments*, such as winning an event in the Special Olympics, or unusual or admirable *abilities*, such as a command of several foreign languages or acknowledged cooking skills. Or someone might be interesting simply because he or she is already *famous*, like Michelle Obama, or even *infamous*, such as the convicted swindler Bernie Madoff.

 **What's the difference between fame and notoriety?**

Fame results from *good* things you've done, whereas notoriety (or "being notorious") results from *bad* things you've done.

When speaking about a person, you might want to consider these tips for making your speech relevant and compelling:

- If the person is already well known, seek out new information your listeners might not know in order to hold their interest. What was the person like before he or she became famous? What does he or she do when not in the spotlight? For example, former President Jimmy Carter has worked extensively with Habitat for Humanity, and you could give an informative speech on that organization, focusing on the personal angle of how one does meaningful work *after* being president.
- If the person isn't well known, find a way to convey his or her essence to the audience. Instead of a tedious list of facts, however, begin with the quality, characteristic, or achievement of this person that's most relevant to the audience, or that speaks to your listeners' values, and structure your speech around that. If, for instance, you wanted to give an informative speech about why you love music, you might tell a story about how you loved to sit on the porch and play guitar with your late uncle.

An informative speech about a person should include a brief biography, but the speech shouldn't be *only* a biography. Your audience should come away feeling that they know your subject as a person, that they understand what motivated your subject to do great (or terrible) things, and that they might even have some insight into why the person made the life choices he or she did.

Processes

It can be challenging to give an informative speech about a process, but this type of presentation can also be most useful or helpful to your audience. The process you choose to speak about might be relatively uncomplicated, like applying to graduate school, or very complex, like following the Olympic scoring system for figure skating. How does a piece of software get developed from concept through training of users? A process might be abstract, like the process of evolution, or very concrete, like the series of events in an actual case of natural selection. Processes are, by definition, continuous, so your description must cut that continuous flow into a discrete series of steps. For example, if you wanted to give a speech about how to perfectly poach an egg, you might organize the speech into selecting an egg, controlling the water temperature, timing the cooking process, and serving the egg.

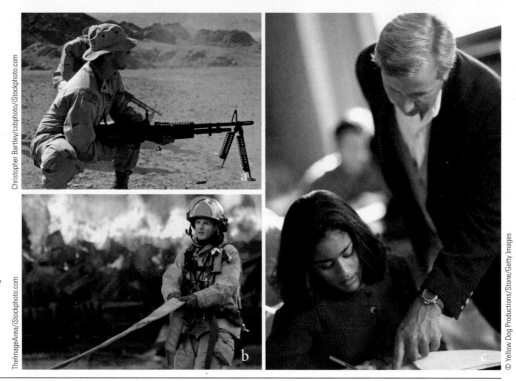

Informative speeches about people we admire—soliders, teachers, firefighters—allow us to illustrate values that are important us—and to the audience—with vivid examples drawn from their lives.

Ideas

Sometimes, you'll want to talk about an abstract concept: freedom, morality, courage, gender. The more abstract and philosophical your topic, the more challenging it may be to find ways to make it real to your audience. Several strategies can help you:

- *Connect your topic to familiar ideas.* If you connect an abstract idea to a concrete one familiar to the audience, it will be easier for the audience to follow. So, for example, if you wanted to talk about the federal budget deficit, you might start with talking about setting a personal budget, talking about the implications of overspending, and then connecting these ideas to the broader concept of the budget deficit.

- *Use detailed examples.* If you wanted to give an informative speech about courage as a character quality, you might start with an example of someone showing courage under fire, for instance, a soldier who braved gunfire to save a wounded comrade. The more detail you provide, the more dramatic and concrete your definition by example of what you mean by "courage."

- *Compare two similar cases.* What if you wanted to give a speech about the idea of justice? It might get boring quickly if you just gave definitions of justice. But you could start instead by comparing two stories: "Rasheed was an African American teenager who was shot on the street late at night. Amy was a white college woman who was shot on the way home from class. Rasheed's murder went

FAQ *How do I find a good informative topic?*

A good informative topic gives the audience information that is both new and useful. If the information is not new to the audience in some way, listeners will be bored. If it is not useful (even if the only use is entertainment or satisfying curiosity), they will not care.

A few questions can get you on your way to finding a good topic:

- What are you interested in that others might not know about? What interesting facts have you stumbled across that you think others might profit from or be interested in?
- What does your audience need to know to improve their everyday lives? What information would be useful to them?
- Can you think of instances where conventional wisdom or common sense about a topic are either wrong or misleading? How could you demonstrate this to an audience?

largely unnoticed by the police and media, labeled as yet another casualty in gang warfare. Amy's murder, on the other hand, created a firestorm of police and media activity. The question here is, what is the nature of justice in these two situations? Doesn't justice imply equal treatment for similar circumstances?" Comparing two specific examples provides your audience with a set of concrete concepts to help them engage and interpret the information.

Techniques of Informative Speaking

What are some of the specific ways in which informative speakers can present the facts surrounding their topics? Defining, describing, and explaining are some of the concrete techniques you can use to compose an informative speech that achieves your goals in a responsible way.

Defining

New and unfamiliar terms should be defined for two reasons. First, audiences aren't impressed by technical vocabulary. They just say to themselves, "Doesn't the speaker understand the topic well enough to explain it to me?" Second, **definitions** help set up arguments and explanations. So, for example, in the speech about the murders of Amy and Rasheed, the speaker defines justice as similar treatment for similar people, this definition can be used to bring up some of the controversies about justice. For example, should justice be affected by considerations of place and context?

definition A statement of the relevant meaning of a word, phrase, or term.

You can define terms and concepts in several ways. For example, if you were trying to explain credit hours in a speech about financial aid, you could offer any of the following types of definitions, all of which are correct:

- *Logical* (an abstract definition): A weight assigned to a course grade.
- *Operational* (the concept in practice): The hours your class meets per week.
- *Authority* (based on a rule): The college catalog defines a credit hour as . . .
- *Negation* (by contrast to something else): Credit hours are not the same as courses, because courses can have anywhere from 1 to 6 credits.
- *By example* (a concrete, relevant instance): You get three credit hours for your public speaking course.

Defining is an important strategy in an informative speech, because it can create an important theme to organize your reflections.

Describing

Much of your success in informative speaking depends on your ability to describe things—objects, events, people, and ideas—in concrete and memorable terms. Concrete details and mental pictures are two techniques for effective **descriptions**.

description A set of vivid and concrete details that characterize an object, event, person, or idea.

Concrete Details Telling your audience that "The economy is in bad shape," however accurate, is uninventive and bland. If, on the other hand, you say, "Factories are closing, people are out of work, and some people, like Adam Schmidt of Pleasantville, USA, are struggling to even put food on the table," you have a much more detailed and evocative statement of the problem. Vivid and concrete details, such as factory closings and the struggles of an individual citizen, take advantage of the idea, first put forward by ancient rhetoricians, that the mind works by dealing with images.

Mental Pictures   Concrete details in your speech help you create a picture in the mind's eye of audience members. You can also create a mental picture using images your audience has already seen. Ask them to call up these images and put them together in a way that serves your purpose. If you have a fairly abstract topic, such as how the Federal Reserve sets the discount rate, it helps to suggests an image. You might compare the Fed's "discount window" to a bank window, where people can walk up and deposit or withdraw their money. The Federal Reserve is the "bank," but ordinary people can't walk up to its window; only large banks can. You explain the point with this mental picture:

> **Imagine a bank: a tall building, big bronze doors, and lots of marble on the floor—an old-fashioned, really impressive building. But as you walk up to get in line, you notice a sign above you that says "You Must Be This Tall to Stand in This Line"—and the sign is more than seven feet off the ground! Suddenly you realize that although this looks like a regular bank, it's not. The vast majority of people aren't even allowed to get in line. It's very exclusive, and you'd like to know what kind of services Big People get at the teller's window.**

Good speakers create vivid images for audiences. When explaining the functions of the U.S. Federal Reserve, the nation's central bank, pictured here, it's helpful to call up images of more familiar banks and walk the audience through them.

Jonathan Larsen/Shutterstock.com

Try It!   *Make a Mental Picture*

Here is a description of a situation: "Poverty has negative health effects."

- What are synonyms for *poverty* might you employ? And what are synonyms for *negative* and for *health effects*?
- Create three different versions of this sentence, making the description more engaging.
- Compare them with the ones your classmates come up with. Which descriptions are the most engaging? Why? Which, if any, descriptions are overdone? Why?

Detailed, visually evocative explanations can not only make your speech more interesting, but they provide your audience with specific points they can connect with their everyday experience.

FAQ *Is it always better to use vivid language?*

Only as long as it in proportion to your topic and goals. To say, "It is hot today" is fine, and to say, "It is a flaming inferno out there today" helps your audience call up a dramatic vision of heat and identify with it. On the other hand, if you say, "The blazing hot sun sizzled my flesh more intensely than the proverbial fires of Hades," your audience might think you're overdoing it.

■ Explaining

You can use a number of strategies to explain something complex, including breaking a process or set of events into smaller parts and using analogies and examples. The goal of these **explanations** is to give your audience easily digestible concept.

explanation A statement or account that makes a process or complex concept clear.

Breaking It Down A process or set of events can be broken into smaller units. For example, if you were giving an informative speech about global warming and you wanted to explain how carbon emissions increase the net temperature of the earth, you could say, "Increasing carbon dioxide levels absorb heat radiated from the earth's surface," but this might not be entirely clear to everyone in the audience. To make the idea easier to grasp, you might explain it this way:

> **Sunlight enters the earth's atmosphere and warms the surface of the planet. The surface then radiates heat back into the atmosphere. As levels of carbon dioxide increase near the surface, however, heat is trapped by the earth's polluted atmosphere. This trapped heat increases the overall temperature of the earth.**

By explaining the rise in temperature as a step-by-step process that begins with the arrival of sunlight into earth's atmosphere, you've helped your listeners to understand the relationship between the specific claims you have made in the speech, and you have made your evidence (in this case, scientific evidence) more accessible to the audience.

Using Analogies When a process is difficult to grasp, you can try explaining it with an **analogy**. Analogies help audiences understand complex information because they liken the topic to something your listeners already understand. Here's an example:

analogy A comparison based on similarities between something familiar and something unfamiliar.

> **Global warming is sometimes referred to as the "greenhouse effect." A greenhouse is a glass structure that a gardener uses to help to keep plants warm during cold months. The glass lets sunlight inside to warm the air and traps the heat the sun generates, because glass is a good insulator. Global warming works the same way: Earth's atmosphere allows sunlight in, and the bigger the blanket of carbon dioxide and other gases, the more readily the atmosphere retains the sun's heat.**

Using Examples When a complex explanation might be too long or too abstract for your audience or speaking situation, a specific example is often helpful. Imagine you are giving an informative speech about the collapse of the housing market, and you want to explain how the collapse of home values made it difficult for some homeowners to avoid bankruptcy. You could say "Declining home values made it difficult for some people to refinance their way out of bad loans," but your point might not be immediately clear to an audience. An example could clarify the meaning:

> **Martina Case was unsure that she could afford the $500,000 price tag on the new home she wanted. Her monthly payments would be too high if**

As chair of the Congressional Oversight Panel of the U.S. Troubled Assets Relief Program, Elizabeth Warren spoke often about the U.S. mortgage crisis. She took big, abstract issues and restated them concretely in terms of the individuals affected by the crisis.

Stephen Crowley/The New York Times/Redux Pictures

she tried to finance the purchase using a conventional mortgage loan. A quick-talking loan officer convinced her she could take out a loan with a low initial interest rate (and therefore low initial payments). Sure, the loan's interest rate would double in a few years, and the payments then would skyrocket, but Martina thought she would surely find a way to refinance the loan at a lower interest rate before then, since property values would continue to increase.

But then something devastating happened: the real estate market collapsed. Two years later, Martina's $500,000 home was worth only $325,000. She couldn't afford the payments on the house because the interest rate had gone up; she couldn't refinance because the house was worth less than the amount of the loan she already had on it; and she couldn't sell it without taking a huge loss. Declaring bankruptcy was her only option.

What happened to Ms. Case has happened over and over in the past few years as declining home values made it difficult for homeowners to get out from under bad home loans.

Although it may not be necessary for economically savvy listeners, an example like this can be helpful for many in the audience because it personalizes an abstract concept and allows the audience to digest the information more easily.

Try It!   *Explanation Techniques*

We have suggested breakdowns of complex processes, analogies, and extended examples as three techniques for explaining a complex idea.

- Pick a topic you might like to speak on.
- When should you employ each of these tactics in a speech about that topic?
- How do you decide?

Choices That Make Information Effective

As audience members, we usually know who is an effective informative speaker. It's someone who is *clear* and *interesting*, who helps us easily understand something new, and who makes us want to know more about it. In addition to the techniques of defining, describing, and explaining, there are several other ways to maximize the clarity and interest of an informative speech:

- keep things simple,
- use supporting material well,
- connect your topic to your audience,
- organize your presentation to inform and captivate, and
- choose effective language.

Keep It Simple

It's natural to want to share *everything* you know about a topic after you've spent so much time researching it. However, you will often have too much information for the time allotted, and you certainly won't want to wash away your audience's interest with a deluge of information.

The more you know, the harder you must work to make sure you are editing your information to suit your purpose and the audience's level of understanding. Some speakers seem to think, "Well, if my audience can't follow along, they'll at least be impressed by how much I know." But audiences are like students: If a teacher is too complex or presenting too much at once, they get bored and annoyed.

Better to keep your message and its presentation as simple as possible to meet the information needs of your audience and the situation. Suppose you want to inform your listeners about the three factors you believe have contributed to a reduction in traffic fatalities in your town: increased police enforcement of the ban on cell-phone use while driving, the city council's new public service messages about the hazards of drunk driving, and the addition of traffic lights at several hazardous intersections. Although it might have been fascinating to research, you will probably not need to describe, for instance, the process by which the city council chose a marketing firm to help create its anti-drunk-driving campaign.

Connect Your Topic to Your Audience

How can you best create a relationship between your topic and your audience? First, consider what might make listeners care. What are their needs—for example, money, self-esteem? What are their motivations—success, pride, passion for new experiences? Are they interested in people, high-tech gadgets, nature, or something else?

Some needs are nearly universal: Everyone wants to be healthy, do meaningful work, and have satisfying relationships. Some needs are specific to an audience: Students want better grades and cheaper tuition, whereas parents may want better schools and safer streets. Your informational claims need to take the motives and experiences of your audience in account.

Likewise, in presenting your evidence, you should take your audience's knowledge and experiences into account. A good way to do this is to start with something familiar that is similar in some way to your unfamiliar topic, because people learn new information by relating it to what they already know or experiences they've already had.

If, for instance, you wanted to inform listeners about the benefits of yoga, you would first ask yourself, "What sorts of activities or experiences similar to yoga might my audience already know about?" Because yoga can enhance health, one possibility would be alternative medicine, which is also believed to improve health. But many people are not very familiar with alternative medicine, so that probably wouldn't be a good angle. The benefits of yoga are both physical and spiritual, so another possibility is choosing to frame yoga as a particular kind of exercise combined with a kind of meditation. Using this framework, you could draw links to other experiences that might illuminate for your listeners what participants claim about the health benefits of yoga.

Use Supporting Material Wisely

supporting material Research-based examples, analogies, and explanations.

A big part of any informative speech is the **supporting material** you discovered in your research and use as examples, analogies, and other kinds of explanatory information. How can you make the best use of it in shaping an effective informative speech? (Chapter 12 will cover presentation aids and visuals, which are another kind of supporting material.)

Don't Overdo It   Examples are wonderful for interest and often necessary for clarity, but sometimes less is more. One or two may provide understanding, while six or seven will be confusing. An analogy will take you just so far, and pushing it until it breaks down doesn't help your audience. For example, yoga is a form of meditation, and meditation and prayer are similar. But some world prayer traditions, such as the idea of "talking to God," are quite different from meditation and would lead your audience away from understanding yoga.

Turn the *Ear* Into an *Eye*   The biggest problem with speech is that it's not visual: The audience can't *see* what you're talking about. You can help, however, with specific and visual examples, as well as concrete language that suggests an image, as we discussed earlier in the section "Mental Pictures." Do yoga practitioners put themselves in positions that look like pretzels? Not exactly, but the image of a pretzel gives a good visual hint about how difficult some yoga poses are.

Own It   Information won't be compelling to an audience if it is only about imaginary or hypothetical people. To help your audience relate to your speech, *personalize* it. Talk about *your* relationship to the information ("When I first heard people talking about yoga, I had no idea what they were talking about . . ."), why it interested you ("I was fascinated by the difficulty of yoga"), and the audience's potential relationship to it ("We all deal with the stresses of school, work, and family life and wonder what would relieve some of it,").

Choose Effective Organizational Patterns

We'll discuss organizational patterns thoroughly in Chapter 9, which will explain the different patterns you can choose: the *topical pattern*, which takes listeners from one subtopic to another; the *chronological pattern*, which moves from the

Phil Date/Shutterstock.com

Because many in your audience would have only a dim idea of what yoga looks like, you would have to use metaphors and clear descriptions to communicate more precise ideas in a speech about yoga.

past through the present to the future; the *spatial pattern*, which moves from near to far or far to near; the *cause and effect pattern*; and the *problem-solution pattern*.

Once you choose an organizational scheme, stick with it. You will confuse your audience if you begin with an introduction about yoga and *physical* health and then segue to subpoints about meditation's *mental* benefits. And, as we've said before, don't start with the most difficult concepts but rather with ones that are simpler and closer to the audience's understanding and experience.

Choose Effective Language

Clear language is essential to informative speeches. Your audience needs you to translate or define unfamiliar and technical terms. Chapter 10 will discuss many more points about language and style.

Translate the Technical Talk It's all too easy to fall into talking like an expert when you've done good, extensive research on a topic, but that also means leaving your audience behind. To avoid doing so, explain all the technical terms and spell out all abbreviations the first time you use them. If you end up with a long list of technical terms to define, you may want to think twice about whether they're all necessary for your audience. For example, in a discussion of yoga, you may decide it's important to include *chakras*, but depending on the length and focus of the speech, choosing to call them "energy centers" rather than defining *chakras* might be a better decision. The translation does a pretty good job of communicating what they are without requiring the audience to learn new vocabulary.

Define Your Terms   Sometimes a term is important enough to define because a simpler one will create a misunderstanding. For example, if you are talking about the flexibility benefits of yoga, most people think of them in terms of "stretching their muscles," which is true, but it's also important to know that sustained yoga practice will stretch tendons and ligaments as well as muscles. To distinguish these tissues from muscle tissue, you would want to define tendons as "connective tissues that link muscle and bone" and ligaments as "connective tissues that link bones to bones." That will help you clarify the flexibility benefits (and disadvantages) of stretching tendons and ligaments.

Some choices work for every speech, and some are specific to a purpose. By keeping things simple, connecting to your audience, and using appropriate support and organization and clear language choices, you can ensure you'll be delivering a well-understood and well-received speech.

Summary

Access an interactive eBook, chapter-specific interactive learning tools, including flashcards, quizzes, videos and more in your Speech Communication CourseMate for *Public Speaking*, accessed through CengageBrain.com.

A skilled informative speaker presents information to an audience in a way that is easy to digest and remember. The information may even make a difference in how audience members think about the world. Informative speeches introduce new information, perspectives, and emotional connections to the audience, so informative speakers need to take responsibility for the choices they make. They are not just conduits for information but actively shape it for the audience. The topics for informative speeches include objects, events, people, processes, and ideas. Definition, description, and explanation are important techniques for informative speeches. Skilled speakers also know the importance of simplicity, connecting to the audience, and choosing supporting materials, organizational pattern, and language wisely.

QUESTIONS FOR REVIEW

1. What is the difference between a persuasive and an informative speech?
2. What are the responsibilities of informative speakers? To the audience? To themselves?
3. What is the role of *defining* in an informative speech?
4. Why is it important to use vivid descriptions and careful language choices in an informative speech? What kinds of techniques can you use to make your descriptions more vivid?

QUESTIONS FOR DISCUSSION

1. Can any speech ever be simply "informative?" Is an informative speech in part persuasive? Is there a sense in which *all* communication is persuasive? Explain your answer.

2. If you are presenting new information, you'll present your topic differently than if you were encouraging a new perspective or creating a positive or negative feeling. How exactly do the different goals of informative speaking change the choices you will make in a speech? Give some examples.

3. Suppose you have a big topic and could talk about it for 30 or 40 minutes, but you have only 7 minutes available to you. How do you choose what to put in to your informative speech and what to leave out? Identify a couple of principles, and then, using a topic that interests you, illustrate how they would help you make choices.

LEARNING GOALS

- Explain the difference between information and proofs
- Identify the dimensions of ethos, and why they matter for a speaker
- Assess the role of emotion, or pathos, in persuasion and the role of frames in producing emotion
- Explain the purposes of reasoning, or logos, in persuasive speeches
- Choose different types of arguments, according to when they are most effective
- Explain the benefits of addressing counterarguments and show how to deal with them

CHAPTER OUTLINE

Jeff Greenberg/Alamy

Being Persuasive

Heather always disliked arguing with Apurna. They both were political science majors, and they always got into arguments in class about the role of the government in solving social problems. Heather felt she had sound arguments with research and facts to back them up, but somehow Apurna always managed to sway her classmates by what seemed to Heather like manipulation. Heather felt passionately about her beliefs, and she believed they were well thought-out—but how could she convince her classmates to get behind her positions?

Overview

In this chapter we'll analyze the choices you make in designing a persuasive speech, a speech that moves the audience members to change their actions or the way they think about your topic. You've already learned, in the previous chapters, how to choose a topic and present compelling information. Now you'll see the kinds of arguments that are used to shape information to create a persuasive speech. ❯

Introduction: Giving the Audience Proofs

Persuasion is an everyday tool. We regularly persuade, or attempt to persuade, others to do what we would like them to do. Asking for a raise, arguing for a rule change, and trying to convince a customer to buy a particular item all are forms of persuasion. And all can be successful or unsuccessful depending on how well we present our arguments to our audience.

persuasion The use of speech to influence others through reason, credibility, and identification

Persuasion is the use of speech to influence the actions of others through reason, credibility, and identification. That is, when we persuade someone, we do it largely by presenting better or more believable arguments or by getting the person to identify with or see an argument from our perspective.

The dark side of persuasion is manipulation. *Manipulation* means using deception in your speech, making unsound arguments appear strong, or attempting to appear to be someone you are not.

Persuasion attempts to influence an audience in the context of an ethical speaking relationship, and the speaker undertakes this task with the good of the audience in mind. Instead of trying to pull the wool ever someone's eyes, as in manipulation, persuasion gives people reasons to believe or act differently than they currently do.

> ### Try It! *Information vs. Persuasion*
> Imagine you are the speaker and the topic is crime on campus.
> Write two short paragraphs, one in which you describe or outline an informative approach, and one in which you describe a persuasive approach. How do the approaches differ? Why?

Explaining persuasive communication has a long history, dating back to Aristotle's *Rhetoric* (written about 2,400 years ago). Some ancient Greeks were skeptical about rhetoric, or principles of speaking and writing persuasively, believing it was too often used for manipulation. But others, including Aristotle, believed rhetoric was the substance of high-quality public dialogue.

Persuasion is common in written communication as well as verbal. When you hand in a paper, you are attempting to persuade your teacher. The op-ed (opposite the editorial) pages of the newspaper are examples of written persuasion, or journalism that goes beyond reporting and explaining facts to take a position on the issues of the day. If you like to read blogs, you'll know that (depending on the author) they are often a mix of personal experience and arguments intended to sway the reader.

FAQ *Who was Aristotle?*

Aristotle was a Greek philosopher (384–322 BCE) who systematized many academic disciplines from biology to astronomy, ethics, and rhetoric by creating definitions for them and outlining how they work. He was also the *pedagogue* (personal teacher) of Alexander the Great.

In the public speaking realm, citizens use persuasive techniques when speaking at local school board or city council meetings for or against a proposed policy. Another familiar example of persuasive speaking is the opening and closing arguments presented by the prosecution and the defense in a courtroom. Each side attempts to persuade the jury that its view of the case should prevail.

We sometimes think that if others could only understand the situation, or "see things the way I do," they would quickly agree with us. If that were the case, just being informative would be enough to be persuasive. But most of the time, disagreement is due to more than lack of understanding; it goes deep enough that new facts aren't enough to change people's beliefs or actions. What's needed is to turn facts into reasons to change, which takes us out of the informative speech and into persuasion.

Courtrooms, in both real life and *Law and Order* episodes, are good places to find persuasive speaking techniques in use.

Persuasion doesn't seek change only through establishing the "truth"; persuasion appeals to the relationship between arguers, to the listeners' emotions, and to the listeners' reason. These three appeals together are the tools of persuasion, or **proofs**. They are called ethos, pathos, and logos.

proofs The three kinds of persuasive appeals: ethos, pathos, and logos.

Ethos is the attempt to establish a relationship of trust with your audience and convince them you are someone they should listen to. The audience needs to see the persuader as ethical, practical, and knowledgeable about the subject. A speaker who belittles others is not likely to be regarded as an ethical or responsible arguer. A speaker who argues that colonizing the moon is the only way to save the planet is not to appear practical. And a plumber trying to persuade the audience to endorse nuclear energy will probably have little credibility.

ethos An appeal based on the speaker's trustworthiness and expertise.

Pathos is the speaker's attempt to put the audience in the right frame of mind to accept his or her argument. Pathos is used to show the audience both how it is reasonable to feel a certain way about a topic and how those feelings can translate into the actions and beliefs. A speaker who shows an audience pictures of the victims of a war, in an effort to get listeners to support humanitarian aid, is likely to get an emotional response from the audience. If listeners think, "What terrible pain those people have suffered; I feel I should send money to help," the speaker will have successfully and appropriately evoked the audience's emotions.

pathos An appeal to emotions of the audience.

Logos is the use of reasoning to persuade an audience. Statistics, surveys, polls, authorities on a certain subject, and the use of historical evidence are examples of logos. But they are only some of the types of reasoning that can be used in an argument. Presenting well-organized materials and drawing conclusions through an orderly sequence of claims and reasons also contribute to a logical case. Later in this chapter, we will discuss different types of arguments. (Chapter 9 will discuss the details of organizing and concluding your speech.)

logos An appeal based on reasoning.

To be successful, a persuasive argument cannot use just one or two of these appeals or proofs. For example, if an argument were eminently rational (logos) and even evoked an emotional response (pathos) in the audience, they would still not be likely to change if they thought the speaker had no credibility (ethos). Similarly, if a speaker seems trustworthy and also plays on our emotions, we are still likely to resist if we feel like the speech is based on nonsense.

As an appeal based on ethos, George Clooney can cite his work with the humanitarian group he co-founded, Not on Our Watch, when he speaks about human rights abuses in Africa.

A persuasive argument should demonstrate a balanced use of all the proofs, woven together throughout the speech. It is ultimately their coherence that persuades. Consider an appeal for humanitarian aid. If the speaker mentions that she is a United Nations relief worker who spent time in the region in need, she demonstrates her credibility on the subject. If she also presents casualty statistics and identifies the sources of all her information, she is also being logical, supplying the audience with reasons to give money. If her case relies on how serious the problems are in the post-war country, she can gain the sympathy and pity of the audience through photos and stories that demonstrate the conditions of ordinary people there.

Ethos: Why Audiences Should Believe You

The word *ethos* means "the character or knowledge of the speaker." A speaker has ethos if there is reason for audiences to think he or she is believable, reliable, or trustworthy. For the ancient Greeks, the word *ethos* meant "habit," because speakers are judged partly on whether they are in the *habit* of telling the truth, judging wisely, and making good arguments.

When you seek to persuade, you are asking the audience to trust you, and you have to provide reasons for them to do so. Some of these reasons are related to expertise: Have you done your homework? Do you know your subject? Do you have the sources and research to back up what you say? Organize your information clearly and cite sources in your speech. Much of your ethos is built into the speech from the ground up in this way. Chapter 8 will help you locate credible sources and cite them in your speeches.

But there are other dimensions of ethos for speakers. Ethos also means that *you*, a real live person, are standing in front of others, speaking words in your own voice and name. Naturally, audience members will ask themselves *why* you have chosen to speak to them about this topic and *who* you are that qualifies you to speak on it. If you can't show why playground accidents concern *you*, you probably won't be able to convince the audience that such accidents concern *them*, because, as you know from the chapter on audiences, good speakers always try to construct an inclusive "us" to address as their rhetorical audience.

FAQ Is ethos *the same word as* ethics?

No, but our word *ethics* comes from a closely related word in the ancient Greek, a word which meant "habits." You can easily see the relationship, because ethical people have good moral character and habits.

Demonstrating to the audience why you are speaking can be a challenge for students. There's always a temptation to say, "Whatever. It's just an assignment. I had to come up with something, and I don't care." But don't be surprised if you can't construct a good speech with that attitude. The audience can tell if you don't care. Get in the habit of investing yourself in your speech and your topic. Audiences value commitment in their speakers.

To integrate yourself into your speeches, look at your materials and ask yourself what you would be thinking, doubting, or wondering about if you were in the audience. You'd be asking yourself why this speaker cares about clean water, acquaintance rape, student government, rising tuition costs. The choice is yours. You can leave your audience wondering what your personal connection is to the topic, or you can build ethos into the speech by explaining your reasons and credentials to the audience.

ZUMA Press, Inc./Alamy

Stephen Spielberg is a speaker who has ethos, or believability and trust, in the field of filmmaking.

Classical Dimensions of Ethos

Aristotle, in the second part of his book *The Rhetoric*, discussed the dimensions of ethos, emphasizing that it is not just a quality a speaker possesses but also one that audience members attribute to the speaker. That means it's your responsibility to *prove* to the audience that you are worthy of their trust. Aristotle's three dimensions of ethos—good judgment, excellence, and goodwill—illustrate how to show you are trustworthy.

Good Judgment   Good judgment could also be called "common sense," but as is often pointed out, common sense isn't all that common. If you expect people to believe you have good judgment, make sure you display its hallmarks:

- a balanced and fair treatment of opposing points of view,
- thoughtful adaptation to your listeners so you can take account of what they believe without talking down to them, and
- a judicious use of evidence.

Excellence   To believe you, listeners also need to believe you are a virtuous person. What Aristotle meant by this is that you strive to be excellent. Excellence doesn't mean that you're never wrong, but rather that you are oriented toward your better self. Excellence also means a high level of competence ("virtuosity"): Are you good at communicating? Connecting to the audience? Do you have other skills or knowledge you are sharing with the audience? You can probably think of public speakers or people you've known who communicate a sense of mastery that creates respect for them.

Goodwill   Have you shown your listeners that you have *their* best interests in mind? Part of the reason salespeople are sometimes mocked in popular media is that people assume they are always looking to make an unfair profit at the buyer's expense. When your listeners decide, perhaps because of a one-sided presentation or poor adaptation, that you are in it for yourself rather than advising them in a fair way, they will believe that you lack goodwill toward them.

Why Are You Speaking on This Topic?

Even though you could reasonably see your classroom speeches as just assignments, other speaking contexts are different. You are speaking for a reason, and the audience wants to know what that reason is. Think about Aristotle's definition of goodwill: Does your reason for speaking converge with the audience's interests?

People listening to you *assume* you have a connection to or interest in the topic. If you don't say what it is, they will speculate about it. Suppose you're giving a speech on rising tuition costs. Your listeners may be wondering, among other things:

- Does this speaker have trouble paying tuition?
- Do her parents pay her tuition?
- Does she have loans?
- Does she have a car (because cars are expensive)?
- Would she have gone to a more expensive school if she could have afforded it?

By addressing thoughts like these and relating your personal story to the subject of the speech, you will bring immediacy to your speech. Of course we're not saying you should build ethos by talking about yourself for 10 minutes. Instead, we're warning that speakers who remain aloof from their speeches, who just provide disembodied information, will likely have low ethos compared with those who show the audience their investment in the topic. Speakers have higher ethos when they share their firsthand experiences and concerns with the audience—when they make their speech appropriately *personal*. Of course, balance and appropriateness are the keys. Your persuasive speech isn't just a "research report," it is your chance to speak on something you care about. Make sure the audience knows that.

> ## FAQ — *What factors influence a speaker's credibility?*
>
> Writer Sherron Kenton lists a number of perceptions that influence an audience's belief about a speaker's credibility[1]:
>
> - Perception of the speaker's intelligence
> - Perception of the speaker's motivation to make "valid assertions"—that is, to build a careful, well-supported case
> - Suspicion of speakers who seem too eager to persuade instead of being sincere
> - Perception of "expertise" due to speaker's age, position, and/or shared values and needs
> - Perception that the speaker is kind, friendly, calm, patient, and enthusiastic

Pathos: The Framework of Feelings

Pathos is the proof that appeals to emotion. However, simply generating a lot of raw emotion by being outrageous or provocative is not going to be very successful, and neither is generating too little emotion, which can come across as boring. Rather, your goal should be to put your audience in a frame of mind consistent with your persuasive purpose. You're trying to evoke *appropriate* emotion.

Your audience's emotional reaction will be guided by what you are saying about your topic and how you're saying it. If you'd like to have a state legislator removed from office, you don't want the audience thinking to themselves, "Hey, but he's such a nice guy!" Rather, you want to portray his actions in a way that will rouse appropriate and justified indignation in the audience—indignation consistent with approving his removal from office. If you have *only* indignation (or some other emotion) but no arguments to back it up, you're not likely to change anybody's mind. And if you overdo the appeals to emotion, your audience may doubt your objectivity and judgment, which can harm your ethos, their trust in you as a speaker.

Emotion can provide consistency to your whole presentation. To incorporate pathos (or, more technically, "pathetic proofs") into your speech, begin by asking yourself, "How do I *expect* the audience to feel about my arguments? What do I feel? What emotions are appropriate?" Then make choices about language, examples, and arguments that support that frame.

There are as many ways of appealing to pathos as there are human emotions. However, one useful appeal to pathos that can go wrong if misused is creating fear.

John Lund/Paula Zacharias

Effective speakers make an effort to shape audience emotions, such as fear, pity, hope, anger, disgust, fascination, or curiosity.

Before we examine why, let's look at a few possibilities for eliciting positive emotions that you might include in your pathos toolbox.

Appeals to Positive Emotions

By appeals to positive *emotions*, we mean appeals that connect your topic or thesis with emotions that people typically want to feel, such as sympathy, nobility, and empowerment. Appeals to positive emotions work because people are predisposed to feeling these emotions and they give an audience a sense of participation in an issue.

Sympathy   Audiences may identify with a claim based on *sympathy*, for example, in a speech about a social problem. One of the best ways to invoke sympathy is to argue by example, picking a specific person or group of people who are affected by a problem and telling their story in a vivid way. To evoke sympathy, you invite audiences to identify with the people affected by helping them to imagine themselves in the same position. For example, television commercials for organizations that promote animal welfare earn your sympathy by showing images of animals that look sad or lonely.

Nobility   Sometimes you can convince an audience to do something by claiming that by taking up your cause, they are following their own best instincts. A speech that appeals to *nobility* usually frames the values you assume the audience already holds and then implores them to live up to the best version of these values. For example, you might frame a controversial freedom of speech issue, such as the right to silently protest against war at a soldier's funeral, by pointing out how important freedom of speech is to our democracy, and by extension to the audience. This strategy works because it compliments the audience by crediting them with good intentions or beliefs, while simultaneously challenging them to live up to these values.

Empowerment   One of the most common responses audiences have to a speech goes something like this: "I agree with what you are saying, but what can I do about it?" Audiences may be fully on board with your claim but frustrated by the fact that they

Empowering audiences by relating small steps they can take is a powerful speaking strategy, as Michelle Obama demonstrates when she addresses audiences about making good food choices.

Gerald Herbert/AP/Corbis

can do little to change the state of affairs. To use this situation to your advantage as a pathos-oriented appeal, focus on what the audience *can* do, such as making individual lifestyle changes or getting involved in the political process. Empowering the audience in this way is effective because it reaffirms that audience members are not, in fact, powerless, and they can be effective in making big and small changes toward solving a problem.

> ### Try It! *Look for Pathos*
>
> Think of a speech that moved you. Why was this speech effective for you?
>
> - List three qualities of the speech that you connected with on the level of pathos.
>
> Next, think about one or two great speeches you have seen in a movie or TV show. What specific elements of these speeches still stick with you?
>
> - Try to rewatch or find the speech online and take notes about some of the compelling phrases, imagery, and ideas in the speech.
> - What emotions did the speech evoke for you? Why do you think it evoked these emotions?
> - What lessons can you take for your own speaking practice from these examples? Note three lessons.

◾ Fear and Other Negative Appeals

In persuasive speeches, you often want people to change their behavior, to do something. One of the standard, and often appropriate, ways to do this is to use *fear appeals*.[2] Fear appeals identify a threat and then let audience members know what actions will prevent them—or someone important to them—from being harmed. If obesity, political advertising, global warming, or rising tuition costs can hurt us (physically, politically, financially), we naturally want to take steps to avoid the harm.

A related negative emotion is outrage, an emotional reaction to something we deeply feel is morally wrong. Sometimes we can be outraged by unfairness and injustice, sometimes by hearing about violence or aggression.

If you give just a clinical recitation of statistics, audience members may have no feeling of fear and not do anything differently. You need to make the problem seem threatening or scary, but fear appeals need to be gauged carefully, because they are specific to each audience and can backfire. If you crank the fear level too high, the audience might be turned off to the topic and maybe to you. Your audience could feel manipulated and just tune you out.

If you make people fearful of something they feel they can't change, they'll have to ignore you to reduce the discomfort of their fear. Or if your fear appeals are over the top ("We are destroying the Earth!"), yet you only offer a limited course of action, your speech won't make sense to the audience. For example, many students end their speeches by advising their audience to contact their senators and representatives and request that they vote a particular way. But that may not be enough. You should present solutions and actions steps that are in reasonable proportion to the size of the problem you've described; that might mean getting students organized, donating money, attending a demonstration, or something else.

Your speech has to arouse enough fear to make it reasonable for people to act, but not so much fear that they just ignore you. How do you find the balance? You'll want to create a level of fear or tension that's in proportion to your audience's ability to actively change the situation. So you can either tone down the fear (from "Coal-based pollution will destroy our world by the end of the century" to "Greenhouse gases will change our climate unless we act soon"), or you can increase the perception that audience members' individual actions do make a difference ("Every plastic bottle you recycle cuts down on our use of crude oil for manufacturing . . .").

■ Framing

Emotional reactions can help guide our interpretation of speakers (and situations), and so they become a frame for a speech (as we discussed in Chapter 1). Imagine that you're walking down the sidewalk, and you see two people rolling around on the ground together. Quick—how do you feel? What do you do? At this point, nothing—because you don't know what's going on. You don't have a *frame* for interpreting what you see. In fact, there are several possibilities:

- They are fighting.
- One person has picked the other's pocket and been caught.
- It is a practical joke gone wrong.
- They found a really inappropriate place for making out.
- These are students acting out a piece of street theater for an assignment.
- One person is having a seizure and the other is helping him.

The problem here is interpretation. If you know what's happening, you know whether to be angry or amused, and whether to clap or call 911. In the same way, when you decide to persuade, you can't just present bare facts; you have to also provide a frame for your audience to interpret and understand those facts.

As we'll discuss in Chapter 9, much of the work of framing happens in the introduction to your speech. The way you set up your topic will determine, in part, how your audience hears it. Framing gives your audience perspective, a place from which to evaluate the information and what it means to them. And framing usually imply values, or judgments about what's important, and what actions follow from those values. To build on our example of two people on the ground, if one of them really is being

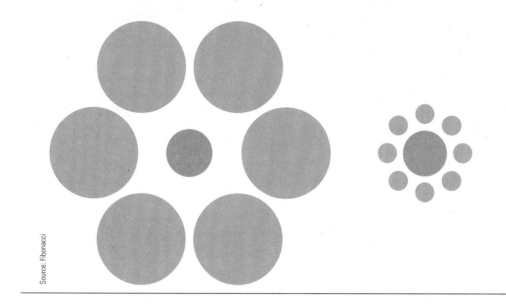

This optical illusion illustrates the principle of framing. The two center circles are the same size, but they appear to be different sizes because of the size of the circles that frame them.

mugged or having a seizure, most onlookers will call 911 because they value health and safety, and those values imply that they should help others.[3]

Often you can communicate a frame by using a mental image, as in the example above. Not only does "painting a picture" make your frame easy for the audience to understand and remember, but your picture can also make an emotional appeal. President Ronald Reagan was the first to create an analogy between the federal deficit (which is hard to picture) and your "checkbook," which stands in for your personal bank account. Of course, the federal budget is nothing like your personal finances, but if you think about your checkbook and a billion-dollar deficit, you will find that very alarming and scary.[4]

Not every audience or public will find the same frames meaningful and emotive. Remember, in Chapter 3, when you identified a rhetorical audience for your speech (asking the audience to listen with a particular set of interests, as a consumer, as a citizen, or as some other role), you were picking out a set of interests a frame might address.

Suppose you are speaking about a new medical procedure. If the rhetorical audience is consumers, then a frame focusing on cost or savings or money will be effective in sparking appropriate emotion. If the rhetorical audience is people who care about being healthy, then a frame focusing on health and avoiding sickness will be most effective. The contrast between "look how much you'll save" and "look how much sickness you'll avoid" is a contrast between two frames for the same material.

The frame should be visible "all the way down"—throughout your entire speech. For example, if you choose a health frame, while not completely ignoring cost, you'll probably want to organize your points around health and sickness, find more evidence to support those, and draw a conclusion about health. Chapter 8 will show you how to find evidence to fit your topic and your frame, and Chapter 9 will show you different ways of organizing your points.

Logos: Who Needs an Argument?

Usually we think of an argument as something we would like to avoid—few people enjoy "having an argument," especially when it means shouting and getting red in the face. However, the arguments in a persuasive speech are not the type that leaves you frustrated and

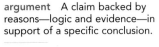

FAQ — *Is logos just logic?*

The English word *logic* does indeed come from the Greek word *logos*. But the word *logos* in classical Greek had a much broader meaning. It meant "reasoned speech" (a logographer was a speechwriter) and "theory or rationale" (as in the many English words that end in *–ology*, such as *psychology* and *sociology*), and it could also mean "argument" (reasons given in speech), which is the sense we'll use here.

hoarse. By **argument**, we mean logos, or a statement or claim backed up with reasons. These reasons may be based on evidence, statistics, other forms of data, or the opinion of experts. Thus, this kind of argument is quite different from a shouting match. Making a good argument is one of the most important steps in giving a persuasive speech.

What makes a good argument? Well, you may not be surprised to hear that making good arguments is a matter of choices. That means you choose not just what you want to say but also how to defend your points. Making a good argument means giving a clear statement of a position and backing up this position with reasons. An argument addresses questions such as "Why is that statement true?" "Why should we believe you?" "How do you know that?" or even "So what?"

Here is an example of what we mean by making good argument choices. Imagine the sleepy guy in the back row—we'll call him Fred—gets up to give his speech in class one day. Fred has been paying some attention in class but perhaps not enough. He at least knows that a speech needs an introduction, a body, and a conclusion, so he stands up and delivers the following speech:

> **Today we get much of our entertainment from free file-sharing services. I would like to address the issue of downloading music and movies. We should not download music and movies off the Internet that we haven't paid for. In conclusion, I think that everyone who is using free file-sharing services should stop.**

Obviously, that speech is a little on the short side. Are you persuaded? Probably not. Why not?

Obviously, Fred's speech has no significant details, and it contains no attempt to engage the audience or grab their attention. There is not even a hint of support for his main point that we "should not get music and movies off the Internet that we haven't paid for." In the absence of supporting evidence, how do we know that we should agree with him?

With just a little more work, Fred could make a much more compelling case for his central point. To do this, he needs to introduce some supporting evidence. He might say,

> **We should not download music and movies off the Internet that we haven't paid for.** *Free music and movies from the Internet are destroying the entertainment industry.*

Now Fred is approaching an argument, though he is not quite there yet. He has now provided a reason to support his statement "We should not download . . ."—that free file sharing is destroying the entertainment industry.

Of course, we still might not be convinced: How do we know file sharing is destroying the music industry? Fred's next step is to get more specific and cite some sources:

> **We should not download music and movies off the Internet that we haven't paid for. Free music and movies from the Internet are destroying the entertainment industry.** *Recent reports from the RIAA (the Recording Industry Association of America) and the MPAA (the Motion Picture Association of America) indicate that the practice of file sharing has significantly reduced the profits of musicians and filmmakers.*

Finally, Fred is on the right track, and the third version of his speech is shaping up as a decent argument. We can now see the line of reasoning that supports Fred's point about file sharing. Of course, we still might object that Fred has not really made a compelling case for his point, because we might ask, "So what?"

CHRISTINE CHEW/UPI/Landov

Irish musician Bono argued forcefully in an interview with *USA Today* against file-sharing websites, calling the current system "madness."

Fred makes one final attempt:

We should not download music and movies off the Internet that we haven't paid for. Free music and movies from the Internet are destroying the entertainment industry. Recent reports from the RIAA (the Recording Industry Association of America) and the MPAA (the Motion Picture Association of America) indicate that the practice of file sharing has significantly reduced the profits of musicians and filmmakers. *Good profits for creative production in entertainment are important because they create a significant incentive for musicians to make the best music they can and for filmmakers to make great films.*

If you enjoy the things you are downloading from file services, you shouldn't jeopardize the future of the entertainment industry by undermining the profit motive that drives good-quality work. You get what you pay for, after all.

Regardless of your opinion about file-sharing services, or even about Fred's line of reasoning, the final version of his speech is clearly much better than the original. In the final version, Fred has made a complete argument—he has

- made a statement,
- supported it with evidence, and
- related the argument to the concerns of his audience.

Let's explore the techniques that distinguish Fred's first try from his developed speech by addressing the relationship between arguing, persuading, and informing.

Try It!   *Look for Logos*

Go to http://www.whitehouse.gov/briefing-room/speeches-and-remarks and pick one of the president's speeches that advances an argument for change in policy or belief. Identify the primary claim made in the speech. Next, identify the supporting claims. Do the supporting claims adequately justify the main claim? Why or why not?

You've been making arguments and giving reasons your whole life. "Why are you going to college?" "Because _____" and whatever fills in the blank are your reasons for going. Reasoning is basically about *linking* things together: a claim ("I should be going to college") and some kind of support or justification for it.

In preparing a speech, it's helpful to think of argument as a *movement* from reasons to claims, or conclusions. You start with what the audience already knows, believes, or values (the reasons) and move to what they should believe or value (the claim or conclusion).

Every speech also needs a *pattern of argument*: How are you going to support the claim you'd like the audience to believe with reasons and evidence? There's much more to argument than citing a lot of statistics. Facts and statistics are not useful unless they fit into a pattern of argument. All too often, speakers fire a barrage of numbers at their audiences that amount to nothing, because they haven't made clear what argument the numbers fit into, and how. There's nothing wrong with having the numbers to prove your point, as long as you start with an argument.

Finally, keep in mind the saying that "the best persuasion is self-persuasion." Rather than imagining your arguments will magically win over the audience, think about giving your audience real reasons to believe and act differently than they do now. Think of empowering rather than conquering them.

Now, we'll move to six common types of reasoning that you can use to structure the arguments in your speeches. You can mix these types of argument; the typical speech contains several of them. The six types are

- inductive argument (or argument from examples),
- formal (or deductive) arguments,
- causal arguments,
- arguments from analogy,
- arguments from signs, and
- arguments from authority.

We'll conclude the chapter with a look at counterarguments, or the ways you can respond to arguments against your position—either other speakers' arguments or arguments circulating elsewhere—so you can effectively make your case. There is always another side to an issue, and by acknowledging it, you not only assert your own side but also weaken the other side in the audience's mind.

Types of Arguments

For each one of the six common types of argument, we'll define it and then explain how it works and when it will be useful to you as a speaker.

▨ Arguments From Examples (Inductive Reasoning)

inductive reasoning Argument from form; a claim based on specific examples.

In **inductive reasoning**, you draw a conclusion based on examples or instances. You're making a general claim based on a number of examples. The examples serve as evidence for the claim.

How It Works If you want to argue that Milwaukee has good restaurants, you could base that claim on the restaurants you know: Kopps, Maders, Pizza Shuttle, Oakland

Gyros, and so on. If each of them is good, it increases the strength of your general claim about Milwaukee's restaurants. If you gather even more information—making sure it is about different kinds of restaurants—you increase the strength of your support even more.

If you have only one or two examples, then your argument can fairly be dismissed as anecdotal. If you have many examples, and they are varied in terms of time, populations, and circumstances, then you can support your claim inductively.

You can often use statistics to good effect here: you might discover, for instance, that 80% of Milwaukee restaurants get a two-star or higher rating. Be sure, however, that the statistics are clearly connected to your claim and that the audience knows exactly what your argument is.

You should also be careful to tailor the strength of your claim to the strength of evidence. The claim can't be any stronger than the evidence for it. Depending on how good your evidence is, there are a number of ways to state the claim (in order of decreasing strength):

- Milwaukee *certainly has many* good restaurants.
- Milwaukee *undoubtedly has many* good restaurants.
- Milwaukee *has many* good restaurants.
- Milwaukee *probably has many* good restaurants.
- Milwaukee *might have many* good restaurants.
- Milwaukee *has some* good restaurants.

Especially if your evidence is statistical, your claim needs to match it. If only 15% of Milwaukee's restaurants have achieved a four-star rating, a claim that the city "certainly has many good restaurants" wouldn't hold up.

When It's Effective   Inductive reasoning is most useful when you are trying to support a general claim, often as a part of a larger argument. For example, if you were speaking about the problem of student cheating, you'd need to establish some facts, ones that address the following questions:

- How many students cheat?
- What types of students cheat?
- How often do they cheat?
- In what ways do they cheat?

Each of these questions is answered by an inductive generalization about students, such as "80% of U.S. college students reported that they cheated last year." Notice the generalization here: The "80%" is an extrapolation from the number of students who completed a survey. If the sample was good one, this is a valid generalization. Notice also that the statement of the fact is qualified by the method ("they reported") and time ("last year"). A different method might produce a different number, and the number of cheaters might change over time.

To see the power of inductive reasoning, contrast the statistic with your personal experience. You might know a couple of students who cheat, but your description of your experience with them wouldn't help you prove that there is a *widespread* problem with cheating. With inductive reasoning, you rely on a large number of examples taken from a reliable source.

Formal Arguments (Deductive Reasoning)

Sometimes the *form* of an argument persuades us. Any argument, no matter the content, with an *if-then* format is likely to be convincing. **Arguments from form** are also called deductive arguments. Deductive reasoning, which is the subject of the field of

argument from form   Deductive, or if-then, reasoning.

logic, is a huge topic, and we can only touch on it here. Although it can be challenging to set up a deductive argument correctly in a speech, it's very convincing when it works.

How It Works   Deductive reasoning typically has an if-then form: If X is true, then so is Y. To create a deductive inference using this form, you establish the relationship between the "if" and "then" statements and the conclusion you want to draw.

1. If there are five 4-star restaurants in a town, then it is a good restaurant town.
2. Milwaukee has six 4-star restaurants.
3. Therefore, Milwaukee is a good restaurant town.

Statements 1 and 2 are called the *premises*, and 3 is the *conclusion*. The word *therefore* in Statement 3 asserts that there is an *inferential relationship*: You can logically infer the conclusion from the premises. In fact, the relationship between the conclusion and premises is *very* tight. If the premises are true, the conclusion *must* be true also.

The if-then form or pattern is straightforward. You state the relationship between two actions, situations, or characteristics (*if* one is true, *then* the other is true). Then you show the first one is true—and so the second one must be true also.

1. *If* you are an adult, *then* you need health insurance.
2. We're *all* adults.
3. *Therefore*, everyone here today needs health insurance.

If the first two statements are true, the conclusion must be also, creating a powerful argument.

When It's Effective   The challenge in formal reasoning is justifying your premises. In the health-insurance example, you can do it through logic (everyone gets sick) and the nature of the occasion (we're all adults). Other ways to establish premises are reasoning from authority (discussed later) and reasoning from examples (discussed above).

Although deductive reasoning can be powerful, it can be hard for an audience to follow. So make it very clear, and avoid overwhelming the audience with a long chain of involved reasoning.

Causal Arguments

We often need to be able to show *why* something happened—not what its purpose was, but what caused it. **Causal arguments** try to demonstrate that an event or a situation has a cause and that changing the cause or causes would change the situation.

causal argument   A claim that one event, situation, or attribute causes another.

How It Works   Especially when you're talking about problems and solutions in your speech, you will want to establish the *causes* of situations or actions. Knowing the real causes allows you to propose effective solutions. What you're trying to do in causal reasoning is show that two events, situations, or attributes

- occur together,
- vary together, and
- are connected by a describable mechanism.

For example, if you want to claim that studying hard causes better grades, you'll need to show that studying and grades are associated *and* that they vary together (more study produces higher grades, less studying produces lower grades) *and* that there is some reasonable explanation for this relationship (studying produces more understanding, which enhances performance on exams).

If you were talking about a disease, the mechanism would be underlying physical process that explains how we get (or treat) the disease. For instance, smoking and

Jeffrey Wigand, the whistleblower played by Russell Crowe in the movie *The Insider*, revealed to Congress that tobacco companies secretly increased the amount of nicotine in cigarettes, causing them to be more addictive. A speaker could cite his testimony in a causal argument about tobacco's effects.

lung cancer occur together, heavy smokers have a higher incidence of lung cancer than nonsmokers, and over time, the chemicals in cigarette smoke damage the DNA in lung cells, causing them to reproduce wildly, resulting in cancerous tumors.

When It's Effective   When you show that two things are associated, you have demonstrated a *correlation* between them. Sometimes, you'll be able to find statistics to show correlations between events. There are two kinds of causal claims: weak and strong.

In a *weak causal claim*, you know only that two situations or actions are associated, which doesn't always mean there is a causal relationship. For example, your heart is beating every morning when you get up and the sun comes up every morning, but that doesn't show a causal relationship. Your heart isn't beating just because the sun came up (or vice versa). When you have strong statistical data but no good account of how the causality happens, limit your claims.

A *strong causal claim*, on the other hand, relies on a clearly proven mechanism, which is usually a scientific explanation of a physical or biological process: how solar power cells convert light into electricity, for example, or how your body converts food into the energy that moves your muscles.

Arguments From Analogy

As you saw in Chapter 6, *analogies* are comparisons that link unfamiliar things to familiar things by highlighting a similarity. When you say, "Doing my math homework is like throwing myself against a brick wall," you're using an analogy to convey the challenging quality of the experience. Sometimes *as* rather than *like* announces an analogy: "This homework is as hard as nails." If you omit the *like* or *as* and say, "I'm hitting a brick wall on the math homework," then you'd be using a *metaphor*, wherein the comparison is only implicit.

An **argument from analogy** compares two things and asks the audience to believe that one of them has the characteristics of the other. If your body is like a machine, and if a machine needs fuel, then your body needs fuel as well.

argument from analogy   A claim that a similarity exists between two objects or actions.

How It Works   You can use analogies to argue; by claiming a similarity between two things, you can claim that something true of one must be true of the other. George Washington said that "Government is . . . like fire, it is a dangerous servant and a fearful master." Accepting this analogy would mean that you could infer that although government is useful (fire/energy is of course useful), we should be careful with it because it can be dangerous, and it can overwhelm us if we don't keep it under control.

When It's Effective   For an analogy to work, it has to be appropriate ("The body is like a bowl of ice cream" is inaccurate and so probably wouldn't be useful in arguing anything). It also has to start with something your particular audience will find familiar (like a machine as an analog for the human body).

There are two types of analogies:

- *Literal*: The comparison has a factual basis.
- *Figurative*: The analogy is suggestive and useful but not based in fact.

For an argument, a literal analogy is more useful than a figurative one. Your body *is* like a machine in many ways. But if you were to argue that the negotiations between the United States, the United Nations, and the European Union are like a ballroom dance, you could push the analogy only so far (for one thing, ballroom dance has only two partners).

Analogies have their limits. Don't push them past what's plausible or helpful to your argument.

■ Arguments From Signs

Sometimes in a speech, we're trying to predict the future. How can we know what might happen? **Arguments from signs** try to show that an event, condition, or characteristic is a sign of some future event.

argument from signs   A claim that one event, situation, or attribute precedes another.

How It Works   Arguments from signs work when we're discussing relationships that are highly correlated but not causal. If you look for one thing, will you (almost) always find another? If so, then the first is a *sign* of the second. Dark clouds are a sign of rain, because although they don't cause the rain, they are a reliable signal that it is approaching.

Signs can be conventional or realistic. A *conventional sign* is a human-created symbol, like the white flag as a sign of surrender, or SOS as a distress signal. Conventional signs aren't usually useful for persuasive speeches. A *realistic sign* reflects a relationship in the actual world. For example, dark clouds mean rain, and if the leading economic indicators are down three quarters in a row, that is a sign that a recession is likely in the next year.

When It's Effective   Signs require some support, because it's always possible that the relationship we've inferred is false or inappropriate. For instance, dark clouds could be smoke from a forest fire and not a sign of rain. Racial and gender stereotypes are signs we sometimes use for predicting what other people will do—but we shouldn't use them because they are inaccurate and unethical. For example, if women truly were worse drivers than men (the stereotype), their auto insurance rates would be higher (though in fact they are lower).

However, one subject which extensively uses argument from signs is economics; certain kinds of economic arguments rely on signs that, for instance, prices are going to rise, the Federal Reserve may change interest rates, and so on. These arguments are often based on a good deal of support in the form of research and understanding of the history of the economy.

■ Arguments From Authority

When you are speaking from expertise on a subject based on research or experience, you may make an **argument from authority**. The crucial thing is to figure out how to make your expertise clear to your audience.

argument from authority A claim that a statement is true because of the expertise of its source.

How It Works   When you do library research, you're finding out what other people, who presumably know more than you do, have said about a particular claim. You can bring their authority to bear on factual claims in your speech, and sometimes on value claims, too—claims that something is "better" or "worse," "right" or "wrong."

If you want to argue that you know the mostly likely reason that students drop out during their first year of college, you'll have to cite an authority in the field of higher education research. If you want to know how many students drop out of your particular school, these figures should be available from the university administration.

Because your knowledge of any interesting topic is probably limited, you'll rely on authorities quite a bit. Make sure you're using them appropriately. For the most part, stick to factual claims; claims about values or policy are harder to support with an appeal to authority. For example, researchers can tell you how many people are killed each year in handgun accidents, but they can't tell you, in an authoritative way, how many accidents are morally acceptable to society (you'll have to make your own decision and claims about that). Make sure too that your authority is a specialist in the topic of the claim. You wouldn't cite a theologian about gun statistics, nor a chemist about a point of Christian theology.

When It's Effective   It's very important to ensure that your authorities aren't biased and don't have self-serving motives. Organizations now routinely create websites, hire impressive-seeming "experts," and post lots of information. But even though a site may come right to the top in a Google search, it may be biased, so you can't use it. Of course, such a site may refer you to legitimate sources of research. (See Chapter 8 for more about how to evaluate online sources).

Greg Mankiw of Harvard (left) and Paul Krugman of Princeton University (right) are experts on economics who frequently speak from authority on issues of the day.

What About the Other Side? Dealing with Counterarguments

counterargument An argument in opposition to your or someone else's argument.

The way you think about **counterarguments** makes a difference to the way you approach public speaking. Normally, when we think about presenting our position on something, we tend to de-emphasize counterarguments. Objections to our positions often make us uncomfortable, and we may try to avoid them. And then some speakers are more concerned with getting their way or pulling the wool over the audience's eyes than with providing all the facts to help the audience make a wise decision. But if you've internalized the idea that an argumentative speech is always in dialogue with its audience, you might want to approach counterarguments differently.

If your speech is in a process of dialogue and discovery with an audience (and we hope you think of it that way), then it is often better to deal directly with counterarguments to your position. If the goal of your speech is to help the audience make a more informed choice about your topic, laying out the possible objections to your position gives the audience a sense of the full range of issues at stake. More importantly, if you address the counterarguments to your position, you give the audience the essential tools to work with you in a dialogue.

Why Addressing Counterarguments Is Persuasive

Dealing directly with counterarguments can also make your speech more persuasive. By laying out the objections to your position and countering them, you can achieve three goals that will help you persuade your audience:

1. *You recognize that your audience is smart.* They are probably already thinking of a number of the important counterarguments to your position. By naming and addressing the counterarguments, you open up an opportunity to persuade them on these points that you wouldn't otherwise have had.
2. *Addressing counterarguments adds to your credibility.* Your audience will be listening for evidence that you have researched your position thoroughly and thought through the main objections to your points. Addressing counterarguments explicitly demonstrates that you have done the groundwork to support your position. It also shows your audience that you are in control of the issues surrounding your speech and that despite the objections, there are still good reasons for them to believe your position is defensible.
3. *You can control and frame the terms of the discussion.* The way you choose to introduce the counterarguments helps define them in the mind of your audience. If you frame the counterarguments a way that benefits your claims, you will have gone a long way towards persuading your audience even before you have presented your primary conclusions.

Tips for Dealing With Counterarguments

Let's imagine we are coaching Nathan, who is arguing with Heather about the benefits of welfare. Nathan is to give a speech in class that defends his position that expanding welfare is economically beneficial. Here are some tips we might offer him:

Seth Weing/AP/Corbis

Counterarguments are clearly visible in a debate, such as between presidential candidates Barack Obama and John McCain, as speakers make their case and refute others, but counterarguments are equally important in a speech without a formal rebuttal.

1. *Reference the counterargument specifically*, and define who is making it. Nathan might say,

   Conservative critics of welfare argue that welfare benefits decrease the incentives for people to work.

2. *Give a charitable version of the counterargument*, one that the other side might make, preferably by citing a specific source. This will add to your credibility by showing that you understand the counterargument, and it will help set up the reasons why you disagree. Nathan might say,

   For example, John Q. Taxpayer argued in last week's *City News* that people have no incentive to work when the government is willing to pay their living expenses.

3. *Point out that although the counterargument has merit, there is a reason why the audience should not accept it.* Some of the best techniques of rebuttal are to say that the counterargument ignores an important fact, oversimplifies the case, or runs contrary to empirical evidence. For instance, Nathan might say,

   There is a certain logic to what Mr. Taxpayer is saying. After all, who would work if the resources to achieve their loftiest aspirations were provided free of charge? But what criticisms like this ignore is that the purpose of these programs is not to provide a luxurious lifestyle, but to provide their basic needs so that they can get a job. For instance, the program that Mr. Taxpayer is criticizing provides housing assistance so that people have an address to put on a job application, job training so that they have a marketable skill, and basic subsistence needs so that they can focus on a job search.

4. *Finally, remember the benefits of framing.* The way you choose to represent the counterargument helps to define its power for your audience. Nathan could frame the counterargument that welfare hurts economic productivity in a number of ways. Which of the following is the best frame?

   The vast majority of qualified economists who have studied welfare demonstrate that it does depress economic productivity.

Economists argue that welfare reduces the incentives for work.
Some economists claim that providing the basic subsistence necessary for a job search might also risk reducing the incentives for people to work.

Counterarguments are important in maintaining the dialogic framework we discussed in Chapters 1, 2, and 3; they anticipate your audience's interaction with what you say. If you are going to engage the audience, you need to engage their arguments—especially the ones that attack your claims and your reasons.

As you design your counterarguments, ask yourself the following questions:

- What are the main objections to my argument or position? (You probably know this from your research.)
- How can I integrate my response into my speech? (At what point in the speech will audience members be likely to think about objections?)
- Can I frame my position as a way to answer the counterarguments that might come up?

For example, a counterargument to the claim "Wisconsin should lift the ban on smoking in public places" is that smoking bans protect public health (which is one of the primary reasons for the ban in the first place). You could narrow the claim to deal with this counterargument by arguing that "Wisconsin should lift the smoking ban only in bars." Smoking would still be prohibited in public places such as schools and restaurants, but bar owners would be able to regain valuable smoking customers. Thus, narrowing the topic from lifting the smoking ban in *all* public places to lifting it *only* in bars better positions the speaker to answer the counterargument of public health.

You can also answer counterarguments by saying your position is better than the other side's (technically, this is called a "comparative advantage" case). Using the smoking example, you could argue that bars are important local businesses that supply jobs and pay taxes, and in tough economic times, their need to grow and profit should be valued more than public health.

> **Try It!** *Using Ethos, Pathos, and Logos*
> Find the outline and notes for a speech you have already given. What was your primary strategy for projecting a sense of credibility? What primary emotional appeals were you employing? Can you define your primary argument strategy? How would you compose and deliver the speech differently with these three modes of proof in mind?

Summary

Giving a persuasive speech requires attention to ethos, pathos, and logos—three important factors that classical rhetoricians labeled "proofs" because they contribute to the persuasive force of your speech. A persuasive speech requires attention to presenting yourself as credible, well researched, and well intentioned—all the reasons why an audience should not only listen to you but believe what you are saying. Rhetoricians call this quality of a speaker ethos. To be persuasive you also have to use pathos, or connect with your audience emotionally, by moving them to connect positive or negative emotions with your topic, your description of the world, your thesis, and the action that you are calling for.

Finally, it is to your benefit to make arguments that rely on solid logical connections between your claims, evidence for them, and the ways that you use them to paint a picture of the world or call an audience to change their beliefs or actions. Rhetoricians call this proof logos. Six types of reasoning you can employ are inductive arguments, formal (deductive) arguments, causal arguments, arguments from analogy, arguments from signs, and arguments from authority.

Finally, speakers must be prepared to address, in their own speeches, what others will say about a topic. There is always more than one side to an issue, and even though you have the floor during your speech, it should address some of the arguments against your side accurately and cogently.

Access an interactive eBook, chapter-specific interactive learning tools, including flashcards, quizzes, videos and more in your Speech Communication CourseMate for *Public Speaking*, accessed through CengageBrain.com.

QUESTIONS FOR REVIEW

1. What are pathos, ethos, and logos? Why are they called "proofs"?
2. What characteristics give a speaker credibility?
3. What kinds of emotional appeals might a speaker employ in a speech?
4. What are the six types of argument? How does each one work?
5. How do speakers benefit from addressing counterarguments?

QUESTIONS FOR DISCUSSION

1. Sometimes, speakers seem like they are working too hard to make an emotional connection with an audience, and audiences are put off by it or feel manipulated. What, in your opinion, makes the difference between a successful and an unsuccessful emotional connection?
2. There is a fine line between a well-supported argument and one that loses the audience in details. What makes a speech seem well argued to you? Can you identify some consistent strategies that make arguments seem engaging?
3. Speakers appear credible to audiences for a number of reasons. What qualities make speakers seem believable to you? What qualities make speakers less credible to you?

LEARNING GOALS

- Describe the importance of responsible research choices
- Outline an effective, efficient research strategy
- Create search terms for focused online searches
- Gather relevant research materials
- Discover the note-taking approach that works best for you
- Evaluate the credibility and usefulness of different sources
- Effectively organize research materials and choose the most useful ones
- Correctly cite your sources

CHAPTER OUTLINE

Ferenc Szelepcsenyi, 2010/Used under license from Shutterstock.com

Research

ack followed the news enough to know that rising medical costs were a problem, both as a hot-button political issue and as a more general social problem. Because there was so much energy around the topic, it seemed like a great choice for a public speech. But after a little searching, he encountered a problem: Pundits on all sides of the political divide were offering suggestions that seemed to be directly contradictory. Though Jack had some firm political beliefs of his own, the harder he looked, the more confusing the issue became. He wanted to give an informed speech, not only because he wanted to know about medical costs as a citizen but also because he was tired of listening to abstract partisan arguments. Jack didn't just need a few facts to fill in the major points of a speech—he needed a strategy for sorting through the conflicting information and deciding what he should think and say.

Overview

Research is necessary for an effective public speech. This chapter will help you make responsible, well-crafted, and carefully executed research choices. First, we will help you figure out what you already know and translate that knowledge into a research strategy. Next, we will provide some concrete tips on where to go for research (including other people as well as the Internet and the library), how to design a good search query for search engines and databases, and how to narrow your search. After that, we will address what you need to do once you have collected your research material, including how to read through it, take notes, and evaluate which sources are worthwhile. Finally, we will deal with how to use your research process to refine your arguments, choose and organize your quotations, and give proper credit for the sources you use in your speech. ❯

Introduction: Becoming an Expert

Your task in researching, composing, and delivering an effective public speech requires that you acquire some expertise on your topic. You do not have to be the kind of expert who can produce original facts, figures, and data and publish groundbreaking work regarding your topic. You should, however, become at least a local expert on the topic—or the expert for your audience's purposes. Put differently, you should cultivate enough expertise on your topic to bring new insights to your audience and to speak with confidence and credibility.

Your audience may know nothing about your topic. If this is the case, what you say could help shape their opinions, so your words should be backed up with some reliable information. Or you may be speaking in front of an audience that already has a good base of knowledge about your topic. In this case, your credibility depends on having a good grasp of the literature about your topic.

Expertise matters. For example, consider how a few medical experts changed the way we think about vaccination. In 1998, the prestigious British medical journal *The Lancet* published a study claiming there was a strong link between autism and early childhood vaccination for measles, mumps, and rubella (MMR). The findings were widely publicized, and a movement against vaccination emerged. Parents worried that if they vaccinated their children, they were putting them at risk of developing a serious developmental disorder. Immunization rates declined significantly. According to an investigation by London's *Sunday Times*,[1] in Britain before the study, 92% of children were vaccinated against measles, mumps, and rubella. After the study, vaccination rates declined by 12%, and similar declines were reported in the United States. In Britain, the number of cases of measles rose from 58 in 1998 to 1,348 in 2008, and similar increases occurred in the United States.

Yet it turns out the study reported in *The Lancet* was based on flawed evidence, and there were a number of good reasons to question its claims. For example, although there has been a significant increase in autism in the last few decades, there has been only a slight increase in MMR vaccinations. Children who are not vaccinated have just as much risk of autism as children who are vaccinated. Moreover, the increase in autism did not start at the same time that the MMR vaccination did.[2]

What does a story about bad laboratory research have to do with the kind of research you will conduct for public speaking? Plenty. Even though you probably will not be presenting laboratory research to the public, the way you put together your research about your topic—including the quality of your arguments and the sources you choose—will make a difference in the way your audience thinks about your topic.

The sources, ideas, and arguments speakers use to justify a position in public have public implications, guiding the way people think about important problems. The question to keep asking yourself is whether the research you present in your speech helps your audience to make better choices, perhaps changing their habits, their votes, or the way they think about the world. Citing bad research can perpetuate dangerous myths, and it might cause your audience to jump to unsafe conclusions. You have the choice and the responsibility to make sure the conclusions you come to in your speech are well founded and well supported by high-quality research.

Researching Responsibly

In a good presentation, the points are delivered in an articulate, well-organized manner using high-quality research from reliable sources, which are cited properly. Whether you undertake your research conscientiously can make the difference between misinforming your audience and providing them with truly helpful answer to an important problem. In other words, you have choices about how you find and use research in your speech. Because these choices have implications, you need to engage in the process of researching, citing, and using information in your speech as if it matters to your audience.

Sometimes research seems like an annoyance—necessary for an assignment, but not all that important if your topic isn't obscure or controversial. But you should not think about research as a process you can complete by just going through the motions.

Geoffrey Canada, award-winning founder of the Harlem Children's Zone, carefully assembles data before making presentations about HCZ's community-building programs, because his audiences expect him to have evidence of their effectiveness.

No matter how well you think you know a topic, responsible research will always reveal new possibilities for argument and invention, giving you more choices. You might find incredibly persuasive support for your opinion, or you might change your mind as you unearth the best counterarguments against your position. The fact that you do not know the outcome is the best reason to research—in fact, it is *the* reason to research.

Need more reasons to conduct responsible research? You probably cannot be clear and persuasive about your topic if you have only a hazy understanding of it. In fact, haziness in their speech is one of the ways to spot people who are trying to manipulate or deceive others into agreeing with them. We are naturally suspicious of a speaker who does not offer good evidence for his or her claims. Conversely, when speakers demonstrate mastery of the details in their speech, we tend to trust them more. Having a well-researched speech helps your claims seem plausible and avoids the impression that you are talking about something you don't know much about.

Try It! *Finding Out When Research Is Needed*

Is it possible for unsupported claims to be persuasive? Try this experiment:

- Choose a topic and write an outline for a speech about it in about a minute, without researching or checking any facts.
- Then share it with a classmate or friend, and see how persuasive he or she thinks the speech would be.
- What does your friend's reaction tell you about research?

If your credibility is one more reason for responsible research, another is that your evidence is the audience's evidence; your listeners use the evidence you give them to persuade themselves. The impression made by a charismatic speaker fades quickly, but compelling bits of evidence, useful information, and well-chosen examples may stick in the audience members' minds for a long time.

The Research Process

Research can seem like a formidable task if you throw yourself into it without a plan. But if you break the process into a series of manageable steps, you will be well on your way to an effectively researched speech. The keys are knowing where to start and being able to manage the process. The basic elements in the research process are these:

1. Figuring out what you already know about your topic
2. Designing a research strategy
3. Organizing a search strategy for the various databases and resources that you will use
4. Gathering your materials, with complete source information
5. Reading and evaluating your materials and taking notes
6. Revising your claims and selecting the information you will use
7. Organizing and selecting research information and integrating it into your speech
8. Generating citations for your materials

In this chapter, we will walk through each of the steps in this process, focusing on practical advice for sharpening your research skills. Although there are many valid ways to engage the research process, having a well-thought-out plan and an organized approach to finding and using your materials is the key.

Figuring Out What You Already Know

Once you have chosen a topic that matters to you (or one has been assigned), start your research process by detailing what you already know about your topic. Make your existing knowledge work for you by forecasting what you would say given just what you know about the topic.

Draft a brief outline of what you might say if you had to give the speech right now, without doing any research. Ask yourself a few questions in preparing this outline:

- What is your opinion on the topic as it currently stands?
- What are the reasons you hold this opinion?
- What arguments and ideas do you think your audience will expect to hear in support of the topic?
- What are the best counterarguments to your position?

Don't worry about making the outline perfect; just get down on paper what you already know. For example, if you were to argue that marijuana should be legalized, you might write down this thesis and three-point outline.

Thesis: Marijuana should be legalized, because the costs of keeping it illegal are too high.

1. Enforcing marijuana laws costs too much and takes up valuable law enforcement resources.
2. The dangers of marijuana use are overstated, and we should be focusing on more dangerous drugs.
3. Making marijuana legal would allow for better regulation of it and would create a significant new stream of tax revenue.

Now ask yourself the questions suggested earlier. Here they are again, with your possible answers.

- What is your opinion on the topic as it currently stands?

  I believe marijuana should be legalized because enforcing marijuana laws has large social and economic costs.

- What are the reasons you hold this opinion?

  Because it seems like a lot of law enforcement costs are associated with marijuana laws, and I think these resources could be used elsewhere.

- What arguments and ideas do you think your audience will expect in support of the topic?

  They might expect me to say I am a marijuana user, but I am not, so I probably want to present the case in terms of the public policy costs. They might expect a defense that marijuana is harmless, and they might expect me to argue that enforcement is not effective in reducing marijuana use.

- What are the best counterarguments to your position?

  Keeping marijuana illegal lessens marijuana use, and marijuana use creates significant social problems due to addiction and its associated criminal behaviors.

An important part of the research process is figuring out what you already know. For instance, for a speech advocating the legalization of marijuana, you may already know that the use of marijuana for medical purposes is legal in some states but is still contrary to federal laws.

You might notice that a few themes have popped up in your outline. Circle or make a list of them and think about the ways they connect to your thesis. The following points connect with the thesis that marijuana should be legalized because the costs of enforcing marijuana laws are too high:

- Marijuana enforcement
- Rates of marijuana use
- The harms of marijuana use
- The economic and social costs of marijuana laws
- Sources and uses of tax revenue

With this list, you are ready to begin researching. Your goal is to be sure you know something about these themes and that you have facts to back up what you say. With any luck, you will find that your opinion has been confirmed by others, or you may find that you need to change your opinion.

Designing a Research Strategy

Once you have sketched what you already know about the topic, the next step is to design your research strategy, which consists of answers to three basic questions:

- *Where are you going to look?* A good answer to this question requires more than just saying you will go to an Internet search engine. Good researchers rely on a number of different resources to find the best facts, data, evidence, and support for their claims. The next section, "Deciding Where to Go," describes the variety of sources you could try.

- *How will you look for your sources?* What search terms will you employ, and how will you modify them to get the best results? The section "How to Conduct an Online Search" will offer helpful hints.
- *What do you expect to find?* It is a good idea to have at least some sense of the kinds of facts, data, and evidence you will be looking for. Your initial outline can serve as a useful resource for this, but you should be constantly doing a mental update of arguments that may turn out to be important for your speech.

Your answers to these three questions, which you can write down for reference if you find it helpful, will help you orient your research strategy. First, they will give you a focus and a goal to return to if you feel you are getting lost in research or wandering too far afield. Second, they will help you compare your research practice to your research goals. At every point in the research process, remind yourself of your answers to these questions. It is easy to get sucked down a research rabbit hole, pursuing leads that take you farther and farther from where you wanted to go. This is normal, and you may even revise your approach midstream (more on that later, in "Revising Your Claims"), but you also want to make sure you are staying disciplined and connected to your original plan.

Deciding Where to Go

Where should you go, virtually or physically, to look for materials? Three kinds of resources are available to you:

- electronic media (web-based articles, blogs, and multimedia resources),
- print materials (newspapers, journals and books), and
- people (informational interviews and other kinds of conversations).

Which is best to start with? The answer depends on the topic you have chosen.

Web-Based Search Engines   The big search engines, like Google, Yahoo!, and so on, are a useful place to start, and they will provide you with a wide range of sources. Google has functions for doing not only general web searches but searches of blogs, news sources, and scholarly articles, and books. For each of these search engines, do a general search, a blog search, a book search, and a search for scholarly articles. There are two good reasons to do all these searches: One, you want your sources to be as diverse as possible, and two, for certain topics you might find relevant evidence in only one area. For example, if you have chosen a current-events topic, news sources are probably your best bet because books and scholarly articles may be outdated, except for general and theoretical backup. On the other hand, if you are talking about a relatively specialized topic—for example, something scientific or about legal or public policy—a news search may not be your best bet.

Google (www.google.com) is one of the easiest and best places to start a research project. However, as you've probably discovered, the main problem is not the lack of sources but rather the need to appropriately narrow your search. A generic search will give you a broader range of different kinds of sources, linking to homepages for various organizations, news stories, blogs, and other online content. Two more specific functions, Google News (news.google.com) and Google Scholar

The expansion of search engines like Google has made research easier than ever, but the challenge is to get the best results from a sea of information.

Annette Shaff/Shutterstock.com

(scholar.google.com), can help target your search for materials a bit more narrowly. Google News (as well as Yahoo! News at news.yahoo.com) integrates news stories from many newspapers, TV stations, magazines, and wire services. It is a good place to search for topics that are either relatively recent (such as an ongoing political debate) or specific to an individual locality or event (for example, the rising crime rate in your city).

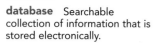

database Searchable collection of information that is stored electronically.

peer review Prepublication evaluation of scholarly articles by other scholars or researchers in the field.

Academic Databases for Journals and Other Periodicals Searching in Google Scholar retrieves academic journals and reports in a single convenient feed, and it will also link you to a number of the major scholarly **databases** (such as JSTOR and Project Muse, whose articles are accessible through your campus library). These large collections of journals will give you a variety of sources in most academic fields. The coverage may not be as specific as you would like for some topics, but academic publications can be helpful in giving you a broader perspective.

The journal articles and reports accessible through academic databases are peer-reviewed with solid theoretical grounding—the gold standard for good expert commentary on a topic. So, for example, if your topic is "climate change is induced by human carbon consumption" or "free downloads have hurt the music industry" or any other topic where a degree of technical expertise would be useful in sorting out a question, such databases can be extremely useful. **Peer review** is important because it means the accuracy and fairness of the source does not rely solely on the expertise of the person who wrote it, but it has also been reviewed by other experts in the field. If you need help finding relevant scholarly articles, check the FAQ box on databases, refer to your school library's web page, or talk to a librarian.

FAQ What are the best databases for scholarly articles?

Your campus library will have a database for just about any field that you might find helpful. They include America, History and Life (history and American studies, via EBSCO), AnthroSource (anthropology, from the American Anthropological Association), Business Source Premier (business journals and articles, via EBSCO), Communication and Mass Media Complete™ (communication studies, via EBSCO), and EconLit (economics, via EBSCO)—and that's just a sampling from the first few letters of the alphabet!

The major general article databases include Academic Search Premier, Academic OneFile, the CQ Researcher, LexisNexis Academic (law and public policy journals), JSTOR and Project Muse (humanities), and Science Direct and SpringerLink (sciences). Most college and university library home pages have a list of the databases you have access to as a student and a basic description of each.

Books Searching your library's online book catalog can point you to resources available in extended print format. Searching for books can be a bit more tricky than is searching for online resources because books are organized around broader themes than the topic you are researching. This does not mean you should not use books, but rather that you may have to look at a higher level of generality than you otherwise would. For example, although you may find a number of good books on the topic of marijuana legalization, you might also want to look at more general books about drug policy that contain chapters or sections about marijuana.

Books can be a great resource for your speeches because they are often written for nonspecialist audiences, and their authors have more space to explain their arguments. For each book you think you might want to look at, take a note of the title, the authors or editors, and the call number. You may be able to find the full text of some older books online, but you may also have to track down books at the library, and you'll need all this information.

Interviews and Conversations You may find that you want information that is not available online or in a library. If you know of someone who may have that information, arrange for an interview or conversation. You might interview an author of an article you found, an official who has experience with your topic, or someone directly affected by your topic. Authors and other experts are great sources of information, and they can usually direct you to other research resources. Officials with day-to-day experience with your topic can both tell you the important arguments and issues from their perspective and give you a sense of what directions you might take. Finally, people directly affected by the issues you address can add a personal perspective on what might otherwise be fairly abstract evidence.

To interview someone, you can make initial contact via email or phone. Published scholarly articles are often accompanied by email contact information; if not, they will usually say where the author works, and you can typically find an email contact link on a department home page. Officials of various kinds usually list their email contact information on their organization's web page; if not, you can usually find a phone number for someone in the organization who can direct you. If you are interested in talking to someone personally affected by an issue, the

Auremar/Shutterstock.com

Personal interviews often yield information about local issues you won't find anywhere else.

problem is finding a person who meets you criteria—usually by asking, emailing, or calling around.

When you contact the person you want to interview, clearly identify yourself, say you are calling for a class assignment, and have a list of questions prepared. You should record the interview, if possible, for transcription after the conversation. If this is not possible, take notes that are as extensive as possible without losing attention to the conversation. You should also assure the person that you will send them your notes after the interview if they would like. If you would like to quote sources you've interviewed or corresponded with, let them know you are going to quote them and where, and give them a draft of the quote so they can review it for accuracy. Also be sure to cite them by name and title in your speech.

Making a Methodical Search

To ensure you have a solid grasp on your topic, and to convince your audience you have done the work necessary to be a minor expert on your topic, you'll want to read and cite evidence from as many different kinds of sources as you can. You'll notice in class that the best speeches seem very complete: The speaker has tracked down information that silences each doubt you had in mind as you listened. You need to do the same. If you don't already feel skilled at library research, whether online or in person, take this opportunity to participate in one of tutorials your college library offers and get know a reference librarian or two; they can be extremely helpful.

You should also be organized and methodical. Keep a running list of the places you have turned to for research. Note the search engines you have gone to, the specific versions you have used (for example, a general Google search, a Google Scholar search, a Yahoo! news search), and any other databases you have consulted (compilations of academic journals, websites that have been particularly helpful, library catalogs that you have used), so you can make sure you've researched all the resources you would like to use and so you can return to a resource in case you want to double-check a fact or get more details.

How to Conduct an Online Search

Once you have decided where you would like to look, think about how to execute your searches. Online searching offers ease and efficiency, provided you remember a couple caveats: You cannot make your searches too general, because there are far more sources on most topics than any one person could read, and search engines are not yet very good at giving you the results you want unless you invest a little thought and effort in creating search terms and focusing your search.

Creating Search Terms

To start your search efficiently, create a list of search terms to use on the Internet and in your library's electronic catalog. You can add to, modify, or eliminate terms as you go, based on how productive they are. The common themes that popped up in your initial outline about your topic can be converted into your initial search terms. Your list can have as many subcategories as you have themes for your topic, and if your research moves you in a new direction, you can add new themes and search terms.

Designing a good search requires trial and error. If your search terms are too broad, you will waste time picking through useless sources to find a few gems. If your terms are too narrow, you will miss many useful sources.

Start with one of the common themes as a search term and read the first few articles that turn up from that search. You could also try an "and" search, such as on *marijuana and law enforcement*, or *marijuana and its health effects*. Do terms of art (that is, terms that people in the field use frequently) or other concepts occur with any regularity? In working through a first search about our topic example of marijuana legalization, you would find some search terms to add to your list, because you would get a sense of what phrases people are using to talk about the issue. For example, after scrolling through the first few search results, you might add terms like the following:

"Marijuana reform"
"Marijuana prohibition"
"Marijuana decriminalization"

You can also experiment with synonyms and subtopics. For example, if you started with the theme of "social and economic costs of marijuana laws," you might try "marijuana enforcement" and "marijuana and war on drugs" instead of "marijuana laws." For "social and economic costs," you might try "prison overcrowding," "law enforcement resources," "drug use," and "drug rehabilitation."

Try this process with a few of your themes, substituting search terms that appear in articles you find in your early searches. What new terms do you find? Don't hesitate to modify your list and return to it to brainstorm new approaches if you get stuck.

Focusing Your Search

To provide yourself with a good introduction to the material but not get lost in a multitude of sources, you will have to continually narrow the focus of your search terms, moving from more general to more specific searches. If you simply type "marijuana legalization" into a search engine, you will get many sources—indeed far too many to manage (there were more than 440,000 hits on Google for that search term at the time of this writing). You may want to skim a page or two of the results of this search, but the search term is too broad for your purposes.

In your first general searches, look for any political advocacy organizations, think tanks (advocacy organizations for specific topics that produce materials for the public to use), or other groups that have a specific interest in your topic. Make a note of these websites and organizations and return to them later; they are often a treasure trove of good, though partisan, information. See the FAQ box for more about think tanks and advocacy organizations.

As you continue to narrow your searches, you will find interesting new angles and arguments on your topic, and you can begin to revise and refine your outline accordingly. Your goal is to have a good quotation or statistic to back up each of the major claims in your speech. (Chapter 9 will discuss more details about creating an outline of your speech.)

FAQ *What are some go-to think tanks and advocacy organizations?*

There are so many think tanks and advocacy organizations that it isn't feasible to list them all. Here are a few examples organized by area of expertise and political persuasion that can help give you an idea of where to start.

	Generally Conservative	Generally Progressive
Foreign Policy	The Heritage Foundation	Brookings Institution
Domestic Policy	The Cato Institute	Pew Research Center
Economic Issues	American Enterprise Institute	Center for American Progress
Higher Education	Foundation for Individual Rights in Higher Education	American Association of University Professors

Speakers from advocacy organizations, such as John Podesta of the Center for American Progress, can supply important research and information, though it tends to support their preferred side of an issue.

Ramin Talaie/Corbis

Gathering Your Materials

If you have patiently followed a research strategy, you should be compiling a number of interesting leads for research. At this point in the process, however, you should not be reading your sources closely, nor should you be taking detailed notes on their contents. At this stage, you should simply be gathering materials in an organized way and getting ready to engage them more fully.

You can gather materials electronically or in printed form. If you gather them electronically, you can download the materials (articles, news stories, blogs, and so on) to a folder and then open them individually when you decide to read them. Or you can cut and paste all the materials into a Word document. Compiling one big document of research materials has a couple of advantages: You can easily search the whole of your research results for key terms using the *Find* command. You can also move quickly between individual documents once you have combined them into a single document.

If you prefer to collect materials in printed form, you will need to have a system for physically organizing the materials (a set of folders or an accordion file works well), and you will probably have to pay for and copying or printing the files. Although collecting in hard copy may be a necessity for various reasons, it also increases the amount of work you will have to do later, because you will have to transcribe quotations and statistics you would like to use into the body of your speech.

Regardless of your method, make sure that you have the complete citation data available to you for later use. This includes

- the title of the piece,
- the author,
- the journal or book title,
- the publication date,
- the Web address,
- and page range of the piece, if it is available.

If you download your research materials, usually this information is part of the package. If you are cutting and pasting into a single document, be sure you include this source information or enter it manually. If you are working with hard copies, write the citation data directly on the hard copy or keep a running document that is easy to cross-reference with the hard copy.

Reading Your Materials and Taking Notes

Now that you have a good-sized pile of materials, dozens of files, or a long research document, you can turn to reading and taking notes. Here your challenge will be to read efficiently and to make your reading count by ending up with good notes that you can use for your speech. In other words, you want to be able to locate the quotes, facts, and figures you pull from the individual documents without having to spend time rereading everything.

To begin, let's talk about reading strategies. Of course you need to read carefully, but you also want to read efficiently. Here are some tips:

- *For journal articles*, read the **abstract** (a summary at the beginning of the article), the first few paragraphs, the section titles, and the concluding paragraphs first. You can use the same approach for long news articles, except they won't have an abstract. Reading in this way will give you a sense of the overall argument, and it will clue you in to which sections are most relevant for your purposes. You may even choose to skim or skip a few sections on the basis of this preview.

abstract Summary at the beginning of a scholarly article.

- *For news articles*, read the first four or five paragraphs carefully. Because news articles typically begin with the most important information, these paragraphs will usually give you the basics of the story. You can skim the later paragraphs to see whether there might be anything useful in them.
- *For a book*, reading the introduction or preface and the table of contents will usually save you work. Introductions will typically walk you through the

Design Pics/Jupiter Images

Newspaper articles usually answer the questions who, what, when, where, why, and how in their opening paragraphs, so when researching newspaper articles, pay special attention to the beginning.

organization of the book, and you can choose to ignore the portions of the book that are not relevant for your purposes. If the book has an index, you can use it to look for specific pieces of information.

- *Blog entries* do not have a standard format—and so there are not as many reliable techniques for reading them efficiently.

As you read, take notes that will remind you how the research will be relevant for your speech and make it easy for you to fit it into your speech. What kinds of information will be relevant?

- *Arguments* that directly support points in your original outline are obviously helpful, perhaps to quote directly.
- *Background information* can provide context for your speech. In an informative speech, you might note general information about the object, process, or event you are talking about. In a persuasive speech, you might note information that describes current thinking about the problem you are addressing.
- *Facts, statistics, and data* can show the significance of your issue or be memorable because they are unexpected or make a particularly apt comparison. In an informative speech, you might make a note of data that describe how widespread or important an object, event, or process is. In a persuasive speech, you might note facts and data that speak to the scope and implications of a specific problem.
- *Quotations* from notable people with whom the audience might connect or regard as important can give you or your argument credibility. Other quotations are worth noting because they provide a rhetorically powerful justification for a major point or add explanatory value by using just the right words.

You can manage this part of the process several ways. One efficient method is to compile a *working document*, or a running list of important facts, quotes, stories, and other arguments that might fit into your speech. There is no need to organize these entries yet.

Another method is to identify each note with a *tagline* (Figure 8.1). The tagline is a short phrase that describes the role the fact, figure, or quote might play in your speech. It precedes the actual fact, quote, or paraphrase of an argument, which is followed by a page number and other relevant source information so you can find it in the original document. It is useful to separate the tagline from the material you are borrowing by

FIGURE 8.1
The Tagline Method of Taking Notes

	Tagline
Marijuana laws increase prison overcrowding	
"By taking away criminal penalties for low-level marijuana possession, we would be able to keep people out of the prison and the criminal justice system, where they are frequently harmed in various ways."	Material
American Civil Liberties Union, "Marijuana Law Reform" page, last modified 2012, date accessed 5/16/12, p. online. http://www.aclu.org/criminal-law-reform/marijuana-law-reform	Source note

putting one of them in bold face if you are keeping a Word document, or using two columns if you're compiling your list by hand. To reiterate, at this point the entries need only to be distinct from one another; they do not need to be organized yet—that part comes later. Figure 8-1 shows what a typical tagline note might look like.

Keep a running list of arguments, facts, and quotes distilled from your collection of research materials in this smaller, more usable research document. As long as your taglines are clear, succinct, and consistently worded, you will be able to retrieve the information you need by using the *Find* function if you are working in Word.

Your goal should be to produce five to ten pages of important arguments for the average speech, with each entry containing a small fraction of the total words in the original research documents. If you make good choices, once you work all the way through your collection of research materials, you should be able to write your speech from the smaller, more distilled research document.

Of course, there are other ways to take notes. Some people use note-taking software like Evernote. Others use an index card system or more elaborate written notes. However you choose to distill your reading into a more usable form, the same requirements apply—you need to be able to quickly access arguments, find individual items so you can quote or paraphrase them in your speech, and have all the necessary information to properly cite each piece of material you use.

Evaluating Sources

As you distill your research into more usable form, you will be making a number of choices, including the arguments you would like to use in your speech and the evidence you would like to muster to prove them. However, you should not choose quotes, facts, or arguments just because they confirm the case you would like to make. You need to consider the credibility of the source. You may have found some powerfully worded, on-topic, quotations, but if they are not from a credible source, you use them at your peril.

blog A web log, or personal journal, by an individual or a group of authors.

Let's take a look at how to evaluate the credibility of different kinds of sources.

■ Blogs

Blogs can be helpful sources of information, but only if the contributors are knowledgeable and trustworthy. You will want to find out what the blogger's qualifications are before you decide to quote from a posting. If the reasons for the blogger's expertise are not included in the About section of the blog, you can try a web search for the author's name. A world of difference exists between a blog conversation among qualified academic or public policy sources and one among random members of the public. Because blogs are not edited or peer reviewed, you should treat the information and arguments you find there with some skepticism; blogs often represent a specific point of view.

FAQ *What is bias?*

Bias is usually contrasted to objectivity, which roughly mean the source is either "interested" or "disinterested." *Interested* means the source has a stake in the outcome and would like to see things turn out a particular way. *Disinterested* means the source is neutral and will accept whatever conclusions evidence points to.

Even if neither bias nor objectivity exists in a pure form, we can examine whether a source, an expert, or an institution has a bias, relatively speaking, toward one side or another of a controversy. For example, a source may be biased if it has a significant financial, personal, or other incentive to make a particular argument.

Bias does not mean that the position of the source must be dismissed as wrong, but it does mean that you should pay extra close attention to the evidence that supports its arguments, because an interest in a particular side or conclusion can (often unintentionally) cause people to misrepresent arguments and evidence.

■ News Articles

News sources can range from highly credible to extremely biased. Nationally recognized, award-winning newspapers and magazines usually have experienced reporters, excellent research staff, dependable fact checkers, and skilled editors. Some examples include *The New York Times*, *The Chicago Tribune*, *The Wall Street Journal*, and *The Economist*. But journalists are not necessarily experts in every area they cover. Staff writers for local newspapers and wire services may not have expertise in every topic they have to write about. Once again, you can go online to research the journalist's background. If he or she is not a specialist, let the article guide you to research done by more qualified writers.

■ Opinion or Advocacy Pieces

Editorials, position papers, and other opinion or advocacy pieces can give you someone's take on a topic, but you need to be careful about two issues here: bias and qualification. If you cite a really powerful article about legalizing marijuana from www.blazed.com or www.Iheartpot.org, you may not only be citing a poorly qualified author, but you may also be undermining the perception that you have done careful research on your topic, because these sources are not unbiased.

Journalist Jane Brody, author of several books on health and nutrition and the long-running Personal Health column in *The New York Times*, has substantial education and writing experience in the fields of health and medicine. Her expertise is evidenced by the many speaking engagements described on her website.

Henry S. Dziekan III/Getty Images

Scholarly, Peer-Reviewed Articles

Peer-reviewed articles by scholars and researchers are available on general Internet search engines and in databases like InfoTrac and Academic Search™ Elite, available at your local library or on your college or university library's web page. As we mentioned earlier, Google has a specific search portal for academic publications (Google Scholar).

Peer-reviewed articles can be great sources because they have been subjected to a rigorous editorial process and are likely written by people with strong qualifications. Though they are highly credible, however, they may be too abstract or specialized to be useful for a general audience. You'll need to consider your audience when you consider presenting information for a scholarly publication.

Research studies are usually presented in peer-reviewed articles and are generally good sources of information. Empirical data on your position can help answer questions and provide solid real-world evidence for your claims. Be careful to cite the conclusions of the study appropriately; you can run into problems if you are either mischaracterizing or exaggerating a study's conclusion.

Wikis

Wikis, like Wikipedia, are websites whose content is written and edited by the general public. They can be helpful for an introduction to a topic and sometimes can point you to other, more credible sources. However, because wikis can be written and modified by anyone, they cannot be relied on to present accurate information.

wiki A website whose content can be created and edited by its users.

In general, *Wikipedia is not a reliable source* except as a possible starting point for your research. Citing it in your speech can damage your credibility by making it seem that you have taken the easy way out and that you did not bother to find more authoritative information to support your claims.

Websites and Web Pages

Websites and web pages can be a useful source of information and evidence, depending on the objectivity and expertise of their author or sponsor.

- Web pages maintained by faculty, research groups located at universities, and think tanks (such as the Cato Institute or the Brookings Institution) are generally reliable.
- Websites of nonprofit organizations such as the American Cancer Society and government research organizations such as the National Institutes of Health are also generally reliable.
- Corporate web pages are often full of promotional material. Do not use them as your only source about a product or a corporation.

 FAQ *Researching online is just like going to the library, isn't it?*

No. The first rule of Internet research is always this:

Consider the source. *Anybody can post anything.*

Unlike book and journal publishing, where a professional system of editing and fact checking ensures the quality of what's published, Internet publishing is cheap and private. What people post is limited only by their time and imagination. Although many print publications have an editorial stance (The *New York Review of Books* is somewhat liberal, *The Economist* somewhat conservative), they still have to adhere to standards of evidence and argument to maintain their readers' trust. Internet materials do not have to meet these standards, and their authors do not have to respond to criticism.

This is not to say that all corporate or personal pages are dubious or irresponsible, just that it's up to you to figure out which ones are. Let the researcher beware! Be suspicious of what you find online, especially if it seems too good to be true. For example, if you go to www.townhall.com, you might think, "Oh, town halls, OK, this should be a good, neutral source of information on public debate and discussion of political issues." You'd be wrong, however; this site is a portal to many ultraconservative websites. There's nothing wrong with one-sided sites—unless you think you're getting a balanced view from them.

- Personal or private web pages can have links to an immense amount of information on a topic, or they can be one person's ranting. Cite these as a source only after you have checked the author's credentials.

See the FAQ box for some additional insights about researching online.

Revising Your Claims

Now that you have begun to read the research you collected, you may want to refine your argument. If you have researched effectively, you may want to modify your claims, or maybe even change your opinion on the basis of the work you have done. You may need to go back and forth between your arguments and your research several times. Your research may suggest new or better arguments, or you may find that some of your arguments require a little more research.

 What If I Change My Mind Mid-Topic?

The big-picture answer (though not the comforting one if you have a deadline) is that changing your mind based on your research is a good thing. It means you learned something, and writing a speech should be easy now because you have a good understanding of both sides of the argument. You can still use many of your first ideas by introducing them and then explaining why the research or force of a better argument means that you, and therefore the audience, should think about the topic in another, better way.

Sometimes when you have collected and read all the sources you planned to, you can declare victory and say that you have found enough good support for your original proposition to write a speech. Other times, the evidence does not cooperate—either because you do not find as much information as you would like, or because the majority of your research points in a different direction from what you originally intended. These bumps in the road do not represent a failure; they represent the success of your research: You looked and you could not find good, credible support for the case that you wanted to make.

If this happens, ask yourself what speech you could write on the basis of the research that you have already collected. You may be able to write a solid outline for a slightly different speech than you originally intended. If you need to go back to the beginning with a revised research plan, however, write a new projected outline with the arguments you *are* finding, and look in some new places, using new search terms. By being persistent, methodical, and flexible enough to change your plans a bit, you should be able to create a nice base of research in quick order and arrive at a robust, well-argued case for your speech.

Organizing Your Research Information

Once you have a good selection of quotes, facts, and data that you are comfortable with, you can decide how to integrate them into your speech. The easiest way to do this is to look at all your taglines and group them into like categories. You can take note of the most frequent themes and group them into sets of like arguments. If you have been consistent with your taglines, you should even be able to write a new outline with your taglines serving as the specific points. So, for the hypothetical marijuana legalization topic, the organization outline might look something like this:

I. Basic facts about existing marijuana laws

  Tagline/Quote

  Tagline/Fact

II. Social costs of criminalized marijuana

    A.   Overloads the criminal justice system

        1. Prison overcrowding

           Tagline/Quote

           Tagline/Fact

        2. Takes up law enforcement resources

           Tagline/Fact

    B.   Increases criminality

        Tagline/Quote

III. Economic costs of criminalized marijuana

Obviously, such an outline will put you ahead of the curve in terms of writing an outline for your speech (see Chapter 9). But do not be concerned if organizing your research does not automatically produce a speech outline or if your speech outline doesn't end up exactly matching the organization you chose for your notes. Your goal here is to organize all your research materials so you can access them quickly when you start writing your speech.

You should have a number of facts, quotes, and other pieces of supporting materials for any given point you plan to make. Order the supporting materials from most useful to least useful, so you can easily pick and choose between them. What makes supporting evidence good? The quality of the source, the degree to which it supports your claim, and other considerations including, for example, how good the quote sounds, or how robust the study data are. To choose the supporting material for your speech, ask whether the individual fact, quote, or piece of data advances your goals given the specific audience and situation Let's look at this question in a bit more detail.

Choosing the Sources for Your Speech

You don't want to cram *all* your research into your speech. You need to decide which pieces of information will make the cut and appear in your speech. When you write a rough draft for a paper, for example, you do so realizing you are not going to keep all of it. Some material will be great as is, some will be good but in need of improvement, and some will be destined for the recycle bin. In the same way, you need to gather a large enough body of research so that you can make some good choices about what to include in your speech and what served only as background information helping you to understand the topic. (Your instructor might want this material to appear in the bibliography you turn in, however.)

How do you choose? For each piece of evidence you are considering for your speech, ask yourself three questions.

- First, what purpose does the information serve for your overall goal? What will your audience understand about the topic if you include this quotation, fact, or statistic? Would the audience miss the information if you did *not* include it? If the material advances an argument that is crucial to your speech, use it. But if it's on a side issue, even if it's a great quotation, it will distract listeners from your argument.
- Second, what kind of evidence is it? You probably will serve your purpose best if you have an appropriate balance of facts, quotes, and statistics, because

If you are speaking about the trend for corporations to purchase naming rights to sports stadiums, your home team's win-loss record might make you proud but is probably not relevant evidence for your speech.

John Biever/Contributor/Getty Images

audiences tend to get bored if you include too many of one kind. A speech that is all quotes or all statistics can be difficult to listen to.

- Third, how good is the evidence? This is not only a question of whether the information helps you prove a point or convince your audience. Evidence is only as good as its source, and, as you've seen, not all sources are strong ones.

When you have polished your research skills, you will find that you will easily discover more sources than you can possibly cite in your speech, so it's important to choose carefully, and cite the sources that best help you make your case to your audience.

Citing Your Sources and Avoiding Plagiarism

One of the important choices in research is giving credit where credit is due. There are two reasons for this. First, showing that qualified people support your claims helps to prove the credibility of your case. Second, giving the audience the necessary information to track down your sources shows that you are confident in your claims and allows the audience to continue the conversation you have started. Perhaps most importantly, academic life is based on the principle that everyone should get credit for ideas he or she introduces, giving us strong practical and ethical reasons to avoid plagiarism.

In Chapter 2, we made the case for not plagiarizing other people's work. That rule most directly affects you when you are turning your research into a speech. Because the audience will not usually receive a written copy of your speech, it can be easy to plagiarize.

FAQ **What does APA citation style look like?**

Here are some examples of APA citations for different types of materials you may find in your research.

Book (one author): Ivie, R. L. (2007). *Dissent from war.* Bloomfield, CT: Kumarian Press.

Book (two authors): Keith, W. M., & Lundberg, C. O. (2008). *Essential guide to rhetoric.* New York, NY: Bedford/St. Martin's.

To avoid this problem, you should give credit in two different places. First, you should say in the body of the speech, where you got the fact, quote, statistic, or argument. This is as simple as naming the person, publication, or organization that produced the information. For example, you might say in your speech: "The National Organization for the Reform of Marijuana Laws said in a 2004 report that . . ." The important thing is to give your audience a cue that you are relying on someone else's hard work.

Second, you should list the sources that you cite in your speech in a bibliography. A **bibliography** is record of all the sources where you found your information. Think of it as a way for somebody to look up and verify your information, making sure it is just as you said. Your bibliography has to be complete enough to allow someone to go to a computer or the library and look up whatever he or she doubts.

A common style for organizing the information in a speech's bibliography is the American Psychological Association (APA) format, which is standard in the social sciences. See the FAQ box for some examples. You can think of a bibliography citation as answering four of a journalist's "w questions":

Author = who?
Year = when?
Title = what?
Publication = where?

Your instructor may prefer a different style for your bibliography, but whatever style you use, be consistent, so all the entries are formatted in the same way. Make sure your citations complete, so your audience will have not trouble tracking them down should they choose to do so. If you have more questions about how to compile a bibliography, talk to your instructor or a research librarian, or take advantage of the online research and citation resources at Purdue University's Online Writing Lab (OWL) at http://owl.english.purdue.edu/.

Book (edited volume; entire book): Inness, S. A. (Ed.). (2004). *Action chicks: New images of tough women in popular culture.* New York, NY: Palgrave Macmillan.

Book (chapter in edited volume): Chao, P. S. (2006). Tattoo and piercing: Reflections on mortification. In L. J. Prelli (Ed.), *Rhetorics of display* (pp. 327–343). Columbia: University of South Carolina Press.

Journal Article (one author): Bowers-Campbell, J. (2008). Cyber "pokes": Motivational antidote for developmental college readers. *Journal of College Reading and Learning, 39,* 74–87.

Journal Article (two authors): Mitchell, R. K., & Nelson, C. L. (2007). Don't drink and speak: The relationships among alcohol use, practice, motivation, anxiety, and speech performance. *Communication Research Reports, 24,* 139–148. doi:10.1080/08824090701304865

Journal Article (three to five authors): Foulger, T. S., Ewbank, A. D., Kay, A., Popp, S. O., & Carter, H. L. (2009). Moral spaces in MySpace: Preservice teachers' perspectives about ethical issues in social networking. *Journal of Research on Technology in Education, 42,* 1–28.

Magazine Article (no author, accessed online): Study reveals gap in HIV testing knowledge among college students. (2008, August 28). *Science Daily.* Retrieved from http://www.sciencedaily.com/releases/2008/08/080827164039.htm

Newspaper Article (one author, accessed online): Morgenson, G. (2009, November 11). From an idea by students, a million-dollar charity. *The New York Times.* Retrieved from http://www.nytimes.com/2009/11/12/giving/12STREET.html

Blog Post: Robert Hariman. (2011, May 9). Floods and federalism [Blog post]. Retrieved from http://www.nocaptionneeded.com/2011/05/floods-and-federalism/

Video Blog Post: UW Madison LGBTCC. (2010, November 22). Stop the silence [Video file]. Retrieved from http://www.youtube.com/watch?v=YFW63cjN6xk

bibliography A record of all the research sources for a speech.

Getting Help From a Research Expert

Sometimes when you are conducting your research, great materials seem to be falling off the page or computer screen. Other times, it can take some additional searching and revision to come up with a well-researched speech. No matter what, keep trying! If you don't give up the first time you hit a snag, and if you are flexible enough to revise your speech based on the research you find, you will be in great position to give a well-supported speech. Obviously, you can go to your classmates, TA, or instructor to compare notes, strategize, and look for more solutions.

The librarian is one of your best resources for helping you efficiently find the information you need.

But going to the library and talking to a research librarian is one of the easiest ways to get over a research hump. Most college and university libraries have a dedicated staff of people who are eager to help you compile research. Do not be afraid to take advantage of this easy and free way to hone your research strategy. You may save a substantial amount of time and effort by consulting a research expert early in the process, and the skills you gain by doing research alongside a qualified instructor will have benefits for the rest of your academic career.

Summary

Access an interactive eBook, chapter-specific interactive learning tools, including flashcards, quizzes, videos and more in your Speech Communication CourseMate for *Public Speaking*, accessed through CengageBrain.com.

Research requires you to make a number of choices about how to support the claims in your speech and to make it persuasive and useful for your audience. Saying what you think in a clear, organized, and persuasive manner is important, but you also have a responsibility to make sound arguments that are well supported by facts, figures, statistics, and expert opinion. If you are organized and persistent, you will eventually find what you need or make a reasonable revision of your initial hypothesis.

Engage in research with a strategy in mind, combining the knowledge you already have about the topic with techniques for learning new information, balanced against the time you have and the research demands of the project. Decide where you will go for information and how you will execute and refine your search. Next, make choices about how you will gather, evaluate, and organize materials and how you will translate them into notes, or usable chunks of information that you can transform into a speech. After reading the research you've collected, consider whether you need to revise the arguments you intended to make. Finally, choose the quotes, facts, and data to include in your speech, and make sure you properly credit the work of others that you have used.

One last and important reminder: Take advantage of the many resources on campus for helping you learn to research more effectively. Seeking them out early in the research process will pay off.

QUESTIONS FOR REVIEW

1. What are your research responsibilities?
2. Describe the process for researching a speech topic. Why is it important to have a strategy?
3. How will you generate search terms for your research?
4. How should you keep track of your research?
5. How do you properly cite a source, both in a speech and in a bibliography?

QUESTIONS FOR DISCUSSION

1. What are the various ways you might use research in your speech? What, for example, determines whether you need to directly quote someone? When do quotations distract, and when do they help?
2. What makes a good source? What makes a poor source? What are some ways you can tell the difference?
3. What are the biggest roadblocks to research in your experience? What strategies have you used to overcome them?

LEARNING GOALS

- Identify the three main parts of a speech and their functions
- Master the use of previews, internal previews, and transitions
- Describe the patterns of organization and their advantages and disadvantages
- Choose main points and their order
- Justify choices of supporting material and their placement in your speech
- Construct clear and useful outlines

CHAPTER OUTLINE

Jeff Greenberg/Alamy

Organization

As a nutrition major, Felicia had many things to say about making better dietary choices, but she also had a problem. As soon as she sat down to figure out what she would like to tell her audience, she found she had too many points to fit into a short speech, and it was hard to imagine doing anything with her material other than reading a giant list of dos and don'ts. But who would want to listen to that? How could she decide what points to include? How could she weave all the points she wanted to make into a coherent scheme that told an interesting story?

Overview

You've picked your topic, thought about audience, and done your research. Now you can start figuring out how to actually put your speech together. Where do you begin? That's the task of *organization*, where the structure of the talk you'll give actually takes shape. A strong grasp of structure allows you to take control of the material, to make your information interesting and understandable, and to more easily remember and deliver your speech. ❯

Introduction: Getting Organized

organization The logical progression of a speech.

Public speaking lies in the middle of a continuum. It is less flexible and improvised than conversation, but it is less permanent than books and documents. Your task in organizing your speech is to choose a structure for your ideas that makes them as coherent as a formal written document, while allowing you to deliver them in a conversational way. But listening is very different from reading, because the words are gone once they are spoken—your audience can't scroll back to see what they missed.

Organization allows your audience to follow the logical progression of your speech and helps both you and your audience to remember your ideas. It demonstrates that you are in control of your material, and it can also add persuasive force to your words. You can organize your speech to begin with the overwhelming evidence in favor of your position, to progressively build your argument to a crescendo around your conclusion, or simply to report the facts. Organization is a crucial tool in creating a compelling communication experience for an audience. It combines the immediacy and power of a person speaking with the structure and clarity of a written text.

So organization is much more than settling for clichés for speech introductions. It is a powerful set of tools for connecting your arguments and information to the audience. But here is the important point, one that we emphasize again and again in this book: For speech to be truly public, that is, for you to speak as a member of a community and for the good of the community, you must make appropriate choices and take responsibility for them. This rule applies to organization as much as to the other parts of the public speaking process. You make choices about how to organize your speech, and those choices have implications for how you present a case, and for how your audience responds to your speech.

To choose responsibly, you should be aware of the different effects you produce by organizing your speech in different ways, which we look at in the following pages. Your choices can add to the clarity of what you are saying, improve your ethos as a speaker, and make the information more useful and easily digestible for your audience. As you'll see, we'll talk about structure in two stages. First, we'll cover the overall structure of the speech—beginning, middle, and end—and in the second half of the chapter we'll go over the structure of the body of the speech.

The Basic Three-Part Structure

Not every public speech has an easily identifiable introduction, body, and conclusion. Sometimes, people just tell stories, and in some speeches, like the President's annual State of the Union address, the speaker works through a number of issues, a list. The audience has expectations for how the State of the Union or a personal narrative speech will go and often has more information about the speakers and their purposes than the audience does for public speaking classroom assignments or for speeches that aim at public advocacy.[1] As in all public speaking, your audience and their expectations should guide the choices you make—after all, the President would look a bit silly introducing the State of the Union speech by saying, "Hello, I am the President of the United States, and today I am here to talk to you about the state of the union."

For your class assignments and other public speaking, we recommend adhering to the three-part structure. This isn't just a convention of speech and writing teachers but a fact about how communication works: You can't start in the middle or abruptly stop and walk away. You have to do some work to get the speech going (the introduction) and do some work to finish up properly (the conclusion). It is always safest to at least provide your audience with a sense of who you are, what your goals are, and what you will be talking about, and to end with a conclusion that tells listeners what you want them to do with the information you've provided. Thinking in terms of introduction, body, and conclusion will help you *manage* the process of beginning to speak, speaking, and finishing speaking.

The Introduction

Your **introduction** allows the audience to listen knowledgeably for the important points you will make. Audiences need a bit of structure to help them understand where you are going with a speech and what you would like them to do with it.

introduction The first section of a speech, consisting of the statement of the topic, thesis, and preview.

Without answers to the following questions, the audience won't be sure how to process or respond to the rest of the speech. The introduction meets some important communication needs.

- Who is the speaker?
- Why does she want to speak?
- What is she speaking about?
- Why should we listen?

Though the introduction is the part of your speech you deliver first, it may well be the last part you will draft. Why? Well, an introduction can only come after you have done your research and decided what you want to say in the body of your speech. You may find it's more efficient to save writing your introduction until you have fully laid out what you want to say with the rest of the speech.

◼ Functions of an Effective Introduction

Here's what an effective introduction should do for your speech. Remember, the introduction isn't just a throwaway chunk of talk at the beginning of your speech; it has some specific tasks.

- *Get the attention of the audience:* Give people a reason to listen. Cheesy ways of catching attention (rude jokes, shocking images, strange delivery) aren't

Although he was once president of the United States, when Bill Clinton speaks now, he does so in several different roles, and each time he has to make clear what his relationship to the audience is.

needed and aren't helpful. The idea is to catch the audience's imagination (especially their visual imagination, their "mind's eye") with a snappy and appropriate presentation of your topic.

- *Define the audience and the speaker:* Tell the audience the role you want them to take in listening to this speech (their rhetorical role); define the role you are taking as the speaker.
- *Show why the audience should listen:* Tell the audience what's in it for them and why this topic is relevant to them. You need to make the case that it is worth their effort to listen to you through the rest of the speech.
- *Develop common ground:* Offer a context that makes sense of your topic. What's going to be the basis for your argument or persuasion? It might be a belief, a value, or an institution, something audience members all share or belong to. For example, if you are speaking in favor of relaxed environmental laws, you might want to base your speech in arguments about the value of capitalism, free enterprise, and the ability to pull oneself up by the bootstraps. So the introduction should introduce these themes.

These functions don't correspond to separate sections of the introduction—you won't have an attention point, a common-ground point, and so on—but they should all be accomplished in the course of the introduction.

A tip: It's best not to start with a quotation. Because *you* are standing there, the audience expects *your* words to come out. Beginning with someone else's words can confuse them.

Elements of the Introduction

The whole introduction should not be too long. Usually, it's about 25% of the speech, and it consists of the narration, the thesis, and the preview.

Narration   A narrative (from the Latin *narratio,* "something told or related") is a story. The narration is the part of the introduction where you begin to set up what will follow in the rest of the speech. Its purpose is to pique the audience's interest. It does not have to be a story (though it can be); it can also be a question, an analogy, or a verbal image that gets listeners acquainted with your take on the topic and elicits their attention.

Narrations can take two general forms. You can introduce your topic by moving from a general claim to a specific topic in an **inverted pyramid**, or you can use a specific example to illustrate a general theme, which is called the **Sunday feature** method. Here are examples for a speech about dangerous playground equipment.

 Why not start with a joke?

Speakers are commonly advised to start with a joke. Jokes and funny stories make a good beginning, but only if you meet three conditions:

1. You must actually be funny (you might seek feedback from others on this).
2. You must have a good joke or story.
3. It must add an insight relevant to understanding the topic.

Most speakers cannot meet all three conditions in every speech, so beware!

Inverted Pyramid

> **It's a terrible thing when a child is killed. Children may die from illness, deliberate violence, or accidents. Some accidents are just that and can't be avoided. But others are preventable, and their occurrence is even more tragic when they involve playground toys intended to give pleasure to kids. Statistically, slides over four feet high are as dangerous to children as guns, and we need to do something about them . . .**

inverted pyramid A strategy of moving from a general claim to a specific topic.

Sunday feature Use of a specific example to illustrate a general topic.

This narration does several things well. It establishes the topic and the speaker's orientation to it. It places the topic in a category—"avoidable deaths of children"—which marks it for action by the audience (as opposed to "horrible stuff we just have to deal with," a category that doesn't require action). It introduces a comparison—guns—which helps the audience see that the slide isn't just playground equipment but something very dangerous.

For a group that is very familiar with kids, such as parents, this is a good introduction because the category itself will certainly compel their interest. However, if the audience is a group of 19- to 20-year-olds without an immediate interest in kids, it may leave them a bit cold. Remember, the audience is thinking, "What has this got to do with me?" In that case, the Sunday feature approach to narration might work better.

Sunday Feature Example 1

> **Bobby Brady was a pretty average kid. He liked video games, ice cream, and going to the water park. He loved going to the neighborhood playground and trying out all the equipment. He'd swing on the swing, going as high as he could. He and his friend Jorge would rock on the teeter-totter for hours. But Bobby especially enjoyed the slide, climbing up, up, up to the top and sliding down as fast as possible. He doesn't enjoy it any more. Bobby Brady died last year, after falling from a slide. I wish I could say he was the only one—but I can't. Thousands of children are killed or injured each year at playgrounds, and we need to do something about that . . .**

This narration makes the problem very concrete and helps the audience get beyond the abstraction of "thousands of deaths and injuries" by using a single case, Bobby, to stand for all the deaths and injuries. It makes the speaker's position clear, but it doesn't bring in a clear policy frame at the start, asking only for sympathy until the very end. That may be acceptable, but it will mean more work on policy implications later in the speech. This introduction grabs and holds our attention by creating a little bit of mystery—what is interesting about Bobby? Nothing yet—so the audience, whether parents or not, will keep listening to find out the rest of the story.

Sunday Feature Example 2

You wouldn't think so but swing sets or slides can be deadly. Sure, kids need to be careful, but they shouldn't get hurt on playthings. We need to do something about the problem of unsafe playground equipment.

This narration is weak. It doesn't develop the problem in any kind of vivid detail, and it doesn't establish the speaker's perspective. If "kids need to be careful," then playground equipment isn't the only or primary problem, so the audience isn't clear about what the actual topic of the speech will be or the speaker's position on it. Its attention-getting power is limited by abstraction and ambiguity.

Thesis   Recall that the thesis is a clear statement of your subject and/or your argument. You should always assume you are asking for the audience's time and attention—and you need to work to deserve it. A primary frustration for an audience is not knowing the *point* of a speech—what is it about? Your audience can't tell how the parts of a speech relate to each other until they know the central point. So, early in the speech, you need to make a clear, one-sentence statement of your main point.

The thesis is the hinge point on which everything else in the speech turns. Aristotle claimed that organization was simple: "State your point and prove it." But you've got to have a clear point in order to do this.

Compare the following thesis statements for the playground speech introduced earlier:

1. Playground equipment must be improved to make it less dangerous.
2. Playgrounds need to be made safe for kids.
3. Playground equipment manufacturers must be held accountable for the safety of their products.

Each of these would be a fine thesis statement—for very different speeches. The arguments needed for each thesis would be different because the diagnosis of the problem is different. The second thesis just states the problem, whereas the first and third ones suggest a solution.

FAQ   *What makes a good thesis statement?*

Strong thesis statements are clear, direct, and related to the content of the speech. Refer to Chapter 5 for pointers on how to write a good thesis statement.

The Preview   The **preview** is a thumbnail outline of the speech, a road map that will help both you and your listeners stay on track. Giving a preview for a speech is sometimes called *signposting*, because it signals the road ahead. Classically, the preview was called the "division of points," because it alerted the audience to the major divisions or sections of the speech.

preview   A brief outline of a speech in the introduction.

The best way to think about the preview is this: The body of the speech is divided into two or three main arguments (or groups of arguments), and you'll need to tell the audience what they are, so the listeners can recognize them—and how they fit together—when they come along in the speech. The preview should therefore be a quick, memorable sentence or two that exactly describes the organizational structure of the speech. Here are two previews, each for a different speech about playground equipment.

We'll see that playground equipment poses two main dangers to kids, *falling* and *crushing*.

To solve the problem of playground equipment, we'll have to look at the *dangers* it poses, the *reasons* safety has not been a priority, and the *actions* we can take to ensure that playground safety improves.

The narration, the thesis, and the preview are a way to introduce your topic and speech to the audience, introduce yourself to the audience, and introduce the audience to themselves. These elements of the introduction are also preparation for the substance of the speech, the body.

The Body

The middle section of the speech, the **body**, is likely to be the longest part of the speech, because it is where you present the bulk of your arguments and evidence to the audience. It's the core of the speech; if you don't have the content for the body, there's not much to introduce or conclude. Although the introduction and conclusion build a framework, the body fills that framework in.

body The core of a speech, where the arguments and evidence are presented.

The body needs to make information and arguments clear and, in particular, the *relationships* between information and arguments. As your speeches get longer and more complex, the responsibility to help the audience understand and see connections becomes greater.

Two goals should guide your choices when developing the organizational structure for the body of the speech: attention and understandability.

- *Attention:* The order of your points and the organizational structure that frames them can help or hurt your how compelling your speech is. For example, if there is a common objection to or misunderstanding about your thesis, you might want to structure your speech to address it in the first point, because the audience may be discounting your (very good) points until the objection has been met. Or suppose you know the audience is extremely uncomfortable with solution proposed in your problem-solution topic. You could structure your speech to spend more time on the problem to better prepare the audience to hear your suggestion for dealing with it.

- *Understandability:* Understandability arises not only from a thoughtfully organized body but also from everything that helps your audience see how the parts fit together: introduction, preview, transitions, internal previews, review, and conclusion. Creating a compelling speaking experience requires you to make sure audience members always know where they are in the speech and understand the relationship of the current point or argument to the whole.

- You *always* have choices about how to organize a body of material, and no matter how natural or easy an option looks, you should always ask, Why this way? Why not another? How does this organization fit my purposes and

Audience members can quickly become confused, inattentive, and distrustful if they feel lost in your speech or don't know where you are going.

audience? Audience members shouldn't walk away scratching their heads or feeling their main questions went unanswered because they were bewildered by your choice of organization. That's where responsibility comes in.

Functions of the Body

- What purposes does the body of your speech fulfill?
- *Development:* It develops the two or three main points identified in the preview: the same points, in the same order. Not only does this make listening easier for the audience, but it also forces you to carefully organize your material, instead of just randomly listing it.
- *Arguments:* The body presents arguments for and addresses arguments against your thesis. You can organize counterarguments within each point or incorporate them into the structure of the body. (Chapter 7 discusses the details about handling counterarguments.)
- *Supporting Materials:* The body develops your arguments and make cases by presenting supporting materials. The bulk of your evidence and examples appear in the body.

The three main elements of the body of your speech are its points, transitions between them, and internal previews.

Points

Your speech should have no more than four or five points, and ideally just two or three. Why? If you would like the audience to understand and remember the basic structure of your information or argument, it's much easier if there are fewer points.

Also, you need to be able to *organize* the information you've researched. If you have 14 points in your speech, you're probably just listing it. (In a few pages, we'll discuss organizational patterns.)

Points should be relatively balanced in terms of length and development, including arguments and supporting materials. An outline, which will be discussed at the end of chapter, is a useful way to check for structural balance.

Transitions

transitions Words, phrases, or sentences that link a speech's sections or points.

Transitions are words, phrases, or sentences that link your speech's arguments, points, or sections together. They not only signal the movement from one element to another, but they also alert listeners to where you are in the speech. Effective transitions between points of a speech can help the audience understand the flow of your argument more clearly.

You are probably already familiar with the transitions used between clauses in a sentence: *and, but, yet, while, moreover, in spite of.* Notice that grammatical conjunctions like these link clauses or sentences in different ways:

- *And* establishes a parallel relationship between clauses ("We need to stay informed, *and* we need to vote").
- *But* establishes a contrast between clauses ("We need to be partisan *but* reasonable").
- *Since* makes one clause a reason for another ("We all should vote, *since* democracy depends on participation").

TABLE 9.1	Transition Words and Phrases by Relationship	
Similarity	**Part-Whole**	**Consequence**
Additionally	A case in point	Because
Also	A particular X is . . .	Consequently
And . . . as well	Another example	Due to
Another	For example	Hence
Equally important	For instance	If . . . then
Moreover	Specifically	Since
Not only . . . but also		So
		Therefore
Similarly		Thus
Contrast	**Whole-Part**	**Series**
Although	Altogether	After
But, yet	In all	First . . . second . . . third
Conversely	In short	Following
However	More generally	Next
In spite of	Nevertheless	Then
On one hand . . . on the other hand		
On the contrary		
While		

Speech transitions work in a similar way. Choose from the groups in Table 9.1, depending on what relationship you want to indicate between arguments or points in the speech.

Transitions are important because they provide the redundancy needed in oral communication. Although you indicated the structure in the preview, listeners need to be reminded all the way through. Even if the audience members were looking at a list of the points in your talk, they might still need transitions, because it might not be obvious when you had moved from one point to another.

Tetra Images/Jupiter Images

Good transitions should be like the passing of a baton between runners in a relay race. When the baton is passed correctly, both runners have their hands on it for just a moment. In the same way, a good transition briefly connects the point before and after for the audience.

Internal Previews

As your speeches get longer and more complex, you may find that to help the audience out, you need to give previews *within and between your points* just as you do for the

FIGURE 9.1
Basic Speech Outline

I. Introduction

    A. **Narration:** A day at the polls

    B. **Thesis:** Low voter participation is a serious problem

    (Preview)

II. Body

    A. **(Major point)** Low turnout makes democracy ineffective.

        1. Elected officials don't have a mandate.

        2. Special interests might prevail.

    B. **(Major point)** Low turnout makes democracy unfair.

        1. Law and officials lack legitimacy.

        2. People don't have an investment in outcomes.

III. Conclusion

    (Review)

    Conclusion: We should not tolerate low participation.

    Peroration: *Your* day at the polls.

whole speech. An eight-minute speech with two major points will certainly be complex enough to need internal previews within the main points to guide listeners through them.

For an example of a speech that is complex enough to need transitions and internal previews, see the speech outline in Figure 9.1.

With transitions and internal previews added in italics, the body of the speech would look like Figure 9.2.

FIGURE 9.2
Speech Body with Transitions
and Internal Previews

I. (Body) The problem of low participation

    A. Low turnout makes democracy ineffective.

    (Internal preview) *Low-turnout elections harm **both** those elected **and** those who vote.*

    1. (Substance of point) *Elected officials* don't have a mandate.

    (Transition) *If the elected officials don't have the mandate, who does? It might be special interests.*

    2. (Substance of point) Special interests might prevail *in policies that affect voters.*

    (Transition) ***Not only** are low-turnout elections ineffective for democracy, **but** they can **also** create an unjust democracy.*

    B. Low turnout makes democracy unfair.

    (Internal preview) *The unfairness of these elections derives from questions about legitimacy and outcomes.*

    1. Law and officials lack *legitimacy.*

    (Transition) *An illegitimate election may not command the obedience of voters, and for good reason.*

    2. People don't have an investment in *outcomes.*

Transitions and internal previews make a complicated speech easy to listen to. When even the outline looks complicated, these elements will make it clear to the audience.

The Conclusion

The **conclusion** is your last chance to pull your arguments and ideas together for the audience, come to a satisfying conclusion, and leave a good final impression. One way you *don't* want to conclude your speech is to suddenly stop speaking and walk away. The audience needs to be told the speech is over, and what it all meant for them. Your conclusion is therefore just as important as your introduction and the body of your speech, and you'll want to think it through in advance.

conclusion The last section of a speech, consisting of the review, the restatement of the thesis, and the peroration.

Functions of the Conclusion

You'll want to draw the speech to a close by restating your major points, like your preview did in the introduction. This is the *review*. Similarly, take this last opportunity to make yourself clear, and restate your thesis. Finally, leave the audience with an appropriate image or emotion as their final impression, which is called the *peroration*.

The conclusion also allows you to finish speaking. Sometimes, if speakers haven't written a conclusion, they trouble stopping. Without a conclusion, the speech doesn't sound finished, even to the speaker's ear, and he or she may just keep going, trying to avoid the awkwardness of just suddenly stopping and saying, "Thank you." Use the following elements to put together a solid conclusion.

Elements of the Conclusion

Three elements can help you structure your conclusion into a satisfying wrap-up.

Review The **review** is a restatement of the major points; it parallels the preview without exactly repeating it. For example,

> **We've now looked the dangers of playground equipment from both falling and crushing.**

review A restatement of a speech's major points in the conclusion.

Restatement of the Thesis The **restatement of the thesis** allows you to reiterate the point of the entire speech. Here, you can show how the main points fit together and tell the audience once more how you want them to think about this material and what you want them to do with it. The conclusion parallels the thesis but states it more fully, because the audience now knows more than they did in the introduction. Here's an example built on thesis statement 2 in "The Introduction" section of this chapter:

> **The available evidence shows that playgrounds are dangerous for kids.**

restatement of the thesis The second element in the speech's conclusion, which elaborates on the thesis statement in the introduction.

Peroration **Peroration** comes from the Latin term for the final summary of your position. It draws together the gist of the speech and gives a sense of finality and completion. Here, you might make an emotional appeal, one last push for your argument, as a final invitation to the audience to engage with your speech and your topic. This word is often used to describe the final summations that attorneys make in a jury trial.

peroration The final summary of a speaker's position in the conclusion.

Writing a good peroration requires some thought. The best way to begin is to look back to the narration. If you return to the beginning, then the listeners will perceive that the circle has been closed and the speech must be over. Here are two examples:

- **Yes, it's inevitable that there will be accidents, and that kids will die in playground accidents. But they don't have to. Accidents are preventable, and they don't have to happen at the playground.**
- **Bobby Brady lost his life to a swing, but we can swing into action to save other kids. Let's fix the playground problem.**

Notice that the second example also incorporates an *antithesis*, a sentence with a reversal of elements (from *life/swing* to *swing/action*), which is often an effective way to end a speech. (Chapter 10 has more about how to write an antithesis.)

The three parts of a speech—introduction, body, and conclusion—form the skeleton that supports all the information and arguments you will want to present. Mastering this level of structure will help make you a confident and effective speaker.

Let's turn now to the basic elements of organization you can choose for the body of your speech and advantages and disadvantages of each one.

Patterns of Organization

Some speeches, such as a eulogy or a commencement address, will follow patterns that we will discuss in Chapter 13. For other speeches there are a variety of organization patterns you can choose to fit your purpose, the subject matter, and the audience.

A speech isn't just a set of boxes into which you put information—it's an attempt to connect with the audience. So patterns of organization are often patterns of argument. Even in an informative speech you are arguing in a sense, because you are trying to relate information to the audience and make a case about the best way to understand it. Making choices about organization is making choices about how best to present your case or your information. Each organizational structure we describe below helps pull your points together and show the relationships between them in a different way.

Your choice of organizational pattern will make a difference not only in the way you present your case to your audience but also in the way your audience thinks about your topic and responds to your conclusion. We'll look at five basic organizational patterns—chronological, spatial, cause-effect, problem-solution, and topical—and their advantages and potential drawbacks.

▇ Chronological

chronological pattern Time-related sequence of points.

The **chronological pattern** orders ideas and arguments in a time-related sequence. There are three possibilities: historical, past-present-future, and step by step.

Historical Development   With a historical pattern, you can explain the chronology of a series of events, such as this:

Topic: The History of Recess in Elementary Education
   I. The one-room schoolhouse
  II. The 20th-century elementary school: Teeter-totters and rocket ships
 III. The 1990s: Revolution in surfaces

Past-Present-Future   Start with what happened or conditions in the past, describe the present, and then say what the future will or should be like. This can be an alternative to a problem-solution organization, especially if you are not trying to get the audience to take a specific action but only get them to agree with the basis for action.

> **Topic: From the 1950s to the 2000s: How Kids Play Outside**
>
> I.   **1950s: Running and biking**
> II. **1990s: Skating and blading**
> III. **2020: Toys of the future**

Step by Step   Explain the various parts of a process in order. For example, if you wanted to criticize the voting system, you might describe the process of voting (how things get on the ballot, how ballots get printed, how voters are registered). This will allow you to place your criticisms of the process in a framework that will be easy for the audience to remember and understand.

The following outline breaks down the way kids move as they grow, from babies' beginnings of locomotion to how young children play outside. Even though the main heads are parts of the process, the speech is basically chronological, because the process changes through time.

> **Topic: Play and Physical Exercise**
>
> I. **Crawling/Toddling**
>   A. **New babies**
>   B. **6–12 months**
>
> II. **Walking**
>   A. **1-year-olds**
>   B. **2-year-olds**
>
> III. **Swinging**
>   A. **Backyard toys**
>   B. **Playground toys**

Advantages   A chronological ordering helps to convey a strong narrative for your speech by connecting events over time. It may add to your ethos as a speaker by demonstrating your grasp of your topic area, whether history or child development. Chronological orderings also tend to be easy to remember, and they give the audience an easy-to-grasp and intuitive framework for your speech.

Disadvantages   Sometimes, chronological orderings can be dull. They might make you seem to be less interested in what can be done today and more interested in things that have gone before. Be careful not to get too mired down in the minute details of history or descriptions of the present day. Instead, remember that the audience wants to do something with the information you give them, and limit the historical facts to ones that help them understand the topic and decide what they think about it, or what to do about it in the future.

Spatial

A **spatial pattern** organizes points by location in space. Because most people easily follow and remember visual information, spatial organizations are extremely effective. The space can be global, local, or personal.

spatial pattern   Organization of points by location.

Geography   You can specify geographic areas that will be the points of your speech. Be sure they are familiar enough that the audience can easily imagine them.

East-Midwest-West
Urban-rural-suburban
City-state-national

Familiar Locations   If you were explaining student involvement on your campus, you might organize your information around the *buildings* that represent opportunities for students to be active. You might talk about the kinds of activities that go on at the student union and other places where people meet. Because everyone in your audience will have a mental picture of these places, your points will be easy to remember.

Student involvement at our university
1. In the residence halls
2. In the student union
3. In town

Physical Parts   If you're talking about computer etiquette, you might organize your speech around the keys on the keyboard: "The keys to good email are the Send key and the Delete key."

From head to toe is also a form of spatial organization. For example, you could structure a speech on the benefits of yoga by listing the mental benefits of controlled breathing and meditation and then move on to improved heart rate, increased flexibility and stamina, better posture, and so on.

Yoga and your health
I. Joints and muscles
II. Lungs
III. Brain

Advantages   Spatial ordering helps your audience remember elements of your speech by connecting your points to locations they might know and experiences they share. It adds to your speech's effectiveness by inviting your audience to mentally picture the points you are making.

Disadvantages   You need to make sure the spatial organization will maintain the audience's interest. Not everyone will be interested in a regional breakdown of a public policy problem, for instance. Avoid spatial ordering if you have to stretch your material too far to match the space you are talking about. Other potential drawbacks are the opinions the audience has of the locations you mention and lack of familiarity with the locations.

Cause and Effect

cause-and-effect pattern Organization of points that describes the origins and then the symptoms of a condition.

The **cause-and-effect pattern** identifies the origins or causes of a condition and then the ways in which it manifests itself. With a cause-effect argument, you can establish why something happens, so that you can talk about changing it. Linking cause and effect is important if, for instance, you're trying to show there are problematic results of an ordinary action, such as e-waste caused by frequent purchases of new smartphones.

Organizing by cause and effect is well suited to speeches aimed at understanding, agreement, or enlightenment rather than overt action. For example, if you're talking about the problem of drug abuse, you could try to establish an argument like this:

> Decreases in government spending on social programs, housing, job training, and support for education [cause] *have resulted* in an increase in drug use and abuse, particularly among lower-income people.

Or you could create an argument outlined like this:

Laws that allow licensed citizens to carry a weapon ("conceal-carry laws") cause an increase in accidental shootings.
I. Carrying a hidden gun
   A. With/without a license
   B. With/without training
II. Increased shootings
   A. Accidental discharges
   B. Mistaken discharges
   C. Discharge during a crime

This argument is an interesting one, in that it's possible to argue a different cause-effect argument ("conceal-carry laws reduce crime"), which isn't quite the opposite argument but is evidence for the opposite conclusion about whether we should have these laws.

Advantages   The cause-and-effect pattern is effective because it helps your audience understand the practices and decisions that have led to the situation you are addressing, so it has some of the advantages of historical organization without the risk of getting lost in the history. If listeners are likely to feel powerless to address the circumstances you are pointing out in your speech, identifying the causes can show them how they can take action. Cause-and-effect speeches also help your audience remember the content of your speech, because when the cause and the effect are linked, they are both easier to recall.

Disadvantages   Sometimes, audiences resist cause-and-effect thinking. They might disagree on the causes or believe the situation is more complex than the picture you are painting. Speakers may also mistakenly fix on elaborate descriptions of a cause,

Former White House press secretary James Brady speaks frequently on the subject of gun violence, despite having been paralyzed by a gunshot during the assassination attempt on President Ronald Reagan in 1981.

losing sight of the larger picture. Also, if the causes of a problem are well entrenched, audience members may feel there is little they can do to change things.

Problem-Solution

problem-solution pattern Organization of points that describes a problem and then suggesting a solution and audience action.

The **problem-solution pattern** allows the speaker to examine the symptoms of the problem, suggest a solution, and then propose what the audience can do to get involved. Speakers use this type of organization to advocate new policy or a specific course of action. The justification for the change must be strong enough to support the action called for. Figure 9.3 is an outline for a speech about the problem of bullying gay kids and possible solutions.

Advantages Once you have identified and framed the problem, you may not have to do much work to convince your audience because our natural response to an identified problem is to call for a solution. Problem-solution speeches are persuasive because if you can get the audience to agree with you about the problem, it is relatively easy to lead them to a solution. This organization is good for motivating action. It also has the virtue of being relatively simple organizationally, so it is easy for you to remember and to sum up for your audience.

Drawbacks The problem-solution speech can seem simplistic, and if the audience disagrees with you about the nature and extent of the problem, they may be hostile to your solution. Conversely, audience members who agree with you about the problem might disagree with you about the solution. Finally, the problem-solution speech can be problematic for the same reason that it is persuasive: It demands a call to action, and sometimes audiences are put off if they feel manipulated or forced into agreeing with you.

Topical

topical pattern Organization that relates points to the topic, such as part to whole, types, or reasons.

The basis of the **topical pattern** of organization is only that the points have a relationship to the topic. It is the most frequently used pattern but also one of the most difficult because its success depends on the range and limitations of the subject, the purpose of the speech, and the characteristics of the audience.

The topical pattern is not necessarily a random list. Here are some types of topical patterns.

Part to Whole The points add up to the argument for the thesis.

Gun control is wrong because it's

unconstitutional + ineffective + dangerous

Types The points give two or three types of examples related to the thesis.

Three types of academic dishonesty plague universities: collaboration, fabrication, and plagiarism.

Reasons Each point is a subargument.

There are two valid reasons for going to war: to protect our country and to protect other countries.

Advantages Topical organization is always appropriate to your topic area. It is derived from the research you did and directly frames and organizes the content you have worked on. It is also good for your ethos as a speaker, because it

FIGURE 9.3
Outline for Problem-Solution Speech

I. Introduction

   A **Narration:** "Boys will be boys." "That's so gay." "Sticks and stones can break my bones, but words will never hurt me." What do all these phrases have in common? All point to attitudes contributing to problem of lesbian, gay, bisexual, transgender, queer (LGBTQ) bullying and violence.

   B **Thesis:** LGBTQ bullying is a widespread problem that affects all of us.

   C **Preview:** We'll discuss today the problems of bullying and some easy solutions we can all do to prevent it.

II. Body

   A **Problem**

      1. LGBTQ bullying is increasing

         a. Lots more incidents

            i. Verbal

            ii. Physical

         b. Incidents happening all over country; also locally

      2. Causes societal problems

         a. Dropouts

         b. Problems at work

         c. Depression

         d. Suicides

   B. **Solution**

      1. Awareness; stand up against injustice

         a. Speak out

         b. Report incidents (many schools have ways to report incidents: UWM's is http://hatebias.uwm.edu)

      2. Be a straight ally

         a. As in the civil rights movement, didn't have to be part of the group in order to participate.

         b. Martin Luther King, Jr.: Injustice against one is an injustice against all.

         c. Stand in solidarity against bullying/violence.

         d. Today I'm coming out as straight ally.

      3. Lobby for change

         a. Congress members to step up anti-bullying campaigns.

         b. Local school boards to implement anti-LGBTQ violence into their anti-bullying campaigns.

showcases your research and thus conveys the sense that you know what you are talking about.

Drawbacks Topical organization asks the most from your audience, because they are not as close to or as invested in the materials as you are, so they have to work harder to engage with and remember an organization scheme that is not immediately or intuitively apparent. For them to remember your content or be motivated to act, you will need to keep things interesting.

Combination

You can combine different organizational patterns within one speech. You can use different patterns to develop your subpoints than you've used in the main outline; they do not need to echo the structure of the main outline. For example, in a problem-solution speech, the first main point might be historical, and the second might be spatial.

Here is an example with two main points that combines cause-effect and problem-solution for the body of the speech. Note how transitions guide the listener through this complex structure.

Cause → effect leading to *problem → solution*

Kids watch lots of TV.
Therefore,
they are not developing their reading skills.
This is a problem because
they will be the underemployed of tomorrow.
To remedy this,
parents should limit viewing time.

This is a common combination structure that allows you urge a particular solution after establishing its cause.

Advantages   A combination of formats puts you in control of what you want to say and how you want to say it. You can draft your speech in the way that is most fitting for your audience and your topic.

Disadvantages   A combination approach can ask too much of the speaker and the audience. You have to manage more elements in your speech, and with each new organizational element, the audience can lose track of the structure of your speech. Combination speeches require more time to set up and deliver, so you either have to give a longer speech or cut details that might be important.

Because they will not immediately recognize the structure of a combination speech, the members of your audience might be a little more skeptical about your content than they otherwise would be. If you choose this approach, be careful not to make the structure too complex: You might ask yourself how you would take notes on this speech if you heard it for the first time and, further, whether you could reproduce

> ## Try It! Choosing an Organizational Pattern for Your Topic
>
> Think about one of your favorite topics, perhaps even from a speech you have already given. Make an outline or quickly reconstruct your original one.
>   Now imagine that speech in at least two other organizational patterns.
>
> - How would you fit the speech into each of the new patterns?
> - How would it change the content and character of the speech to organize it differently?
> - What choices would you have to make in redrafting the speech?
> - With each of the new patterns, is it a better or worse speech?
>
>   Many of your speeches can be organized in different ways. If you always keep in mind the other possibilities, you will be able to recognize what your current organization pattern is built to maximize, and you can focus all your choices on making the best elements of that organizational schema work for you.

In speaking about current events, news anchor Anderson Cooper has to be selective in choosing his points and support from the flood of information in the news every day.

an outline of it from memory. If you do not feel you would be able to do this, the structure of your speech might be too complex. Keep in mind that your goal is not just to present information but to connect with your listeners by making the contents of your speech digestible and persuasive.

Choosing the Order of Points: Primacy vs. Recency

In some organizational patterns, it's obvious which points should come first and last. In a problem-solution speech, the problem needs to come before the solution. In chronological speeches, you need to have the points move forward or backwards in time. In spatial and topical organizations, however, you have a choice; you can put the points in whatever order you like—but which one?

This choice depends on which characteristic is most important for your speech: **primacy**, which means putting your strongest arguments first to show their importance, or **recency**, which puts them last so they will be the most recent in the audiences' memory. The traditional answer favors recency: Your speech should build toward the strongest arguments and the most salient and important facts or ideas.

The only time you wouldn't put your best or most important material last is when you think you may have a problem with an audience assumption requiring

primacy Organization that places strongest arguments first to show their importance.

recency Organization that places strongest argument last so the audience will remember them.

counter-information or a counterargument. For example, if you were advocating for a conceal-carry law, your strongest argument is that people are safer. However, because the main fear people have about concealed weapons is that they may be hurt, your audience might not be listening carefully until you establish, in the first point, your evidence that the average person is safer in a community that has a conceal-carry law.

Arranging Your Supporting Materials

Not only do you have to decide the pattern for your main points, but you also need to figure out where to put the facts, figures, quotations, and the other supporting materials you will be using as evidence for your arguments. Obviously, supporting materials should appear with the claims they are supporting, but here is more specific advice, in the form of five principles, to guide you in figuring out the best places for evidence of various kinds in your speech.

- *Highlight your best quotations, facts, figures, and research information in a prominent place.* Inexperienced speakers sometimes bury their most compelling evidence somewhere in the middle of their speech, the place where audiences often tend to pay less attention. If you have a really good quotation or fact, don't be afraid to highlight it in your introduction or conclusion, as long as you refer to it with the appropriate point in the body of your speech. If you decide you must put it in the body, at least place it early and in one of your main points.
- *Avoid long strings of the same type of evidence.* Audiences tend to tune out long lists of facts, statistics, or quotations. The more of similar types of evidence you put together, the less effect any one of them has.
- *Follow numbers or data-heavy evidence with an explanation that helps the audience interpret them.* Often audiences do not know what to do with numbers or statistics (like social scientific research) or do not immediately understand the implications of your evidence. Providing a simple explanation after numbers or other raw data can assist the audience in drawing appropriate conclusions. If you are pointing out the average college student spends 1.84 hours in front of a computer for gaming purposes,[2] you can put the statistic in perspective by adding, "That means almost 10% of your waking time is spent on gaming."
- *Vary the types of evidence you employ.* A speech with quotations from experts, statistics, personal narratives, and historical facts is more compelling than a speech that cites only one kind of evidence. Put multiple types of evidence into each of the sections of your speech. For instance, you can cite the number of drivers in fatal accidents who were texting, you can quote someone who was injured in such an accident, and you can explain a study on the psychology of attention that shows how distraction actually happens.
- *Don't be afraid to give the opposition a fair hearing.* If you found great numbers, quotations, or other materials that support *counterarguments* against your position, quote them in your speech. Take this opportunity to frame the debate for the audience. This will assure your audience that you are familiar with opposing arguments and are ready to address them head on. Keep in mind that your citation of opposing positions should be brief, fair, and to the point.

For an overview of your main organizational pattern, the order of points, and the integration of supporting materials, outlining, covered in the next section, will help you immeasurably.

Outlining

An outline is a way of organizing knowledge, both for you and for your audience. Your outline is midway between your research and the speech that you will give, and it helps you improve both. An outline creates a picture of your speech's *structure.*

First, it helps objectify the speech. Getting your speech down on paper makes it easier for you to examine it for flaws in its organization, in assumptions you've made about the audience, or in your line of reasoning. Now you can "eyeball" the speech to evaluate its tightness and structure:

Check for tightness

- Is all material related to the purpose of the speech?
- Is all necessary supporting material included?
- Is all unnecessary material expunged?

Check the structure

- *Balance:* Are all main points roughly the same size?
- *Completeness:* Is anything missing?
- *Logic:* Is the argument apparent and plausible?

Second, an outline can serve as a memory aid through visualization. If you can see the structure of the speech, like a picture, it's easier to remember it.

Third, an outline is easier to revise and rearrange than a fully written-out manuscript of the speech.

Finally, because for most speeches, you'll be speaking from notes rather than a full manuscript, an outline, which contains the "bones" of a speech, gives you a perfect starting place for putting your notes together.

Outline Structure

When you begin writing and revising your speech, your outline *is* your speech; as you revise the outline, you are revising the speech. What does a good outline look like? First, it needs to *look* like an outline: It should be as short as you can make it and still include all your points and evidence. (Your instructor may have specific requirements for outlines, especially whether they are full-sentence or keyword outlines.) The structure of a speech needs to be obvious at a glance. The *shape* of the outline lets you see the shape of the speech—the forest and not just the trees.

The outline of the body is the most important part. You don't need as much structural detail for the introduction and conclusion, though you may want to fill these in as you get closer to the end.

Outlines have two kinds of points. **Coordinate points** are points at the same hierarchical level. For instance, these two are coordinate points:

> **coordinate points** Points at the same level in an outline.

I. Good students
II. Weak students

Subordinate points are one level down from main points; you will always have at least two subordinate points below any one of your main points. For example, here are the two coordinate points again, this time with two subordinate points each:

> **subordinate points** Points supporting a main point

I. Good students
    A. Those who study
    B. Those who seek the help they need

    II. Poor students
     C. Those who hope for the best
     D. Those who can't get their acts together

Notice that every hierarchical level in the outline is indicated in *two* ways: with a different *coordinate symbol* (the type of letter or number we use for each level) and with a different *indent* (each level is indented more than the level above).

■ Preparation and Delivery Outlines

Because you will usually be speaking extemporaneously (see Chapter 11), your outline substitutes, during the speech preparation process, for a full manuscript. A first version of your outline serves as your "blackboard" for developing and refining ideas; a final version gets turned in; and another version goes on your cards.

During the process of preparation, you can use outlines in several different ways. First, you'll need a *working, or research, outline.* This is basically a best guess of what your speech is going to look like. As you do more reading and find out more about your topic—and think through your audience's assumptions and expectations—this outline will change frequently, and that's good. Think of this process as a loop: Your research strategy depends on the outline, but once you've done your research, your outline will change. That new outline generates new research questions, and so on, until you feel you've got it right.

For an extemporaneous speech, "writing" is really just a metaphor, because it's typically counterproductive to actually write out a manuscript. If you write out the sentences, you may struggle to recall them when you're speaking from an outline or some note cards. It's best to write only short phrases that will remind you of what you want to say. So until you get to the finishing touches of devising particular stylistic elements, "writing" means putting ideas and arguments into a form you can look at and evaluate, which usually means on paper or in a computer file you can print.

In addition, for the extemporaneous speeches you'll usually be giving, you'll be speaking from an outline, so you need to be able to put together an outline that meet your needs for the delivery of your speech. You should consider several factors:

- Is the print large enough for you to read?
- Have you used different fonts, colors, or a highlighter to distinguish different sections of the outline, to help you find your place when you look down?

Some speakers help the audience by showing portions of their outlines as slides or other visuals, which is especially effective in long speeches.

Dennis MacDonald/Alamy

- Is there enough white space on the page or the cards to make the outline easy to follow?
- Have you kept your outline minimal, except for the few places where you have a quotation or a line to read word for word?

Summary

Organization is a critical element in the success of your speech. The choices that you make in arranging your materials have real consequences for the persuasive value of your speech, the listeners' ability to remember it, and their motivation to implement the changes in practice, worldview, or opinion that you would like them to make. Effective organization requires you to understand the functions and elements of the three mains parts of a speech: the introduction, the body, and the conclusion. You'll have to master the various patterns of organization for the body, and add transitions, internal previews, and supporting material to them. Finally, you'll also need to become a proficient outliner, creating representations of your speech that help you perfect and deliver it.

Access an interactive eBook, chapter-specific interactive learning tools, including flashcards, quizzes, videos and more in your Speech Communication CourseMate for *Public Speaking*, accessed through CengageBrain.com.

QUESTIONS FOR REVIEW

1. What are the basic parts of a speech? What role does each of them play in helping your audience to connect with your material?
2. What is a transition? What makes a transition effective? Why are good transitions important for a speech?
3. Compare and contrast the patterns of organization for the body of a speech.
4. What are some ways you can order the main points in a speech, especially in topical organization? What are the advantages and disadvantages of different orderings?
5. What role does outlining play in composing a good speech? What are the best techniques to use?

QUESTIONS FOR DISCUSSION

1. Think of a speech you have heard that seemed to lack a logical order or structure. How did you respond to it? What difference does a good organizational pattern make in an audience's ability to engage a speech?
2. How might the ineffective organization of a speech affect the speaker's ethos, the credibility of his or her arguments, or the persuasiveness of the speech? Why?
3. What organizational pattern do you prefer for speeches? Why?
4. Go to an Internet video site and take a look at either a presidential speech from the last 20 years or a TED Talk (www.ted.com/talks). Try to take notes and identify the organizational pattern. Is it similar to one we've outlined in this chapter? How effective is it?

LEARNING GOALS

- Discuss the importance of language that is concrete, lively, and respectful
- Distinguish figures and tropes
- Explain the figures of repetition and contrast, and construct your own
- Explain the tropes of comparison, substation, exaggeration, and voice, and construct your own
- Describe principles for matching verbal style to the topic and the occasion

CHAPTER OUTLINE

Verbal Style

Edward was just the kind of person you would want to do your taxes. He was smart, detail oriented, and organized. But as a speaker, he had one glaring problem: He tended to put his audience to sleep. Even though he was never less than immaculately prepared, his topics were interesting to him, and his speeches were well argued, he always found himself speaking to the glazed, uninterested stares of his classmates. His presentations seemed to be a bit too abstract or, worse yet, simply boring for his listeners. What could he do, Edward wondered, to make his speeches easier to digest and more appealing to listen to?

Overview

Many speakers worry about the way they say words, which is important (in fact, delivery is the subject of the next chapter). But the words you choose to say are just as, or more, important. In ordinary life, we don't think about our words too much, we just talk. Yet when we want our words to have impact, we should choose them carefully. In addition, we have to take responsibility for our words, and words can sometimes be hurtful or offensive. In a public speaking situation we when expect people to remember our words and take them seriously, we have to spend more time thinking about them and choosing them.

Introduction: What Is Style, and Why Does It Matter?

style Word choices made to achieve the goals of a speech.

Now that you have figured out what you want to say and how you want to organize and support it, the next challenge is to figure out exactly how to express the ideas you want to convey—in other words, the considerations of **style**, or the wording choices you will make to achieve the goals of your speech.

In this chapter we'll give you a set of formal techniques for making word choices that you can integrate into your speeches. We cannot tell you how to phrase *everything* in your speech, since so much about phrasing is unique to you as a speaker and to the audience you are addressing, but we can offer a number of tried-and-true stylistic forms that have been used to effectively in great speeches. In the next chapter, we'll complete our discussion of delivery by discussing the nonverbal parts of speaking; of course, there is sense in which that is a kind of "style," but for this chapter (and this book) "style" means the choice of words and use of language.

Style exploits one of the most powerful features of language, the fact that there are many different ways of saying the same thing. For instance, you could say, "It's hot outside, and I am tired." Or you might say, "It's an oven outside. I'm beat." Or perhaps you have a penchant for poetical expression: "Oh, this insufferable heat—it has left me feeling fatigued." If you try, you could probably come up with dozens of different ways of saying the same thing.

Expressing your thoughts in words is an art. You have choices about how you say what you want to say, and they are important, not least because, as in the example in the previous paragraph, different choices can convey different impressions about your topic. Striking just the right style for your topic and the occasion helps you achieve your speaking goals. Perhaps you want to evoke a straightforward informational tone; perhaps you want to convey some particularly significant material in a playful and even artful way. Whatever you want to achieve, the style you choose does matter.[1]

Characteristics of Effective Style

As a speaker, you will use language as your primary tool. No matter how wonderful a speaker's delivery may be, if she begins her speech "La oss snakke i dag om problemet med nettkriminalitet," you will not have any idea that this is a speech about cybercrime, unless you speak Norwegian. No amount of work on topic choice, organizational patterns, or delivery can make up that gap—language matters. Language matters to being understood, to being interesting, to convincing the audience you are worth listening to.

The study of verbal style, how to choose and use the right words, is key to communicating effectively. The second part of the chapter will discuss how you can choose words to achieve your communication goals, but, first, in this section we cover the basics. To be an effective speaker, you need to use language that is concrete and lively, that reduces abstraction and makes ideas come alive for listeners, and that is respectful and doesn't unintentionally exclude some audience members.

If you're not clear and interesting, you've lost the audience, no matter what else you do right. If you are perceived as disrespectful, you've lost the audience. We'll talk about each of these characteristics in turn.

Concrete and Lively Language

Holding the interest of the audience and making yourself understood depends to a large extent on making abstract ideas and relationships concrete, so the audience can more clearly imagine what you're talking about. When people complain that a speech was dry, they usually mean the material was presented in a way that was abstract and theoretical rather than concrete and vivid. When concepts, numbers, ideas, and arguments are couched in language that creates a picture in the audience's mind, they become almost as visual as a movie, and the speech in turn is more interesting.

Painting images with words—detailed, three-dimensional, persuasively real images—is a skill you can learn. For instance, compare these two sentences. Which one creates a picture in your mind?

1. He cut it up.
2. Swiftly and silently, Jim hacked the watermelon into small pieces.

Clearly, sentence 2 provides much more detail than sentence 1 does. The mental images that audience members construct from sentence 2 would be more similar than their mental images from sentence 1.

The language of public speaking is not the same as the language of everyday chitchat. Using language that departs somewhat from everyday speech, while remaining appropriate to your audience, makes the occasion special and can inspire listeners to pay closer attention.

Language that is interesting and lively is also easier to remember. Because self-persuasion is the best persuasion, the audience needs to remember what you've said so they can mull it over later. Dry and abstract language will not do help them do this. You must turn people's *ears* into *eyes*, so they "see" what they are hearing.

Try It! *Making Language Lively*

How could you make each of the following sentences more concrete and vivid?

- We should do something about immigration.
- U.S. consumers have a responsibility to reduce their environmental impact.
- Better nutrition is in everyone's best interest.

Respectful Language

Because public speaking is designed with an audience—and a public—in mind, you need to speak in way that includes as many people as possible. You shouldn't, deliberately or accidently, make any audience members feel excluded by using language they find disrespectful. Both off-color language and sexist and racist language can create disrespect and exclusion.

Off-Color Language Is it permissible to use foul language? Of course you can say whatever you like. But is it smart to do so? In the vast majority of cases, you should avoid it.

The usual argument offered for using foul language is that it helps speakers convey the depth of emotion they feel about a topic or import a bit of pathos they would not otherwise be able to convey. It is true that using, say, a four-letter word to describe a bad situation conveys a very different meaning than saying it is "disappointing." But swearing almost always a bad choice, for three reasons.

First, you cannot know in advance how much rude epithets might undermine your credibility with your audience or get in the way of their hearing your argument. In general, the more you deviate from the speaking norms your specific audience expects, the more likely you are to create unintended resistance.

Second, when we speak in public, we model how we think people *ought* to speak in public. What if audience members went away from your speech persuaded that foul language was the best way to convey the emotional frame of your topic? If they did, they might not all use the same careful judgments you did in coming to your word choices, and the quality of public discourse would decline—thanks to you.

Third, many people see the use of foul language as a sign of disrespect toward the audience. As a result, these choices might make it difficult for you to build the kind of ethical relationship with your audience that you would like to have.

Sexist and Racist Language Our language carries assumptions and implications with it. We have to be sensitive to whether the assumptions of the words we use are respectful to everyone in our audience. For example, if you talk about "manpower" in your speech, that seems to imply that women aren't able to work or be productive, whereas talking about the "labor force" carries no such implication. Why not skip the implication? You don't believe it anyway. The same reasoning applies to outdated terms *fireman* and *policeman*, for which you should substitute *firefighter* and *police officer*. Just as you wouldn't use *boys* to refer to a group a college men, you shouldn't

Comedians like Chris Rock often rely on four-letter words for humor, but what works late at night in a comedy club isn't appropriate in public speaking situations.

Bill Waugh/AP Photos

refer to female adults as *girls*. In some parts of the United States, *guys* is used in a gender-neutral way, so "you guys" can refer to both men and women, but you probably want to avoid it in a speech, just to avoid any misunderstanding.

Racist language includes both disrespectful terms for races or ethnicities to common expressions that use the name of an ethnic or racial group in a derogatory way.

Generalizations about a group of people are also unacceptable. When a speaker says, "All _____ people are talented in music," the speaker may mean it to be a compliment, but this statement stereotypes people and denies their individuality.

Language that essentializes people is also disrespectful. When you talk about "the deaf" or "the blind" or "AIDS victims," you have taken one characteristic and made it the essence of a group of people. Perhaps that characteristic is relevant to your speech, but people are much more than their disabilities or illnesses and most prefer to be acknowledged as "people who are visually impaired" rather than just "the blind."

However you use the techniques of verbal style discussed below to make your speech exciting and memorable, begin by striving to use language that is concrete, lively, and respectful to your audience.

Classifying Verbal Style: Figures and Tropes

Rhetoricians and linguists have proposed many theories of verbal style and many different systems for categorizing its elements. In this chapter, however, we'll cover just two special forms of speech that are especially useful for public speaking: **figures**, or changes in the structure of a phrase or sentence that lend an ear-catching quality, and **tropes**, or changes in the way words and concepts are used that give them a new meaning.

figure Ear-catching change in the structure of a phrase or sentence.

You probably already use some figures and tropes in your everyday speech. For instance, only animals have legs and feet, but we routinely refer to "the foot of a mountain" and "the leg of a chair." These common metaphors are a kind of linguistic trope. Some turns of speech, like these familiar images, pass by in conversation without drawing attention to their form, whereas others are uncommon and artful uses of language. It is this second group that is important to public speakers.

trope A figure of speech that gives a new meaning for a word or concept, such as a metaphor or a simile.

Figures

Your goal in choosing figures for your speech is to use them deliberately in order to highlight important content. If you use a figure too frequently, it begins to draw attention to itself rather than to your content, and then it becomes just a distraction for your listeners. Two useful types of figures are those of repetition and of contrast.

Figures of Repetition

From our earliest days as conversationalists, we learn to avoid structured repetition of words or phrases. If we tell a friend we're going shopping, for instance, we don't say, "I'm going to buy eggs. I'm going to buy milk. I'm going to buy ketchup." We say, "I'm going to buy eggs, milk, and ketchup." Yet in public speaking, such repetition, even though it seems redundant, can be used to create structure, lend emphasis, and make words more memorable. A Roman rhetoric textbook, *Rhetorica ad Herennium,* noted that speakers who repeat words and phrases do so not because they are at a loss for words; instead, they are creating something powerful and beautiful: "For there inheres in the repetition an elegance which the ear can distinguish more easily than words can explain."[2]

The following example repeats the phrase "It takes no . . .," giving both emphasis and structure to the passage:

> It takes no compromising to give people their rights. It takes no money to respect the individual. It takes no survey to remove repressions.
> —Harvey Milk, campaign speech for San Francisco Board of Supervisors, 1973. The works of Harvey Milk are owned by L. Stuart Milk and are used for the benefit of the Harvey Milk Foundation.

FAQ *Can I use too much repetition?*

Some of the most memorable speeches in U.S. history rely on repetition. For example, Martin Luther King's "I Have a Dream" speech uses the word *dream* at least 8 times. However, one of the keys to effective repetition is to cluster the repetitions in only one part of the speech. Such a cluster, which may draw on a theme from earlier in the speech, gives the word or phrase more impact than if it were repeated throughout the whole speech.

You can repeat words, phrases, or sounds effectively, and you can repeat at the beginning, middle, or end of sentences. If you repeat initial sounds, it is called *alliteration* ("Peter Piper picked a peck of pickled peppers"). If you repeat final sounds, it is called *rhyme* ("Hickory, dickory dock, the mouse ran up the clock"). Both these repetitions of sounds are more common in poetry and song than in public speaking, which more often uses repeated words and phrases. Let's look at a couple figures of repetition.

Grammatical Repetition   Almost everyone knows the final words of President Lincoln's Gettysburg Address:

> . . . this government *of the people, by the people, for the people,* shall not perish from the earth.

grammatical repetition The use of two or more phrases with the same grammatical structure.

Because the phrases in italics have the same grammatical structure (in this case, preposition + definite article + noun), we call this **grammatical repetition**.

Another famous example of grammatical repetition is the message Caesar sent to the Roman Senate in 47 BC to announce the results of a battle he fought in Turkey:

> Veni, vidi, vici. ("I came, I saw, I conquered.")

Here Caesar gave us three complete sentences with the structure of *I* + verb. It is not only an economical expression but a memorable one (in the original Latin, it is also an alliteration).

Here is another example, this time from Martin Luther King, Jr.:

> You have been the veterans of creative suffering. Continue to work with the faith that unearned suffering is redemptive. Go back to Mississippi, go back to Alabama, go back to South Carolina, go back to Georgia, go back to Louisiana, go back to the slums and ghettos of our northern cities, knowing that somehow this situation can and will be changed.

Go back to + (place) is repeated six times, creating speed and force to King's call for civil rights workers to take action, and the emotion is impossible to ignore if you listen to a recording of the "I Have a Dream" speech. This type of repetition is very powerful and allows you to focus on either the phrase that is repeated or the complement to that phrase.

progression Grammatical repetition that creates a sense of movement.

Progression   **Progression** uses repetition to create a sense of movement. The effect of progression should be that of moving, rung by rung, up a ladder, drawing the listener forward to a conclusion. The following progression become popular during the 2008 U.S. presidential election:[3]

Martin Luther King Jr.'s famous address to the March on Washington on August 28, 1963, is known as the "I Have a Dream" speech, because of the repeated phrase at the core of the speech. In fact, King uses repetition often throughout the speech.

Rosa sat so that Martin could walk,
Martin walked so that Barack could run,
Barack ran so that our children could fly.

Generally, progression leaves the most important item until the end and builds to the word or point you want the audience to remember.

All this will not be finished in the first 100 days. Nor will it be finished in the first 1,000 days, nor in the life of this administration, nor perhaps in our lifetime on this planet.
—John F. Kennedy, inaugural address, January 20, 1961

Some possible progressions include the following:

Minutes → hours → days
Great → greater → greatest
Local → state → Federal
Low → middle → high
Bad → worse → worst

You can also use progression to structure the points of your speech, so the preview will itself be a progression. For example, if your thesis were "Taxation is unjust," then structuring your argument as a progression might yield this argument:

If taxation is unjust for the federal government, then it is unjust for a state, and if unjust for a state, then it is unjust for our town.

Like repetition, progression uses ordinary words and their normal meanings, but it arranges them to create a striking and memorable effect. You can use these figures to create emphasis for points you are trying to make.

Figures of Contrast

Think about the difference between these two sentences:

> **It's often hard for people to change their cultural assumptions, even when they make major geographical and sociological moves.**

> **You can take the boy out of the country, but you can't take the country out of the boy.**

They have much the same meaning; the difference is in the choice and arrangement of the words. The second version makes the contrast clear and memorable. There are several different ways to use contrast. Let's look at antithesis and a couple of its variations.

antithesis The use of two contrasting or opposing words or meanings.

Antithesis Antithesis means "putting opposites together" by creating a sentence with two contrasting or opposing parts. Here's a famous example:

> One small step for a man; one giant leap for mankind.
> —Neil Armstrong, as he set foot on the moon, July 21, 1969/James Dickey

By putting the contrast of ideas into the structure of the sentence, antithesis makes the point in more than one dimension.

Consider this example from Richard Nixon's eulogy for Senator Everett Dirksen in 1969; it is part of Nixon's argument that Dirksen was an outstanding politician:

> A politician knows how to make the process of democracy work and loves the intricate workings of the democratic system. A politician knows not only how to count votes but how to make his vote _____.

Because you can easily guess what the last word of this passage must have been, you know that you, like the audience, were following the structure of the sentences, and listening/reading closely.

Consider the final sentence of this passage from a speech by Carrie Chapman Catt, a leading advocate of women's suffrage, to Congress in 1917 on why women should have the vote:

> If parties prefer to postpone action longer and thus do battle with this idea, they challenge the inevitable. The idea will not perish; the party which opposes it may.

The antithesis fills out the meaning of *inevitable* from the previous sentence in a clear and compelling way.

You might think that only someone with poetic abilities could write this way. Not at all. Anyone can come up with effective antitheses in a few minutes. When you compose an antithesis, don't try to write it from beginning to end. Instead, start by thinking about a couple of ideas that are crucial to the argument or point you're trying to make. Then, try this: Draw a line, and put an arrow in the middle to serve as the fulcrum of your scale, as in Figure 10.1a.

If your ideas were about trust and money, think about their opposites: trust/betrayal and wealth/poverty. Put the opposing words on either side of the fulcrum (Figure 10.1b). Then play around with the words to shape them into phrases; in Figure 10.1c, it seemed that reversing the order of the concepts worked better. In a speech whose theme is "money can't buy happiness," this might be an effective way of making the point.

Try to keep about the same number of words and syllables on each side of the fulcrum, as Charles Dickens did in a famous antithesis that begins *A Tale of Two Cities* (see Figure 10.2).

The basic way to create the opposition in an antithesis is to use words with opposite meanings, like *best* and *worst*. The plain double antithesis and the double-reverse antithesis are slightly more complex ways to structure an antithesis.

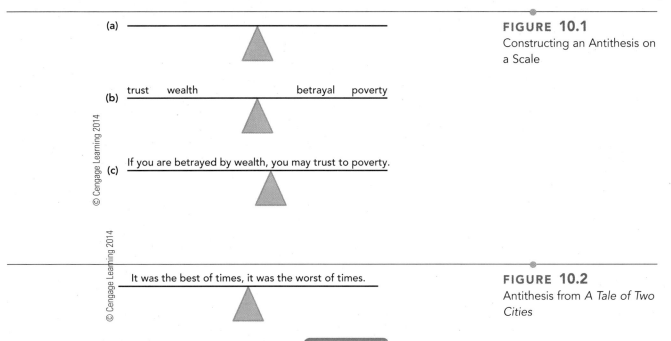

FIGURE 10.1
Constructing an Antithesis on a Scale

FIGURE 10.2
Antithesis from *A Tale of Two Cities*

Plain Double Antithesis In **plain double antithesis**, the contrast is double, between two or more pairs of terms, such as between *all* and *none*, between *virtues* and *vices*, and between *dislike* and *admire* in this example:

> He has all the virtues I dislike and none of the vices I admire.
> —Winston Churchill, describing a political opponent

Here are a couple of other examples:

> [We have] made the most difference in people's lives when we've led not by polls, but by principle; not by calculation, but by conviction.
> —Barack Obama, op-ed, *Des Moines Register*, November 27, 2007

> Extremism in defense of liberty is no vice, moderation in the pursuit of justice is no virtue.
> —Barry Goldwater, accepting the Republican Party's nomination for president, 1964

The double-antithesis has all the virtues of the simple antithesis, but it allows you to put more ideas in play.

Double-Reverse Antithesis A **double-reverse antithesis** achieves opposition by reversing the order of key words, which creates the opposite meaning, an AB-BA structure.

> Let us never negotiate out of fear, but let us never fear to negotiate.
> —John F. Kennedy, inaugural address, January 20, 1961

> A pessimist sees the difficulty in every opportunity; an optimist sees the opportunity in every difficulty.
> —Winston Churchill

> When the going gets tough, the tough get going.

FAQ *How can I use contrast effectively?*

Figures of contrast work best if you stick to a few rules:

- Keep the contrasting figures compact, that is, relatively close together and preferably in the same phrase.
- Use contrast sparingly—save it for important points. You wouldn't, for example, use a contrasting construction in a transition ("Now, the first point, as opposed to the second").
- Look for real opposites—contrast works best when it is stark. Don't try to force an opposition between things that are not actually opposites.

plain double antithesis Two pairs of contrasting words.

double reverse antithesis Key words repeated in reverse order, in AB-BA structure.

John F. Kennedy's inaugural address is filled with powerful antitheses.

The double-reverse antithesis is a little more difficult to compose that these other types, but they are really memorable, which is why they get used for commercial jingles.

Aristotle claimed that "popularity of style is mainly due to antithesis," and he was certainly right that antitheses are impressive and memorable. They are especially useful in your peroration (see Chapter 9), where they can help you end your speech clearly and definitely. Because you can usually predict the end of an antithesis after hearing the first half, you are anticipating the end, and it's clear the speaker means to be absolutely done.

Try It! *Recognizing Figures of Repetition and Contrast*

Almost everyone knows Abraham Lincoln's Gettysburg Address, delivered on a battlefield in Pennsylvania after a Civil War battle in which many thousands of soldiers died. Most people find the speech very powerful, but they're not sure why. The reason might be Lincoln's skill with figures of speech. Find out for yourself. Here is the text of Lincoln's speech; see how many figures of repetition and contrast you can find in it.

Fourscore and seven years ago our fathers brought forth on this continent a new nation, conceived in liberty and dedicated to the proposition that all men are created equal.

Now we are engaged in a great civil war, testing whether that nation or any nation so conceived and so dedicated can long endure. We are met on a great battlefield of that war. We have come to dedicate a portion of that field as a final resting-place for those who here gave their lives that that nation might live. It is altogether fitting and proper that we should do this.

But, in a larger sense, we cannot dedicate, we cannot consecrate, we cannot hallow this ground. The brave men, living and dead who struggled here have consecrated it far above our poor power to add or detract. The world will little note nor long remember what we say here, but it can never forget what they did here. It is for us the living rather to be dedicated here to the unfinished work which they who fought here have thus far so nobly advanced. It is rather for us to be here dedicated to the great task remaining before us—that from these honored dead we take increased devotion to that cause for which they gave the last full measure of devotion—that we here highly resolve that these dead shall not have died in vain, that this nation under God shall have a new birth of freedom, and that government of the people, by the people, for the people shall not perish from the earth.

How hard was it to find these figures? Do you feel they helped make the speech powerful and memorable? Which ones would you personally change?

Tropes

Tropes are words or phrases that we use to convey a message other than their usual, literal meaning. As we pointed out earlier, you may not realize it, but you use tropes in your daily speech. The challenge for your public speaking is to choose tropes that serve your purpose and are understandable to the audience.

Tropes are surprisingly easy to create and use, and they are very effective with audiences. Tropes can serve several purposes in your speech, including comparison, substitution, and exaggeration (see Table 10.1). We'll begin with the comparative tropes, metaphor and simile, and then move to the tropes of substitution (metonymy), exaggeration, and voice.

FAQ *Why is it called a "trope"?*

Trope comes from the Greek word *tropos*, which means "turn." A trope is a turn of meaning that is somehow meaningful to the audience. If you "turn" a phrase to say something in an indirect but artful way, you have used a trope.

▮ Tropes of Comparison: Metaphor and Simile

Every time you get up to speak, you are telling the audience something they don't already know. How can you help them understand it? You'll have to start with things they do know and lead them into the new information. Tropes of comparison are a great way to accomplish this, because they allow you to compare the unfamiliar to the familiar.

TABLE 10.1 Types of Tropes and Their Functions	
Comparison	*Exaggeration*
Metaphor	Understatement
Simile	Overstatement
Substitution	*Voice*
Metonymy	Personification

Metaphor A **metaphor** is an assertion that is not literally true but is still understandable. In essence, it is a comparison that does not use the word *like* or *as*, and it is a particularly important trope. When you say of a favorite football player, "Oh, he's a monster," you don't mean it literally (he's a human being, not a monster); you mean it metaphorically (he's a really large, intense, tough player). Metaphors shift or transport meaning from one context to another. Although what you've said isn't literally true, it invites the listener to transport or transfer meaning from *monster* to the football player.

Metaphors can make unfamiliar things familiar. For instance, you can say,

> **College basketball teams are the minor leagues of professional basketball.**

This is not literally true, because the professional teams don't fund or control the college teams, but the metaphor points out the structural relationship between student athletes and professionals.

Metaphors can also simplify complicated things. The statement "Your body is a machine, so it needs regular maintenance in the form of checkups" lets your audience apply their knowledge about cars to health issues. Metaphors are so common you may not realize how often you use them. Knowing how to create or find good ones for a particular speech is the challenge.

Here are some sample metaphors, continuing the example of the speech about blood donation from Chapter 1:

> **Turn on the light for someone without hope—give blood.**
> **Donating blood opens the door to hope.**
> **Blood is life.**
> **Giving your blood is giving yourself.**
> **That little tube is a lifeline to others.**

Notice that metaphors can clarify what you're doing when you give blood ("blood is life"), or they can express the benefits of giving blood ("opens the door to hope"). Which you would choose depends on the point you are trying to make in your speech.

Sometimes entire speeches can even be structured around a metaphor: If the audience understands and remembers the metaphor, then they will understand and remember the entire speech. For example, suppose you are talking about educational reform, particularly for underachieving students, and your points are the needs to improve home life, classroom facilities, and after-school activities. You might choose the metaphor of an ailing tree. What could we do to improve it? First, we'd look at the roots, the part we can't see (home life), and be sure the soil was right and properly balanced (appropriate opportunities at home). Then we'd attend to the trunk of the tree (the classroom) and make sure it was whole and pest-free (good facilities and no distracting students). Finally, we'd look at the leaves (after-school programs) and make sure they were healthy and able to nurture the rest of the tree (extracurricular opportunities that enhance the rest of the educational process).

Although it's not always possible find an appropriate controlling metaphor for an entire speech, it's often worth the effort. Just make sure that all the parts fit (if the metaphor falls apart or contradicts itself at some point, it's like a flat note for a singer and can spoil the audience's impression of your speech). Also make sure the metaphor isn't so strange or obscure that you'll confuse the audience.

Simile A **simile** is an explicit comparison between two things that uses the word *like* or *as* to connect them. Less subtle and complex than metaphors, similes are most useful when you are trying to help the audience to immediately see the clear relationship between something they know about—for instance, "beating your head against the wall"—and a new or unexplored idea or experience—"taking a math class too advanced for you." The simile would be "Taking a math class too advanced for you is like beating your head against the wall." Clearly, taking this class is going to prove painful and frustrating.

Similes are related to metaphors, yet they can be more precise, because you can fill out the similarity as specifically as you need to, helping you make your point clearly. Compare these examples of similes about blood donation to the examples of metaphors about blood donation in the previous section:

Giving blood is like making a deposit in a bank.
Giving blood is as important as giving time or money.

Similes are also useful when the object of comparison has parts you can use to explain aspects of the main idea. Here is a simile for a speech about changing our diets:

Your body is like a machine: You take fuel in, you produce heat and do work, and you produce waste products. We need to look at the kinds of "fuels" we use and how efficient they are for our "machines."

Similes can be useful because they are familiar, but if they are trite or clichéd, they may not make a strong impression on the audience. Like a stone worn smooth through long handling, they no longer create much mental friction. If you've heard it a million times, you often just don't hear it. Here are some classic similes that you should probably avoid in favor of something fresh:

brave as a lion	sick as a dog
blind as a bat	silent as the grave
busy as a bee	gentle as a lamb
cold as ice	good as gold
dry as a bone	hard as nails
pretty as a picture	strong as an ox
quiet as a mouse	sweet as honey

Try It! Using the blood donation example as a model, design a metaphor that is appropriate for the topic of your next speech.
- Now, take that metaphor and reframe it as a simile.
- Which of the two is more effective for your purposes?
- Which is more powerful?
- Why?

The Trope of Substitution: Metonymy

Metonymy (pronounced *meh-TAHN-ah-mee*) is an expression that substitutes a part for the whole, or a property of something for the thing itself. An example is a television executive saying, "We need to double the eyeballs in this timeslot." Obviously, the programmer is talking about viewers, not actual eyeballs, but substituting the relevant part of the viewers' anatomy creates metonymy.

Metonymy is not only a kind of shorthand, but it also directs listeners' attention in a particular way (the eyes are the important part, because television executives want people watching TV). The metonymy in which sailors are called "hands" ("All hands on deck!") is rooted in the days when ships were controlled by ropes, which the sailors worked with their hands. Journalists sometimes refer to infantry soldiers as "boots on the ground," because traditionally the infantry advanced on foot.

metonymy An expression that substitutes a part or a property for the whole.

As a member of the 2012 American Red Cross Celebrity Cabinet, Jackie Chan communicates the importance of blood donation.

Associated Press

How could metonymy help a speech on blood donation? Suppose your argument is that giving blood is a small inconvenience that has a huge positive impact. To sum up that argument in a memorable way, you could use metonymy:

That tiny pain can save a life.
Every bare arm saves a life.
Blood donation is community in a pint-sized bag.

In each of these, some feature of the experience of blood donation stands in for the larger meaning of giving blood.

Tropes of Exaggeration: Overstatement and Understatement

Another way to get your point across is by using overstatement and understatement.

hyperbole Extreme overstatement that is obviously untrue.

Hyperbole is an overstatement, a claim so over the top is it obviously not true:

I have a million things to do today.

Litotes (pronounced *li-TOE-tees*) is an understatement, expressing something in a way that is obviously out of proportion with the facts.

litotes An exaggerated understatement that is obviously untrue.

The United States has just a small army.

Both hyperbole and litotes are means of ironic exaggeration that put a particular perspective on an event. Litotes usually includes a kind of reversal, in which the understatement serves to emphasize the magnitude of the truth, without making the speaker seem overly passionate or concerned; the audience gets to draw the conclusion.

Here are examples of litotes and hyperbole about blood donation:

Giving blood takes just a second.
A drop of blood from you can do an ocean of good for someone else.

These tropes put the experience of blood donation in perspective, highlighting how a small sacrifice can yield an important result.

◼ The Trope of Voice: Personification

Personification is the process of giving human qualities to abstract or inanimate objects, allowing them to speak, feel, or think.

> **The cost of this school building speaks volumes about its importance to the community.**

Personification is an effective way to position an argument or point of view by shifting from the actual speaker to an imaginary one. For example, if a speaker on a Civil War topic wants to avoid seeming partisan, she might attribute certain arguments to the locations themselves.

> **The battlefields speak to us, eloquently. They ask us to consider the meaning of disagreement, and sacrifice, in a democracy.**

If you were going to make an argument about the impact of blood donation, you could give agency to the blood or illustrate that without donations, people won't get the surgeries they need:

> **Your blood might go out and save a life.**
> **All these empty hospital beds whisper, "Where were the blood donors?"**

Thanks to modern film animation techniques, talking objects are very familiar, and speakers should make creative use of them.

personification Human qualities ascribed to an abstract or inanimate object.

Matching the Style to the Topic and the Occasion

We've given you many new choices about language in this chapter. Making these choices means considering how to coordinate them with your goal, with the occasion, and with the topic. For example, if your speech is about an everyday topic, your style should be simple, reserving metaphors and examples for difficult concepts. You would not, for example, talk about the "tyranny" of cilantro-haters or the "bloody massacre" of class registration. On the other hand, if you are talking about a subject with a significant emotional charge, you might use a more elaborate style. No one should give a speech about genocide in Sudan and say that it was "kind of a bummer."

Similarly, your style should fit the occasion and the audience. If you are giving a toast in front of a crowd of college friends at a wedding, you will need to strike a balance between the customary ribbing, old stories, and something sweet (often metaphorical) about love. If you are giving a pitch at a business meeting, you wouldn't use too much figurative language, and only if it relates to your goal. For example, you might use a poker metaphor to invite someone to "double down" on an investment, but you would likely not talk about how an investment made your "heart take wing." (We'll discuss special-occasion speeches like these in Chapter 13.)

As you think about language and your speech, remember: Novelty is like salt; a little goes a long way. If every sentence is overwhelmingly interesting, the audience will burn out and probably stop listening well. Use figures to highlight your most important points, the ones you absolutely want the audience to walk away remembering. Look through your speech and ask yourself, "If they remember only two things, what would I want them to be?" Figures are helpful when you move from one idea or point to another: as transitions and in the introduction, conclusion, or anywhere you're trying to draw attention to main ideas and relationships.

The speeches you give in class will primarily be designed to inform your audience about something important or interesting to you or to persuade them to get on board with a policy or other course of action. As a result, although you have some room to use strongly figured language, you will have to pick your places. For example, stylistic figures work well in stories that serve as an example of a larger issue and in your call for action.

Summary

Access an interactive eBook, chapter-specific interactive learning tools, including flashcards, quizzes, videos and more in your Speech Communication CourseMate for *Public Speaking*, accessed through CengageBrain.com.

Language matters. Choosing the right words is a choice about style, even more than delivery is. Although there's no secret verbal jiu-jitsu that can enable you to persuade people by just choosing the right words, presenting your arguments in smart and compelling language helps to make you an effective speaker and communicator. Excellent speakers start by ensuring that their language choices are as concrete, vivid, and respectful as possible. They then go on to look for places in their speeches where they can arrange words (as *figures*) to make a point or use a turn of phrase (a *trope*) to enable the audience to see their point. All these choices need to be made *appropriately*, taking into account the audience, the occasion, and the topic.

Having good ideas and good arguments in your speech is important, but people are not simply data processing units. The way you use language to convey an idea makes a big difference in how your audience will receive your ideas. Stylistic choices can be difficult, but the most important thing for good style is to think about your choices and to select wisely.

QUESTIONS FOR REVIEW

1. What is style? How do the choices you make about language influence your audience's reception of your ideas?
2. What are the different types of figures?
3. To what uses can tropes be put? Give examples.
4. Give an example showing how you would integrate tropes and figures into a speech.
5. What should guide your choices in using tropes, figures, and other stylistic elements in your speech?

QUESTIONS FOR DISCUSSION

1. Can someone use too many tropes and figures? How would you tell whether a speech was over the top?
2. Which kind of trope seems to be the most common, in everything from famous speakers to advertising jingles? Why do you think it is so popular?
3. Take a simple statement like "This course is difficult." Now, invent as many different ways of saying it as you can. Which of the ones that you invented might be effective in a speech? Which would not? Why?
4. Go to www.americanrhetoric.com and select a speech. Choose one section of the speech (the introduction, conclusion, or a particular argument), and make a list of all the tropes and figures you find in it. Then write a brief paragraph explaining which ones served the speaker's purpose and which ones didn't. Compare results with your classmates.

Presenting a Great Speech

Diana Ong/SuperStock/©Getty Images

- Distinguish speaking from talking
- Explain the techniques for creating focus and energy from anxiety
- Compare the different types of delivery and connect them to appropriate situations
- Demonstrate the principles of good vocal delivery
- Demonstrate the principles of good physical delivery
- Explain the best ways to practice your speech
- Describe ways of engaging audience questions

CHAPTER OUTLINE

Jeff Greenberg/Alamy

Delivery

"**S**ome of them look like they don't want to be here, and most of them look bored," thought Kelli as she gathered her notes and approached the podium. "I hope I don't screw this up." As she looked out on what seemed like a sea of people, her heart began to race. "How do people do this?" she thought. She heard the quiver of her own voice as she began her introduction, convinced that each person in the classroom saw every bead of sweat on her forehead and heard every slip and stumble. Her classmates all seemed to be so much more at ease at the front of the room. Hurriedly taking her seat after her speech, she mumbled to herself, "That was awful. How can I get better at doing this?"

Overview

For most people, what seems scariest or most difficult about public speaking is the performance—actually getting up to speak. The hard work (described in the previous 10 chapters) really comes before you get up. Moreover, having a well-organized speech you care about and that is also correctly adapted to your audience will make you more comfortable. In fact, it is the best thing you can do to improve your delivery experience. Yet there are reliable methods of improving delivery, moderating fear, and preparing to speak. We'll examine them in this chapter, starting with strategies for dealing with your anxiety and then moving to the different types of delivery. After that, we will look how to use your voice and your body effectively and how to communicate credibility. The chapter concludes by discussing the most effective ways to practice your speech and how to handle audience questions about it. ❯

Introduction: Stand and Deliver

So far in this book, we have discussed what goes into writing a good public speech. We have discussed how you should think about your audience and the purpose of your speech, how you can organize your speech, how you should support your arguments, and how to choose the best way to say what you want to say. Now we're ready to discuss how to actually stand up and give your speech.

Delivery is the most rewarding, and for some the most challenging, part of the public speaking process. But like all the other parts, delivery depends on some basic choices about how you present your material. Though doing all the work necessary to put together a good speech improves your chances of giving a successful speech, the way you deliver it—your choices and your practices in giving the speech—matters to the way your audience receives it.

For evidence of this, think of Martin Luther King, Jr.'s famous "I Have a Dream Speech." Here is the conclusion from that speech:

> When we allow freedom ring, when we let it ring from every village and every hamlet, from every state and every city, we will be able to speed up that day when all of God's children, black men and white men, Jews and Gentiles, Protestants and Catholics, will be able to join hands and sing in the words of the old Negro spiritual, "Free at last, free at last! Thank God Almighty, we are free at last!"

If you listen to this speech (it's available in many places online), you will notice a number of things about how Dr. King delivers it. First, you might observe how crisply and distinctly he delivers each of the words. Note also how effective he in using the pace and tone of his voice to emphasize certain words: Anyone who transcribes the speech knows exactly where to put the exclamation points ("free at last!"), and no listener can doubt how important it is to Dr. King that *all* "God's children" be free.

But imagine someone else giving the same speech under very different circumstances, a disheveled speaker who stands in front of an audience, fumbling with his notes. Speaking in a mumbling monotone, he inserts excess words and awkward pauses:

> **When we . . . um . . . [pause] allow freedom, you know [scratches cheek] . . . to ring, from every village, and every hamlet, and from every state and . . . uh, every, um . . . city . . .**

We don't have to butcher this great speech any further to make the point: The way a speaker delivers a message makes a big difference to the way an audience responds to it, and even the most skillfully drafted speeches about the most crucial topics can fall flat if the speaker does not pay attention to the finer points of delivery.

Speaking or Talking?

What are the obstacles to good delivery? The first is that you may not have been trained to deliver a public speech. Good public speaking is the result of practice and training. In the course of this chapter, we will provide some important tips for practicing and delivering a good public speech.

The second but perhaps more significant obstacle is anxiety about public speaking. Jerry Seinfeld once said,

> According to most studies, people's number one fear is public speaking. Number two is death. Death is number two. Does that sound right? This means to the average person, if you go to a funeral, you're better off in the casket than doing the eulogy.[1]

It's commonplace that some people fear public speaking more than anything else. Yet as long as the label "public speaking" is not attached to the event or occasion, most of us are really quite comfortable talking in public. You usually spend a large part of each day talking to other people, and you take for granted your ability to do it. Consider, for instance, how often you do the following:

- Order a complicated coffee drink, making yourself clear, while others in line watch and listen.
- Speak up in a class, with the rest of the class listening.
- Give directions to someone who stops you on the street.
- Deal with an irate customer at your workplace.
- Persuade your mechanic to fix your car just a little bit sooner.

Each of these events is, in a sense, a kind of public speech. You decide (perhaps subconsciously) what you are trying to do, note who the audience is, and then say the right words, with the right look on your face, in the right tone of voice. You're so good at this everyday communication (because you've been doing it for years) that you tend to think it's easy and that it's natural rather than a learned skill. But it's the result of years of practice since you were young, learning to interact with others.

Anyone who's traveled abroad and spent time in other cultures soon realizes that successful communication is not just saying the words of the other language but embedding them in the right kind of performance. Greeting a shopkeeper in France isn't merely saying the word *bonjour* ("good day/hello") but saying it in the right upward intonation, eyebrows up but without actually smiling—learning to *perform* the greeting that native speakers give without thinking.

The point of public speaking training is to *extend* and *enlarge* your communication performance skills, not create them from scratch. You are already a much better communicator than you realize, and in working on your public speaking, you're building on years of resources and skills you've developed. What makes some people nervous about public speaking is thinking it is something different from everyday communication that takes years of study and practice to do competently. Of course, being a *great* speaker takes years of practice, but being a good and effective speaker is within everyone's ability. We'll turn next to the main obstacle: anxiety.

Creating Focus and Energy From Your Anxiety

The biggest concern for most speakers is anxiety about speaking. How can you deal with it? How can you overcome it to create focus for yourself and communicate energy to the audience? Here are 11 effective strategies that will start to work for you right away.

1. Remember, we are all in the same boat.

Keep in mind that almost everyone is anxious when they speak, even the most seasoned speakers. But no one has ever died of public speaking anxiety—you will get through it! Take comfort in knowing that you and your fellow classmates are all negotiating a degree of nervousness in speaking. You can work together to create a supportive atmosphere for everyone. This means not only that you each need to think about how you will speak in front of others but also that you all need to work on being a charitable and responsive audience.

2. Manage your expectations.

One of the reasons people fret so much over public speaking anxiety is that they secretly think they can eliminate all their anxiety. This is unlikely, so the most productive mind-set is to go into a speaking situation accepting that you will be nervous and that being nervous is OK. The question for you is not "Will I be nervous?" or "How can I control my feelings?" but rather how can you respond to your nervousness.

3. Recognize that nerves make you a *better* speaker.

Nervousness is a good thing, because it means you care about what the audience thinks. If you didn't care, you wouldn't be nervous. And you'd be a boring speaker, because you'd be speaking only to please yourself. Instead of aiming

Audiences want to see you give a compelling speech, and you can legitimately see them as being on your side.

to be entirely without nerves or completely comfortable, try to turn your nerves into energy. That way, nerves often look like excitement and enthusiasm to the audience. How do you do this? By not reacting to your nerves. For many people, feeling nervous (flushed face, quicker breathing, thumping heartbeat) starts a cycle: nervous, nervous about being nervous, nervous about being nervous about being nervous, and so on. Instead, your strategy should be to notice your nerves and then turn your attention, calmly and deliberately, back to speaking. That little bit of nervous energy is still there, and the audience may notice it, but you are in control and communicating.

4. Keep in mind that you don't look as nervous as you feel.

Very few people are stunningly articulate and at ease their first time in front of an audience. However, looking nervous and feeling nervous are two different things. Though you may feel like a bundle of nerves, this is not what the audience sees. They see a person who would like to do a good job of giving a speech and who is attempting to impart useful information to them. So take comfort in the fact that your feeling of nervousness is nearly all subjective and is not what the audience is perceiving about you as you speak.

5. Learn to see the bigger picture.

Your public speaking course is a learning process. Every time you speak in front of an audience, you are in the *process* of learning to speak more effectively. This means you need to be easy on yourself when you don't give a perfect speech. Instead of focusing on your shortcomings, focus on what you can do better next time.

6. Remember that your topic is more important than your nerves.

Presumably, you have picked a topic that is important to you, one you believe should be important to your audience, too. Recognize that what you want to say is important. One thing that will help your motivation trump your nerves is the conviction that what you are saying is more important than the nerves you may feel.

7. Practice!

As it does for any other skill, good practice can help you get through the tough points in your speech. You can practice in two ways: (a) Run through the speech in your mind and ask yourself what parts are potentially difficult—focus your practice efforts on these. (b) Give the speech in front of a friend or family member. This will not only give you a chance to get some valuable feedback; it will also help you get used to speaking in front of other people. "How to Practice Delivering Your Speech" later in this chapter will offer additional recommendations.

8. Let your preparation speak for you.

If you are giving an unprepared speech off the cuff, you have reason to feel unsure of yourself. If, however, you put in the work required to draft a well-ordered, coherent speech, you can rely on your notes and the concepts you have organized as supports to get you through any nervous moments. If you have a well-conceived outline and a good central concept for your speech, it will be easy to pick up the flow even if you get lost or stumble.

9. Visualize your success and believe in it.

Many times speakers will, before the speech, get lost in daydreams about screwing up and feeling humiliated. Not only are these unlikely to come true, but they make it harder for you to deal with your natural and useful nervousness. Instead, visualize a successful speech, where you feel nervous but move past it to a great performance.

10. Remember the audience is on your side.

No one wants to see a bad speech. In fact, the audience is hoping for a great one. If you envision an audience of people you are comfortable with (regardless of who is really sitting there) and act as if you are giving the speech to them, This can help you manage any anxiety about whether the audience is friendly. Trust yourself and trust your audience. Keep in mind that audiences do not want to see speakers fail—your audience wants you to succeed, especially because they have been or will be in the same position soon.

11. Act "as if."

If all else fails, keep in mind that it is not how you feel but how you act that dictates the success of your performance. As the saying goes, "Fake it until you make it." You don't have to *feel* calm; you just have to get through the speech. So the best thing you can do is act as if you *belong* in front of that room. This will also convey a sense of authority that will make you feel better.

Types of Preparation and Delivery

The biggest obvious difference between conversational communication and public speaking is that you typically prepare carefully for public speaking—both for the content and the performance of it—whereas conversation seems to happen without our even thinking about it. Speakers can choose among several methods to prepare for performance; each one has its strengths and weaknesses. Different methods of preparation will put different demands on your delivery.

▪ Speaking From Memory

speech from memory   A speech that is written out and delivered from memory.

In a **speech from memory**, the speaker writes out the text of the speech and then memorizes it. Speakers in antiquity used this technique a great deal—in classical Greek and Roman education, students memorized enormous chunks of text—but hardly anyone does anymore. Why? Because it's very difficult, and there's not much need for it. With the development of books and computers (and the teleprompter), we no longer need to memorize texts we want to remember.

For the *appearance* of spontaneity you can't beat speaking from memory—*if* you have the gift of making a rehearsed speech sound spontaneous. But memorization is a lot of work, and you run the risk of forgetting your material, getting lost, or sounding rehearsed and mechanical. Speaking from memory comes very close to acting and is the mode of performance farthest from daily conversation.

▪ Speaking From Manuscript

manuscript speech   A speech that is written out and read to the audience.

For a **manuscript speech**, the speaker writes out the text and then reads it. Although this is a common method and easier than memorization, it still requires a great deal of skill. Many speeches not written by professional speechwriters are not designed to be read aloud, and most people read aloud so poorly that the audience is left wondering, "Why couldn't he give me the text and let me read it myself?"

Many politicians use the manuscript delivery technique by reading from a teleprompter, which shows them an electronic text at eye level. Thus, they can read without ever looking down, giving an impression of naturalness, which also may be the result of long practice.

President Ronald Reagan was famous for his extraordinary ability to read from a text while making it sound as if he was thinking up the words in the moment.

Some new speakers convince themselves that a manuscript will solve their performance problems and reduce their anxiety. That's possible, but these speakers often stare at their manuscript, reading in a robotic monotone and never looking at the audience. They may *say* they're less nervous, but it's hard to believe that from looking at them.

Extemporaneous Speaking

In an **extemporaneous speech** the speaker relies on limited notes and supplies the specific words and sentences as he or she speaks. If the speaker were to deliver the same speech again, the words would be slightly different. Extemporaneous speaking is the most common type of formal speaking you will do and, therefore, the most important type for you to learn.

Preparation for extemporaneous speaking can be very individual. Some people can speak from just a list of words (their topics); others prefer a detailed outline; and still others use something between the two. Even if you are using one of these kinds of notes, however, you may well write out certain parts of the speech. If you have a really great metaphor or antithesis, you should write it out word for word, because the exact words matter. Many people also like to write out the first and last couple sentences of their speech, because it helps them in the places they are most likely to be nervous or unsure.

extemporaneous speech A speech delivered from written notes or an outline.

Impromptu Speaking

Impromptu speaking is speaking off the top of your head. You already use it every time you are called on in class or in a meeting, and it is not as difficult to do in a public

impromptu speaking A speech delivered on the spot, without preparation.

speaking situation as you might think. Many important moments in your work career (from the job interview onward) will be impromptu.

In impromptu speaking, you use the same skills of organization and argument you would in a normal speech, but you have to plan the structure very rapidly in your head instead of preparing it ahead of time. The more experience you have speaking, the more likely you have a stock of arguments, anecdotes, and even evidence that you can bring out on the spot.

Try It! *Are You a Better Reader or Speaker?*

If you have or have access to a video camera or a video-enabled computer, try the following exercise:

- Deliver a three-minute chunk of your speech from a manuscript. Now try to deliver the same chunk from notecards and then from memory.
- Track the differences you notice as you give the speech using each of the three techniques.
- Watch the video of each delivery. How did your impressions of your performance match up with the video? What does this exercise tell you about the process of speaking?

■ Staying on Time

"There was never a speech too short" is an old saying about good public speaking. As the quip ironically reminds us, many speakers go on longer than they should.

Staying within your time limit is an important skill for competent, ethical speaking. It demonstrates your respect for your audience's time and that of any other speakers on the program, as well as your accurate understanding of the speaking occasion or context. Audiences have little patience with speakers who abuse their time, and they have trouble paying attention to such speakers. In many situations, you will have a set amount of time in which to speak, and if you go over that limit, either you'll be very unpopular with your audience or you might even be cut off before you can finish!

If you've designed your speech carefully and practiced it consistently, it's usually not too hard to get it within a minute of the allotted time, but it's important to be aware if you're going too quickly or too slowly so you can adjust your pace and avoid going over time. In many speaking situations, either you'll be cut off when your time is up or you will commit the serious error of stepping on someone else's speaking time. It makes sense to have someone give you time signals (holding up fingers or cards with numbers) to show you, in countdown style, how much time you have left in the speech. Once you have practiced this way for a while, it's easy to stay in control of how long you speak.

Each preparation method has its own dangers for straying beyond the time limit. If you are using or manuscript or have memorized a manuscript, you are likely to be consistent in your timing, but there is always the chance you'll speak more quickly, or slowly, in the real speech than in practice. In impromptu speaking, you probably need to be looking at a clock, because you are creating the speech as you go along, and you may have to edit on the fly to stay within your allotted time. The biggest difficulty comes with the most common preparation method, the extemporaneous speech. Because you're speaking only from notes and previous preparation, your speech can easily go too short or too long. However, if you prepare carefully and practice in all the ways suggested later in this chapter, you should be able to control the length very well.

Types of Speaking Aids

Unless you are giving a memorized speech, you will have to think about what kind of speaking aids you are going to use to help you keep track of what you plan to say. Each type of aid has advantages and disadvantages. In some cases, the choice is a matter of preference, but in other cases you may be forced by the situation into a particular choice. Remember, however, you still have to *know* and *remember* your speech. Speaking aids just help you stay on track.

If, as is almost always the case, you're giving an extemporaneous speech, you have some choices about your performance aids.

- You can use an outline, printed on 8.5″ × 11″ paper, making sure it's in a large enough font and has enough white space that it's easy to read. The disadvantage is that you're stuck at the podium, since it's hard to carry a floppy piece of paper around and consult it effectively.
- If you are going to walk around, your notes or outline printed on 4″ × 6″ or 5″ × 8″ cards is effective. You can hold the cards in your hand, walk around with them, gesture with them, and put them down if you need to. Like the outline on a sheet of paper, the print on the cards needs to be large enough to read easily.

Your next choice is what to put on the cards or notes. You should start with your outline (see Chapter 9). Because the outline reflects all your research and thinking, you will usually need just a word or phrase ("Facts about student loans") to help you recall what point is next. In addition, the more you practice, the less elaborate your speaking outline will need to be.

Some things should be written out word for word in your speaking notes:

- Because *quotations* are someone else's words, it's important to get them exactly right.
- If you are giving the audience *quantitative information*, you'll want to be sure you get the numbers straight.
- The *names of scholarly journals* can be long and complicated (for example, *Transactions of the American Entomological Society*, a journal about insects).

Image Source/Jupiter Images

Notes on cards or paper can help you keep track of what you want to say.

- If you have taken the trouble to create a wonderful antithesis or other figure, you need to get the exact wording to have the full effect.

You may also want to customize your cards and notes to improve your delivery. After you print your speaking outline, you can write in delivery notes to yourself ("Breathe!" "Look up"). Or you can use highlighters or color printing to symbolize different delivery reminders. For example, a green dot might mean "Breathe!" and a blue dot might mean "Look at the audience." You'll get used to your own system as you practice.

Some speakers use colors to guide them through a complicated outline. For example, main points are blue, subpoints are green, and citations are orange; then when you glance down at the card, your eye is drawn immediately to where you want to be in the speech.

If you are giving a manuscript speech and you don't have a teleprompter, you'll have to read from a set of pages you bring with you. Make sure the font size is large enough to read easily at a glance without squinting or bending your head toward the text. Most professionals double-space their "reading" manuscript, so their eyes can more easily find their place on the page. It's common for these scripts to be printed entirely in uppercase, though some people find all capitals harder to read.

The most commonly used presentation aid is PowerPoint slides, and they can be a blessing or a curse (see Chapter 12). Although they are intended to help the audience follow the presentation, you can also think of them as a set of extemporaneous notes for yourself as speaker. If you know your material well, the slides may be all the reminder you need. You can also print up the slides for yourself and add delivery notes to them (either by hand or in the Notes panel), just as you would your cards or outline.

Using Your Voice Effectively

Your voice is your most supple and important performance instrument. The vibrant richness of the spoken word gives us our ability as speakers to create emphasis and shape meaning. The aspects of your voice that you control during speaking are volume, speed, articulation, and inflection. Let's see what each one adds to your delivery.

Volume

If you can't be heard, your speech won't be effective. Your voice needs to be loud enough for the room, but not overpowering. (Most aspects of delivery are about finding the golden mean between extremes.) There are basically three sizes of rooms based on volume needs:

1. *About 5 to 10 people in a small room.* In this case, a natural conversational voice will be fine, or maybe a bit louder than normal to catch people's attention. Using a "big voice" in this setting will be distracting.
2. *About 10 to 50 people in a larger room.* In this case, you are going to have to speak up and create more volume than normal. You're still close to conversational delivery, but you have to speak loudly enough that people in the back can hear you. You may have to slow your pace a bit to achieve this (see the discussion of speed, in the next section).
3. *More than 50 people in a big room or auditorium.* Here you face a choice. The best option is to use a microphone (or a lapel mic, if one is available). The other option is to shout without sounding like you are shouting. With a little practice, this is not too difficult. You'll need to slow down and insert enough

Exactostock/SuperStock

A lapel mic has the advantage of amplifying your voice while giving you the freedom to move around in front of the audience.

pauses to give yourself breathing breaks. It's best to write speeches for this setting in shorter sentences and phrases (campaign speeches typically use this strategy).

In order to turn up the volume of your voice in the larger settings, *relax*. Try not to tighten your throat or put any stress on the muscles there; it's common for your voice to strain as you "speak up." Unlike the muscles you use in athletics, your vocal folds (the muscles in your larynx that vibrate to produce sound) work best when at ease. Just like a singer's, your throat should be relaxed. Your voice works like a trumpet or clarinet: The sound coming out of it doesn't get louder because you tighten your lips (or fingers) but because you increase the air pressure going through it.

You can increase the air pressure going through your throat by taking deep breaths, and by taking in and pushing out air as low in your abdomen as you can. If your breathing is shallow (just your collarbone is going up and down, known as "clavicular breathing"), then you can't push enough air to gain volume. Think of planting your feet flat on the floor and pushing your voice out from your diaphragm, the muscle that stretches across the bottom of your rib cage (see Figure 11.1), rather than from your throat. That will require breaths that seem to go all the way down to your stomach and lower abdomen, or you won't be sufficiently activating your diaphragm.

For a more public-sized voice, the sound also needs to resonate through your head sufficiently. Your voice sounds best when it resonates normally, meaning through your sinuses. The Try It! box tells you how to find out whether you're resonating.

Try It! *Test Your Resonance*

You can test your resonance by laying your hand lightly on top of your head while you increase your volume. As you get louder, you should feel the vowels in your speech vibrate slightly up top. If you don't, experiment until you can. Your voice will be richer and stronger for it.

FIGURE 11.1
The Diaphragm

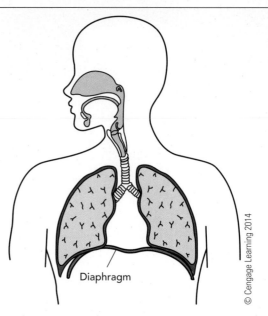

Diaphragm

© Cengage Learning 2014

■ Speed

Some people speak a little quickly, but we can understand them; others a bit slowly, but we can understand them as well. So there isn't one perfect pace, but people have to be able to understand you. As you practice, you need to get regular feedback about whether your speech allows you to be understood.

If you go too fast, it all runs together. If you go too slow or with too many long pauses, the audience loses the thread of your thought. For most people, the best pace for public speaking is just a bit slower than their normal pace, because this allows for clear articulation (see the next section).

If you are in a setting with a microphone, you may have to adjust your pace to accommodate the amplification. The larger room, the longer it seems to take for your amplified voice to reach the back, so words that are perfectly clear to the front row seem mushed together and hard to understand in the back row. You'll need to practice to get used to the slower pace and pauses needed with a microphone in a larger room.

■ Articulation

articulation The clarity with which words are pronounced.

Articulation is the clarity with which you pronounce the sounds in words and make them distinct and intelligible. If you don't articulate enough, people may miss or mishear important words or phrases in your speech. Because they can't back your speech up like a DVR or CD and listen again, they'll just be lost.

On the other hand, you can also go wrong by overenunciating, pronouncing sounds that aren't normally pronounced in English (linguists call this "hypercorrectness"). For instance, *often* is usually pronounced "offen"; the *t* is silent. Speakers who are trying too hard to articulate will add the *t* sound, thinking that is somehow more correct. Similarly, some clusters of words run together when spoken. Creating a distinct gap between the words in the phrase "an hour" sounds strange. Not only does it make listeners work harder, overenunciation can also be irritating and make the speaker sound pretentious.

Find a mean between the extremes. Ideally, your articulation will be just a bit more crisp than usual, stepped up just a notch so people in the back row catch it as clearly as those in the front.

Inflection

Inflection is the emphasis you put on words to shape meaning for the listener. As you say a sentence out loud, you naturally speed up and slow down, become louder and softer; you shape sentences with your voice the way a singer shapes a musical phrase. When people complain that a speaker is monotone, what's missing is *inflection*; the speaker has failed to make his or her speech rise and fall and, in effect, to more musical.

Try an experiment with a famous phrase from the end of the Gettysburg Address, given by Abraham Lincoln during the Civil War:

> . . . that this nation, under God, shall have a new birth of freedom—and that government of the people, by the people, for the people, shall not perish from the earth.

Most people today read the phrase in the following way, emphasizing the italicized words:

of the people, *by* the people, *for* the people

What if you read it the way Lincoln read it, with the emphasis on the nouns instead of the prepositions?[2]

of the *people*, by the *people*, for the *people*

The difference is huge. Instead of being about abstract relations ("of . . . by . . .for"), the phrase now drives home a central point of Lincoln's political philosophy, that democracy is a form of governing in which the government serves the people even as they create it.

Now try reading this sentence (from Lincoln's second inaugural address) out loud; Lincoln was trying to urge the worn-torn country to unite.

A house divided against itself cannot stand.

When you put stress on a word, it creates either focus or contrast. **Focus** signals that, of all the words in the sentence, *this* particular word tells you what the sentence is about, what's the relevant context for the sentence. **Contrast** helps establish what the sentence *isn't* about.

A *house* divided against itself cannot stand.

Contrast: But something else could stand.

A house *divided* against itself cannot stand.

Focus: This sentence is about division.

A house divided against *itself* cannot stand.

Contrast: But divided against something else, it could stand.

A house divided against itself *cannot* stand.

Contrast: Being divided is linked to the impossibility of standing.

If you try out all the various possibilities of stress in this sentence, the one that best matches Lincoln's meaning in the speech is stress on both *cannot* and *divided*. Obviously, you won't work quite this hard for every single sentence in a speech, but for important ones, and maybe for quotations, it is worth your trouble.

Because people sometimes lose their natural inflections and fall into a monotone when they are nervous, practice is your best friend for speech performance. For key sentences in your speech, try out different inflections and see how they sound, both to you and to your practice audience. Mark your notes or cards with emphasis if it helps you remember. You need to get used to the sound of your voice when it is at public volume *and* inflecting.

inflection Verbal emphasis on particular words to reinforce meaning.

focus Verbal emphasis on a word, signaling that it is the key to a sentence's meaning.

contrast Verbal emphasis on a word, signaling an opposition.

Using Your Body Effectively

In addition to using your voice effectively, there are three things to think about for physical delivery: standing, walking, and gesturing. Standing is important because that's what you do while you speak; walking can make a difference because a little bit of movement is interesting and can help the audience follow your speech; gesturing allows you to be both expressive and focused.

Standing

Standing before an audience isn't quite the same experience as standing at a bus stop. You don't want to stand at attention, but you'll want to consciously choose to present yourself in the best possible posture, which can improve your delivery and prevent distracting motions. You'll look—and feel—more confident if you practice the following suggestions.

● *Stand straight:* Keep your back straight and tall as you stand before the audience. This stance both confers and conveys self-confidence and helps you better project your speaking voice, as we've just discussed. Don't stoop to see your cards on the podium; if you hold them about chest high, you'll be able to see them easily. (This is also a good strategy when the podium is too low or too high for you or you elect not to use it.) Establish your stance as you step up to begin your speech, and remain conscious of your posture as you continue your presentation. Quietly correct your position if you sense you are slouching.

● *Keep your chin up and shoulders down:* It's easier to breathe (and therefore to speak) and to see the audience when you lift your chin slightly. The most common delivery problem is not making eye contact (see below); if your chin is on your chest, you won't be able to see the audience even if you remember to look for them. Keep your shoulders back and down, however.

● *Settle your weight on both feet:* If your weight isn't evenly distributed over both feet, you not only throw off your posture, but you risk letting your free foot do unexpected things like wiggling, tapping, or shuffling when you're not paying attention. You might also start shifting back and forth or side to side, something many people do when they're nervous. These motions are distracting to the audience, even if you are not aware you are doing them. Keeping your weight firmly on both feet is the best way to avoid such problems.

General Colin Powell, speaking without a podium, commands the stage through posture and movement.

Walking

Though you'll be making a conscious effort to stand tall and keep your weight on both feet, you needn't feel nailed to the spot. Unless you are speaking into a fixed microphone, you should feel free to move around a bit, in a way that feels natural to you. Not only will this help relax your muscles, which is useful in reducing nervousness, but it will also keep the audience's attention on you and add visual interest to your presentation. Coming out from behind the podium (if you can) brings you physically and psychologically closer to the audience, too, which can help you get your important points across to them. As you can probably guess, there is a happy medium between standing stiffly in place and moving around too much. How do you find it? Read on.

- *Avoid pacing:* Walk purposefully; don't keep walking back and forth, back and forth. You can even return to the podium occasionally and stay still to be sure you aren't overdoing it. And you needn't walk far; a few steps in either direction is enough to keep the audience's eyes on you. Walk at your normal pace, or a bit slower; there's no need to rush. Audiences find too much movement, as well as rhythmic movement and pacing, annoying.
- *Don't trip yourself:* When you do walk, put one foot straight in front of the other. Don't cross your feet and risk tripping yourself—because your main attention is elsewhere, you should limit the chances of making a silly mistake.
- *Face the front:* No matter where or how far or when you walk about, avoid turning your back to the audience, particularly while you're actually speaking. If you are using visual aids (see Chapter 12), you may need to turn away from the audience very briefly to set your visuals up or to point to something, but generally you should face the audience from beginning to end.

- *Move with your speech transitions:* The transitions, or "joints," in your speech are the best times for you to move around, because pausing to take a couple of steps and then starting again signals to the audience, "We're on a new point now."
- *Move from front to back to front:* Generally, in whatever space you have to move around in as you speak, start out toward the front of it, move to the back and sides during your speech's transitions, and return to the front for the conclusion (returning to your physical starting point visually parallels the way your conclusion recalls the thesis, and your peroration recalls the narration).

Using Gestures

Gesturing is highly individual. Some people move their hands a lot when they speak, and some don't; some people come from cultural backgrounds that value lots of gesturing, and others don't. The best choice for you, in public speaking, is to be yourself—be natural. If you normally don't gesture much but you try to during a speech, the gestures will probably look robotic and strange. If you naturally gesture quite a bit and try to hold still, you'll look like you're *trying* not to gesture, and the audience will notice it. If the audience is paying attention to whether you are gesturing or not instead of listening to you, it defeats your purpose in speaking.

Hands are very expressive, and you've spent a lifetime learning to use yours. The only reason you have to think about gesturing is to adapt what you normally do to the public speaking situation. The basic rule is that your hands should either be at your sides, hanging naturally, or in front of you, between your shoulders and waist. If you are holding cards, they should be about chest high, so you can see them without stretching your neck to look down.

Pockets are a problem, especially for men. If your hands are in pockets, they are still visible to the audience, along with all the stuff in your pocket—the loose change, the thumb drive, the car keys, the sunglasses, the pack of gum. Some speakers play with these items when they are nervous, and if you do, the jingling and movement will be distracting to your audience. A little formality is in order here, because you need to appear more focused and engaged.

Your hands should be in front of you, not be behind your back or covering your groin (like a "fig leaf"). Keep them between your shoulders and waist, and use whatever movement is natural to you. Intentionally illustrative gestures, such as holding up two fingers for "two options" or pointing upward for "inflated prices," often look contrived and can be distracting. Unless you are a skilled and experienced performer who has learned to make practiced gestures look natural, you need to trust your own good sense and communication ability. If you are focused on the audience and engaged in communicating with them, your gestures will be appropriate.

Communicating Credibility

How do your delivery skills help to project your credibility? Essentially, you are asking the audience to make a judgment that you are engaged enough with them that they should make the effort to engage you and your ideas. You can signal your engagement in two important ways: through eye contact and through appropriate dress.

▪ Making Eye Contact

Eye contact is a normal part of our every-day communication. In fact, it's so important that in a casual conversation, if you don't make eye contact, you may seem shifty or untrustworthy. That same judgment may be applied to speakers who don't look at their audiences. (Obviously, this doesn't apply to speakers who are blind or visually impaired.) When you are nervous and thinking hard about what to say, you may not focus on eye contact, so it's best to make it a habit.

eye contact Meeting the gaze of people in your audience.

- *Begin your speech with a pause and eye contact:* It's not effective to begin speaking while looking at your notes or cards. Doing that seems to communicate to the audience that you don't want to be speaking, or at least not in front of them. Maybe you feel that way, but the best antidote to that feeling is to act as if it weren't true. Before you begin speaking, take a deep breath and look around the room and make eye contact with the people looking at you.

- *Make actual eye contact:* Keep your chin up, look at the audience, and look them in the eyes. Yes, they can tell if you aren't. Looking over their heads or at their shoes makes a poor impression. If you make a habit of looking people in the eye, it becomes effortless.

- *Sweep the room:* Look at everybody by scanning the room side to side and back to front. Sometimes, it's helpful to seek out the faces of those wonderful audience members who look like they care about what you're saying; they are smiling and nodding and giving you the feedback you need. If you find one person like this in each quarter of the room, take turns talking to each one and looking briefly at the people in between as you shift your gaze. Try not to stare at any particular audience member, but share your gaze around the room so everyone feels included in your speech.

AP Photo/Julio Cortez

Actor Mark Ruffalo, who often speaks out against the natural-gas drilling practice known as hydrofracking, is well versed in the successful use of natural gestures and eye contact.

Choosing Your Appearance

appropriate dress Appearance that fits the occasion and gives you credibility.

Your **appropriate dress** and the way you present yourself will depend on the occasion on which you are speaking. A funeral or wedding may require you to be dressed fairly formally, whereas jeans and a clean T-shirt might be acceptable at a neighborhood meeting or the school board. In general, you would like your clothes to attract as little attention as possible, so your words speak more loudly than your appearance. That doesn't mean you have to dress in a bland or dowdy way. It means that in each speaking context, you shouldn't stand out from others because of your clothes. Instead, you should shine because of how smart and compelling your speaking is.

In particular, sexy clothes don't help speakers communicate effectively. A tight T-shirt on a muscular guy or a seriously short skirt on an attractive woman may look good or not, but either way it creates a problem in the public speaking context. The clothes can attract more attention than the speaker's words.

In general, professional clothing choices are clothes that are neat and clean and don't attract much attention, allowing the audience to focus on what's being said. As a speaker, you want to be taken seriously for your words

Some clothing choices are just not very functional for speakers. You'll want to wear reasonably comfortable clothes that you don't have to worry about. High heels can make you more likely to trip; heavy shoes may thud across a stage. Anything that jangles or dangles (such as loose or heavy jewelry, ornamental zippers, and so on) is likely to be distracting, especially if the sound will be picked up by a microphone.

It goes without saying that you shouldn't be chewing gum while speaking. Traditionally, it is impolite to wear a hat while speaking, but just as important, a ball cap covers your face when you look down at your cards, or even at the front row.

How to Practice Delivering Your Speech

Rehearsal is important for every speaker and every setting. Quite simply, practice helps you gain confidence, which helps you focus on and engage with the audience instead of with your nerves. It also allows you to edit and refine your speech and to see which parts work and which don't.

Sometimes, speakers think that unless they have a word-for-word manuscript, they can't really practice, so they'll just have to wing it. This is not the case at all. Extemporaneous speeches do get better and better with practice from speaking notes; you might use slightly different words each time, but you get better and better at communicating your points.

When people get nervous, they tend to lose their conscious focus and go on autopilot. If you have practiced your speech, then you already know what you want to say and how you want to say it, so you'll be fine. (But you may not remember much about it afterward!) People get stuck only when they're nervous *and* trying to give their speech for the first or second time. Here are some tips for effective practice sessions.

Practice, All the Way Through, at Least Four Times

You should practice your speech a minimum of *four times*. The first and possibly the second times, your delivery might be shaky, but don't worry. You will have at least two more opportunities to improve it as you get more comfortable with your speech. At first, you may be very dependent on your cards and notes. In your later practices, as you get better, you can focus on voice and eye contact, and ask your practice audience (discussed in the next section) for feedback on things you've worked on since the first practice. You'll be amazed at how much less effort and how much more control comes with repeated practice.

Sitting at a desk, looking at your cards, and muttering the speech under your breath does not count as practice. It isn't close enough to actual speaking to do you any good. It might help you memorize your points a little better, but to be as comfortable as possible and do a good job in your actual speech, you have to approximate giving it: standing up, speaking from your notes or cards, with a few people present, and using whatever technology you'll be using in your speech.

Practice in Front of an Audience

Most people find that practicing in front of a mirror does more harm than good, because it tends to make you focus on how you look rather than on what you're saying. Experienced speakers may find the mirror helpful for fixing small problems in their delivery, but beginning speakers usually have bigger goals for their practice sessions than just a few minor fixes.

Practice by *talking to* somebody, not thinking about yourself. The speech is for the audience; if you focus on them, you won't be as likely to think, "Geez, how am I doing?" and make yourself nervous. Instead of using a mirror, therefore, practice in front of a couple of trusted friends, classmates, or family members. Ahead of time, ask your practice audience to be ready to give you specific feedback about your content and your delivery. One of your practice audience members should be giving you time signals each time.

How you choose the people in your practice audience depends on what you want your practice sessions to achieve. If you want your rehearsals to be as comfortable as possible, invite people with whom you don't feel any nervousness. If you want to get used to feeling a little bit nervous and practice dealing with that, you might invite people who will make you a little nervous—whether those are friends who will give critical feedback or relative strangers like classmates. The second strategy is usually more effective, because performing smoothly when you're nervous is a skill you need.

If you can't find people who can help you for a few minutes by listening to you practice your speech, you can rehearse at least a couple of times in front of a wall or in an empty room and imagine the presence of the audience. But make every effort to provide yourself with a live audience for at least two or three of your sessions.

Practice Making Mistakes

Everybody makes mistakes in speaking, all way from a slightly mispronounced word, to mixing up the order of points, to becoming completely blocked and forgetting the topic of the speech for just a moment (that last one happens to even very experienced speaking teachers). Such mistakes are going to happen during practice, and how well you deal with them during practice will determine how well you will deal with them in your speech.

If you slip up, take a deep breath, pause a moment to compose yourself and begin again when you are ready. The pause may seem like an eternity to you, but it is brief from the perspective of the audience. If you don't pause and get your bearings, you may go rushing ahead and make the situation worse.

It's best not to comment on your own speaking ("Wow, that was stupid"). That attracts attention to something the audience might not even realize was an error, because they didn't prepare your speech and haven't seen your outline. You've seen television broadcasters make mistakes many times, but you don't really notice because they respond so professionally: "Back in 1898, sorry, 1998, a large company founded by . . ."

Paying too much attention to the little hesitations, stumbles, and stutters that happen almost every time we speak can cause a speaker to lose focus on the audience. Instead, simply move on. Even the most experienced speakers occasionally trip over their words. What matters is how you respond to these minor stumbles, and that is something you have complete control over.

Breathe, Breathe, Breathe

Stage fright can disrupt your breathing, and if you can't breathe, you can't speak. So as you practice your speech, if you find that you can get to the second point without taking a breath, you'll be out of breath. It's a good idea to mark your cards with reminders to breathe every point or so. If you find your breath coming in shallow gasps, try to slow down and breathe from your diaphragm rather than your upper chest. Again, you can practice proper breathing as you practice your speech.

Answering Questions from the Audience

In many situations, you will have a chance to take questions from the audience and thus extend your speech into an actual conversation. It's a tremendous opportunity to enter into dialogue with your audience, and you should make the most of it. Here are some ways to prepare for and manage the process of taking questions from the audience.

Although you are unlikely to face the press, as Jennifer Lopez does here as she becomes the national spokesperson for Boys & Girls Clubs of America, taking questions from the audience is an important part of being a skilled public speaker.

◼ Anticipating Questions

There are several strategies for anticipating the questions you might receive.

- First, think about where you struggled with the topic when you were developing the speech. Go back through your notes. Does something jump out that you spent a disproportionate amount of time on? If it was difficult for you, then it will probably be difficult for your audience as well.
- Second, if you are working with technical material, you can always expect to be asked to repeat or amplify complicated concepts or numbers. If you had a slide with a chart or diagram up for a minute or less, be prepared to put it back up.
- Third, think about the specific strategic decisions you made in putting your speech together. You only had so much time for your speech, so you had to decide which topics to focus on and which to treat more superficially. You can expect questions on those topics, asking you to expand and deepen them.
- Finally, you can always ask the audience at your practice sessions what their questions are.

◼ Interpreting the Questions

When you get questions, the first rule is to slow down, and take your time. You'll never give a good answer if you don't fully understand the question.

First, make sure you understand what the person is asking. The best way to do this is to use the active-listening technique of restating the question: "So it sounds like you're asking if I think we should eliminate government-funded student loan programs. Is that right?" If the asker doesn't agree, go back and forth until you've got it.

Second, before you answer, think for a second about the question-behind-the-question. In many cases, the question asked is a cover for the person's real concern. If your answer can address that concern, you'll do a better job of answering the question. So, to take the previous example, a question about canceling loan programs might conceal the question, "How am I supposed to pay for college if you take those programs away?" If you weren't advocating elimination of these programs, you can correct that perception and address the question-behind-the-question. If you were advocating elimination, you can not only restate your point, but you can also address this concern.

The basic point is to take your time and be sure you understand the question before you jump in with answers that could just increase confusion.

◼ Giving Your Answers

When you begin answering questions, there are some easy tips that will make you more successful.

- *The question is public, and so is the answer.* Just as the question was addressed to the entire room, your answer should be also. Look directly at the questioner while clarifying the question, but then look around the room as you would normally during a speech. This helps prevent the exchange from becoming personal.
- *Respond to all questions as friendly questions.* Even if the tone of voice or manner of expression might lead you to think otherwise, treat all questions as friendly and helpful. Thank the questioner, and as much as you can, praise the question ("That's a great question," "You make a really interesting point,"

"That's very helpful, thanks"). In fact, all questions are helpful. If somebody has a question, it means that as a communicator you did your job well—that person is engaged enough to want to continue the dialogue.

- *You don't need to have all the answers.* If you don't know something, then say you don't know. Be generous in praising questions that advance the public dialogue even further.

- *Answer questions, not speeches.* In public settings, there are always people who use the question period to make speeches on their favorite topics, whether it is relevant to your speech or not. Don't twist yourself into a pretzel trying to make a speech into a question. Simply thank the person for the interesting insight and call on the next person.

- *Focus.* Many times, questions that are asked with sincerity and goodwill lead you away from your topic. Sometimes that's OK, but sometimes it takes away time from the more pertinent questions that others want to ask. You will usually have to "referee" this yourself, but it's not too hard. If the question doesn't seem to lead anywhere for your audience and topic, then you can say something like "That's a really interesting point, and I'd love to talk to you about it afterward." Or, if you think you can make a connection, especially to a question-behind-the-question, you can always say, "I'm not sure if this is what you're getting at, but here's what my argument would be about your point," and then go on to reiterate or expand on a point you've already made.

Sharing a dialogue with an audience that has engaged you and cares about your topic—even if some of them disagree with you—is one of the most satisfying and important parts of giving a public speech.

Summary

Access an interactive eBook, chapter-specific interactive learning tools, including flashcards, quizzes, videos and more in your Speech Communication CourseMate for *Public Speaking*, accessed through CengageBrain.com.

Creating a good speech means delivering it in a way that engages the audience in your message. Speaking in public differs from chatting or conversation in important ways, because it is addressed to more than one or two people. Because of the larger audience, most speakers experience a certain level of anxiety, which can be turned into focus and energy that improve their performances. Different kinds of preparation (memory, manuscript, extemporaneous, and impromptu) affect the nature of your delivery. To deliver a speech effectively, you need to understand how to use your voice and body in front of a group and how to create credibility with eye contact and appropriate dress. Delivery improves with practice, which will be most effective if you practice your speech at least four times from beginning to end in front of a practice audience. If you have the opportunity to answer questions from the audience, welcome their engagement and the opportunity for dialogue.

QUESTIONS FOR REVIEW

1. What is the difference between speaking and talking?
2. What are techniques for turning anxiety into focus and energy?
3. What makes a speaking voice effective? How is an effective voice produced?
4. How can you use delivery to communicate credibility?
5. Why should you practice? What makes practice effective?

QUESTIONS FOR DISCUSSION

1. Go to www.ted.com/talks, and find two talks that interest you. Compare and contrast the delivery of each. Which one is better? Why?

2. How do the content of a speech, the occasion, and the expectations of an audience factor into delivery choices? Give examples.

3. Why do you get nervous speaking? What is your best technique for managing it?

4. For one of the speeches you chose for Question 1, create a list of five questions you would expect this speaker to get from the audience. These are not just *your* questions, but questions you would expect to others to ask. Do you think the speaker could have anticipated most of these questions? Why or why not?

LEARNING GOALS

- List the goals of using presentation aids

- Identify the basic principles for employing presentation aids

- Describe the basic elements of composition for the content of presentation aids

- Explain how to employ handouts, posters, charts, and other non-electronic media

- Describe how to give an effective demonstration speech using presentation aids

- Use various forms of digital media

- Describe how to deliver a speech with presentation aids

CHAPTER OUTLINE

© Corbis Super RF/Alamy

Presentation Aids

Taye was excited to give a speech about what the United States could do to respond to the humanitarian crisis in Sudan. He had been following the story in the news for a long time, and he felt that something had to be done. His upcoming public speech seemed like a great opportunity to raise awareness and engage others. But every time Taye tried to describe why he felt so strongly about the topic, he felt that words alone were insufficient to convey its magnitude and the reasons for his concern. Of course, Taye knew that one way to help engage his audience was to show them just how significant the crisis was, and he knew of a number of good pictures and video clips he could use. But he certainly didn't want to play second fiddle to a projection screen, and he felt that the most compelling thing about his presentation was his personal passion. At the same time, he knew that showing the images would be incredibly helpful. So, wondered Taye, "How can I make these images work for me?"

Overview

This chapter addresses the use of presentation aids—that is, anything you use to communicate with the audience other than your voice, gestures, and body language. Presentation aids can be digital or physical, visual or audio. Like any element of a good public speech, they require that you make deliberate and responsible choices for engaging your audience. To help you understand these choices, we discuss goals for their use and general principles for integrating presentation aids into your speech. Next, we offer pointers for effective visual and audio elements and for non-electronic media (such as handouts, posters, flip charts, and objects). There's also a section specifically about demonstration speeches using an object. An abundantly illustrated section on presentation software comes next. Finally, we offer concrete advice for integrating presentation aids into your speech, rehearsing with them, and developing a backup plan for digital media—all the while maintaining good public speaking fundamentals. ❯

Introduction: Adding Media to Your Message

Public speaking is an art with ancient roots, but it is also an art that evolves to meet the demands of changing times. Audiences increasingly expect that speakers will present images, videos, and audio clips that allow them to directly experience the objects, events, people, and ideas that make up a speech.

In this chapter we will describe how to develop and use handouts, objects, posters, charts, presentation software, videos, audio clips, and anything else you might employ to engage the full range of the audience's senses in communicating your message. Your presentation aids, sometimes also called supplemental media, should follow all the same principles for public speaking that we have outlined in the other chapters of this book. The choice whether to use presentation aids and what kind is determined by your goals for the speech and for the audience, your analysis of the audience that informs your speaking choices, your ethical goals, and the message about your topic that you would like to convey to your audience.

Images, videos, audio clips, and other forms of presentation aids can make the public conversation clearer and increase its impact: For example, *showing* the magnitude of an environmental or social crisis like an oil spill or a famine can help galvanize public action. But these media must be used effectively. Have you ever sat

> ## Try It! *What Goals Might Presentation Aids Serve for My Speech?*
> Think about the speech you are currently working on.
> - Make a list of the elements that might be strengthened by some kind of presentation aid or supplemental media.
> - Next to each, write the medium that would be most appropriate and which goal for your speech it might advance.
> - Were you able to find a goal for each presentation aid?

through a presentation in which the speaker simply read his or her PowerPoints to the audience as if they were a script? Poorly handled visual aids can be an impediment to effectively communicating with an audience.

Why Use Presentation Aids?

Like all the other choices you make in composing and delivering your speech, your use of **presentation aids** needs to intentionally advance a specific and well-defined goal. You should not include supplementary media just because it seems like the thing to do. If you lack a defined purpose or goal, presentation aids are likely to either become a crutch or get in the way of your speech, instead of enhancing its power and influence.

So what are the primary reasons that you might want to integrate supplementary media into your speech? Here are a few you might consider:

presentation aids Media to supplement a speech, including handouts, objects, posters, charts, presentation software, videos, and audio clips.

- *To help the audience directly experience something you are speaking about.* Hearing or seeing the object, image, process, event, or sound you're discussing can make your audience feel connected to your topic. A presentation aid can help engage your audience by calling upon more of their senses. For example, your comparison of the musical styles of Beyoncé and Adele would benefit from audio clips of each singer's work.

- *To simplify explanations.* Sometimes, the task of explaining a complex event, idea, object, or process is easier if the audience can see or hear it themselves. For example, a simplified diagram of a nuclear reactor can serve as a reference point for a discussion of its safety features.

- *To increase audience engagement and attention.* Properly used, presentation aids can increase the audience's attention by offering images, text, or sounds to complement your spoken words. For instance, you might begin a presentation about the work of director Alfred Hitchcock by playing a bit of the familiar musical theme from his long-running television show.

- *To increase audience retention.* Giving the audience more than one way to engage with your speech increases their ability to follow it and to recall its major points. One study found that the combination of spoken and visual data significantly increased an audience's ability to recall the major points of a speech long after listening to it.[1] For that reason you might want to graph some before-and-after statistics to illustrate the effect of an increase in the school district's budget on students' reading scores.

- *To increase your credibility.* Proper use of supplemental media can increase your credibility by enhancing the audience's connection with you and your materials and by showcasing your expertise. For instance, a 2006 study found that the use of presentation software in a classroom presentation significantly boosted the speaker's credibility with the audience.[2] So your demonstration of yoga poses that improve flexibility would lend authority to your presentation about yoga's benefits.

If you decide to use presentation aids, eight basic principles can help you maximize their benefits.

Principles for Integrating Presentation Aids

Presentation aids that work well for the speaker and the audience do so because the speaker chose them with care and envisioned them as highlighting the best qualities of the speech.

Principle 1: Presentation aids are not mandatory. Use them only when you have a goal in mind and time to prepare them well.

One of your public speaking class requirements may be to incorporate presentation aids, in which case you should find most of this chapter very helpful. If you aren't required to use aids, however, you can avoid weakening an otherwise fine presentation by *not* adding poor or distracting aids as merely a crutch to help you get through a speech.

Principle 2: The focus of the presentation is the speaker, not the presentation aid.

You should use the presentation aid, as opposed to it using you; the focus of your speech should be you and not the aids you are using. For example, if you are using presentation software, you might be tempted to read text off the screen as if it were a script, or you might break eye contact with the audience by facing the screen most of the time. Or you might be tempted to passively play your video and let it make your arguments for you without actively using, engaging, and interpreting its contents. But your speech should not just repeat the content in the presentation aid; the aid should supplement and extend what *you* are saying. You have the job of actively interpreting its relevance and role in your speech.

Principle 3: Presentation aids are an invitation to interact with the audience, not a barrier between the audience and you.

Used well, presentation aids allow the audience to see or hear something that confirms what you are saying in your speech. They are never an excuse for neglecting public speaking fundamentals: You still need to signpost; you still need to maintain eye contact and adjust your nonverbal behavior; and you still need to build a relationship with your audience by considering their needs and the occasion.

Principle 4: Presentation aids require good composition, just like any other element of a good public speech.

As we'll see in the next section, good composition is clear, uncluttered, topical, and simple (think of the acronym CUTS).

- *Clear:* The supplemental media you choose needs to be easy for your audience to see or hear and easy to digest while you are speaking (or afterward, if it is a handout). A packet with pages in the wrong order is a poor choice for a handout.
- *Uncluttered:* The images or sounds you present should have one specific purpose and be without any accompanying "noise"—that is, without extra visual elements or sounds that interfere with your audience hearing what you would like them to hear. One large picture is more effective than a collage of small images that are hard to see.
- *Topical:* Your aids should have a direct and readily understood link to your topic or to some significant element of your speech. A photo of the local airport would not be obviously relevant to a speech about the benefits of curbside recycling programs.
- *Simple:* The more streamlined the composition of your presentation aids, the less likely they will get in the way of your speech (see Figure 12.1).

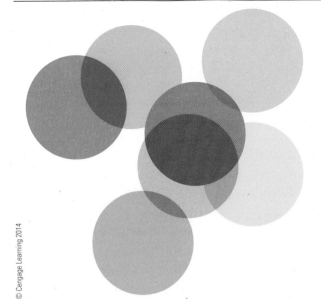

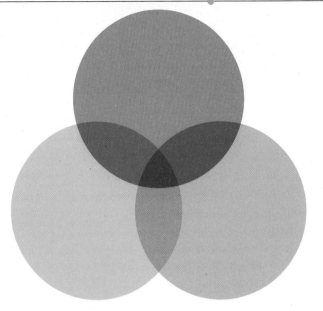

FIGURE 12.1
Simply designed visuals (such as the one on the right, not the one on the left) are easier for your audience to engage.

As we'll see later in this chapter, some types of information lend themselves better to certain kinds of diagrams than others.

Principle 5: Effective and ethical use of presentation aids means the image, video, or sound clip is appropriate to the room and the audience.

Video and audio clips should be short, and you should test the volume ahead of time to be sure it's appropriate for the setting. Good public speaking practice also dictates that the aids you use must not be offensive or dangerous. Avoid images in questionable taste, and be more than scrupulous in adhering to rules about the presence of weapons and harmful or illegal substances—here, a picture, instead of the actual object, can be worth a thousand words.

Principle 6: Supplemental media should solve a problem or deal with a challenge you face in giving your speech.

Your enthusiasm is part of the reason audiences will enjoy listening to you, but when they aren't as familiar with the abstract concepts in your speech as you are, like Taye in the chapter-opening story, you may need a picture, chart, or other aid to make them seem real and concrete. For example, if you are giving a speech about refugee camps, you can *say* the conditions in them are bad, but if you can show a picture or video that documents these conditions, your claim becomes much more concrete. Suppose you want to make the claim that foreign aid investments to prevent water scarcity in developing countries can do much good for a relatively low cost. You could read a list of budget numbers,[3] but a pie chart showing the tiny sliver of the federal budget that goes to international affairs gives your audience a more concrete and easily digestible means of grasping a set of potentially complex relationships (see Figure 12.2).

A good presentation aid can also help your audience stay engaged with and better comprehend a long speech or one with complex organization. A handout or some simple slides of your outline can allow people to see the overall structure of your speech, keep better track of your arguments, and visually follow the progression of your points.

FIGURE **12.2**

Pie chart of the fiscal year 2011 proposed federal budget, with 4% for International Affairs (*Source*: Office of Management and Budget Historical Tables, FY 2011)

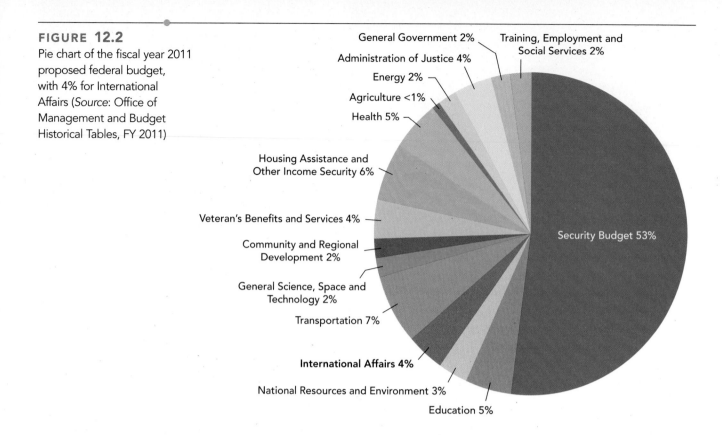

Principle 7: Less is more.

Technology's vast capabilities can seduce us into using presentation aids more than we need to. To guard against this, remember that when it comes to supplements for your speech, less is always more. Why use 20 slides if 10 will do? Why use 10 if 5 suffice? Why show an extended video clip when an excerpt can tell the story? Remember that aids are there to solve problems. Ask of each one, "Is this solving a problem for me? Is there any way I could do without it?" The simpler and more streamlined your presentation, the more compelling a speaker you will be.

Principle 8: Credit your sources.

As with any element of a public speech, if you borrow an image, photo, graph, chart, or audio or video clip that someone else has made, you need to credit the author verbally in your speech, visually on the image itself if possible, and also in the outline or bibliography you hand in if your instructor requires one. By the same token, If you take a picture to use in your speech, make sure to ask anyone who appears prominently in it for their permission to use it in your speech. And if you create your own graph, chart, or diagram, be sure to properly document the source of your information.

These principles and the goals that underwrite them apply to every presentation aid. Whether you are putting pictures on a poster, drawing graphs on a flip chart, or using presentation software with text and embedded video, you have choices to make regarding the goals you have in mind. Keep your speech the focus of the presentation, maintain your engagement with the audience, employ good composition and sound ethics, and address specific challenges presented by your topic and your speaking situation. With this foundation in mind, let's look at some of the common elements that appear in different kinds of presentation aids.

Static Visual Elements

Images that do not move, like photos, pictures, graphs, diagrams, and maps are effective when carefully tied to the content of your speech, where they can visually confirm your claims.

Pictures and Photos

Whether you are using pictures or photos on a poster, a flip chart, or projecting them on a screen, always remember that a picture or photo needs to be topical: that is, it must fulfill a specific purpose that advances your goal. Speakers are often tempted to include images that are tangential to their goal but are visually compelling. Pictures and photos also need to be appropriate for your audience and the situation, so, for example, you should avoid images people might find offensive or difficult to stomach.

Second, photos and pictures are most effective when they demonstrate good visual composition. Here are a few simple rules for making sure you get maximum impact from your pictures.

1. *Size and image resolution count.* Pictures, or the elements of the picture you would like your audience to see, should be large enough to be visible without straining and with good enough image resolution for the image to be clear. If a picture is too small for your purposes, or if enlarging it degrades the quality too much, do not use it.

2. **Cropping** is the process of selecting a portion of an image in order to draw the viewer's eye toward the important subject. The main subject should be clearly visible, usually near the center of the frame, Ineffective cropping choices omit important elements or make the image look crowded, for instance. Other choices simply reflect a difference in emphasis that can affect what your audience takes away from the picture. For examples of how cropping choices change the emphasis, see the three versions of a photo of California governor Jerry Brown addressing a conference about climate risks.

cropping Selecting a portion of an image to focus on the important subject.

Pick images that are appropriately sized and that have good resolution. The one in the middle here meets these criteria.

This is a photo of California Governor Jerry Brown (right) addressing the Governor's Conference on Extreme Climate Risks and California's Future at the California Academy of Sciences in San Francisco, with Rajendra Pachauri (middle), chair of the United Nations Intergovernmental Panel on Climate Change, and billionaire philanthropist Richard Branson (left). Although Governor Brown is the one speaking in this photo, he is not in the center. Framing the image this way emphasizes the event, the exchange of ideas on the stage, and the importance of the conversation for the audience members.

Here is the same photo cropped to put Governor Brown in the center of the image, de-emphasizing the audience and the occasion. This photo not only focuses on the governor as the speaker, but it highlights the intensity of his engagement with his audience and the topic. Although this version of the photo emphasizes different things, it represents another effective choice.

Here is one more cropping choice. Even if the goal was to focus on the man sitting in the middle (Dr. Rajendra Pachauri), the scene is cropped a bit too closely, so the viewer may feel that some elements of the event are missing, and there is not enough room to comfortably contain the whole of the shot. This version is not pleasing to the eye and may distract listeners from the message.

Images that are bright and in crisp focus add impact to your presentation, whereas those that are dark or blurry will obviously detract from your words.

Smit/Shutterstock.com

3. *Brightness and focus* are important. Use only photos that have an appropriate level of brightness and are in good focus so they are easy to see and interesting to look at. If your photo is too dark or blurry it will be difficult for the audience to get the full benefit from it.

Much more could be said about visual composition, but if you pay attention to size, resolution, cropping, and brightness and focus, you will at least avoid picking photos that distract the audience or that detract from the polish of your presentation.

Try It! *Cropping and Framing a Photo*

Find a photo online that you would like to use in a speech, and open it in picture software (even MS Paint would work). Manipulate the frame and size to produce three versions of the image.

● What are the differences among the versions?
● What does each highlight or downplay?
● Which would be most appropriate for a speech about the topic? Why?

■ Charts and Graphs

Charts and **graphs** can show up in posters, handouts, and projected images. They are an effective way to visually represent relationships between data points even though they may not technically add new content to your speech. For instance, if you want to tell your audience how many voters favor the legalization of marijuana, how many oppose it, and how many have no expressed opinion, you will say the numbers, of

chart A diagram that shows the relationship of parts.

graph A pictorial representation of numerical data.

course, but you can also show the data in a chart. This lets your audience take in the relative sizes of these three groups in an instant.

Graphs and charts can also add visual impact to your presentation by showing data in a way that is colorful and memorable. Here are some tips for employing them:

- *Make sure your charts and graphs are not too data-rich.* If you have a data point you would like to represent visually, you probably want to show a relationship between it and a larger whole. So, for example, in the pie chart in Figure 12.2, the point was to visually represent the relationship between one data point (the percentage of the federal budget that goes toward international affairs) and a specific context (the whole federal budget). Charts and graphs work best when they focus on no more than one or two relationships. Making them do more usually both muddles your point and draws your audience's attention away from your speech.
- *Use color for contrast and clarity.* The graph you select or produce should have a just a few contrasting colors that are easy for the audience to see and that help to distinguish the various elements of the graph.
- *Pick the right kind of chart or graph to support your point.* Line graphs, pie charts, and bar charts (see Figure 12.3) all have their best uses.

FIGURE 12.3
Line graphs (top left and right), a pie chart (bottom right), and a bar chart (bottom left)

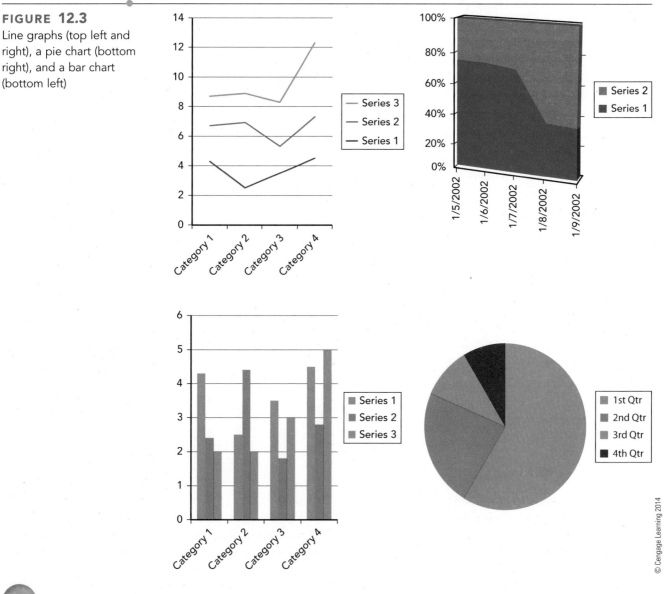

© Cengage Learning 2014

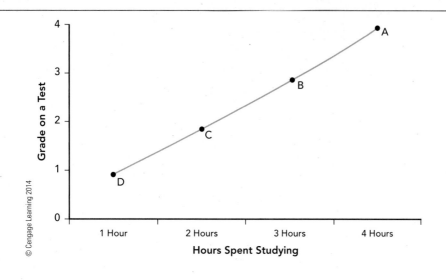

Line graphs (top left and right in Figure 12.3) are particularly good at showing trends or correlations between data points so that audiences can see how two variables relate to one another. Graphs are usually organized around two axes (plural of *axis*). For example, for a graph showing the relationship between the amount of time you spend studying and your grade on a test, you could plot your grade on the vertical axis and the amount of time you spent studying for it on the horizontal axis (Figure 12.4). The graph shows (of course) that the more hours you study, the higher your grade.

You can probably see how a line graph could show the relationship between, for example, the number of free music downloads and music industry profits, or between class size and academic performance. Graphs have the virtue of being simple and easy to understand, and they present a powerful visualization of a trend or a strong relationship between two factors.

Bar graphs, like line graphs, allow you to show a trend or correlation over time. Bar graphs have some advantages over line graphs. For instance, they can show comparisons of magnitude or size, especially if the category you are showing contains subtypes. For example, if you wanted to compare the number of blockbuster action films, horror films, and comedy films over the last four decades, a bar graph would allow you to show these trends side by side (Figure 12.5).

Pie charts are a good way of showing the relationship between one data point and its context, or of showing the allocation of a resource such as time, money, or interest.

line graph A graph that displays numerical information as a series of data points connected by straight lines.

bar graph A graph that displays numerical information as rectangular bars whose lengths are proportional to their value.

pie chart A circular chart that displays numerical information as slices whose sizes are proportional to their value.

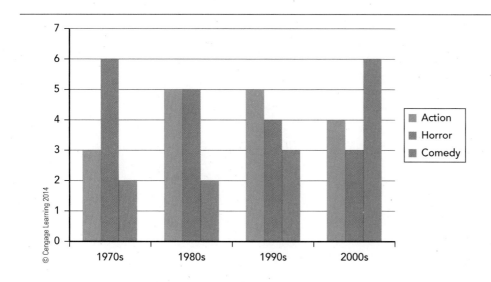

FIGURE 12.6

Pie chart showing hours
spent on laptop during finals
week.

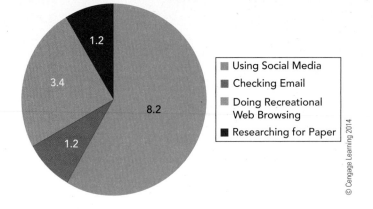

By their nature, pie charts show a whole and the individual components that make up the whole, so they are effective for giving the audience the bigger picture for an individual data point, especially an allocation that's complex or characterized by great disparity. For instance, if you wanted to show a relationship that involved disparity, say, between the amount of time you spend checking email, using social media, fooling around on the Internet, and actually doing research for a term paper on a given night during finals week, you might use a pie chart like Figure 12.6.

Try It! *Using Different Formats for Presenting Data*

Pick a part of a speech that requires you to use some data. Experiment with representing this data as a line graph, a bar graph, and a pie chart.

- Does the data fit into each of these formats?
- In which format does it make the most sense? Why?
- Which format would be the best choice for presenting this data in your speech? why?

Pie charts can also show complex allocation of a resource among many different uses. For example, if you were giving an informative speech about the energy usage of the typical U.S. household, you could show a pie chart that breaks usage down into discrete categories as in Figure 12.7.

FIGURE 12.7

Pie chart showing residential
energy consumption by end
use for U.S. households.
[*Source*: U.S. Department
of Energy. (2012, March).
Residential sector. In
Buildings Energy Data Book
(Chapter 2, introduction).
Retrieved from http://
buildingsdatabook.eren.doe
.gov/ChapterIntro2.aspx]

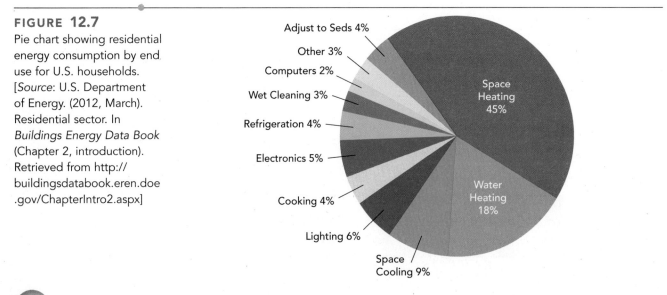

Though you could use this chart to show the disparity between space heating and other energy uses, it also demonstrates the broad variety of different kinds of energy use that factor into household energy consumption. This is what makes pie charts useful—they can both show a stark visual representation of relationships between elements of a category, and they can show the diversity of the category.

Maps and Diagrams

If your speech relies on making a point about geography—for example, if you want to show the geographic distribution of new AIDS cases—or if your speech requires listeners to have familiarity with the geography of a place—such as Yellowstone National Park—a good map can add visual impact to your presentation and give your audience a useful point of reference. Maps follow many of the same rules as other static visual images, but they also require that you provide a visual context. Either the map must be large enough for the audience to see the particular geographic area in its context, or you should show other images that provide that context. Yellowstone, for instance, is mostly in Wyoming but also occupies parts of Montana and Idaho, so you would need to show at least these three states in one or more images to provide the park's geographic context. Maps should also be labeled appropriately, with just enough information to support your points and in easily readable form.

Diagrams are visual schemas that show, for example, the parts that make up an object, as in Figure 12.8. A diagram is like a map in that it represents spatial relationships, but it shows these relationships in regard to an object, like a camera or a lawnmower, for instance, as opposed to a place. Like other images, diagrams should be simple enough for the audience to digest in the context of a speech, with both high enough resolution and strong enough contrast to allow the audience to read the image easily.

diagram A pictorial representation of the parts of an object.

Exactostock/SuperStock.com

FIGURE 12.8
This diagram shows the parts of a long-case pendulum clock and their spatial relationships to one another.

◼ Text

A number of different kinds of presentation aids can use text—including handouts, posters and flip charts, videos, and presentation software. Here are a few tips for using textual elements effectively:

- *Make textual elements clear and easily readable.* If the audience has to strain to read text on a slide, flip chart, or handout, most of their attention goes into deciphering it instead of listening to your speech. All text you present should be of a size, color, and font that allows the average viewer in your particular audience to read it easily. Allow plenty of white space around the text as well for high legibility.
- *Use text sparingly.* The primary focus of your audience's attention should be your speech, not the text in your presentation aid. If the audience has to spend more than 10 to 20 seconds reading, your visual is likely to interfere with your speech.
- *Use text for specific purposes, not as a transcript of your speech.* Text in a presentation aid should have one of a few specific functions.

  - *Summarize or outline.* Bullet points give the audience a visual map of where you are going or highlight the important points. An individual bullet point should contain only four or five words.
  - *Highlight a quotation or important phrase.* Remember, however, that text is best used sparingly in visual aids, keep quotations in presentation aids to about 10 or 12 words. For example, if you were giving a speech about Rwanda and you wanted to show a slide quoting Roméo Dallaire, commander of the UN peacekeeping force for Rwanda, 1993–1994, on the absence of international media coverage, you might be tempted to show all of the following:

"The international media initially affected events by their absence. A tree was falling in the forest and no one was there to hear it. Only those of us in Rwanda, it seemed, could hear the sound, because the international media were not there in any appreciable numbers at the outset."

  - Although you would likely *read* the quotation in its entirety, you would make more effective use of it in your presentation aid if you showed just this portion:

"Only those of us in Rwanda . . . could hear the sound . . . "

  - *Define a central concept or idea.* If there is an argument or point you believe your audience must understand, you can dedicate a slide or a poster to it, but present it in as brief a form as possible.

In short, the guideline for using text in presentation aids is to do the majority of your explanatory work by speaking, not by making the audience read.

Moving Images

Video, animation, and other moving images can add impact and interest to a presentation. They provide a dynamic visual element that can grab your audience's attention, and they can forge a connection among images that might not be as effectively conveyed through words alone.

Of course, the basic recommendations for any supplemental media apply to moving images. They should follow the principle of CUTS we described earlier: They need to be clear (free of interference), uncluttered (focusing on the action you want to discuss), topical (supporting of one of your speaking goals), and simple (free of unnecessary elements or information).

It's particularly important for video to be topical and simple. To make sure a video is truly topical, ask yourself whether it adds to your audience's understanding of your topic. If you cannot imagine your audience fully grasping the power, complexity, or detail of what you are saying without the supplemental video, then you should definitely show it. If the video does not advance the power of your claims, or if showing it does not give the audience something they cannot get from your speech alone, then there is no reason to show it. Simplicity is important too, because each element of the video should support the broader point you are making. Extraneous content will distract listeners from your speech.

Audio

Audio clips add an extra dimension to your speech, particularly if you are addressing a musical element or quote from a great speaker that you might not be able to fully do justice to in your own words. Audio, like video, also needs to follow the rule of CUTS: clear (able to be easily heard), uncluttered (free of other noise or interference), topical (both directly related to your speech and necessary for making your point), and simple (without excess content).

Now, we will turn to the specific ways you can incorporate static visual elements, moving images, and audio into a presentation aid. We will start with presentation aids that have been around for a long time—non-electronic aids including handouts, posters, flip charts, and objects, with a special focus on demonstration speeches, which require you to interact with an object. We then turn to presentation software, and conclude the chapter with suggestions about preparation and delivery with presentation aids, especially digital aids.

Non-Electronic Media

Not every effective presentation aid requires a power supply. In fact, traditional presentation aids such as handouts, posters, flip charts, and objects have a number of advantages over their digital counterparts. They are less likely to cause hiccups in your presentation, like problems with setup or equipment, and they provide a tangible physical presence on the speaking stage that allows you to give a direct, face-to-face presentation of important contents in your speech.

FAQ *What are the best ways to use a handout?*

A handout is best suited to provide

- a complete outline or a summary,
- an outline for taking notes,
- important quotations,
- data that might be cumbersome to present thoroughly in a speech, and
- reference to more resources for understanding your topic.

Handouts

If you decide to use a handout, your first decision is when to distribute it. One school of thought argues that you should not hand out anything that might distract the audience while you are speaking. Handouts can be useful, but they also give the audience something to read or even doodle on instead of paying attention to your speech. The other school of thought holds that a handout can provide your audience with valuable resources, such as an outline they can follow or quotations you can refer to in your speech. In addition, a handout can be a nice takeaway for the audience, and it allows them to engage your speech by reviewing your points or looking at some of the sources you cited.

Like any decision about a speech, you can make the correct decisions about handouts only in the context of your overarching goals. Most of the time, the risk of distributing a handout outweighs the benefit, especially if you believe the primary goal of a speech is to have a conversation with the audience. However, if your speech requires an audience to read and engage with a somewhat complex quotation or text—for instance, if you are giving a speech about why Martin Luther King, Jr.'s "I Have a Dream" is such a great speech—it may be worth the risk to provide the audience with a few portions of the speech on a handout so you and they can refer to them in the course of your speech.

If you do choose to employ a handout, and regardless of when you decide to distribute it, a few tips can help ensure its effectiveness. First, following the principles of visual use of text we established earlier, a good handout should have lots of white space. If it is too dense with text, it will almost certainly distract the audience during your presentation, because they are working so hard to read it. Second, the handout needs to be closely targeted to your purpose and omit extraneous information.

Posters and Flip Charts

Posters and flip charts can add power and clarity to a presentation by giving the audience images or text to connect with during the course of the speech. They are easy to set up and risk none of digital media's equipment failures.

Posters should be placed in an easily visible position near the center of the speaking area, which means they're not well suited to a large room or audience. Follow the basic principles for the display of any visual media by making posters large enough to be seen easily by the entire audience, to be visually interesting and relevant to your topic, and not to be so complex that the audience will have to work hard to digest them. Posters should usually contain one major theme or support one major point in the speech, rather than a series of images or a significant amount of text. If you would like to present multiple images supporting independent points, or if you want text that accompanies multiple points in your speech, consider using multiple posters. A series of posters can tell a linear story or showcase orientation points for the individual elements of a speech.

Another way to achieve this effect is to use a flip chart. Flip charts are another low-tech way to control what the audience is seeing, but it can be difficult and sometimes expensive to make a set of flip charts (or even a poster) large enough for a medium-sized audience to comfortably see.

Objects

If you would like to talk about an object or something you do with an object, you can simply describe the object, you can show a picture of it, or, if the object is portable and appropriate for the speaking situation, you can bring it and show it directly to the audience. There are limits (you shouldn't bring anything that is dangerous, offensive, or against the law or campus rules), but given these, any object that is small enough for you to bring in and large enough to be seen by an audience is worth considering as a presentation aid.

Of course, the object must help meet one of your speaking goals. Ordinary items that everyone is familiar with are unlikely to hold audience interest or tell listeners anything new. A plain piece of paper isn't a good presentation aid unless, for example, you are giving a speech about how to fold it into an origami swan.

Using an object as a presentation aid has certain risks you should be aware of and work to counteract. One tendency is to play with the object as you are speaking. This is distracting and will draw the audience's attention from your speech. Manipulate or gesture toward the object only when there is a good reason to do so—for example, if you are pointing out the fine craftsmanship of a handwoven basket or talking the audience through the steps of a process, such as how to blend oil paint on canvas. Having a table to place the object on while you are not referring to it will help you avoid playing with it.

Second, you may be tempted to look at the object as you are speaking. Of course, you'll need to glance at it occasionally, but it should not become an excuse for you to break eye contact with the audience.

Demonstration Speeches and Presentation Aids

Let's discuss demonstration speeches in a bit more depth before we move on. A **demonstration speech** is a specific type of informative speech, and most of the techniques for giving an informative speech about an object or process apply to demonstration speeches (see Chapter 6). The added wrinkle for a demonstration speech is that you are also presenting a tangible physical object to the audience as a presentation aid.

demonstration speech An informative speech about an object or process that uses a physical object as a presentation aid.

The risks you need to avoid in demonstration speeches are using the object as a crutch or talking to it instead of talking to the audience *about* it. To avoid this danger, organize your speech to achieve the following goals:

- *Introduce the object.* Say what the object is and where it is from. For instance, you have a movie prop from a classic film.
- *Give some background on the object.* Describe how it is made, how old it is if its age is relevant, how you came to have it, and any other interesting background about it. Perhaps you bought the prop on eBay, and the film's stars all autographed it.
- *Talk about what makes the object unique and relevant.* This is the heart of your demonstration. What does the object do, and how? Why are you showing it? What makes it noteworthy enough for a speech? What makes it interesting to the audience? Your movie prop might be one of a kind; it might have appeared in an iconic scene in the film; or perhaps it has inspired you to pursue a career in set design.
- *If you are speaking about a process using the object,* describe the steps in the process one by one, and indicate or demonstrate, if possible, how the object is part of the process. If you are describing how to re-pot a houseplant, for instance, you can demonstrate how to use a trowel to loosen the plant in its current pot first.
- *Conclude your speech by recapping* why the object is speechworthy and why you chose to present it.

If you follow these suggestions, use good presentation-aid technique, and keep in mind the elements of informative speaking from Chapter 6, you will be well prepared to give an effective demonstrative speech.

Presentation Software

Presentation software such as PowerPoint, Keynote, and Prezi can be a powerful supplement to a speech, unless the speaker is simply reading the slides to the audience. There are two basic kinds of presentation software: spatial mapping and slide based. **Spatial mapping software** creates a large idea map of your presentation (see Figure 4.3 in Chapter 4 for an example of an idea map) and allows you to move between various elements of the map as you present. **Slide-based presentation software** moves in a sequence from one image or slide to the next.

Whichever kind of presentation software you are using, the CUTS principle still applies. Each individual slide or part of your spatial map needs to be *clear* enough and large enough for the whole audience to see easily. Each slide should be *uncluttered*, presenting only one theme at a time with the fewest possible images and text elements. Every element should be *topical*, that is, directly related to and necessary for your speech. Finally, each slide needs to be *simple*, so it can be digested with little effort.

Prezi, available in a free academic version at www.prezi.com, is spatial mapping software for creating a "map" or structure of your ideas and arguments. You can move around it and zoom in just by clicking the mouse. The size of the circles in your map indicates the relative importance of the topics, and circles that touch each other indicate topics that are related, as Figures 12.9 shows. Not only do they display information to the audience about your specific points (the cost of various curriculum options, in Figure 12.9a), but they also showcase the organization of those points (Figure 12.9b) and allow you to zoom in on the images (Figure 12.9c) as you move through your presentation.

PowerPoint, Keynote, and other slide-based software packages offer a platform for giving your audience a multimedia experience. You can integrate audio, video, images, and text to engage your audience through multiple senses. Edward Tufte, an emeritus professor of political science, statistics, and computer science known for his work on the presentation of visual information,[4] cautions against letting the slides control the speaker (and thus the audience). The problem is that slides are linear and allow the speaker to move through the material in only one direction.

You can avoid this problem, however, by following some simple principles, some of which we have already outlined.

- *Make your presentation image rich, as opposed to being text rich.* Using an image-heavy presentation forces you to interpret and contextualize the images for the audience, as opposed to reading aloud a series of lists.
- *Make sure each slide is absolutely necessary for the audience to understand what you are saying.* Don't feel pressured to include a slide or bullet point for every element of your speech. Use slides sparingly instead, only when they are necessary to help the audience understand a point.
- *Remember that fewer slides are better than too many.* Many speakers create huge presentations and then feel compelled to speed up their speech or shorten their explanations to get through the slides. Because you, not your slides, are the focus of your speech, you need to select the smallest number of slides possible to maximize your speech time.
- *Don't leave slides up when you are not talking about them.* If you use slides sparingly and only for a specific purpose, you will find there is a good bit of time in your speech when you are not talking about anything that's on the screen. Cut in a number of blank slides, so when you are not talking about

spatial mapping software Presentation software that creates an idea map.

slide-based presentation software Presentation software that allows images or slides to move in a sequence from one to the next

text or image on a slide, the screen is dormant and doesn't distract the audience from you.

Figure 12.10 demonstrates a number of other points to consider when composing slide-based presentations, especially when they contain text-heavy elements.

Cengage Learning

PowerPoint:
Slide Structure – Bad

○ This page contains too many words for a presentation slide. It is not written in point form, making it difficult both for your audience to read and for you to present each point. Although there are exactly the same number of points on this slide as the previous slide, it looks much more complicated. In short, your audience will spend too much time trying to read this paragraph instead of listening to you.

FIGURE 12.10A
DON'T have all text and no structure.

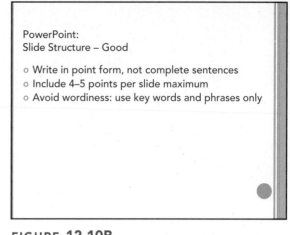

PowerPoint:
Slide Structure – Good

○ Write in point form, not complete sentences
○ Include 4–5 points per slide maximum
○ Avoid wordiness: use key words and phrases only

FIGURE 12.10B
DO have clear, simple structure on your slides.

PowerPoint:
Slide Structure – Bad

○ Do not use distracting animation
○ Do not go overboard with the animation
○ Be consistent with the animation that you use

FIGURE 12.10C
DON'T use distracting animation.

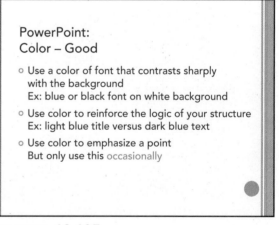

PowerPoint:
Fonts – Good

○ Use at least an 32-point font
○ Use different size fonts for main points and secondary points
  • This font is 28-point, the main point font is 32-point, and the title font is 36-point
○ Use a standard font like Times New Roman or Arial

FIGURE 12.10D
DO use simple, clear text.

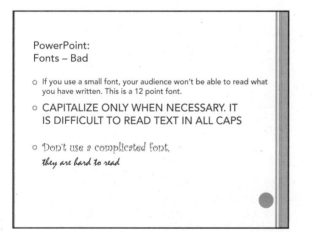

PowerPoint:
Fonts – Bad

○ If you use a small font, your audience won't be able to read what you have written. This is a 12 point font.
○ CAPITALIZE ONLY WHEN NECESSARY. IT IS DIFFICULT TO READ TEXT IN ALL CAPS
○ *Don't use a complicated font, they are hard to read*

FIGURE 12.10E
DON'T use small or hard-to-read fonts.

PowerPoint:
Color – Good

○ Use a color of font that contrasts sharply with the background
  Ex: blue or black font on white background
○ Use color to reinforce the logic of your structure
  Ex: light blue title versus dark blue text
○ Use color to emphasize a point
  But only use this occasionally

FIGURE 12.10F
DO keep color simple and functional.

FIGURE 12.10
Continued

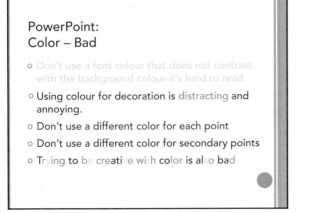

FIGURE **12.10G**

DON'T use colors excessively.

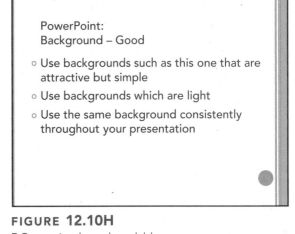

FIGURE **12.10H**

DO use simple and readable backgrounds.

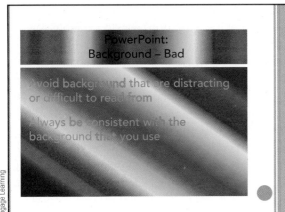

FIGURE **12.10I**

DON'T use backgrounds that overpower text.

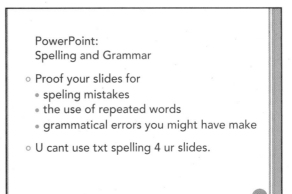

FIGURE **12.10J**

DO proofread your slides.

FIGURE **12.10**

Dos and Don'ts for Composing Slides

Delivering Your Speech With Presentation Aids

Finally, here's how to ensure that your presentation aids support your speech rather than overpowering you as the speaker.

- *Always rehearse.* Perhaps even more than other public speeches, a speech with presentation aids requires rehearsal. Rehearsing will increase your confidence; allow you to check that your aids are clear, uncluttered, topical, and simple; and give you enough familiarity with them to maintain eye contact with the audience. It also enables you to work on timing, making sure you move smoothly from speech content to presentation aid and back again while staying within your time limit.

- *Remember that your aids are not self-interpreting.* Avoid falling into the trap of thinking that when you show something, you do not need to explain it.

Whether it is your grandfather's violin or a line graph of changing population demographics, any visual or audio element requires (1) an explanation of what it is, (2) some sense of where you got it, and (3) a statement of what it means and why it is important to your audience.

- *Maintain eye contact.* It is often tempting to look at your visual aid, or worst of all, to turn your back on the audience to look at a screen. Avoiding hiding behind your technology. No matter how nervous or insecure you feel, you are more interesting and a better communicator than your slides.

Preparing to Use Digital Media

Digital media, when you use them effectively, can add a powerfully dynamic element to your presentation. Equipment that doesn't work can sabotage your planned speech. No matter what media you are using, these preparatory steps will help you minimize that risk:

- Make sure the room contains the right equipment for your needs, and that you will have access to it before your speech so you don't waste valuable speech time setting up.
- Make sure the available equipment will work with your presentation aid. For example, check that there is a DVD player if you have a DVD; if there is a dedicated computer for using presentation software, confirm that the computer has the right presentation software; and if you are using a laptop, make sure your hardware is compatible with the projector.
- Make sure the room can be appropriately configured for your supplemental media. Can you comfortably dim the lights so that the audience can see your slides? Can the chairs be moved so that everyone can see the screen? Can you set speakers to a sufficient volume for your audience to hear?
- If you are going to play a video or audio clip, familiarize yourself with the controls of the video or audio player you will be using and preset and cue up as much as possible ahead of time.

Getting access to the room ahead of time will help you head off many problems that could interfere with your presentation aids.

Developing a Backup Plan for Digital Media

The only surefire way to protect yourself from the ever-present possibility that your presentation aids will fail is to have a powerful and well-constructed speech that you can present without them. But there also *are* things you can do to recover when you have a digital meltdown.

- You can copy your slides to distribute them as hard copies later.
- You can use a web-based presentation program so that as long as you have Internet access you can show at least the major visual elements.
- You can bring your presentation on a thumb drive in case you don't have Internet access.

Plan each time as if the worst that *can* happen *will* happen. And remember, if you focus on and hone your speaking skills, you can be fantastic even during a power failure.

Summary

Proper use of presentation aids or supplemental media allows you to make complex points simpler, engage more of the audience's senses, and demonstrate objects and processes that are difficult to describe with words alone. These aids are effective only when they assist you in the larger task of giving an effective speech. As a responsible speaker, you must make deliberate and ethical choices for engaging your audience, guided by the goals you want to achieve with your audience and the principles for good use of supplemental media. Whether you are using a simple poster or the most sophisticated digital media, make sure each one achieves a concrete purpose, follows good design principles, and supports you as a speaker instead of displacing you in the audience's attention.

Access an interactive eBook, chapter-specific interactive learning tools, including flashcards, quizzes, videos and more in your Speech Communication CourseMate for *Public Speaking*, accessed through CengageBrain.com.

QUESTIONS FOR REVIEW

1. What are the principles for effective use of visual presentation elements?
2. What kinds of problems can presentation aids help solve? What problems can they create?
3. What does "less is more" mean in the context of presentation aids?
4. What does CUTS stand for, and why is it important?
5. List three dos and don'ts for PowerPoint slides.

QUESTIONS FOR DISCUSSION

1. What kinds of speeches need presentation aids? What kinds of presentation aids help you in digesting a speech?
2. What is the difference between a presentation aid that supports a speech and one that substitutes for the speech?
3. What is the best use of presentation aids you have seen? Can you think of the worst? What made the difference?

LEARNING GOALS

- Identify the differences between special speaking situations and informative and persuasive speeches

- Describe speaking techniques and strategies for special situations such as weddings, graduations, and memorials

- Explain appropriate communication techniques associated with ceremonial speaking situations

- Describe the kinds of cooperation and coordination required for group presentations

CHAPTER OUTLINE

Special Types of Speeches and Presentations

Calla had to give a bridesmaid's toast at her sister Annabeth's wedding. The night before the big event, she woke up with a burning question: What was she going to say? Calla had given a number of speeches in her public speaking class in college, but this seemed different: The stakes were higher, and all her family and closest friends would be watching. More to the point, it felt a bit corny to say, "I would like to tell you three things about how great my sister is." She had seen a number of her friends babble on or otherwise crash and burn giving wedding toasts. She wanted to do a great job—this was her sister's big day, after all. How, Calla wondered, should she approach this big moment?

Overview

This book has focused on the most basic types of public speeches: informative and persuasive speeches. The skills you've learned in constructing these speeches can be transferred to other speaking situations. In this chapter we'll be examining what those situations require and how you can boost the skills you have to be successful in them. In addition, we'll look at the additional needs of group presentations. ❯

Adapting Your Skills to New Challenges

In an informative speech, you'd like to create understanding, whereas in a persuasive speech, you'd like to inspire a change in belief or action. Yet on many occasions, you don't really want either of these, and your goal is to honor a person, a community, or some common values. Although you may still create feelings or beliefs in your listeners, you'll do it in a different way than we've discussed so far, You still have choices to make, but ones that are appropriate to the goals of wedding toasts, eulogies, graduation ceremonies, or other special occasions.

How do you have to refine your skills to succeed at the speech types discussed in this chapter? Basically, you need to increase your ability to adapt to the constraints of these situations. Ceremonial speeches are often called **occasional speeches**, not just because they happen only once in a while, but because so much about them depends on the nature of the occasion on which they are given—wedding, funeral, graduation, awards presentation, and so on.

occasional speeches Speeches given "on the occasion" of ceremonies, including weddings, funerals, graduation, and birthdays.

In occasional speeches, special constraints emerge from the expectations about the life transition involved. A graduation celebrates an accomplishment, and a wedding a life to come, and a funeral usually celebrates a life well lived. In each of these cases, you can imagine rhetorical constraints on what can be said (obviously, these are not times to deliver criticism or say anything negative). In many cases, these constraints are embodied in traditions about what to say, which therefore offer a guide to appropriateness in the particular context. However, traditions can, over time, curdle into a set of meaningless clichés. It is the speaker's responsibility to identify the constraints on appropriate speech, and then find a way to say something fresh and new within them.

You should regard the audiences of occasional speeches, even if they are mainly friends and family, as publics. Why? Because at each of these special occasions, you are celebrating values that are shared by communities (which, understood rhetorically, are publics), and you can address the people present as members of the relevant public. For example, if you were giving a eulogy for a person deeply devoted to environmental activism, you don't have to assume that all the friends and family present feel the same. Instead, you can address them as part of a public that benefited, and continues to benefit, from this person's good works.

Group presentations, although not ceremonial, have their own set of challenges in that you, as an individual speaker, do not have total control over the entire presentation. You have to collaborate and cooperate with others to create a unified whole. It also means that you do not, for the most part, speak as "I" but as "we," which will change your approach to ethos. Group presentations are the topic of the last section of the chapter.

Speeches at Life Transitions

Every culture has customs in which family, friends, and others come together to mark important life transitions. Some of these transitions create anxiety or sadness; some create joy or reason for celebration; still others arouse in us a mix of emotions. Your job as a speaker is to find fitting words to address the occasion, and perhaps even to help yourself and the members of the audience to experience the occasion in a meaningful way.

We'll first look at the main goals of occasional speeches—celebrating, praising, and inspiring. Then we'll look in detail at some specific kinds of occasional speeches. The basic principles that make you an effective speaker in informative and persuasive speaking all apply here: You still need to think carefully about the choices you make, and you want these choices to produce good results for your public even if the only effect is to enrich a celebration or to honor someone.

The most important factor that guides your choices in an occasional speech is the character of the occasion. Each occasion provides a *reason* for people to get together, and your remarks need to address that reason, amplifying it, extending it, making it specific to the time and place, making it personal for you and your audience. For example, every wedding toast has the same audience: two people who've made a commitment and a group of people who would like to honor and celebrate that commitment. So in a way, every wedding toast is the same—yet because every wedding is unique, every wedding toast will be different.

The goals of praising, celebrating, and inspiring require identifying a value and connecting it to the person or thing at the center of the occasion. A graduate may be praised for achieving an outstanding academic record, for instance, and a graduation is inspiring because it represents overcoming hardships and difficulties and the possibility of change and improvement. What values might we invoke in this setting? Table 13.1 lists some qualities, characteristics, and achievements we value.

If you think carefully about the person you'd like to praise or celebrate, you can usually find that one or more of the values in Table 13.1 describe what you think is important about the person. Because many people share these values, they create an automatic connection for you between the person, the occasion, and the audience. Let's look at specific types of occasions to see how this works.

TABLE 13.1 Values to Invoke in Settings Calling for Praise, Celebration, and Inspiration	
Bravery, courage, daring, heroism	Growth, maturity
Caring for others, putting others first, selflessness	Hard work
Charity, benevolence, kindness	Having an impact
Commitment	Humility
Compassion, warmth	Humor
Creativity	Making a contribution
Dependability	Mastery
Determination	Open-mindedness
Diligence	Passion
Effectiveness	Perseverance, persistence
Energy, vivacity	Playfulness
Enthusiasm	Poise
Excellence	Receiving an honor or award
Fairness	Resilience
Faith	Spunk
Finishing a difficult task	Teamwork
Flexibility	Wittiness
Frankness	Wonder

Toasts

Traditionally, when a meal is held to celebrate an important life transition, a short speech, accompanied by the raising of a glass (which is the literal "toast"); drinking the beverage at the end of the toast completes it, in much the way that a handshake completes an agreement. Toasts are typically a way to mark the significance of the event and communicate affection and respect for the people present. Toasts are offered for many occasions, including birthdays, retirements, and births, but the situation for which people are most likely to prepare a toast is a wedding.

The wedding toast is an important way for friends and relatives honor the newly married couple. A toast can be 2 to 3 minutes and is traditionally given by the groom, the best man, the maid or matron of honor, or one of the parents. However, many people now choose more informal arrangements, where toasts are given by best friends and relatives who have been notified in advance. The key things to remember if you expect to be speaking in this setting are the following.

Prepare Think about what you want to say in advance. Write two or three words on a slip of paper if you think you'll be nervous; glance at it before your turn comes, and then put it away.

Stand Up to Speak It is traditional, though not obligatory, to stand when giving the toast. Standing makes it easier for people to hear you and gives your words importance and dignity.

Introduce Yourself Begin by very briefly giving your name and stating your relationship to the couple—for instance, "My name is Mike Rogers, and I went to college with Jim."

Keep It Short Shorter celebratory speeches and toasts are more memorable and enjoyable than long, rambling ones.

Keep It Personal Abstract definitions or explanations of big ideas, such as "love" or "commitment," aren't very effective in this moment. Instead, because this is *your* toast, make it about *your* relationship with the bride and groom. You might want to think about what makes them special, such as one or more of the values in Table 13.1. Looking to their future, is there a particular value that comes to mind? Resilience? Compassion? Wonder?

> **David and Beth, we all started out on this journey together six years ago. From the bowling league where you were the best team and beat me easily, to graduation where you had the highest grades and outshone everyone, I've taken enormous pleasure in your successes. And now I am proud to take pleasure in your latest achievement: becoming the most beautiful and happy bride and groom in the world at this moment.**

A wedding toast allows guests to express their joy in the marriage and remind those present of the values it represents.

© Corbis

Stay Original   Keep any quotations very brief and relevant. Please leave song lyrics to the wedding singer.

Use Only Appropriate Humor   Witty and clever remarks can be great, but crude ones never are. Sometimes, guests who a little overwhelmed with the intensity of the moment try to lighten it, but embarrassing the bride or groom doesn't do much to honor them. Jokes about lazy husbands or nagging wives are best left at home.

Speak Directly to the Couple   Ignore the photographer or videographer if there is one, and speak directly to the couple. Hold a glass in your right hand, raise it as you finish speaking, and then take a sip. Your toast is basically a wish that their lives will contain this value or that virtue. For this reason, the conclusion of a toast usually starts with "May you . . ." or "May your . . ."

Be Pithy When Possible   Often a toast is expressed as an antithesis or repetition (see Chapter 10). No limericks, please. Here is a traditional toast as an example:

May you be poor in misfortune,
Rich in blessings,
Slow to make enemies,
And quick to make friends.
May you never forget what is worth remembering,
Or remember what is best forgotten.
May you live each day like your last, and live each night like your first.

Here is another sample wedding toast. The speaker begins by introducing himself, explaining his relationship to the couple, and keeps his remarks short and appropriately positive.

I'm Mike Rogers. I went to college with Jim, and I'd like to wish Juanita and Jim much happiness in their new life together and remind them

both that the same formula for success in college will bring success in marriage: Put in the hard work, and enjoy everything.

Toasts, and wedding toast in particular, can seem like a heavy responsibility if you aren't sure what to do with them. But when you use your knowledge about audience, adaptation, and style and keep your message personal and appropriate, you can always create a meaningful and memorable toast.

■ Eulogy

eulogy A speech given to remember and honor someone who has died.

When someone has passed away, those who cared about the person gather to honor the significance of his or her life. Every **eulogy** is thus in some way a reflection on what makes a life meaningful. With a little thought, you can always find original and personal reflections for a eulogy that express how someone's life has been meaningful to you, to others who knew the person, or even to the larger community. Here are some ideas and suggestions to think about in preparing a eulogy:

Make Sure You're Able to Speak If you are still so emotional that you feel you'll break down, it's perfectly acceptable to pass on the opportunity to speak. It is not disrespectful; rather, it is an acknowledgement that the memorial service has come too soon in your personal grieving process.

Say Less Rather Than More Just as in any speech, if speakers haven't thought through what they want to say, they may ramble. At this time of intense emotion, hearing a speech that goes nowhere can be difficult for the audience. Your eulogy doesn't have to be a polished gem, but it's best to decide ahead of time on at least a thematic value (see Table 13.1) and one or two related examples from the person's life. You can't—and shouldn't —say everything about that the person's life. Other speakers will want to make their own contributions.

To organize your thoughts, think about what you found most impressive about this person and his or her life. See whether you can express it in terms of one of the values in the table. This gives you a theme to pull together what you want to say:

Joan was more than anything a compassionate person.

Now you can fill it out with concrete examples, supplying details as appropriate and with an eye to how much time you want to speak.

We all know of Joan's extensive work with the food pantry for the poor . . .
For those of you who don't live in our city, you may not know that Joan trained assistance dogs for the visually disabled . . .
I remember the time I went to Joan with a problem that was just crushing me, and I have been endlessly grateful for what she told me . . .

Share a Memory The departed live on in memory, so we should share our memories with each other. The best memories to share in your speech will be connected to a theme you have chosen from the values in Table 13.1. Say what, in your experience, was exceptional or praiseworthy about this person, and then give examples that vividly display that virtue.

"Sarah was sweet, kind, and loving to everyone" is fine, but it's abstract, and repeating it with variations doesn't bring *you* into the eulogy or help listeners take a specific picture of Sarah away with them. Many people may have noticed

Whitney Houston's coffin is carried to a hearse in Newark, NJ. At the funeral service, filmmaker Tyler Perry had drawn upon a memory of a conversation with her to frame a message about grace and forgiveness in his eulogy.

how kind Sarah was, but they have not experienced *your* particular memories of her kindness. Choosing to share your memories makes it easy for you to prepare, because all you need to remember are the thematic virtue you've chosen and a story to go with it.

Acknowledge the Community of Mourners   Memorial services are community events. They allow a group of people to recognize and honor the memory of the deceased. So it's helpful to keep in mind that the value you've chosen is not just "your" value but also "our" value, something of significance to everyone's life. The fact that the community shares your value allows you to bring your audience into the eulogy: "We all admired Jorge's determination in the face of life's difficulties," or "All of us struggle sometimes to keep the passion in our work, but Tonya never gave up when a client needed something."

Try It!   *Your Life's Story*

If you were going to write your own eulogy, what would it sound like? It's a useful exercise to find out.

- Start by making a brief timeline of your life, listing accomplishments (which can range from being on a winning sports team to being a caring friend and family member).
- Then go back to Table 13.1 and pick just one value that you think would best capture all you've done and all you are.
- Now create a little outline—and fill in a sentence or so for the narration, two or three points, and the peroration.
- Now try to answer these questions:
  - How hard was it for you to connect the value to the details of your life? Why?
  - Did you need to leave some details out? Why or why not?
  - Did you need to add extra details?
  - What did you learn about the role of values in telling your story?

Eulogies work as a kind of rhetoric. What we all want is to make sense of this person's passing—and life. We do this as a group. People's lives make sense in the context of their communities, of the *publics* they belong to. So eulogies not only invoke values, but they do so with respect to a public, which is an audience, that shares those values. In the same way that in an informative speech you invoke an audience that cares about health so you can talk about yoga, in a eulogy you can invoke an audience that allows you to make public sense of this person's life and accomplishments.

◼ Graduation

Graduations happen from kindergarten and elementary school through middle and high school to college and training programs. These academic accomplishments are often celebrated with a ceremony, and you may find yourself called upon to "say a few words," or even give a full commencement speech, at one of them. Here's how to make your words count,

Recognize Everybody   Even if you're there for just one friend or relative, be sure to congratulate the whole group. Often there will be special honors handed out to a few celebrants, but try to make clear that everyone who graduates is a success.

> **I'd like to thanks everyone for coming today: Graduates, this is your day; friends and family, you are so important to success; and of course our teachers and faculty, without whom we wouldn't be here.**

Oprah Winfrey, speaking at the Duke University graduation in 2012, inspires graduates to excellence and public service.

Use Only Appropriate Humor Appropriate humor adds zest, but inappropriate humor is weird and unhelpful, and it often makes the audience uncomfortable. Humor typically has a target and is to some degree negative, so when you're speaking in praise of others, use humor directed at yourself if you want to be funny,

> **I'm truly honored to be speaking today. And surprised. I know it is probably a big surprise to my parents and many of friends—and to me as well. There are so many talented and impressive people in our graduating class.**

Focus on Values Again, to focus your remarks, decide on the one or two values that will be at the core of your speech. A speech in this setting honors all the students graduating, so pick a value that, to you, is the essence of what all these people have accomplished by graduating. For example, if you choose "courage" as the central value you will speak about, you could develop this theme in several ways:

- The courage to work hard . . .
- The courage not to give up . . .
- The courage to take chances . . .
- The courage to believe in ourselves . . .
- The courage that comes from friendships we'll never forget . . .

Each of these (or just two or three, depending on your time constraints) can be filled out with specific anecdotes about you and people you know, making the abstract value of "courage" concrete and memorable.

Keep Clichés Under Control We've all heard graduation speeches, and we all know the familiar clichés:

- You are the future . . .
- This is the first day of the rest of your life . . .
- Follow your dreams . . .
- You'll always remember these days . . .
- As we look back, we should also look forward . . .
- This is not just an end, but a beginning . . .

These phrases and themes became trite because they are in fact so appropriate. A graduation is a certainly a time to reflect on times past and those to come, to relish what has been accomplished and what can be achieved in the future, and so on. Your challenge is to find a way to express these ideas without using the same stock phrases.

How do you do this? One way is to draw on personal experience. Look back on your own educational experiences and think about specific incidents or stories that can concretely and vividly illustrate the clichés, so you can invoke the truth in them without merely restating them. You might choose a story from current events as well, as long as it is sufficiently well known. But whether you are talking about the latest news or pop culture or music, you have to be sure you know your audience or you'll be leaving some people in the dark.

Consider Metaphors Another rich source for ceremonial speaking is metaphor (Chapter 10). Perhaps you have some area of expertise that

---

FAQ *What should I keep in mind for any speech at a significant life event?*

- *Prepare.* You only get one shot at the toast, eulogy, or other speech, so you should have an idea in advance of what you want to say.
- *Words are a gift.* Your main goal should be to give the couple, the mourners, or the audience the gift of a good or comforting memory, and if you do it right, your speech will become an important part of how they remember the occasion.
- *It's not about you.* Your primary concern should be the person or persons you are honoring, so you should speak in a way that honors and draws attention to them, as opposed to showcasing yourself.

could provide you with a rich set of metaphors for talking about the passage of time, accomplishments, lessons learned, goals for the future, and so forth.

Metaphors or similes from sports can be trite, unless they are enlivened by personal experience. "College (or high school) is a team sport" becomes an effective metaphor when it's filled out with your experience or the experiences and accomplishments of people in the audience.

Graduation remarks and commencement speeches allow you to recognize an important accomplishment of a group of people with reference to the values of that group. A graduation is a public ceremony, and the speech that accompanies it should invoke the relevant publics as the audience for it. Excellent graduation speakers reframe the significance of the experience for the people graduating, allowing them to see the value of their achievement in the context of the larger world outside of school.

Speeches at Ceremonies

As you become more involved in your workplace and community, you will have even more opportunities to use your communication skills. Ceremonial events may take place in a professional context (an awards ceremony at your workplace, for example) or be occasioned by another group you belong to (an annual banquet with a civic group, such as the Independent Order of Odd Fellows, the Masons, the Junior League, or the Rotary). At any of these, there may be speakers that you will need to introduce, speeches of entertainment to give, and awards given and received.

Introducing a Speaker

Although in informal settings, speakers can introduce themselves, in more formal situations, they need someone to introduce them, and that someone might be you. In introducing a speaker, your task is to arouse the audience's interest in the person and to honor him or her in the process. If you do this well, you can help generate excitement and interest in the speaker's talk and make the occasion more enjoyable for the audience. You're trying to connect the speaker to the audience, and the audience to the speaker. In effect you are serving both as an ambassador to the speaker on behalf of the audience, and as an ambassador for the speaker to the group.

In all professional settings, if you are introducing or talking about someone, be sure you pronounce the person's name correctly. If you're not sure, ask in advance, write it out phonetically, and practice. Nothing creates ill will or damages your credibility faster than a mispronounced name. In professional settings, you'll usually be able to contact either the speaker or the organizers, and you can do research not only about correct pronunciation but about other information you'll need to create a great introduction.

The two most important goals for your introduction are to boost the speaker's ethos (see Chapter 7) by indicating why the audience should be interested in him or her and to demonstrate why the speaker either has an interesting perspective on the topic of the speech or is uniquely qualified to address it.

Make It a Complete Speech   Despite the fact that it may take only one or two minutes, an introduction for a speaker has the structure of a complete speech—with a beginning, a middle, and an end—but all in miniature. Just as in any other speech, the body is the important part, in which you need to clarify your topic and purpose and explain why it's important to the audience—that is, why the speaker is especially qualified to be holding forth on this topic.

At an April 2012 speech, University of Colorado student Daniel Paiz worked his personal experience and concerns into his introduction of guest speaker President Barack Obama.

R. Marsh Starks/UNLV Photo Services

Start It Right   The introduction to your introduction speech should be light and brief, and it should have a strong topical connection to either the speaker or the content of his or her speech. For example,

> **We have the privilege tonight of being able to hear a stranger who is actually a friend and who can tell us a lot about improving our service work to the community.**

Give It Substance   You can cover some basic information in the body of the introduction. Here is a basic list, which you should adapt to the specific situation:

- Basic biographical information about the speaker
- The speaker's qualifications or special accomplishments or both
- Information that helps the audience understand why the speaker was invited to speak
- The title or topic of the speaker's talk
- A reflection of excitement about the speaker's talk

When you talk about the speaker's accomplishments, focus especially on the ones that are relevant to this audience. Rather than read a laundry list of awards and milestones, it's often better to pick a couple of them and give a brief explanation of why each is noteworthy.

Clinch It   End your speech of introduction by briefly stating why you are looking forward to the speaker's talk or thanking the speaker in advance. Acknowledging the

---

Try It!   *Creating an Introduction*

Think of two people, one a friend and one a relative. Suppose they are both winning an award for "Best Person of the Year." Write a brief introduction for each.

- How were your introductions similar and different?
- How much information did you feel you needed about each person to create an appropriate speech of introduction?

speaker's generosity in coming to address your group creates an inviting climate that will help put him or her at ease. A good introduction helps the audience understand the speech and puts the speaker in the best position to be compelling and memorable.

After-Dinner Speaking

after-dinner speech A humorous speech given after a meal; discusses an important topic but is not the reason the group has gathered.

After-dinner speaking is just what you would guess: a speech or a talk given at a dinner event or meeting, after everyone has eaten. Typically, if the purpose of meeting is serious and focused on a topic relevant to the group, such as sales reports, new products, or scholarly research, after-dinner speaking is meant to be more like entertainment. But it shouldn't be just comedy or a series of jokes. It should strike a balance between fun and information, and the humor must be gentle.

The best way to understand the after-dinner speech is as a humorous speech with a serious point. Why humorous? Because after dinner, it's hard for the audience to listen. They're full of dinner (and maybe working on dessert), and it's been a long day, so you'll need some humor to wake them up and get their attention. After-dinner speaking may actually be one of the most challenging speaking situations—with a hostile audience, in contrast, at least you can be assured they are listening, if only so they can refute you!

An after-dinner speech needs a topic or theme. It can be related to the purpose of the group or occasion, or you may have the freedom to choose what you want to talk about. In that case, you can find a topic using the techniques we discussed in Chapter 5, by taking inventory of what you know or what you're interested in. For example, you could start with a big-picture issue like global warming and do a humorous take on it:

> **Have you ever thought about all the different places that oil—in the form of energy or plastic—comes up in our daily lives? It heats our homes, fuels our cars. We are even wearing oil, though most of us don't know it.**

You could say several funny things about petroleum-based fabrics and products and then move on to the larger point about our dependence on oil. Or you start with something seemingly ordinary and gradually work toward your real topic:

> **Have you ever noticed how many times a day you check your phone? For email, for texts, for phone messages, tweets, Facebook, and more? It's almost like my phone controls me, and it's saying "Hey. Hey! HEY!" and I just can't ignore it. Wait—maybe our phones do run our lives, and we don't even realize it.**

You could give many different humorous examples, illustrating ways in which technology can turn from a tool into a lifestyle.

After-dinner speeches typically fall flat when they go to one of two extremes: stand-up comedy or an attempt to be completely serious, like a persuasive speech. Instead, use all the skills of audience adaptation you honed for informative and persuasive speeches to find a topic that will be intrinsically interesting, and then give it a light and enjoyable treatment.

What's funny? You have to start, of course, with your own sense of humor and what you find amusing. But then you have to ask hard questions about your ideas because humor can go wrong quite easily. First, avoid political or religious controversy; there is almost no way you can find humor in these topics that won't offend someone in the audience. Second, don't use humor that relies too much on stereotypes—men are like this, women are like that. Instead, try to stick with common human situations,

Neil DeGrasse Tyson, director of the Hayden Planetarium in New York City, brings the romance and importance of astronomy down to earth for audiences.

the grist of what's known as "observational comedy": the challenge of relationships, dealing with difficult people, struggling with technology, finding motivation when things get difficult, learning from travel or a hobby.

Even when you're talking about something which is, in the big picture, a problem, try to keep things relatively positive. Don't try to hammer a point home; just keep the relevance obvious. If you can work in some lightly self-deprecating humor, that will endear you to audiences. Clearly, you'll want to avoid sarcasm and irony, because not only are these often perceived negatively, but also you run the risk of letting the audience feel left out of the joke if you use irony, or worry that it's aimed at them if you use sarcasm. And of course, nothing X-rated or even off-color is acceptable.

Presenting an Award

Sometimes you will find yourself being an award presenter, which is a bit different from being an introducer. Here you will both introduce the person and make clear what the award is and why the person deserves to receive it. To prepare well for a speech in which you will present an award, you need to understand the *meaning* of the award and master the *mechanics* of this special type of speech.

The Meaning of the Award　You will want to begin by saying something about what this award means. Why is it given? What history or traditions are associated with it? Are there outstanding previous recipients who should be mentioned? Are any of them present? You should acknowledge them; do so by name if there are not too many. You should also explain why this recipient is being given the award—what were his or her accomplishments? Who made the decision to give the award? Although you'll want to research the answers to these questions—typically by reading the information provided by the organization giving out the honor—you should try to explain in your own words and make them sincere. For example,

> **It's truly my pleasure to be presenting the 25-Year Length of Service**
> **award to Emily Vanderpool. This award, which comes from the**
> **president of our company, acknowledges the important service**

provided by long-time employees. In a world where people change jobs and careers on a regular basis, it is no small achievement to work 25 years in one company. I know myself—and anyone here who has received a 10- or 20-Year award will back me up—that it takes determination and dedication not only to remain on the job for 25 years, but to do it in an outstanding way. Let me tell you a little bit about Emily's accomplishments . . .

The Mechanics of Presenting It   You can use a few specific strategies to heighten the sense of drama that accompanies the presentation of an award. First, don't call the person up while you're making the introduction; that just forces him or her to stand there awkwardly. If there is a plaque or trophy, hold it where people can see it while you speak, and hold it as if it were something truly precious. Sometimes the name of the winner is known to the audience (and it may be in the program), but in other cases you may be building drama by *not* saying the name until later in your speech. Describing the person and his or her accomplishments before saying the name can be exciting, though you shouldn't let it go on so long that it becomes annoying.

At the conclusion of your speech, invite the winner up with a gesture, look him or her in the eye and smile while shaking hands, and then hand over the award and invite the audience to applaud, if they have not already started. Be sure not to turn your back on the audience, or stand between the audience and the recipient. To continue the previous example:

And so, in light of these accomplishments, I would like everyone to congratulate Emily on her award—not only is it well deserved, but it makes us appreciate her all the more.

Celebrity chef Jamie Oliver, recipient of an award from the Harvard School of Public Health, speaks widely to promote healthier diets for schoolchildren.

© Frantzesco Kangaris/Alamy

People long remember the moment they received an award, and you can use your speaking skills to make it special and memorable.

Many situations in your personal and professional life will require you to "get up and say a few words." With the skills you've gained from this book, you have the tools to master these occasions. Everything you've learned about audiences, adaptation, organization, language, and delivery will enable you be to be outstanding.

Group Presentations

Group presentations are made by two to six speakers; often the group has been doing research or creative work and the members decide to present it together. In a group presentation like this, let's assume you're going to use all the best public speaking skills you have learned through this book: making choices about content, organization, language, and delivery, thinking carefully about audience, and so on. Let's also assume your fellow speakers done their homework and are good speakers too. Now what? Even if you are a fantastic presenter, you're still left with the problem of coordinating everything you want to achieve with the other people you'll be presenting with.

A group has to work hard to make sure it is a *group* presentation, and not just a bunch of people all standing up at the same time. What's the difference? An effective group presentation maximizes the skills of the presenters so that it adds up to much more than just a string of good speeches. It presents a consistent set of ideas and arguments in a compelling way; it is seamless, and the audience doesn't even notice the work that went into coordinating it.

A weak group presentation is chaos; no one is sure who is speaking, what each speaker has to do with the others, where the presentation is going, or what its point is. Here is the danger: Even if everyone is individually a good speaker, the group presentation can still crash and burn.

The keys to excellent group work are *cooperation* and *coordination*. By cooperation, we mean the collaboration that goes into preparing the presentation. Coordination means using effective techniques for managing multiple speakers, and perhaps technologies, in the presentation itself. Because you're not in sole control of the presentation, these strategies must be added to the skills you've mastered for preparing effective informative speeches. Let's look at each in turn.

group presentation A coordinated report by two to six people about their group's research or creative work.

 FAQ *It seems like a lot of work. Are there any advantages to group presentations?*

Yes, there are advantages; the work you put in can pay off for all of you.

- Each person has strengths and weaknesses, and you can set up the group presentation to take advantage of everyone's strengths
- When it is well done, the transition between speakers keeps the audience's interest.
- The transition between speakers creates a sense of forward movement in the presentation.
- Members can support each other, and camaraderie can help reduce nerves—you're not alone up there.
- During the question and answer period, you have the advantage of more knowledge and expertise in answering questions.

Cooperation

Even if the speakers are skilled and knowledgeable, a group presentation's success depends on what happens during the preparation phase. The biggest mistake your group can make is to say, "Let's all go off and prepare, and we'll put the pieces together on the day." That is a recipe for disaster. Why? Suppose your group was putting together a meal, and each person was to make one part, the appetizer, the soup, the

In group presentations, the challenge for each speaker is to make a contribution that will allow the group to be outstanding and effective.

main course, dessert and so on. Without cooperation, what happens? The appetizer is chicken wings, the soup is chicken noodle, the main course is roast chicken, and . . . you get the idea. Even if each dish were well prepared, it's a disappointing and unsatisfactory meal.

Planning In putting together a meal—or a group presentation—the key is planning. The group has to sketch out the parts in advance and make sure they fit together in a satisfying way. First, members have to agree on a topic and purpose: What will we be talking about, and what do we want to accomplish? You might be doing a class project requiring a presentation, or speaking at a sales meeting, or presenting your designs for a better mousetrap to an engineering firm, or outlining to the city council why a new park is needed and where it should be built.

Even when group members work on their own, they should make choices consistent with the common topic and purpose. Of course, in choosing your group's topic and purpose, you'll want to think about all the usual things: relevance to the audience, situation constraints (time, technology), and so on.

Division of Labor Next, divide up the work. You probably shouldn't expect that everyone will give an individual speech, or it may be hard to stay within the time frame you have. It's better to assign one or two people—based on their experience, expertise, or willingness—to each take responsibility for one of the parts of the larger presentation, which include

- Research
- Themes/arguments
- Organization
- Slides/technology

Obviously, after people have done some of their work on these areas, the group will want to gather again to share results and check progress. Sometimes you'll need to adjust your goals or your methods, and more meetings will probably be advisable as you advance in your task.

High-quality group presentations require a lot of discussion and contact. It's immediately obvious when you're watching a group whether they have put the appropriate amount of time into group preparation and cooperation.

Speaking Times   As you divide up the speaking in your presentation, think about how much time each presenter will have. You probably want to try to give everyone roughly equal amounts; otherwise, it may seem that one speaker or one section is far more important than the others. It's also important to minimize transition and not switch between speakers more often than necessary. For example, changing speakers every two minutes is distracting, rather than interesting, and increases the burden of trying to make transitions and keep the presentation coherent.

■ Coordination

The first step in coordinating a group presentation is organizing the presence of more than one person on the stage. You have to figure out how your presentation will become a single coherent presentation from the group and not a series of little speeches that happen one after another. Obviously, everybody needs to practice together, but the bigger question is about the "hand off" between speakers. How do you avoid awkward silence and shuffling, with everyone looking at each other, hoping somebody remembers what's next? Two methods have proved successful: relay presentations and the master of ceremonies.

Relay Presentations   In a **relay presentation**, each person hands off the topic to the next one. You can design your overall presentation as one big speech, with an introduction, a body consisting of two or three points, and a conclusion. Then assign each of these sections to a speaker. If you have four people, let the same person present the introduction and conclusion. If you have only three, someone will present at least two of the points in the body. In this style, the presentation is like a relay race: Each person passes off to the next when finished and then sits down or steps backs.

> **relay presentation**   A group presentation structured as one speech, in which the speakers take one or more of the elements and transition to the next speaker.

Master of Ceremonies   The **master of ceremonies**, or MC, is the person who manages the whole presentation, like the conductor of an orchestra who points to each musician or section when it's their turn to play. If you use a master of ceremonies, you can divide up the presentation however you like.

> **master of ceremonies**   MC; the person who provides the introductions and transitions in a group presentation.

Transitions   In the MC style, transitions are easier for the participants, because the MC does them. In the relay style, each person has to make a smooth and clear transition to the next speaker.

In either case, transitions that work need two things: (1) a really strong preview and (2) transition notes that are written out in advance. Without a strong preview, the audience will already be lost, and good transitions may help but will not save the day. Making up transitions on the fly is foolish, because no matter how well you know the material, they won't be as strong as if you thought them through beforehand.

Advantages and Disadvantages of Each Method   The relay style is simple and direct and probably takes a little less time. But it requires that each speaker be really good at making the transition to the next one. The MC style requires a little more time, as the MC cuts in to make the transition at the end of each segment, but it allows the rest of the presenters to just focus on their particular section.

Delivering the Group Presentation

The many different faces and voices introduce a lot of variety into your group presentation, so it's important to provide continuity that balances it out. Similar structure throughout the presentation will help keep the audience focused. Make your slides or handouts consistent in style. Organize each section of the presentation in a similar way, and make clear to the audience that you're doing so. If the speakers and their content are tied together stylistically and organizationally, they create a presentation whose parts are "cut from the same cloth," meaning that its variation has regularity to it.

Rehearsing the Group Presentation

A group presentation requires at least three full run-throughs, to check for time, transitions, and coordination. You need to do the whole presentation, everyone saying his or her bit, or you won't know what is likely to go wrong or how to fix it. Even more than a solo presentation, a group presentation requires you not only to be good at your speech but to coordinate with others as well. So pay attention not only to the quality of your own performance but also to how it interacts with those of the others.

- Do you go on for too long and take someone else's time away?
- Is someone doing that to you?
- Does some of your material overlap with someone else's?
- Does your part connect to the preceding one in the same way the transition says it does?

These are problems to diagnose and fix at the rehearsal stage.

Whatever technology your group decides to use, be sure to practice with it, too, and make sure everybody in the group knows how to use it. From the laptop to the projector to the slide program, you need to have people back up as well as technology back up to ensure that everything goes well on the day of the presentation.

Summary

Access an interactive eBook, chapter-specific interactive learning tools, including flashcards, quizzes, videos and more in your Speech Communication CourseMate for *Public Speaking*, accessed through CengageBrain.com.

Though occasional speeches impose a number of unique demands on a speaker, the basic rules for composing a good speech still apply. You can use what you've already learned about audiences, publics, and adaptation by thinking about the constraints provided by the occasion. This will allow you to make appropriate choices in deciding what to say at a particular ceremonial event. With cooperation and coordination, you'll be able to extend your skills to the group setting as well.

QUESTIONS FOR REVIEW

1. How do occasional speeches differ from the typical persuasive or informative speech? What advice would you give someone about composing a speech for an occasion like a wedding or a funeral? An after-dinner speech?
2. What are the some of the qualities or characteristics of the speeches that you might give at any of the following life occasions: weddings, funerals, and graduations?
3. How should you give an introduction for a speaker? What factors about the occasion should you consider?
4. What factors should you consider in a composing your part of a group presentation?

QUESTIONS FOR DISCUSSION

1. Which ceremonial occasions are most difficult to speak at? For you? In general?
2. Think of a time when you spoke about someone's life transition—whether to a group or to that individual person. How did you decide what to say? Did you use a formula or cliché, or try to be original? How would you do it differently if you could?
3. What makes group presentations challenging? What makes them rewarding? What are some concrete ways in which you might approach your next one differently?

Appendix: Selected Speeches

Statement to the Iowa House Judiciary Committee

Zach Wahls

January 31, 2011

Good evening Mr. Chairman. My name is Zach Wahls. I'm a sixth-generation Iowan and an engineering student at the University of Iowa and I was raised by two women.

My biological mom, Terry, told her grandparents that she was pregnant, that the artificial insemination had worked, and they wouldn't even acknowledge it.

It wasn't until I was born and they succumbed to my infantile cuteness that they broke down and told her that they were thrilled to have another grandson.

Unfortunately, neither of them lived to see her marry her partner Jackie of 15 years when they wed in 2009.

My younger sister and only sibling was born in 1994. We actually have the same anonymous donor so we're full siblings, which is really cool for me.

Um, I guess the point is our family really isn't so different from any other Iowa family. You know, when I'm home we go to church together, we eat dinner, we go on vacations. Ah, but, you know, we have our hard times too, we get in fights . . . you know.

Actually my mom, Terry was diagnosed with multiple sclerosis in 2000. It is a devastating disease that put her in a wheelchair. So we've had our struggles.

But, you know, we're Iowans. We don't expect anyone to solve our problems for us. We'll fight our own battles. We just hope for equal and fair treatment from our government.

Being a student at the University of Iowa, the topic of same sex marriage comes up quite frequently in classroom discussions . . . you know The question always comes down to, well, "Can gays even raise kids?"

In question, you know, the conversation gets quiet for a moment because most people don't really have any answer. And then I raise my hand and say, "Actually, I was raised by a gay couple, and I'm doing pretty well."

I scored in the 99th percentile on the A.C.T. I'm actually an Eagle Scout. I own and operate my own small business. If I was your son, Mr. Chairman, I believe I'd make you very proud.

I'm not really so different from any of your children. My family really isn't so different from yours. After all, your family doesn't derive its sense of worth from being told by the state: "You're married. Congratulations." No.

The sense of family comes from the commitment we make to each other. To work through the hard times so we can enjoy the good ones. It comes from the love that binds us. That's what makes a family.

So what you're voting here isn't to change us. It's not to change our families, it's to change how the law views us; how the law treats us. You are voting for the first time in the history of our state to codify discrimination into our constitution, a constitution that but for the proposed amendment, is the least amended constitution in the United States of America.

You are telling Iowans that some among you are second class citizens who do not have the right to marry the person you love.

So will this vote affect my family? Will it affect yours?

In the next two hours I'm sure we're going to hear plenty of testimony about how damaging having gay parents is on kids.

But in my 19 years, not once have I ever been confronted by an individual who realized independently that I was raised by a gay couple.

And you know why? Because the sexual orientation of my parents has had zero effect on the content of my character.

Thank you very much.

Rated "D" for Deficiency: The Sunshine Vitamin

Nicole Platzar
Suffolk University, Massachusetts
Coached by Bruce Wickelgren, Jodi Nevola, Bonnie MacEachern, Stephanie Orme, and Tylor Orme

When four month old Jayden Wray suffered severe brain damage and multiple fractures to his arms, leg and skull, his parents, Chana-Al-Alis and Rohan Wray, were left with the blame. According to the January 6, 2012 Huffington Post, Jayden's life ended as soon as the life support respirators were shut off. Many believed that Jayden's bones shattered as a result of vicious blows to his head and from being brutally grabbed and tossed by his parents. An arduous court case played out that left the world in awe, for the "unfit parents" were acquitted. According to BBC News from January 26 2012, Dr. Schiemberg, a pediatric pathologist, proved that fractures in the baby's bones were not caused by shaking but rather the result of severe rickets, a common side effect in individuals who do not get enough Vitamin D.

Vitamin D is critical for the proper functioning of the brain, heart and even the immune system according to a Science News article from July 16th, 2011. And yet Vitamin D deficiency is a prevalent and wildly unnoticed issue in our world. According to the *New England Journal of Medicine* an estimated 1 billion people worldwide, across all ethnicities and age groups have Vitamin D deficiency. As many as 57% of adults have insufficient levels of this nutrient or in other words 6 out of 10 people. Additionally, Dr. Richard Kremer of McGill University Health Center concludes that abnormal levels of this sunshine vitamin are associated with a whole spectrum of diseases. Thus, it is imperative that we examine this issue that affects a vast majority of Americans, most of whom are completely unaware. Today, we will be able to better understand Vitamin D deficiency through first examining the causes and effects before finally proposing solutions to this silent epidemic.

So, why aren't Americans getting their needed doses of Vitamin D? There a generally two main causes for this deficiency: a simple lack of exposure to sunlight and misconceptions about our own nutrition.

First, Vitamin D deficiency largely boils down to one simple fact: we are not getting outside as much as we should. Unfortunately, the sun's ultraviolet B rays are the main and most efficient source of this nutrient. The February 2007 issue of the *Harvard Men's Health Watch* explains that the suns energy turns a chemical in your skin into vitamin D3 which gets carried to your liver and then finally to your kidneys where it gets metabolized and is then able to be sent to its multiple receptors throughout the body. The previously cited Science News article explains that Vitamin D controls cell activity, allowing either activation or deactivation of certain genes that affect immune reactions, muscle maintenance, and calcium absorption. However, Dr. NJ Bosworth, author of "Mitigating Epidemic Vitamin D Deficiency," notes as humankind has become more urbanized, their exposure to sunlight has decreased which results in fewer opportunities for the skin to synthesize Vitamin D. When we are outside we are covered in clothing and sunscreen which keeps us from getting Vitamin D. This is an even bigger concern in the winter or even year-round anywhere north of the San Francisco/Philadelphia latitude, because UVB rays are not direct enough to give us sufficient amounts of Vitamin D.

Next, our misconceptions about vitamin D's presence in our food products have perpetuated Vitamin D deficiency. According to *The New Yorker* from March 2011 most people believe that dairy products such as milk and yogurt are packed with vitamin D. However, in reality they are not. These products are "fortified" which means that critical nutrients are added to them. According to its label, fortified milk contains 100 International Units of Vitamin D, but on average may only contain 50 IU. An increasing amount of experts suggest at least 1000 to 2000 IU daily for optimum health. This means one would have to drink at least 8 glasses of 8oz milk to get near that amount. Additionally, according to the Institute of Medicine few foods are actually rich in vitamin D, only 10% of our levels come from diet. Dr. Edward Giovannuci a nutrition researcher at the Harvard University School of Public Health warns against diet being the only source of Vitamin D.

Not getting enough Vitamin D can have major effects on our health and well-being. To better understand the harms of Vitamin D deficiency, we can first, examine the effects it has on the musculoskeletal system and second, how it increases the likelihood of various diseases.

To begin with, one of the most common physical harms that arise from a Vitamin D deficiency is damage to the musculoskeletal system, which is the organ system that allows for mobility, and includes the muscular and skeletal systems. The American College of Gastroenterology explains that in children Vitamin D deficiency most commonly manifests itself through the childhood disease, Rickets. Rickets, leads to weakened bones that produce deformities such as bowed legs and curvature of the spine, making for consistent and sometimes life-long pain. In fact, the *Daily Mail* article from October 27 2011 states that in the past five years, 85% of pediatric dietitians have seen a rise in rickets cases. In adults, Vitamin D deficiency results in osteomalacia which is a defect in bone mineralization. With severe cases, bone mineral content is lost, causing severe bone pain, which can result in osteoporosis. This escalates the risk for bone fractures, muscle weakness and increased fall risk. Thus, it is imperative that we maintain proper levels of this vitamin so that our musculoskeletal system can thrive.

Furthermore, a lack of Vitamin D is also a catalyst to autoimmune and cardiovascular diseases as well as deadly cancers. A large scale study conducted by the University of Kansas in 2010 revealed that being Vitamin D deficient doubled a participant's risk of death from heart disease whereas those who obtained proper amounts of Vitamin D cut their risk by 60%! Moreover, Vitamin D has found to be crucial in combating the rogue nature of cancer cells. It has the ability to regulate tumor-suppressing proteins that decrease cell proliferation and increases cell differentiation. Additionally, it has been shown to prevent tumors from building through limiting the web of blood vessels they are composed of from receiving nutrients. According to the Clinical Journal of the American Society of Nephrology the risk of developing colon, breast and prostate cancer can be reduced by 30-50% through raising deficient Vitamin D Winning Orations 2012 levels. Researchers found that women who were deficient had a 253% increased risk for developing colon cancer, and women who raised their intake of Vitamin D over a four year period reduced developing cancer by greater than 60%.

Many are unaware of their own inadequate levels and uniformed about the importance of Vitamin D on their lives. And yet, Vitamin D deficiency is a problem that can be so easily solved! The solutions are twofold and can be implemented on a universal and individual level.

To start with, on an institutional level, effective public health measures need to be set in place for combatting Vitamin D deficiency. Movements paved by organizations such as The Vitamin D Council need to be supported. Their mission to end the worldwide Vitamin D deficiency is to bring awareness and educate the general populace, the health industry and policy makers on the importance of Vitamin D. They believe through outreach and awareness, research and activism, this epidemic can be silenced. Education is key to prevention and therefore it is critical to introduce school health classes and programs that would make Vitamin D education part of the curriculum. Additionally, the FDA needs to set stricter labeling regulations for foods containing Vitamin D so that the labels we read on our products are verified and true. The key correlation between Vitamin D levels and disease is its preventative measures; therefore enforcing this fact throughout our world is imperative.

Subsequently on a personal level, a simple change in lifestyle can significantly boost our Vitamin D intake, all by starting with spending more time outdoors. Dr. Hollick of Boston University suggests spending 10 to 15 minutes outdoors with unprotected skin, except for the face, which should always be covered with sunscreen. Doing this a mere two or three times a week can help to achieve healthy levels for fair skinned people. Naturally, those with more pigmented skin or live somewhere where UVB rays are indirect may need to spend closer to 20-30 minutes outside. Everyone's natural levels are different. Ask your doctor for a blood test for the active form of Vitamin D to identify where your levels are and then your doctor can tell you how much you need to intake daily. You can also boost your Vitamin D levels with supplements. Reinhold Veith of the University of Toronoto reports taking a supplement of 1000 IU, which is a moderate amount that can be a solution for a majority of people. Finally, when it comes to diet, oily fish such as tuna, salmon and mackerel are the best sources of Vitamin D.

Conclusively, Vitamin D is not a trivial matter and a deficit of it can result in serious, life altering effects. The young Wray family is only 1 family among a growing population who have suffered a devastating loss as a result of lacking Vitamin D. This is an escalating problem that we all can walk out of this room today and prevent by tweaking a couple small things in our daily lives. Today we discussed the causes, effects and solutions to the Vitamin D deficiency that is sweeping our world. Be proactive, soak up a couple rays and order the salmon at dinner.

Speech at Kensington Town Hall ("Britain Awake") (The Iron Lady)*

Margaret Thatcher

January 19, 1976, London

The first duty of any Government is to safeguard its people against external aggression. To guarantee the survival of our way of life.

The question we must now ask ourselves is whether the present Government is fulfilling that duty. It is dismantling our defences at a moment when the strategic threat to Britain and her allies from an expansionist power is graver than at any moment since the end of the last war.

Military men are always warning us that the strategic balance is tilting against NATO and the west.

But the Socialists never listen.

They don't seem to realise that the submarines and missiles that the Russians are building could be destined to be used against us.

Perhaps some people in the Labour Party think we are on the same side as the Russians!

But just let's look at what the Russians are doing.

She's ruled by a dictatorship of patient, far-sighted determined men who are rapidly making their country the foremost naval and military power in the world.

They are not doing this solely for the sake of self-defence.

A huge, largely land-locked country like Russia does not need to build the most powerful navy in the world just to guard its own frontiers.

No. The Russians are bent on world dominance, and they are rapidly acquiring the means to become the most powerful imperial nation the world has seen.

The men in the Soviet politburo don't have to worry about the ebb and flow of public opinion. They put guns before butter, while we put just about everything before guns.

They know that they are a super power in only one sense—the military sense.

They are a failure in human and economic terms.

But let us make no mistake. The Russians calculate that their military strength will more than make up for their economic and social weakness. They are determined to use it in order to get what they want from us.

Last year on the eve of the Helsinki Conference, I warned that the Soviet Union is spending 20 per cent more each year than the United States on military research and development. 25 per cent more on weapons and equipment. 60 per cent more on strategic nuclear forces.

In the past ten years Russia has spent 50 per cent more than the United States on naval shipbuilding.

Some military experts believe that Russia has already achieved strategic superiority over America.

*Copyright Lady Thatcher. Reproduced with permission from www.margaretthatcher.org, the website of the Margaret Thatcher Foundation.

But it is the balance of conventional forces which poses the most immediate dangers for NATO.

I am going to visit our troops in Germany on Thursday. I am going at a moment when the Warsaw Pact forces—that is, the forces of Russia and her allies—in Central Europe outnumber NATOs by 150,000 men nearly 10,000 tanks and 2,600 aircraft. We cannot afford to let that gap get bigger.

Still more serious gaps have opened up elsewhere—especially in the troubled area of Southern Europe and the Mediterranean.

The rise of Russia as a world-wide naval power, threatens our oil rigs and our traditional life-lines, the sea routes.

Over the past ten years, the Russians have quadrupled their force of nuclear submarines. They are now building one nuclear submarine a month.

They are searching for new naval base facilities all over the world, while we are giving up our few remaining bases.

They have moved into the Indian Ocean. They pose a rising threat to our northern waters and, farther east to Japan's vital sea routes.

The Soviet navy is not designed for self-defence. We do not have to imagine an all-out nuclear war or even a conventional war in order to see how it could be used for political purposes.

I would be the first to welcome any evidence that the Russians are ready to enter into a genuine detente. But I am afraid that the evidence points the other way.

I warned before Helsinki of the dangers of falling for an illusory detente. Some people were sceptical at the time, but we now see that my warning was fully justified.

Has detente induced the Russians to cut back on their defence programme?

Has it dissuaded them from brazen intervention in Angola?

Has it led to any improvement in the conditions of Soviet citizens, or the subject populations of Eastern Europe?

We know the answers.

At Helsinki we endorsed the status quo in Eastern Europe. In return we had hoped for the freer movement of people and ideas across the Iron Curtain. So far we have got nothing of substance.

We are devoted, as we always have been, to the maintenance of peace.

We will welcome any initiative from the Soviet Union that would contribute to that goal.

But we must also heed the warnings of those, like Alexander Solzhenitsyn , who remind us that we have been fighting a kind of 'Third World War' over the entire period since 1945—and that we have been steadily losing ground.

As we look back over the battles of the past year, over the list of countries that have been lost to freedom or are imperilled by Soviet expansion can we deny that Solzhenitsyn is right?

We have seen Vietnam and all of Indochina swallowed up by Communist aggression. We have seen the Communists make an open grab for power in Portugal, our oldest ally—a sign that many of the battles in the Third World War are being fought inside Western countries.

And now the Soviet Union and its satellites are pouring money, arms and front-line troops into Angola in the hope of dragging it into the Communist bloc.

We must remember that there are no Queensbury rules in the contest that is now going on. And the Russians are playing to win.

They have one great advantage over us—the battles are being fought on our territory, not theirs.

Within a week of the Helsinki conference, Mr. Zarodov, a leading Soviet ideologue, was writing in Pravda about the need for the Communist Parties of Western Europe to forget about tactical compromises with Social Democrats, and take the offensive in order to bring about proletarian revolution.

Later Mr. Brezhnev made a statement in which he gave this article his personal endorsement.

If this is the line that the Soviet leadership adopts at its Party Congress next month, then we must heed their warning. It undoubtedly applies to us too.

We in Britain cannot opt out of the world.

If we cannot understand why the Russians are rapidly becoming the greatest naval and military power the world has ever seen if we cannot draw the lesson of what they tried to do in Portugal and are now trying to do in Angola then we are destined—in their words—to end up on 'the scrap heap of history'.

We look to our alliance with American and NATO as the main guarantee of our own security and, in the world beyond Europe, the United States is still the prime champion of freedom.

But we are all aware of how the bitter experience of Vietnam has changed the public mood in America. We are also aware of the circumstances that inhibit action by an American president in an election year.

So it is more vital then ever that each and every one of us within NATO should contribute his proper share to the defence of freedom.

Britain, with her world-wide experience of diplomacy and defence, has a special role to play. We in the Conservative Party are determined that Britain should fulfil that role.

We're not harking back to some nostalgic illusion about Britain's role in the past.

We're saying—Britain has a part to play now, a part to play for the future.

The advance of Communist power threatens our whole way of life. That advance is not irreversible, providing that we take the necessary measures now. But the longer that we go on running down our means of survival, the harder it will be to catch up.

In other words: the longer Labour remains in Government, the more vulnerable this country will be. (Applause.)

What has this Government been doing with our defences?

Under the last defence review, the Government said it would cut defence spending by £4,700 million over the next nine years.

Then they said they would cut a further £110 million.

It now seems that we will see further cuts.

If there are further cuts, perhaps the [Roy Mason] Defence Secretary should change his title, for the sake of accuracy, to the Secretary for Insecurity.

On defence, we are now spending less per head of the population than any of our major allies. Britain spends only £90 per head on defence. West Germany spends £130, France spends £115. The United States spends £215. Even neutral Sweden spends £60 more per head than we do.

Of course, we are poorer than most of our NATO allies. This is part of the disastrous economic legacy of Socialism.

But let us be clear about one thing.

This is not a moment when anyone with the interests of this country at heart should be talking about cutting our defences.

It is a time when we urgently need to strengthen our defences.

Of course this places a burden on us. But it is one that we must be willing to bear if we want our freedom to survive.

Throughout our history, we have carried the torch for freedom. Now, as I travel the world, I find people asking again and again, "What has happened to Britain?" They want to know why we are hiding our heads in the sand, why with all our experience, we are not giving a lead.

Many people may not be aware, even now, of the full extent of the threat.

We expect our Governments to take a more far-sighted view.

To give them their due, the Government spelled out the extent of the peril in their Defence White Paper last year, But, having done so, they drew the absurd conclusion that our defence efforts should be reduced.

The Socialists, in fact, seem to regard defence as almost infinitely cuttable. They are much more cautious when it comes to cutting other types of public expenditure.

They seem to think that we can afford to go deeper into debt so that the Government can prop up a loss-making company. And waste our money on the profligate extension of nationalisation and measures such as the Community Land Act.

Apparently, we can even afford to lend money to the Russians, at a lower rate of interest that we have to pay on our own borrowings.

But we cannot afford, in Labour's view, to maintain our defences at the necessary level—not even at a time when on top of our NATO commitments, we are fighting a major internal war against terrorism in Northern Ireland, and need more troops in order to win it.

There are crises farther from home that could affect us deeply. Angola is the most immediate.

In Angola, the Soviet-backed guerrilla movement, the MPLA, is making rapid headway in its current offensive, despite the fact that it controls only a third of the population, and is supported by even less.

The MPLA is gaining ground because the Soviet Union and its satellites are pouring money, guns and front-line troops into the battle.

Six thousand Cuban regular soldiers are still there.

But it is obvious that an acceptable solution for Angola is only possible if all outside powers withdraw their military support.

You might well ask: why on earth should we think twice about what is happening in a far-away place like Angola?

There are four important reasons.

The first is that Angola occupies a vital strategic position. If the pro-Soviet faction wins, one of the immediate consequences will almost certainly be the setting up of Soviet air and naval bases on the South Atlantic.

The second reason is that the presence of Communist forces in this area will make it much more difficult to settle the Rhodesian problem and achieve an understanding between South Africa and black Africa.

The third reason is even more far-reaching.

If the Russians have their way in Angola, they may well conclude that they can repeat the performance elsewhere. Similarly, uncommitted nations would be left to conclude that NATO is a spent force and that their best policy is to pursue an accommodation with Russia.

Fourthly, what the Russians are doing in Angola is against detente.

They seem to believe that their intervention is consistent with detente.

Indeed, Izvestiya recently argued that Soviet support for the Communist MPLA is "an investment in detente"—which gives us a good idea of what they really mean by the word.

We should make it plain to the Russians that we do not believe that what they are doing in Angola is consistent with detente.

It is usually said that NATO policy ends in North Africa at the Tropic of Cancer. But the situation in Angola brings home the fact that NATOs supplylines need to be protected much further south.

In the Conservative Party we believe that our foreign policy should continue to be based on a close understanding with our traditional ally, America.

This is part of our Anglo-Saxon tradition as well as part of our NATO commitment, and it adds to our contribution to the European Community.

Our Anglo-Saxon heritage embraces the countries of the Old Commonwealth that have too often been neglected by politicians in this country, but are always close to the hearts of British people.

We believe that we should build on our traditional bonds with Australia, New Zealand and Canada, as well as on our new ties with Europe.

I am delighted to see that the Australians and the New Zealanders have concluded—as I believe that most people in this country are coming to conclude—that Socialism has failed.

In their two electoral avalanches at the end of last year, they brought back Governments committed to freedom of choice, governments that will roll back the frontiers of state intervention in the economy and will restore incentives for people to work and save.

Our congratulations go to Mr. Fraser and Mr. Muldoon.

I know that our countries will be able to learn from each other.

What has happened in Australasia is part of a wider reawakening to the need to provide a more positive defence of the values and traditions on which Western civilisation, and prosperity, are based.

We stand with that select body of nations that believe in democracy and social and economic freedom.

Part of Britain's world role should be to provide, through its spokesmen, a reasoned and vigorous defence of the Western concept of rights and liberties: The kind that America's Ambassador to the UN, Mr. Moynihan , has recently provided in his powerfully argued speeches.

But our role reaches beyond this. We have abundant experience and expertise in this country in the art of diplomacy in its broadest sense.

It should be used, within Europe, in the efforts to achieve effective foreign policy initiatives.

Within the EEC, the interests of individual nations are not identical and our separate identities must be seen as a strength rather than a weakness.

Any steps towards closer European union must be carefully considered.

We are committed to direct elections within the Community, but the timing needs to be carefully calculated.

But new problems are looming up.

Among them is the possibility that the Communists will come to power through a coalition in Italy. This is a good reason why we should aim for closer links between those political groups in the European Parliament that reject Socialism.

We have a difficult year ahead in 1976.

I hope it will not result in a further decline of Western power and influence of the kind that we saw in 1975.

It is clear that internal violence—and above all political terrorism—will continue to pose a major challenge to all Western societies, and that it may be exploited as an instrument by the Communists.

We should seek close co-ordination between the police and security services of the Community, and of Nato, in the battle against terrorism.

The way that our own police have coped with recent terrorist incidents provides a splendid model for other forces.

The message of the Conservative Party is that Britain has an important role to play on the world stage. It is based on the remarkable qualities of the British people. Labour has neglected that role.

Our capacity to play a constructive role in world affairs is of course related to our economic and military strength.

Socialism has weakened us on both counts. This puts at risk not just our chance to play a useful role in the councils of the world, but the Survival of our way of life.

Caught up in the problems and hardships that Socialism has brought to Britain, we are sometimes in danger of failing to see the vast transformations taking place in the world that dwarf our own problems, great though they are.

But we have to wake up to those developments, and find the political will to respond to them.

Soviet military power will not disappear just because we refuse to look at it.

And we must assume that it is there to be used—as threat or as force—unless we maintain the necessary deterrents.

We are under no illusions about the limits of British influence.

We are often told how this country that once ruled a quarter of the world is today just a group of offshore islands.

Well, we in the Conservative Party believe that Britain is still great.

The decline of our relative power in the world was partly inevitable—with the rise of the super powers with their vast reserves of manpower and resources.

But it was partly avoidable too—the result of our economic decline accelerated by Socialism.

We must reverse that decline when we are returned to Government.

In the meantime, the Conservative Party has the vital task of shaking the British public out of a long sleep.

Sedatives have been prescribed by people, in and out of Government, telling us that there is no external threat to Britain, that all is sweetness and light in Moscow, and that a squadron of fighter planes or a company of marine commandos is less important than some new subsidy.

The Conservative Party must now sound the warning.

There are moments in our history when we have to make a fundamental choice.

This is one such moment—a moment when our choice will determine the life or death of our kind of society,—and the future of our children.

Let's ensure that our children will have cause to rejoice that we did not forsake their freedom.

Statement on Behalf of the African National Congress, on the Occasion of the Adoption by the Constitutional Assembly of the Republic of South Africa Constitution Bill 1996

Deputy President Thabo Mbeki
May 8, 1996, Cape Town

Chairperson, Esteemed President of the democratic Republic, Honourable Members of the Constitutional Assembly, Our distinguished domestic and foreign guests, Friends:

On an occasion such as this, we should, perhaps, start from the beginning.

So, let me begin.

I am an African.

I owe my being to the hills and the valleys, the mountains and the glades, the rivers, the deserts, the trees, the flowers, the seas and the ever-changing seasons that define the face of our native land.

My body has frozen in our frosts and in our latter day snows. It has thawed in the warmth of our sunshine and melted in the heat of the midday sun.

The crack and the rumble of the summer thunders, lashed by startling lightning, have been a cause both of trembling and of hope.

The fragrances of nature have been as pleasant to us as the sight of the wild blooms of the citizens of the veld.

The dramatic shapes of the Drakensberg, the soil-coloured waters of the Lekoa, iGqili noThukela, and the sands of the Kgalagadi, have all been panels of the set on the natural stage on which we act out the foolish deeds of the theatre of our day.

At times, and in fear, I have wondered whether I should concede equal citizenship of our country to the leopard and the lion, the elephant and the springbok, the hyena, the black mamba and the pestilential mosquito.

A human presence among all these, a feature on the face of our native land thus defined, I know that none dare challenge me when I say: I am an African!

I owe my being to the Khoi and the San whose desolate souls haunt the great expanses of the beautiful Cape—they who fell victim to the most merciless genocide our native land has ever seen, they who were the first to lose their lives in the struggle to defend our freedom and independence and they who, as a people, perished as a result.

Today, as a country, we keep an audible silence about these ancestors of the generations that live, fearful to admit the horror of a former deed, seeking to obliterate from our memories a cruel occurrence which, in its remembering, should teach us not and never to be inhuman again.

I am formed of the migrants who left Europe to find a new home on our native land. Whatever their own actions, they remain still part of me.

In my veins courses the blood of the Malay slaves who came from the East. Their proud dignity informs my bearing, their culture a part of my essence. The stripes they bore on their bodies from the lash of the slave-master are a reminder embossed on my consciousness of what should not be done.

I am the grandchild of the warrior men and women that Hintsa and Sekhukhune led, the patriots that Cetshwayo and Mphephu took to battle, the soldiers Moshoeshoe and Ngungunyane taught never to dishonour the cause of freedom.

My mind and my knowledge of myself is formed by the victories that are the jewels in our African crown, the victories we earned from Isandhlwana to Khartoum, as Ethiopians and as the Ashanti of Ghana, as the Berbers of the desert.

I am the grandchild who lays fresh flowers on the Boer graves at St Helena and the Bahamas, who sees in the mind's eye and suffers the suffering of a simple peasant folk: death, concentration camps, destroyed homesteads, a dream in ruins.

I am the child of Nongqause. I am he who made it possible to trade in the world markets in diamonds, in gold, in the same food for which my stomach yearns.

I come of those who were transported from India and China, whose being resided in the fact, solely, that they were able to provide physical labour, who taught me that we could both be at home and be foreign, who taught me that human existence itself demanded that freedom was a necessary condition for that human existence.

Being part of all these people, and in the knowledge that none dare contest that assertion, I shall claim that I am an African!

I have seen our country torn asunder as these, all of whom are my people, engaged one another in a titanic battle, the one to redress a wrong that had been caused by one to another, and the other to defend the indefensible.

I have seen what happens when one person has superiority of force over another, when the stronger appropriate to themselves the prerogative even to annul the injunction that God created all men and women in His image.

I know what it signifies when race and colour are used to determine who is human and who subhuman.

I have seen the destruction of all sense of self-esteem, the consequent striving to be what one is not, simply to acquire some of the benefits which those who had imposed themselves as masters had ensured that they enjoy.

I have experience of the situation in which race and colour is used to enrich some and impoverish the rest.

I have seen the corruption of minds and souls as a result of the pursuit of an ignoble effort to perpetrate a veritable crime against humanity.

I have seen concrete expression of the denial of the dignity of a human being emanating from the conscious, systemic and systematic oppressive and repressive activities of other human beings.

There the victims parade with no mask to hide the brutish reality—the beggars, the prostitutes, the street children, those who seek solace in substance abuse, those who have to steal to assuage hunger, those who have to lose their sanity because to be sane is to invite pain.

Perhaps the worst among these who are my people are those who have learnt to kill for a wage. To these the extent of death is directly proportional to their personal welfare.

And so, like pawns in the service of demented souls, they kill in furtherance of the political violence in KwaZulu-Natal. They murder the innocent in the taxi wars. They kill slowly or quickly in order to make profits from the illegal trade in narcotics. They are available for hire when husband wants to murder wife and wife, husband.

Among us prowl the products of our immoral and amoral past—killers who have no sense of the worth of human life; rapists who have absolute disdain for the women of our country; animals who would seek to benefit from the vulnerability of the children, the disabled and the old; the rapacious who brook no obstacle in their quest for self-enrichment.

All this I know and know to be true because I am an African!

Because of that, I am also able to state this fundamental truth: that I am born of a people who are heroes and heroines.

I am born of a people who would not tolerate oppression.

I am of a nation that would not allow that the fear of death, torture, imprisonment, exile or persecution should result in the perpetuation of injustice.

The great masses who are our mother and father will not permit that the behaviour of the few results in the description of our country and people as barbaric. Patient because history is on their side, these masses do not despair because today the weather is bad. Nor do they turn triumphalist when, tomorrow, the sun shines. Whatever the circumstances they have lived through—and because of that experience—they are determined to define for themselves who they are and who they should be.

We are assembled here today to mark their victory in acquiring and exercising their right to formulate their own definition of what it means to be African.

The Constitution whose adoption we celebrate constitutes an unequivocal statement that we refuse to accept that our Africanness shall be defined by our race, colour, gender or historical origins.

It is a firm assertion made by ourselves that South Africa belongs to all who live in it, black and white.

It gives concrete expression to the sentiment we share as Africans, and will defend to the death, that the people shall govern.

It recognises the fact that the dignity of the individual is both an objective which society must pursue, and is a goal which cannot be separated from the material well-being of that individual.

It seeks to create the situation in which all our people shall be free from fear, including the fear of the oppression of one national group by another, the fear of the disempowerment of one social echelon by another, the fear of the use of state power to deny anybody their fundamental human rights and the fear of tyranny.

It aims to open the doors so that those who were disadvantaged can assume their place in society as equals with their fellow human beings without regard to colour, race, gender, age or geographic dispersal.

It provides the opportunity to enable each one and all to state their views, promote them, strive for their implementation in the process of governance without fear that a contrary view will be met with repression.

It creates a law-governed society which shall be inimical to arbitrary rule.

It enables the resolution of conflicts by peaceful means rather than resort to force.

It rejoices in the diversity of our people and creates the space for all of us voluntarily to define ourselves as one people.

As an African, this is an achievement of which I am proud, proud without reservation and proud without any feeling of conceit.

Our sense of elevation at this moment also derives from the fact that this magnificent product is the unique creation of African hands and African minds. But it also constitutes a tribute to our loss of vanity that we could, despite the temptation to treat ourselves as an exceptional fragment of humanity, draw on the accumulated experience and wisdom of all humankind, to define for ourselves what we want to be.

Together with the best in the world, we too are prone to pettiness, petulance, selfishness and short-sightedness. But it seems to have happened that we looked at ourselves and said that the time had come that we make a super-human effort to be other than human, to respond to the call to create for ourselves a glorious future, to remind ourselves of the Latin saying: Gloria est consequenda—Glory must be sought after!

Today it feels good to be an African.

It feels good that I can stand here as a South African and as a foot soldier of a titanic African army, the African National Congress, to say to all the parties represented here, to the millions who made an input into the processes we are concluding, to our outstanding compatriots who have presided over the birth of our founding document, to the negotiators who pitted their wits one against the other, to the unseen stars who shone unseen as the management and administration of the Constitutional Assembly, the advisers, experts and publicists, to the mass communication media, to our friends across the globe: Congratulations and well done!

I am an African.

I am born of the peoples of the continent of Africa.

The pain of the violent conflict that the peoples of Liberia, Somalia, the Sudan, Burundi and Algeria suffer, is a pain I also bear.

The dismal shame of poverty, suffering and human degradation of my continent is a blight that we share.

The blight on our happiness that derives from this and from our drift to the periphery of the ordering of human affairs leaves us in a persistent shadow of despair.

This is a savage road to which nobody should be condemned.

This thing that we have done today, in this small corner of a great continent that has contributed so decisively to the evolution of humanity says that Africa reaffirms that she is continuing her rise from the ashes.

Whatever the setbacks of the moment, nothing can stop us now! Whatever the difficulties, Africa shall be at peace!

However improbable it may sound to the sceptics, Africa will prosper!

Whoever we may be, whatever our immediate interest, however much baggage we carry from our past, however much we have been caught by the fashion of cynicism and loss of faith in the capacity of the people, let us say today: Nothing can stop us now!

Thank you.

The Perils of Indifference

Elie Wiesel
April 12, 1999, Washington DC

Mr. President, Mrs. Clinton, members of Congress, Ambassador Holbrooke, Excellencies, friends:

Fifty-four years ago to the day, a young Jewish boy from a small town in the Carpathian Mountains woke up, not far from Goethe's beloved Weimar, in a place of eternal infamy called Buchenwald. He was finally free, but there was no joy in his heart. He thought there never would be again. Liberated a day earlier by American soldiers, he remembers their rage at what they saw. And even if he lives to be a very old man, he will always be grateful to them for that rage, and also for their compassion. Though he did not understand their language, their eyes told him what he needed to know—that they, too, would remember, and bear witness.

And now, I stand before you, Mr. President—Commander-in-Chief of the army that freed me, and tens of thousands of others—and I am filled with a profound and abiding gratitude to the American people. "Gratitude" is a word that I cherish. Gratitude is what defines the humanity of the human being. And I am grateful to you, Hillary, or Mrs. Clinton, for what you said, and for what you are doing for children in the world, for the homeless, for the victims of injustice, the victims of destiny and society. And I thank all of you for being here.

We are on the threshold of a new century, a new millennium. What will the legacy of this vanishing century be? How will it be remembered in the new millennium? Surely it will be judged, and judged severely, in both moral and metaphysical terms. These failures have cast a dark shadow over humanity: two World Wars, countless civil wars, the senseless chain of assassinations (Gandhi, the Kennedys, Martin Luther King, Sadat, Rabin), bloodbaths in Cambodia and Algeria, India and Pakistan, Ireland and Rwanda, Eritrea and Ethiopia, Sarajevo and Kosovo; the inhumanity in the gulag and the tragedy of Hiroshima. And, on a different level, of course, Auschwitz and Treblinka. So much violence; so much indifference.

What is indifference? Etymologically, the word means "no difference." A strange and unnatural state in which the lines blur between light and darkness, dusk and dawn, crime and punishment, cruelty and compassion, good and evil. What are its courses and inescapable consequences? Is it a philosophy? Is there a philosophy of indifference conceivable? Can one possibly view indifference as a virtue? Is it necessary at times to practice it simply to keep one's sanity, live normally, enjoy a fine meal and a glass of wine, as the world around us experiences harrowing upheavals?

Of course, indifference can be tempting—more than that, seductive. It is so much easier to look away from victims. It is so much easier to avoid such rude interruptions to our work, our dreams, our hopes. It is, after all, awkward, troublesome, to be involved in another person's pain and despair. Yet, for the person who is indifferent, his or her neighbor are of no consequence. And, therefore, their lives are meaningless. Their hidden or even visible anguish is of no interest. Indifference reduces the Other to an abstraction.

Over there, behind the black gates of Auschwitz, the most tragic of all prisoners were the "Muselmanner," as they were called. Wrapped in their torn blankets, they would sit or lie on the ground, staring vacantly into space, unaware of who or where they were—strangers to their surroundings. They no longer felt pain, hunger, thirst. They feared nothing. They felt nothing. They were dead and did not know it.

Rooted in our tradition, some of us felt that to be abandoned by humanity then was not the ultimate. We felt that to be abandoned by God was worse than to be punished by Him. Better an unjust God than an indifferent one. For us to be ignored by God was a harsher punishment than to be a victim of His anger. Man can live far from God—not outside God. God is wherever we are. Even in suffering? Even in suffering.

In a way, to be indifferent to that suffering is what makes the human being inhuman. Indifference, after all, is more dangerous than anger and hatred. Anger can at times be creative. One writes a great poem, a great symphony. One does something special for the sake of humanity because one is angry at the injustice that one witnesses. But indifference is never creative. Even hatred at times may elicit a response. You fight it. You denounce it. You disarm it.

Indifference elicits no response. Indifference is not a response. Indifference is not a beginning; it is an end. And, therefore, indifference is always the friend of the enemy, for it benefits the aggressor—never his victim, whose pain is magnified when he or she feels forgotten. The political prisoner in his cell, the hungry children, the homeless refugees—not to respond to their plight, not to relieve their solitude by offering them a spark of hope is to exile them from human memory. And in denying their humanity, we betray our own.

Indifference, then, is not only a sin, it is a punishment.

And this is one of the most important lessons of this outgoing century's wide-ranging experiments in good and evil.

In the place that I come from, society was composed of three simple categories: the killers, the victims, and the bystanders. During the darkest of times, inside the ghettoes and death camps—and I'm glad that Mrs. Clinton mentioned that we are now commemorating that event, that period, that we are now in the Days of Remembrance—but then, we felt abandoned, forgotten. All of us did.

And our only miserable consolation was that we believed that Auschwitz and Treblinka were closely guarded secrets; that the leaders of the free world did not know what was going on behind those black gates and barbed wire; that they had no knowledge of the war against the Jews that Hitler's armies and their accomplices waged as part of the war against the Allies. If they knew, we thought, surely those leaders would have moved heaven and earth to intervene. They would have spoken out with great outrage and conviction. They would have bombed the railways leading to Birkenau, just the railways, just once.

And now we knew, we learned, we discovered that the Pentagon knew, the State Department knew. And the illustrious occupant of the White House then, who was a great leader—and I say it with some anguish and pain, because, today is exactly 54 years marking his death—Franklin Delano Roosevelt died on April the 12th, 1945. So he is very much present to me and to us. No doubt, he was a great leader. He mobilized the American people and the world, going into battle, bringing hundreds and thousands of valiant and brave soldiers in America to fight fascism, to fight dictatorship, to fight Hitler. And so many of the young people fell in battle. And, nevertheless, his image in Jewish history—I must say it—his image in Jewish history is flawed.

The depressing tale of the St. Louis is a case in point. Sixty years ago, its human cargo—nearly 1,000 Jews—was turned back to Nazi Germany. And that happened after the Kristallnacht, after the first state sponsored pogrom, with hundreds of Jewish shops destroyed, synagogues burned, thousands of people put in concentration camps. And that ship, which was already in the shores of the United States, was sent back. I don't understand. Roosevelt was a good man, with a heart. He understood those who needed help. Why didn't he allow these refugees to disembark? A thousand people—in America, the great country, the greatest democracy, the most generous of all new nations in modern history. What happened? I don't understand. Why the indifference, on the highest level, to the suffering of the victims?

But then, there were human beings who were sensitive to our tragedy. Those non-Jews, those Christians, that we call the "Righteous Gentiles," whose selfless acts of heroism saved the honor of their faith. Why were they so few? Why was there a greater effort to save SS murderers after the war than to save their victims during the war? Why did some of America's largest corporations continue to do business with Hitler's Germany until 1942? It has been suggested, and it was documented, that the Wehrmacht could not have conducted its invasion of France without oil obtained from American sources. How is one to explain their indifference?

And yet, my friends, good things have also happened in this traumatic century: the defeat of Nazism, the collapse of communism, the rebirth of Israel on its ancestral soil, the demise of apartheid, Israel's peace treaty with Egypt, the peace accord in Ireland. And let us remember the meeting, filled with drama and emotion, between Rabin and Arafat that you, Mr. President, convened in this very place. I was here and I will never forget it.

And then, of course, the joint decision of the United States and NATO to intervene in Kosovo and save those victims, those refugees, those who were uprooted by a man, whom I believe that because of his crimes, should be charged with crimes against humanity.

But this time, the world was not silent. This time, we do respond. This time, we intervene.

Does it mean that we have learned from the past? Does it mean that society has changed? Has the human being become less indifferent and more human? Have we really learned from our experiences? Are we less insensitive to the plight of victims of ethnic cleansing and other forms of injustices in places near and far? Is today's justified intervention in Kosovo, led by you, Mr. President, a lasting warning that never again will the deportation, the terrorization of children and their parents, be allowed anywhere in the world? Will it discourage other dictators in other lands to do the same?

What about the children? Oh, we see them on television, we read about them in the papers, and we do so with a broken heart. Their fate is always the most tragic, inevitably. When adults wage war, children perish. We see their faces, their eyes. Do we hear their pleas? Do we feel their pain, their agony? Every minute one of them dies of disease, violence, famine.

Some of them—so many of them—could be saved.

And so, once again, I think of the young Jewish boy from the Carpathian Mountains. He has accompanied the old man I have become throughout these years of quest and struggle. And together we walk towards the new millennium, carried by profound fear and extraordinary hope.

Endnotes

Chapter 1

1. For more on rhetorical situations, see Bitzer, L. F. (1968). The rhetorical situation. *Philosophy and Rhetoric, 1*, 1–14; Vatz, R. E. (1973). The myth of the rhetorical situation. *Philosophy and Rhetoric, 6*, 154–161.

Chapter 2

1. Perkins, H. W. (2002). Social norms and the prevention of alcohol misuse in collegiate contexts. *Journal of Studies on Alcohol, 14*, 164–172. Retrieved from http://www.collegedrinkingprevention.gov/supportingresearch/journal/perkins2.aspx
2. Jonsen, A., & Toulmin, S. (1990). *The abuse of casuistry.* Berkeley, CA: University of California Press, especially Chapter 10.
3. Davidson, D. (1984). *Inquiries into truth and interpretation.* Oxford, England: Clarendon Press, especially Chapter 13: On the Very Idea of a Conceptual Scheme.
4. Johnstone, H., Jr. (1965). Some reflections on argumentation. In M. Natanson & H. Johnstone (Eds.), *Philosophy: Rhetoric and argumentation* (pp. 1–9). University Park: Pennsylvania State University Press.
5. Arnett, R. C., & Arneson. P. (1999). *Dialogic civility in a cynical age.* Albany, NY: SUNY Press.
6. Brockriede, W. (1972). Arguers as lovers. *Philosophy and Rhetoric, 5,* 1–11; Natanson, M. (1965). The claims of immediacy. In Natanson & H. Johnstone, Jr., *Philosophy: Rhetoric and argumentation* (pp. xx–xx). University Park, PA: Pennsylvania State University Press.

Chapter 3

1. Booth, W. C. (1963). The rhetorical stance. *Composition and Communication, 14,* 139–145; Brockriede, W. (1972). Arguers as lovers. *Philosophy and Rhetoric, 5,* 1–11.
2. Lake, R. A. (1990). The implied auditor. In D. C. Williams & M. D. Hazen (Eds.), *Argumentation theory and the rhetoric of assent* (pp. 69–90). Tuscaloose: University of Alabama Press.
3. McGee, M. C. (1975). In search of "the people": A rhetorical alternative. *Quarterly Journal of Speech, 61*(3), 235–249.
4. Johnstone, H. W., Jr. (1981). Toward an ethics of rhetoric. *Communication, 6,* 305–314.
5. Dewey, J. (1927). *The public and its problems.* New York, NY: Holt.

Chapter 4

1. Booth, W. C. (1963). The rhetorical stance. *Composition and Communication, 14,* 139–145.

Chapter 6

1. UT Health Science Center. (2011, June 27). Waistlines in people, glucose levels in mice hint at sweetener's effects [News release]. Retrieved from http://www.uthscsa.edu/hscnews/singleformat2.asp?newID=3861
2. Centers for Disease Control and Prevention/National Center for Health Statistics. (2011, November 17). Obesity and overweight. *FastStats.* Retrieved from http://www.cdc.gov/nchs/fastats/overwt.htm (2011, November 17).
3. Health Discovery. (n.d.). Tips for keeping your New Year's. Retrieved from http://www.healthdiscovery.net/articles/Tips_New_Year.htm (2011, November 17).
4. Surgeon General Regina Benjamin, "The Prevention Imperative: Protecting the Health and Well-Being of America's Families," in *America's Health Rankings: A Call to Action for Individuals and Their Communites,* 2011 edition (United Health Foundation: 2011), p. 4. Available at http://www.americashealthrankings.org/SiteFiles/Reports/AHR%202011edition.pdf.

Chapter 7

1. Kenton, S. B. (1989). Speaker credibility in persuasive business communication: A Model which explains gender differences. *Journal of Business Communication, 26*(2), 143–157. A good source for research on source credibility updated to the information age is Andrew Flanagin's and Miriam Metzger's website Credibility and Digital Media @ UCSB: http://www.credibility.ucsb.edu

2. Ruiter, R. A. C., Abraham, C., & Kok, G. (2001). Scary warnings and rational precautions: A review of the psychology of fear appeals. *Psychology and Health, 16*, 613–630.

3. Important work on framing has been done by the linguist George Lakoff: Lakoff, G. (2002). *Moral politics: How liberals and conservatives think* (2nd ed.). Chicago, IL: University of Chicago Press. Lakoff, G. (2004). *Don't think of an elephant!: Know your values and frame the debate.* White River Junction, VT: Chelsea Green Publishing.

4. For different example of a mental image, think about the cliché you've may have heard before. The speaker is talking about a danger growing so slowly that people may not take action until it's too late, and he compares the public to a frog being boiled to death in a pan of water: Supposedly, if the water is heated slowly enough, the temperature will never change quickly enough to cause the frog to jump out and avoid being boiled. The analogy ("in this situation, we are like a frog in a pan of water . . .") serves to frame the problem you're talking about, implying that it's a more serious problem than it seems at any one moment. If you're trying to make a case about cumulative physical, social, or moral damage, this visual analogy would help your audience frame any given instance as part of a larger problem. Of course, frogs do try to escape from boiling water if they can (http://www.snopes.com/critters/wild/frogboil.asp), so it wouldn't be responsible to use this analogy, even though it's a common one.

Chapter 8

1. Deer, B. (2009, February 8). Hidden records show MMR truth. *Sunday Times.* Retrieved from http://www.timesonline.co.uk/tol/life_and_style/health/article5683643.ece

2. Dales, L., Hammer, S., & Smith, N., (2001). Time trends in autism and in MMR immunization coverage in California. *Journal of the American Medical Association, 285*(9), 1183–1185; Kaye, J., Melero-Montes, M., & Jick, H. (2001), Mumps, measles, and rubella vaccine and the incidence of autism recorded by general practitioners: a time trend analysis. *British Medical Journal, 322*(7288), 720.

Chapter 9

1. This set of expectations is often called the *genre* of the speech. For some classic work on genre, see Campbell, K. K., & Jamieson, K. H. (Eds.). (1978). *Form and genre: Shaping rhetorical action.* Falls Church, VA: Speech Communication Association; Jamieson, K. H. (1973). Generic constraints and the rhetorical situation. *Philosophy and Rhetoric, 6,* 162–170; Miller, C. (1984). Genre as social action. *Quarterly Journal of Speech, 70,* 151–167.

2. U.S. Department of Labor, Bureau of Labor Statistics. (2008). *American time use survey.* Retrieved from http://www.bls.gov/tus/datafiles_2008.htm

Chapter 10

1. For examples of scholars who analyze style, see Fulkerson, R. P. (1979). The public letter as a rhetorical form: Structure, logic, and style in King's "Letter from Birmingham Jail." *Quarterly Journal of Speech, 65*(2), 121–136; Carpenter, R. H. (1998). *Choosing powerful words: Eloquence that works.* Boston, MA: Allyn and Bacon.

2. [Cicero]. (1954). *Rhetorica ad Herrenium.* Trans. H. Caplan. Cambridge, MA: Harvard University Press.

3. Representative Cleo Fields may have introduced a longer version in February 2008, which then was shortened by the rapper Jay-Z. Fields, C. (2008, February 23). State of the Black Union 2008, morning session [Video clip]. *C-SPAN Video Library.* Retrieved from http://www.c-spanvideo.org/clip/2156642; Hershkovits, D. (2009, January 23). Sourcing the quote: "Rosa Parks sat so Martin Luther King could walk. Martin Luther King walked so Obama could run. Obama ran so we can all fly" [Web log]. *Papermag.* Retrieved from http://www.papermag.com/2009/01/sourcing_the_quote_rosa_parks.php; yaddab. (2008, October 29). "Rosa sat so Martin could walk, so Obama could run, so our children can fly" [Web log]. *Daily Kos.* Retrieved from http://www.dailykos.com/story/2008/10/29/645922/–Rosa-sat-so-Martin-could-walk-so-Obama-could-run-so-our-children-can-fly

Chapter 11

1. Song, S. (2004, July 19). Health: The price of pressure. *Time*. Retrieved from http://www .time.com/time/magazine/article/0,9171,994670-1,00.html
2. Rarig, F. (1955, November 1). Audio interview. Audio-Visual Register of the WSCA Oral History Project, A0327. University of Utah Archives. Frank Rarig, a professor of speech at the University of Minnesota starting in 1911, recalls talking to someone who was present at the Gettysburg address.

Chapter 12

1. Katt, J., Murdock, M., Butler, J., & Pryor, B. (2008). Establishing best practices for the use of PowerPoint as a presentation aid. *Human Communication, 11*(2), 189–196.
2. Schrodt, P., & Witt, P. L. (2006). Students' attributions of instructor credibility as a function of students' expectations of instructional technology use and nonverbal immediacy. *Communication Education, 55*, 1–20.
3. Norris, J. (2011, April 28). Five myths about foreign aid. *Washington Post*. Retrieved from http://www.washingtonpost.com/opinions/five-myths-about-foreign-aid/2011/04/25 /AF00z05E_story.html
4. These criticisms are taken from Tufte, E. (2006). *The cognitive style of PowerPoint: Pitching out corrupts within*. Cheshire, CT: Graphics Press.

Index